PALESTINE AND ISRAEL

PALESTINE AND ISRAEL

THE UPRISING AND BEYOND

David McDowall

University of California Press
Berkeley   Los Angeles

Published by
University of California Press
Berkeley and Los Angeles, California

Copywright © 1989 by David McDowall
This edition published by arrangement with I. B. Tauris & Co. Ltd.

Library of Congress Catalog Card Number: 89–40444
ISBN 0–520–06902–1

Printed in Great Britain

CONTENTS

MAPS

PREFACE

In spite of its title, this book was conceived and begun before the commencement of the Uprising in December 1987. My reason for writing was not to add yet another prescriptive view to the many already given on the Palestine question. It was, rather, that as a result of a visit made to the region in 1986 I came to the conclusion that the prospects for Palestine and Israel had begun to change in a radical way, or at any rate my own perception of these prospects had. Many Palestinians in the territories were already aware of a change in their fortunes, but this was less well understood by Israelis, by Palestinians living outside, and still less by the West.

Until July 1988 the framework for discussion at an international level remained based upon the *de jure* Armistice Line of 1949, on Jordanian participation in any future political settlement for the occupied territories, and on agreement between Israel and its neighbouring Arab states. The reasons why this was so are clear. The 1949 Armistice Line was a legal benchmark for a solution, and was therefore naturally adhered to by most responsible governments. These governments (whether Arab, Israeli or Western) were naturally reluctant to accord negotiating authority and control to a stateless people and to its representative political institution, for this surrendered too many hostages to fortune, particularly since the institution in question, the PLO, had been so mercurial in its performance so far. Partly as a result of these two factors, Jordan's primacy in any solution was implicitly and explicitly affirmed. It was seen as 'moderate', a term in this context meaning well-disposed towards the West (and largely dependent upon it) and willing to strike a bargain with Israel. The PLO's position was far less predictable, both towards Israel and towards the West's perceived interests. Linked, of course, to this consideration was another one: that a solution based on any principle other than the 1949 Armistice Line would have destabilizing repercussions on Jordan and possibly also on Israel. Finally, the 1949 Armistice Line had been adhered to because of international law which maintains the inadmissibility of acquiring territory by war.

My own view, and reason for writing this book, was that this framework was increasingly untenable. Jordan and the PLO had mutually inimical interests and seemed unlikely to reach a comprehensive settlement without one or the other suffering a severe, possibly fatal, reverse. Even before the Uprising, Jordan had been unable to transact a solution without the approval of the PLO, or in the case of its demise, the assent of those Palestinians living under occupation. The PLO had only been willing to accept a solution leading to a Palestinian state, something which threatened the stability of the Hashemite Kingdom. At an international level peace discussions between the Arab world and the West had been primarily concerned with preventing further destabilization of the region. Achieving a viable solution to the Palestine question had been subordinated to this and other wider goals. Finally, Israel had never really accepted the meaning of Resolution 242 as this was understood by virtually all other parties, whether the latter believed in minor border rectifications or in none. Neither Likud nor Labour was willing in practice to yield sovereignty of a sizeable portion of the occupied territories.

Then came the Palestinian Uprising, which had its own momentum free from outside control or considerations. It is, in my view, the most important political development in the history of the Palestinian people so far. Where the Arab revolt of 1936–9 failed, the Uprising has succeeded in uniting all Palestinians in a common endeavour. Where the PLO – despite its great psychological importance – failed to find a fruitful means for liberation, the Uprising evolved a philosophy for a real people's war which, by its emphasis on civil disobedience, attacked its adversary at its weakest point. Inside the occupied territories an irreversible process began, in which the inhabitants embarked on the painful process of repudiating control by, and dependency on, Israel. By the time this book was completed in mid-December 1988, that process of repudiation had already become the new normality in the territories, with the authorities no nearer to suppressing it than they had been twelve months before.

Outside the territories, too, new realities took shape. The PLO and the Palestinian people returned to the forefront of the Middle East agenda, at a time when some observers had concluded that their fortunes were virtually played out. At the end of July 1988 King Husayn formally renounced sovereignty of the West Bank, just short of the fortieth anniversary of its incorporation into the Hashemite Kingdom. In November two other events of great moment took place: Israel's general election, which reflected deepening division and uncertainty among its citizens; and in Algiers the formal acceptance by the Palestine National Council (PNC) of Resolution 242 and, more symbolically, the declaration of the State of Palestine. Then, in December, the anniversary of the Uprising was crowned when the United States agreed to talk with the PLO for the first time ever. It made this decision only after isolation at the United Nations, and after the PLO's explicit recognition of Israel and renunciation of terrorism.

These heady events made writing – and particularly completing – this book a good deal more difficult than it otherwise would have been. But although I have mentioned the Israeli election, the PNC conference and the United State's decision at various points, I do not believe that they alter the general analysis I have attempted concerning the long-term context in which the struggle for Palestine and Israel takes place.

After 1967 it was natural for a solution to the Arab-Israeli problem to be cast in inter-statal terms, for the quarrel seemed to be between Israel and hostile neighbouring Arab states. But then the PLO sprang up. More important than that, however, certain developments were taking place inside Palestine/Israel which were changing the nature of the struggle from an inter-statal to an inter-communal one. The most obvious manifestation of this was the establishment of Jewish settlements in the occupied territories, and the increasing economic integration of these territories into Israel proper. People started asking whether the 1949 Armistice Line was still tenable as the basis for a settlement.

More important but less noticed, however, was the growth in size of the Palestinian community living inside the 1949 Armistice Line as citizens of the State of Israel. Its existence and continuing proportionate growth are overwhelming reasons for thinking that finding a solution to relations between Israeli Jew and Palestinian Arab must go far beyond such simplicities as the 1949 Armistice Line. The fate of the whole area of Israel/Palestine will remain in doubt until the relations between Jewish and Palestinian Israelis are also resolved.

Finally, there is the vexed question of the Palestine refugees. There has been a tendency ever since 1949 to bow to the inevitable, that Israel will allow none of these back, and to view as unrealistic the Palestinian vision of a return. This view may be correct, but it strikes me as equally unrealistic to suppose that any deal struck which fails to address the refugee question adequately will lead to permanent peace.

Such issues seem distinct from the Uprising, with its main aim of securing freedom for the West Bank and Gaza Strip. Nevertheless, the Uprising is deeply relevant to what this book has to say, for it is the first major development in an unfolding process of disengagement by the Palestinian people from the control system which Israel has applied for so long. It is no longer possible to look at the issues which prompted me to write, except in the light of the Uprising.

I regret that my conclusions are not optimistic but I have tried to resist the temptation to be prescriptive, as if the problem is neatly soluble. Frankly, I do not know if the conflict in Palestine has a 'solution' and, if so, what that solution is or how it could realistically be achieved, and it would be foolish to pretend that I do. It certainly strikes me that justice for everyone is no longer attainable (if ever it was), although it is quite clearly an essential precondition for peace that both protagonists must feel that things are being *reasonably* settled.

The book is divided into three basic parts: the issues – in time and space – outside Palestine today; the present challenge to Palestinian Arabs and Israeli Jews in Palestine; and the future prospects for both. I have tried to clear away some of what strike me as distracting features of the conflict. The first of these is the international dimension. It seems to me that the world powers have not done much so far to resolve the conflict. Rather, they have complicated it with the negative impact of their own rivalries and with the supply of weaponry despite their protestations of peaceful intent. The real issue at stake, as it always has been, is that of relations between Jews and Arabs who actually inhabit Palestine. In this regard the insistence of non-Palestinians that Jordan should represent the Palestinians has struck most of the latter, ever since 1948, as fundamentally misplaced and I have attempted to show why this is so. Another obstruction is what one might call the 'demonology' of Palestine, and I have dealt with this issue as the introduction to the last section, looking to the future. Both protagonists have created their own version of the struggle for Palestine. The real course of events in Palestine has not necessarily been as the protagonists like to view it. For both sides there are some uncomfortable truths about the past which, if more openly recognized, would possibly allow Jews and Arabs to come to terms with each other more readily.

Can Palestinian Arabs and Israeli Jews live peacefully together? For the foreseeable future one must be sceptical. By its prolonged occupation and settlement of the West Bank and Gaza Strip, Israel implied that relatively peaceable relations were possible between Jews and Arabs in Palestine, albeit in circumstances in which one community was firmly subordinated to the other. The Uprising has demonstrated how mistaken this view was and that a strong chord of solidarity exists between all Palestinians everywhere, including those who are Israeli citizens.

How Israel responds to the challenges implicit in the Uprising will depend very much on its own self-image and upon the way in which the Jewish electorate defines its Zionist identity. Undoubtedly a crisis of identity will occur in Israel, made far more painful by the fact that Israel, unlike almost any other country in the world (most of which exist more by accident than design), exists for an express purpose concerned with Jewish identity. As this crisis draws closer, the Jewish electorate seems increasingly divided as to what to do and the prospect increases of successive weak governments which are unable to meet the fundamental challenge posed by the Palestinian resurgence. As a consequence both peoples probably face in the future perils as great as those they have endured since 1947.

I should declare my own position, which is more sympathetic to the Palestinian view than to the Zionist one. However, it is not my concern in this book to plead the case of one party against the other. I have sought – and readers must judge for themselves how successful I have been – to examine the situation as it exists and what this implies for the future.

I should say something briefly about nomenclature. By Palestine I mean no more than the area 'between the river and the sea' as defined during the period of the British Mandate. I do not use Palestine to mean any of the area east of the Jordan river, although a few Palestinians and a more substantial number of Israelis would claim that Palestine includes the East Bank too. I sometimes refer to Eretz Israel (the Land of Israel). This is a vaguer term, but I hope that the meaning is clear in each context. I sometimes use it while discussing Zionist outlooks to distinguish all Palestine from the State of Israel as defined by the 1949 Armistice Line. I also use it instead of the term Palestine where this more happily fits with the issue under discussion. Finally, of course, many Israelis – whether they would actively claim it or not – consider that Eretz Israel could (possibly should) include part of the East Bank, a little more of the Golan, and part of south Lebanon. I hope I have been clear where this maximalist concept is used.

I have also used the term 'Palestinian' to mean Palestinian Arabs. I do not mean to exclude Jews from the right to be described as Palestinians, but I have tried to name each community as it would wish itself to be described, not as others would wish to describe them. Inside Israel therefore, despite its apparent clumsiness, I have usually defined people as either Jewish or Palestinian Israelis. The latter are thus described because they increasingly dislike the official description of 'Arab Israeli' or worse yet 'non-Jews', as implying they have no Palestinian identity. It must also be said that as a result of separation from the rest of the Arab world and disappointment with its political performance, Palestinian Arabs everywhere tend to give increasing pre-eminence to their Palestinian rather than Arab identity. All this may seem like straining at gnats, but I believe that one aspect of understanding the situation is to allow people to be described according to how the majority of them feel. However, the nomenclature is far from perfect, and I can think of categories of both Jewish and Arab inhabitants of Palestine/Eretz Israel who would disagree strongly with the terms I have chosen.

Acknowledgements

Although I have endeavoured to substantiate my argument with written sources, I could not possibly have written this book without an enormous amount of information, advice and guidance from many people. They have made this book happen though, of course, they are in no way responsible for the conclusions I have drawn from their contribution. My primary debt is to a large number of Palestinians living in Palestine. Some would not have minded a personal acknowledgement but I know that it might have put others at risk and I therefore decided to make my thanks general, and include no names. Others I can name more freely, who all – to greater or lesser extent – pointed out what I had misunderstood, directed me to various materials I had not seen, or more generally gave me a view I had not appreciated before. These include Shlomo Avineri, Judith Blanc, Sarah Cave, Peter Coleridge, Abba Eban, Simon Edge, Marisa Escribano, Thomas Friedman, John Gee, Yehoshafat Harkabi, Paul Jeremy, Reuven Kaminer, Penny Maddrell, Moshe Ma'oz, Roger Owen, Ilan Pappé, Gwyn Rowley, Israel Shahak, Arnon Sofer, Benny Temkin, Ralph and Jean Wadge and Kitty Warnock. I should also like to thank the library and staff of the Royal Institute for International Affairs and of the London Library, and Judy Mabro who edited the text. I am also grateful to the Minority

Rights Group for its permission to use excerpts from Report No. 24, *The Palestinians*, in the Introduction.

I owe a different kind of debt to my family. My wife, Elizabeth, kindly read the final draft suggesting changes to make the text easier to follow. She and my sons, Angus and William, endured my obsessive behaviour with patient forebearance for longer than was remotely reasonable, and forgave my mentally abstracted absence from the family hearth.

Finally, I owe a major debt of thanks to two people in particular: Anne Enayat, my editor, who painstakingly and patiently commented on, and helped me shape, no less than three drafts at times when I felt I had lost my way. I am enormously indebted to her. Secondly, I owe an even greater debt to Albert Hourani. He also kindly read an early draft and commented extensively on it. But my debt to him goes further than this, for he has been my teacher and friend for more than twenty years. As for a whole generation of students, he shared with me his understanding of the Middle East unstintingly and long after I had ceased to be his formal student; but also at a deeper level, he imparted what I can only describe as a moral framework in which to place world events. To him, therefore, I should like to offer this book, with great affection and thanks.

PROLOGUE: UPRISING

Balata Refugee Camp, Nablus, 11 December 1987
'Don't hit him with your baton' the Israeli officer screamed at the soldier as the photographer approached the Red Crescent ambulance where a dead girl's body lay on a stretcher, swathed in a rough checked blanket.

It was late yesterday when they brought the four dead and seven injured Palestinians out of Balata refugee camp near Nablus, the largest city in the occupied West Bank.

After another day of clashes with Israelis, scores more wounded were said to be inside the camp which holds about 30,000 people . . . According to the Palestinians the trouble began just after two o'clock yesterday when about 1,000 people came from attending prayers in the camp mosque. 'When we left the mosque, the soldiers began to shoot' one eyewitness said. 'Suddenly everyone was throwing stones at the Israelis. Someone told me that the girl said to the soldiers, "Shoot me." And they did.'[1]

Three days earlier, on 8 December, an Israeli truck had ploughed a car in Gaza killing four Palestinians inside. The following day Gaza had exploded in angry anti-Israeli demonstrations and riots. For many months afterwards Palestinian stone-throwing youths set an agenda of disorder throughout the occupied territories. Young Palestinians, frustrated and angry with the prospect of indefinite Israeli rule, defied the military firepower arrayed against them.

The unrest, which caught almost everyone by surprise, was quickly recognized to be on an entirely different scale from previous disturbances. In Arabic it was called the *intifada*, 'the shaking off', and in the English speaking world, the Uprising. Its significance was intuitively recognized among Palestinians, for it was the first time that the people of the territories had acted with cohesion and as a nation. Most felt that a threshold had been crossed, and that there could be no going back.

The world was assailed by disturbing scenes of Israeli efforts to restore order. Television networks and newspapers around the globe relayed pictures of Israeli troops firing on stone-throwing demonstrators, or beating those they caught with cudgels. It rapidly became clear that many of the latter were not demonstrators at all. One such picture was captioned 'Armed Israelis drag a Palestinian youth from his house yesterday, during a sweep through the town of Khan Yunis on the Gaza Strip. The youth was taken into an alleyway and beaten unconscious.'[2]

Fuel was added to the fire by the coincidental visit of a British minister of state, who gave vent to his own abhorrence at the conditions in the Gaza camps: 'I defy anyone to come here and not to be shocked. Conditions here are an affront to civilised values. It is appalling that a few miles up the coast there is prosperity, and here there is misery on such a scale that rivals anything in the world.'[3] Another visitor, the British opposition spokesman on foreign affairs, Gerald Kaufman, himself a Jew and a long-standing friend of Israel, remarked 'friends of Israel as well as foes have been shocked and saddened by that country's response to the disturbances.'[4] The following week the Under-Secretary-General of the United Nations also visited the territories and expressed dismay at what he saw. Within days Israel's international standing was at its lowest ebb since the siege of Beirut in 1982.

Prime Minister Shamir maintained that the army was making strenuous efforts to avoid bloodshed in the territories, adding in its defence: 'Terrorists and hooligans who attack our security forces are not heroes. But these criminals know that the army is trying not to wound or kill them, so they become more impudent. No one wants bloodshed.' But bloodshed there was, on a greater scale than had been seen before in the occupied territories. By 16 January forty-two Palestinians had been killed. By the end of September 1988 deaths by shooting totalled 257, while another eighty-nine had died from the effects of tear gas, or from injuries inflicted by Israeli troops.[5] But there was no sign of a let-up, either in the Uprising or in Israel's response to it.

The Palestine Liberation Organization and its sympathizers were quick to exploit Israeli excesses. By the end of the first week *Wafa*, the

PLO press agency, reported that Israeli troops had stormed Gaza's Shifa Hospital six times in the space of three days: 'soldiers chased patients, their relatives, and hospital staff through the wards. Patients and others were beaten in the surgical and internal wards. Those injured are being snatched by troops and taken into custody.'[6]

As the days passed the Uprising spread rapidly. Remote villages were encouraged to demonstrate. This widened the Uprising geographically, stretching Israeli forces and making their presence more embarrassingly visible. It also 'awakened' the less politicized rural areas. Civil disobedience became a central feature of the revolt. Repeated general strikes took place in the main towns of the West Bank and Gaza Strip. These strikes, to which some shopkeepers at first reluctantly subscribed, were demonstrations of civil disobedience which Israeli forces endeavoured to break by forcing open shops and beating up shopkeepers who would not co-operate.

In East Jerusalem the Uprising scored a major success by breaking the image of Israel's capital as a united city. Two Israeli banks on the main Arab shopping street were sacked during demonstrations, while strikes and the introduction of a curfew in East Jerusalem (the first since 1967), destroyed the illusion of Arab–Jewish coexistence in the city.

Mosques throughout the territories became vital local focuses for resistance to occupation. The religious sanctity of the mosques gave the Uprising a fresh dimension, demanding sensitive handling by the authorities. However, after Friday prayer on 15 December, Israeli police stormed the most sacrosanct of Palestinian precincts, the Haram al Sharif in Jerusalem, throwing tear gas into the prayer hall where worshippers were gathered, outraging Muslim opinion around the world and triggering another round of international protest and condemnation.

As it became clear that the disturbances had acquired the characteristics of an organized uprising, some commentators thought the PLO was behind it. They pointed to the successful hang-glider attack on Israel's northern border the previous month, which had left six Israeli soldiers dead, as the immediate source of inspiration. However, the nature of the unrest betrayed a local and collective leadership that derived its momentum from popular feeling. The search for a local provocateur led to ill-informed verdicts that the Islamic fundamentalist movement had triumphed over Palestinian nationalism and now directed the masses.[7]

The unprecedented character of the new leadership, however, soon became apparent. A shadowy group calling itself the Unified Leadership of the Uprising (UNLU) quickly emerged claiming authority for its direction. Unlike previous political leaders, this group refused to disclose the identity of its members so as to avoid arrest. It was widely assumed that UNLU was composed of local representatives of the main factions operating in the territories, Fatah, the Popular Front for the Liberation of Palestine (PFLP), the Democratic Front for the Liberation of Palestine (DFLP), the Palestine Communist Party (PCP), and the Islamic revivalists. Members of each of the five groups evenly drawn from the West Bank and Gaza Strip, it was rumoured, formed UNLU's central committee.[8]

Contrary to the expectation of many, UNLU soon demonstrated skill and authority in directing the masses. Yet as the months slipped by, Israel was unable to locate and destroy it. UNLU began issuing leaflets throughout the territories, instructing the people on the conduct of the Uprising. These leaflets, which appeared irregularly but approximately every fortnight, were significant in a number of ways. They told the people what to do and how to organize, through the formation of local committees. The leaflets also provided a unified political programme and the methods which would be used to achieve it. *Communiqué no. 16* of 13 May 1988 gives a characteristic flavour:

To the Masses of our People, forty years have passed since the eviction of our people from its homeland . . . The current national revolution and the sacrifices that it has entailed have succeeded in obtaining international recognition of our legitimate national rights. These include the recognition of the PLO as the sole legitimate representative of the Palestinian people, the right of our people to return to their homeland, and our right to self-determination and the establishment of a Palestinian state under the leadership of the PLO . . . the Unified National Leadership of the Uprising wishes to affirm the following (1) We salute the heroic role the people of the refugee camps in the Gaza Strip have played in escalating the uprising . . . (2) We call upon our fighting people in the Gaza Strip to continue their escalation and to defeat the neo-fascist plan to issue new identity cards. We urge all Gaza Strip residents to boycott this scheme and to refrain from paying taxes . . . (3) We urge the immediate resignation of department heads in the [Israeli] Civilian Administration in the Gaza Strip, and call upon Khairi Ramadan of the Health Department and Muhammad* al Jidi of the Education Department to resign immediately . . . (4) We urge our people to complete the task of forming popular committees without delay . . . [they] are entrusted with organising the requirements of daily life and guaranteeing essential services and supplies such as food, health, education and security. The popular committees represent the people's authority and function as alternatives to the crumbling apparatus of the occupier . . . (5) We urge the intensification of strikes against the police and collaborators . . . (6) We urge the escalation of the refusal to pay taxes . . . (7) We call upon our people to intensify the boycott against Israeli goods for which there are no (sic) local substitutes or with which they can dispense . . . (8) We call upon workers to intensify the boycott against work in the Zionist settlements . . . (9) We call upon lawyers to reduce their fees and to work towards exposing the inhuman conditions under which our people are living . . . (10) We call upon teachers to participate as widely as possible in the popular education effort . . . (11) We call for complete adherence in all areas to the commercial strike and to the schedule permitting the opening of places of business between 9 a.m. and 12 noon . . . At a time when we commemorate the painful anniversary of our dispersion and mark, along with the Muslim world, the Feast of al Fitr we call upon our people to hold prayers in memory of the martyrs of the uprising after the special prayers of . . . Friday 13 May . . . (b) to declare 15 May, the anniversary of the Disaster [the declaration of the State of Israel], a day of mourning and general strike, to refrain from using public or private transport . . . (c) In memory of the fallen martyrs, and in protest against the Arab and Muslim silence regarding the crimes against our people and our holy places, the Unified Leadership has decided to cancel all celebratory aspects of the Feast of al Fitr . . . your people will demonstrate after prayers, place wreaths on the graves of our martyrs, and raise Palestinian flags . . . (d) The second and third days of the Feast . . . we will visit the wounded and the families of martyrs and deportees. We also call upon our people to form committees for the assistance of families in need . . . (e) to declare a general strike on Saturday 21 May . . . The period from 12–22 May should be considered a period of militant nationalist activity. May the banner of the Uprising flutter over the path of liberation and independence. Long live our glorious uprising! We shall be victorious![9]

The popular structure advocated by UNLU soon proved its resilience. The committees which were formed in villages, town neighbourhoods and refugee camps rapidly took control of their areas. Like UNLU itself, these committees remained anonymous but authoritative, and proved impossible for the authorities to contain. When Israeli troops arrested every member of a popular committee in Jalazone camp in January 1988, a new committee was in place within a couple of days to continue the co-ordination of popular action. Mutual support was widespread, with villagers sending vegetables and other produce into the refugee camps, and others sending spare clothes to the areas worst affected.

UNLU had two basic objectives, to persuade Israel it would be too costly to hang on to the territories much longer and to persuade the world that an international conference in which the PLO alone represented the Palestinians was the only possible political way forward.

Israel's response

Israel's political and military leaders had been unanimous on the need to restore authority in the occupied territories regardless of the longer-term implications of the wave of unrest. But they had all been taken by surprise by events and were ill-prepared to deal with them. This quickly became evident by the behaviour of those sent to restore order.[10] Many of these used indiscriminate violence. Israeli Druze 'border guards' shot dead an eleven-year-old boy, a seventeen-year-old girl and a 57-year-old woman in Balata camp on 11 December.[11] '"They are dogs, just dogs, these Druzes" screamed one old man, dragging me to see a middle-aged woman cowering under a blanket in another room, her face bruised and puffy with shock', the *Guardian* correspondent reported.[12] Horror at Druze excesses was shared by some Israelis. One soldier interviewed by the Hebrew daily *Ha'aretz* described his own reactions:

> I break into a cold sweat when I think that I'll have to go back into that filthy place. I'm not the kind of guy who disobeys orders or refuses to serve in the [occupied] territories. But I doubt whether I'm emotionally capable of again seeing the terrible things I saw this time at close quarters. I'll be having nightmares for weeks to come.
>
> What I'm talking about is the way the border police question Arabs they've arrested on suspicion of throwing stones or petrol bombs. I saw them really smashing up 13 or 14 year old kids a

few times and I just felt sick . . . for the first time I really understood what occupation means.[13]

At first it was thought that mass arrests and expulsions from the territories would remove the leaders of the unrest, but after several hundred were detained the demonstrations became if anything more vehement. Expulsion was the last resort punitive action, used to remove emerging leaders of resistance. The cabinet considered the expulsion of fifty or so individuals, but as international pressure mounted against Israeli threats of mass expulsions, the number was reduced to nine. Having expelled four of these, however, Israel hesitated before expelling the other five, fearful of triggering renewed unrest.

Internationally, Israel's resort to expulsion focused attention on its failure to uphold the provisions of the 1949 (IVth) Geneva Convention concerning the protection of civilians under military occupation. Israel reacted with indignation to UN Security Council Resolution 605 calling for its observance of this convention, and to the criticism from Western democracies, particularly that emanating from the United States.

The authorities also attempted to impose curfews on the areas of unrest, especially the refugee camps. At one point all Gaza was under curfew, with over 500,000 inhabitants confined to their homes.

As the death toll rose in the first fortnight of January, amid mounting international protests, Defence Minister Yitzhak Rabin shifted the emphasis of repression away from the use of firearms in favour of physical intimidation and economic coercion to re-establish order. In the short term it was successful. He exhorted his troops to use 'might, power and beatings' to restore order.[14] Soldiers armed with cudgels beat up those they could lay their hands on regardless of whether they were demonstrators, or not, breaking into homes by day and night, dragging men and women, young and old, from their beds to beat them. At Gaza's Shifa Hospital 200 people were treated during the first five days of the new policy, most of them suffering from broken elbows and knees. Three had fractured skulls. Pregnant women were reported to have miscarried after beatings. Tear gas was widely used. Thrown into homes it became a lethal weapon, accounting for numerous fatalities.[15] Young men were seized at random and tied to the fronts of Israeli vehicles to discourage stone throwers. 'We will make it clear who is running the territories,' Rabin declared.[16] There was a rationale for the new policy of physical violence. 'A detainee sent to prison', a government official explained, 'will be freed in 18 days unless the authorities have enough evidence to charge him. He may then resume stoning soldiers. But if troops break his hand, he won't be able to throw stones for a month and a half.'[17]

An attempt was made to break economic disobedience. Sledgehammers were used to force open shuttered shops during strikes and shopkeepers were beaten up. But locksmiths and welders repeatedly repaired the damage enabling the strikes to continue.[18] After the first few weeks Israeli efforts to strikebreak were largely abandoned. Attempts were made to force the 120,000 or so Palestinians who worked in Israel back to work. Refugee camps in Gaza, the chief source of this labour, were put under siege.[19] Those caught bringing food into camps under curfew had it taken from them:

> As the women wept and shouted, soldiers trampled bread and vegetables underfoot and threw a basket of food under a passing car. One soldier threw a cauliflower at one of the women as they turned away, hitting her on the back of the neck. 'We are not punishing them. We just want to give them a reason not to break the curfew' an Israeli officer, named Colonel Avi, told reporters.[20]

These efforts were more successful, since Palestinians depended on earnings in Israel. However, the withdrawal of labour on certain days continued to have a disruptive effect.

The absence of any political consensus in Israel over the causes for the unrest and the long-term solutions to it, was reflected in the way in which the National Unity Government made highly contradictory statements.[21] Everyone put a different significance on the unrest. Shamir qualified his own analysis by suggesting 'There is nothing new in this and nothing to fear. We have overcome this kind of thing in the past and we will do so now and in the future.'[22] His only concession to the trouble was to suggest that Israel might implement its own understanding of the Camp David autonomy plan, but only once order was restored. Peres, by contrast, argued the need to pursue a political solution concurrently with the restoration of order: 'We have to choose between Jordan and the PLO. Those who reject dialogue with Jordan open the way for the PLO.'[23] However, he also inadvertently admitted what the political establishment had denied before, that the PLO had already sought direct dialogue with Israel.[24]

The loudest protests came from the far Left and Right of Israel's political spectrum. The Left protested against troop violence and called for a quickly negotiated abandonment of the territories. The Right argued for tougher treatment of the insurgents and proper protection of the Jewish settlements.[25] Neither the protection of the settlements nor the repression of Palestinian irredentism commended itself to the military commanders responsible for civil order in the territories. While denying that the unrest threatened to become a full-scale rising, the chief of staff blamed the crisis on the failure of politicians to negotiate a solution.[26]

Both main parties, Likud and Labour, faced a high level of internal disagreement. In the former a 'young Turk', Moshe Amirav, who had nearly been expelled from the party for his talks with two leading Palestinians, gathered together a small dovish group calling for the return of Menachem Begin to party leadership and for 'full autonomy to the Palestinians'.[27] Shlomo Lahad, Likud veteran and mayor of Tel Aviv, urged the government to get rid of the occupied territories before it was too late.[28] In the Labour Party Rabin urged tough repressive measures, while Abba Eban, now an elder statesman, warned 'The situation is deforming our youth and degrading our democracy. We have to decide: are we to absorb the Palestinians and turn Israel into a Muslim state, or are we to become, like South Africa, a country in which people are denied their rights.[29]

The overlap between Likud and Labour parties, with hardliners like Shamir and Rabin at one end of the spectrum and Lahad and Eban at the other, reflected the overlap in attitudes between the two parties' supporters. Neither party reflected a coherent position on the Uprising. The immediate result of the unrest was a popular tilt to the Right. Three independent opinion polls in late December showed that the extreme right-wing party Kach, led by Meir Kahane, now claimed 5 per cent of the vote, compared with 1 per cent in the 1984 election. Other parties to the right of Likud gained similarly.[30]

While the tide of Jewish Israeli opinion ran in favour of the political Right, there was also a renewed surge in Peace Now, the broad coalition of left of centre groups seeking an end to Israel's continued confrontation with its Arab neighbours and subjects. Peace Now had been born in response to the negotiations for peace with Egypt, but had scored its greatest success during the Lebanon war of 1982, when it had gathered approximately 400,000 demonstrators to protest the massacre of Sabra/Shatila. On 23 January 1988 up to 50,000 Jewish and Palestinian Israelis demonstrated over the fate of the territories.[31] But Peace Now was better able to express what it did not want than what it did. Its early strength lay in its ability to mobilize protest against troop casualties, demonstrated during the invasion of Lebanon in 1982. The absence of Jewish casualties in the Uprising limited its appeal.

One reason for the general shift to the Right was the alarming and unexpected solidarity of Palestinian citizens of Israel with their cousins in the occupied territories. On 21 December a 'Peace Day' protest took place, with an estimated 80 per cent of the Israeli Palestinians staying away from work or school. Over one hundred Palestinians were arrested, and in two traditional centres of Palestinian nationalism, Nazareth and Umm al Fahm, tear gas was used to disperse the demonstrators.[32]

Although for twenty years most Jewish Israelis considered that the old 1949 Armistice Line had ceased to exist, only 160,000 Jewish Israelis had actually settled in the territories captured in 1967 and other than these few were exposed on a daily basis to the Palestinian presence. Most of the electorate still considered the occupied territories, while part of Eretz Israel, to be beyond the frontiers of daily life. Inside Israel itself most Jewish Israelis scarcely noticed the Palestinians, since almost every Arab population centre lies some way from the main thoroughfares of the country. Furthermore, Jewish Israelis had taken Palestinian unskilled labour for granted, and only noticed it when it was withdrawn.

The shock of the 21 December strike was increased by the participation of hitherto quiescent categories, bedouin in the Negev and Palestinians living in mixed cities.[33] There was an unhappy realization that eradicating the 1949 Armistice Line had cut both ways. If Eretz Israel of the Jews had become reunited, so also had Palestine of the Arabs. As one apprehensive commentator put it 'the Arabs won't settle for Nablus and Ramallah. They want Jaffa, Haifa and Acre too.'[34]

Israelis were also shocked by the economic impact of the Palestinian protest strike. For the first five weeks of the Uprising absenteeism by workers from the territories was approximately 50 per cent, resulting in a slowdown in the construction industry, a breakdown in municipal services, particularly the collection of garbage, and the collapse of agricultural labour at a moment when it was greatly needed.[35] Emergency plans included recruiting schoolchildren to pick the orange crop before it rotted on the trees, and recruiting cheap labour from the Far East to take the place of Palestinians. Some municipalities and commercial employers sent recruiters to remote Palestinian villages offering ten times the going rate in order to help them through the crisis. Tourism, which had surged in 1987 and was a vital foreign exchange earner, faced a massive recession as holiday cancellations flooded in.[36] Before the end of March 1988 the Economy Minister admitted that the Uprising had already cost Israel $300 million.[37]

Israelis had to consider for the first time the implications of a section of the work-force using economic disruption for political purposes. It was hardly surprising that the reaction was strong.

The Uprising and the PLO

The PLO was no less surprised than Israel by the Uprising, and at first was uncertain how to react. It wished to enhance its own standing by taking the credit, but did not wish the unrest to be dismissed simply as a PLO provocation. It was essential that the nature of the occupation be seen as the root cause of the Uprising, but it was also important that the spontaneity of the Uprising should not allow external contestants, primarily Syria, Jordan and the United States but also other Western countries, to dismiss the PLO's role as 'marginal, if not irrelevant' as one Western diplomat put it.[38]

Before the end of December, the PLO itself had announced the formation of the Unified National Leadership of the Uprising inside the territories. But there was an uneasy ambivalence implicit in the new balance of power and authority over the Palestinian movement, between the PLO and the new popular committees. There was something unsettling about the way in which loyalty to the PLO was now being expressed: 'We support the PLO. But the uprising comes from us. Anyway, who is the PLO? The PLO are our cousins. You cannot divide us from them just as you cannot divide the spirit from the body.'[39] Such remarks indicated that the people of the territories no longer took their lead from the PLO in diaspora, but rather led the PLO themselves.

Working together the leadership in Palestine and abroad was able to achieve an unprecedented legitimacy. The PLO outside the territories assisted in the propagation through radio broadcasts of instructions to the people of the territories regarding forthcoming acts of disobedience. Through a clandestine radio station it was able to beam popular music, speeches and accurate details of casualties over a wide area. In the absence of trustworthy alternatives, Israeli and Jordanian Palestinians began to tune in also.

The Uprising in the Arab world

At a meeting in Tunis at the end of January, the Arab states agreed to provide financial support depending on 'the continuation of the

Uprising'.[40] But they felt endangered by its spontaneity. In Algeria, Bahrain, Iraq, Jordan and Morocco unauthorized solidarity demonstrations were banned or broken up, and the organizers arrested.[41] In early June Arab heads of state met in Algiers. That it took the Arab states six months to convene a summit conference to consider the Uprising – the most significant Arab effort to date to recover the territories – suggested reluctance and embarrassment on their part. They found its autonomous drive threatening. Its leadership boldly told their conference to boycott the US Schultz mission, advice they felt bound to follow.[42] Jordan and Syria hoped that the conference would marginalize the PLO, but instead it dramatically restored its standing,[43] to a level it had not enjoyed since Israel's attempt to destroy it in Beirut in 1982. For as long as the Uprising persisted the PLO was likely to enjoy an almost unassailable position in the Arab world. As one refugee in Yarmuk camp in Syria happily remarked, the Uprising was 'stones in the face of the occupation and a slap in the face of the Arab governments.'[44]

In Egypt the explosion in the territories disturbed the progress of President Mubarak towards reintegration in the Arab fold, after its peace with Israel in 1979. While the focus of Arab attention remained on the Gulf war, Egypt, by its support of Iraq, hoped to resume its place at the heart of Arab political life. The Uprising was an uncomfortable reminder to the Egyptian people and to the wider Arab world, that Mubarak's relationship with Israel was embarrassingly different from theirs.[45] 'The only option to stabilise the situation in the Middle East', he announced, 'is an international peace conference.'[46] A conference might not conclude peace but it would help erase the negative impact the treaty with Israel had made in the minds of the Arab masses. Mubarak also proposed a six month halt to the Uprising as part of a package towards international peace talks.[47] The absence of Arab world condemnation of this proposal suggested that he was not alone among Arab leaders in wishing to halt the Uprising.

Syria, too, had grounds for disquiet. The discomfiture of Israel was highly desirable but increased PLO standing was an obstacle to Syria's longer-term ambition to be the unchallenged leader and arbiter among the Arabs in their struggle against Israel. The Uprising also created difficulties with its own surrogate Palestinian factions and on its own hold on Lebanon, where its Shiite allies still besieged the refugee camps of Beirut. Syria was also vulnerable from its Gulf funders, which did not expect it to attack Palestinian refugee camps. Consequently it instructed the siege of the camps in Beirut to be lifted.[48]

However, it was Jordan that had the greatest grounds for unease.

King Husayn welcomed the chance for an international peace conference. He feared with the rest of Jordan's population, East Bankers and Palestinians alike, that if Israel could not contain the situation it might resort to mass expulsion of Palestinians across the river Jordan. He also feared the effect of the Uprising on Palestinians living in his kingdom, in particular that it would fuel criticism of the government's inability or unwillingness to confront Israel or offer the Palestinians any support.[49]

The international arena

Outside the region, the Western powers viewed the Uprising with apprehension, for routine scenes of troop brutality demanded a response. There was a fear that the authority and strength the Uprising gave the PLO would make diplomatic progress more difficult, and that the Uprising threatened to destroy the fragile *modus vivendi* which had persisted in the territories for some years.

Since it had tried to manage the Middle East crisis without the interference or disagreement of other outside powers, the United States was in an exposed position. It could put more pressure on Israel to accept some kind of international forum as the way forward, but it had to ensure that Israel, as its strategic ally, would not be seriously damaged in the process. As a result it followed an ambivalent line at United Nations Security Council meetings to discuss the Uprising.[50] Like almost every other Western country and the Soviet Union, the United States still favoured some kind of international peace conference.

As the Uprising took on an apparent permanency, US Secretary of State, George Schultz, made four trips to the region, in order to instil life into the stalled 'peace process'. But no progress could be made. Both Israel and the USA were preparing for the election of new administrations in November, the Israeli government was hopelessly divided over the issue of international negotiations, and the United States was still unprepared to consider PLO participation or Palestinian self-determination. Without these there was no possibility of Palestinian participation and little chance of Jordanian or Egyptian participation either.

Uprising: the new normality

From the first days of the Uprising it had been clear that the most important political process since 1967 was now in motion. Soon both Palestinians and Israelis began saying, as General Amram Mitzna the Israel area commander purportedly remarked, 'there will be no return to the situation that pertained in the territories before the uprising began.'[51] It also became clear that the Uprising, and the mass mobilization of the Palestinians which it had engendered, was more important than the rise of the PLO itself twenty years earlier and more important, too, than the rebellion of 1936–9 in the struggle of national independence. The Uprising had unified people to an unprecedented extent. Its direction, authority and impetus were rooted in the experience of the common people. This was a new sensation for Palestinian nationalism. The widespread civil disobedience was a people's war in a way the armed struggle had never been, and it commanded universal support in a way the Arab revolt of 1936 had failed to do.

Clashes continued, although the frequency began to abate. One serious case was at the village of Bayta on 6 April 1988, in which a settler shot dead three Palestinians. A Jewish girl was also killed in the affray and it only became clear that she had been killed by another settler after the army had demolished thirteen homes and deported six villagers. Bayta indicated the temper of Israeli opinion. An opinion poll at the time indicated that 12.9 per cent of respondents wanted Bayta destroyed, while 52.4 per cent wanted the demolition of the homes of the 'guilty'. Only 21.5 per cent opposed the demolitions policy.[52] Ten days after Bayta an Israeli commando assassinated Abu Jihad, the senior PLO official with special responsibility for the territories, in Tunis. If the action was intended to discourage the Uprising it was highly counterproductive, for it led to renewed demonstrations.

A war of attrition set in. It was clear on the Israeli side that there would be no swift end to the unrest. Israel attempted to reassert control by widespread arrests. By May 1988 10,000 were imprisoned, more than 1 in every 200, many in a prison at Ketziot in the Negev where conditions were described by a retired US federal judge as 'appalling'.[53] In Gaza the authorities began issuing new ID cards without which it was impossible to get work in Israel. These were available only to those who paid their taxes. When a village tried to pay its water dues through a popular committee, rather than the Israeli-appointed village council, the authorities cut off the water until the village council was reinstated by the villagers and enabled to pay.[54] But Israel's success was limited. In June it admitted that its tax revenue from the territories had fallen by 50 per cent.[55] In August Israel tried to close down Palestinian popular committees, but struck at long established and registered charitable institutions. By the end of October it had demolished around 100 homes 'for security reasons', rendering approximately 700 people homeless.[56] It also began to arrest leading Palestinian moderates, for example Faysal al Husayni who had incurred official wrath by addressing a Peace Now rally, calling for a two state solution.[57] In September Defence Minister Rabin introduced the use of plastic bullets with the statement 'it is our intention to wound as many of them as possible . . . inflicting injuries is precisely the aim of using plastic bullets.'[58] During the course of September eight Palestinians were killed with these bullets.[59] By the end of September, too, a total of 30,000 Palestinians were reported injured during demonstrations, army searches or during arrest or interrogation. One leftist journal reported 'systematic beatings on kidneys, stomach, testicles, women's breasts, hands, soles of feet, burns, beatings and illnesses exacerbated by prisoners being drenched by water or forced to stand for days in the scorching sun, their heads covered by stinking sacks. Dozens of women miscarried, some during and after interrogation, most from the after effects of anti riot gas.'[60]

For the Palestinians the Uprising acquired normality. The semi-official *Facts Weekly Review* declared in April that the popular committees 'are more than just temporary committees which will operate for a limited period of time. They represent a permanent structural change in the form of organisation of Palestinian society.'[61] At the beginning of October the twenty-seventh UNLU leaflet was published, with the authorities apparently no closer to locating the source of these instructions than they had been at the outset.

The Palestinians seemed to be slowly wresting more ground from the authorities. When the authorities closed the schools of the territories, the population organized neighbourhood schools in private homes.[62] Voluntary medical teams increasingly took over health matters. On the economic front there was an enormous growth in the campaign for home production, whereby everyone who could find even the smallest patch of soil would grow vegetables or rear chickens. It was still necessary for workers, especially from the Gaza Strip, to find employment in Israel but there was an increasing determination to keep this to a minimum. By June 1988 Palestinian employment in Israel had fallen by about 40 per cent, and this fall began to look permanent. Some economists believed that with patience it would be possible to generate economic activities in the territories to absorb underemployed and unemployed workers.

The economic aspect of the Uprising became increasingly important. A genuine separation between Jew and Arab in Palestine seemed to be taking place. As Palestinians concentrated on household production as a means of subsistence, the authorities began to apply tougher economic punishments. During the summer months approximately 8,000 olive and fruit trees and thousands of dunums (1 dunum = 1,000 sq. m) of wheat were burnt.[63] This scorched earth policy was intensified by the loss of an estimated 100,000 dunums of woodland in Israel, blamed on Palestinian arsonists.[64] Elsewhere farmers in dissident villages were forbidden to harvest crops. In September the authorities threatened sanctions against the coming olive harvest 'to hit back at villages that are centres of unrest . . . to achieve maximum deterrence'.[65] Halhoul, a town just north of Hebron, was told by the civil administration that it would be unable to export its grape crop if the unrest did not cease.

Meanwhile, with a lack of military success army commanders expressed the view that the Uprising might go on for years.[66] Set in this time span and with both Palestinian Arab and Jewish Israeli attitudes in mind, it was time for a reassessment of the whole Arab-Jewish relationship in Palestine since it had begun to go wrong a century earlier.

INTRODUCTION: THE LEGACY OF THE PAST

Early Zionist settlement

The Uprising occurred a century after the first Zionist settlement in Palestine. In the 1880s, towards the close of the Ottoman period, the first Zionist settlers began to arrive in Palestine, leaving their homes in Russia or eastern Europe as a result of pogroms and persecution. They believed that the twin dangers to European Jewry, persecution in the east and assimilation in the west, could only be resolved by the establishment of a Jewish nation, able to order its own affairs on its own territory. It was natural that these Zionists should fix upon Palestine, in European eyes a relatively undeveloped land closely connected with the last time, 2,000 years earlier, that the Jews had been a nation. By 1914 85,000 such settlers had arrived in Palestine, amounting to 9 per cent of the population. For most, it was only after they had arrived in Palestine that they began to appreciate the central moral and practical difficulty facing the Zionist undertaking: that Palestine was already inhabited by half a million Christian and Muslim Arabs.

These Arab inhabitants quickly appreciated the dangerous implications of Zionist settlement. In 1886 the first land dispute between peasant and settler occurred.[1] It was one of about forty affrays between Arabs and Zionists over the next thirty years. Zionist settlement was a good deal more noticeable in certain cities, particularly Jaffa and Jerusalem. In the decade 1881–91 the Jewish population of Jerusalem increased from 14,000 (almost entirely non-Zionists who were there only for religious reasons) to over 25,000, the balance being mainly Zionist.[2] That same year, 1891, a number of Jerusalem notables wrote to the Grand Vizir in Istanbul asking him to prohibit further Zionist immigration.[3] When the latter did so, however, the European powers acted in concert to force the Ottomans to limit the prohibition to immigrants *en masse*, rather than to individuals, thereby making the prohibition virtually worthless.[4] In 1899 the Mayor of Jerusalem wrote to the Chief Rabbi in France, and implicitly to his acquaintance, Theodor Herzl the leading Zionist of the day, asking 'in the name of God, let Palestine be left in peace.'[5]

In the first years of the new century warnings against the Zionist dangers were more publicly expressed by leading Arab thinkers.[6] Two new local newspapers, *al Karmil* (1908) and *Filastin* (1911) adopted a clearly anti-Zionist stance.[7] By 1914 Zionism was the major political issue in Palestine. Notables, townspeople and peasantry were well aware of Zionist immigration, land purchases, urban settlement and the aims these activities implied. On the whole Palestinian notables kept a sharp distinction between Zionists, who represented one aspect of a more general political and economic European threat, and Ottoman Jews, whose presence and status within the empire was long standing and accepted.

For the inhabitants of Palestine, Zionist settlement took place against a backdrop of unprecedented change, largely resulting from increased European economic penetration. One feature of this change was the transition from a subsistence to a cash crop economy particularly in the coastal areas, accompanied by a growth in sharecroppers and landless labourers, and the beginning of seasonal labour migration from the central uplands of Palestine to the richer coastal areas.

In 1917 British troops advancing from Egypt captured almost all Palestine from the Ottoman forces. In November Arthur Balfour, the Foreign Secretary, wrote to Lord Rothschild that:

> His Majesty's Government view with favour the establishment in Palestine of a national home for the Jewish people, and will use their best endeavours to facilitate the achievement of this object, it being clearly understood that nothing shall be done to prejudice the civil and religious rights of the existing non-Jewish communities in Palestine, or the rights and political status enjoyed by Jews in any other country.

Britain's motive was to encourage colonization of this newly-captured territory under its own auspices in order to secure its political position in Palestine and so undermine the French and Russian stake provided for in the Sykes-Picot Agreement a year earlier. (The Sykes-Picot Agreement, the Allied plan to carve up the Ottoman empire into spheres of control on its defeat, had envisaged Palestine, or most of it, constituting an international zone under joint Allied control.) Britain wanted to control the eastern flank of the Suez Canal, to safeguard its communications with India.

The Balfour Declaration was greeted with enthusiasm by Zionists and dismay by Arabs both in Palestine and beyond. The latter had received both vague and explicit assurances from Britain that they would be allowed the freedom to form governments of their choice.[8] The Balfour Declaration contradicted these promises. A few Zionists, most notably Israel Zangwill,[9] were also dissatisfied since the declaration spoke of a Jewish homeland *in* rather than *of* Palestine, suggesting something less than the whole of the land. Most Zionist leaders, however, felt that the Balfour Declaration was a vital building block in the achievement of their aims. In 1919 they unsuccessfully claimed the right to settle the area they considered Eretz Israel (the Land of Israel), extending beyond Palestine as delimited by Britain and confirmed by the League of Nations (see map 1). This claim was based upon biblical Israel at its apogee, on the water resources of the Litani river in south Lebanon, and on British possession of the East Bank of the Jordan. It disregarded the Ottoman centuries when Palestine had not included any land east of Jordan.

Few Palestinians had expressed any nationalist sentiment before the war. However, faced with the disappearance of the Ottoman government and the advent of a European power apparently intent on encouraging Zionist settlement, they joined with other Syrians in calling for 'a democratic civil constitutional monarchy on broad decentralized principles, safeguarding the rights of minorities', and opposing Zionist colonization of Palestine.[10] However, expressions of Syrian Arab nationalism were short lived in Palestine for two reasons. Palestinians were uneasy at the willingness of Damascene Arabs to consider some kind of compromise with the Zionists, if the latter would unite with them in an attempt to be independent of France and Britain and would also provide capital to develop the Syrian hinterland. Then, in July 1920 France invaded Syria, removed its government and brought it under direct control, thus bringing to an end any hope that Palestine (or southern Syria as it was sometimes called) might still be incorporated into an independent Syrian Arab state.

Palestine under the Mandate

Palestinians felt themselves disadvantaged by British mandatory rule in a number of ways, of which the first was the decision, following

——— Boundary of the British
Palestine Mandate 1922–47

– – – Boundary of the land claimed by
the Zionist organisation, at the
Paris Peace Conference 1919, to
be set aside for Jewish settlement

Damascus

Sidon

Tyre

Acre
Safad
Haifa
Tiberias
Sea of
Galilee
Nazareth

Janin
Tulkarm
Nablus
Tel Aviv
Qalqilya
Jaffa
Lydda
Ramallah
Ramla
Jericho
Amman
Jerusalem
Bethlehem
Dead Sea
Gaza
Hebron
Rafah
Beersheba

0   20
km

Aqaba

Map 1   Palestine

Ottoman *millet* practice, to treat Muslims and Christians as separate political communities. Palestinians wanted to be treated as a single community because they were united on the one issue which gripped them: Zionist settlement of the country. It was felt to be a deliberate ploy to frustrate this unity. When Britain was granted its formal mandate from the League of Nations in 1922, Palestinians felt their position further weakened by the stipulation that a Jewish agency should assist the British authorities to develop Palestine economically.[11] The already existing Zionist Organization (later named the Jewish Agency) was recognized as this agency. The Palestinian Arabs had no similar organization or agency in being, and were not invited by the terms of the mandate to create one. The expectation that the Jewish community, known as the Yishuv, would develop Palestine economically implied growing Jewish economic power in the country, and it was not long before this expectation started to be fulfilled.[12]

The Palestinians' reaction to the British Mandate was divided, but tended to be recalcitrant and uncooperative in effect, since the Mandate legitimized Zionist settlement in Palestine in disregard of their own wishes. Many Palestinians had wanted a parliamentary body in which all Jews living in Palestine before the war would enjoy proportional representation, but they refused to accept the legitimacy of Zionist settlement subsequently. This state of mind determined Palestinian behaviour throughout the Mandate period. Palestinian notable families were disadvantaged without a legal structure equivalent to the Jewish Agency to argue their case, particularly since they refused to incorporate themselves in a way which implied recognition of the legality of the Mandate, since this also implied the legality of Zionist settlement. Their logic excluded the possibility of effective political action.

Not everyone favoured the rejection of all compromise, but the hardliners tended to win the argument. When Britain held elections for a legislative council in 1923, both Muslim and Christian Palestinians boy-cotted them after considerable debate. Their overwhelming objection was that the legislative council would not be able to challenge the terms of the Mandate, thus debarring the issue that vitally concerned them, Jewish immigration and settlement.[13] By refusing to participate Palestinians forfeited their chance to moderate the effect of Zionist settlement.

By contrast, the Zionist leadership was highly conciliatory, asserting that 'the absolute desire of the Jewish people is to live with the Arabs in conditions of unity and mutual honour and together with them to turn the common homeland into a flourishing land, the consolidation of which will ensure each of its peoples undisturbed national development.'[14] Nevertheless, there were plenty of warning signals that Jewish ambition went well beyond what Britain had in mind. For example, in 1921 a leading representative of the Zionist Organization pronounced 'there can be only one national home in Palestine, and that is a Jewish one, and no equality in the partnership between Jews and Arabs, but a Jewish preponderance as soon as members of the race are sufficiently increased.'[15] Such remarks suggested to Palestinians that their fears, despite British reassurances, were not exaggerated.

The inability of Palestinian notables to provide effective leadership for the inhabitants of Palestine stemmed to a considerable extent from the division of these notable families into two broad factions, whose point of view was represented by one of two rival Jerusalem families, the Husaynis and the Nashashibis. The former was associated with a more militant nationalist line, the latter with a more accommodationist one, although there were exceptions to this tendency. The failure of the notable class to direct popular anger into effective political action led to periodic outbursts.

In 1920 a number of Zionist settlements were attacked, and Britain decided to limit Jewish immigration. In 1921 a more serious outburst of anger by an Arab mob in Jaffa led to the deaths of nearly 200 Jews and 120 Arabs. But what the commission of enquiry decided had been a spontaneous outburst was seen very differently by Jewish settlers, who naturally interpreted it as a pogrom, similar in motive and kind to those from which they had escaped in Russia. Unwilling to leave their safety in the hands of the authorities, leading Zionist settlers, notably David Ben Gurion, Israel's future prime minister, began to organize the self-defence of each settlement.

In 1929 far worse attacks, amounting to massacres, took place on Jews in Jerusalem, Hebron and Safad, three of the four sacred Jewish cities in Palestine. These attacks were significant because they were made on Jewish communities which pre-dated Zionism, and because they were made for religious reasons. Their immediate cause was the dispute over Jewish access to the Western (Wailing) Wall and its proximity to the Haram al Sharif, where stands the Dome of the Rock (where Abraham offered to sacrifice Isaac) and the al Aqsa mosque, the site of the Prophet Muhammad's Night Visit. Britain had followed Ottoman precedent which satisfied Muslim but not Jewish opinion. Religious Jews attempted to assert greater freedom for themselves there. The Mufti, Hajj Amin al Husayni, used Muslim tension to strengthen his leadership in Palestinian national affairs, and was undoubtedly behind the build-up of Muslim anger.[16] While many Palestinian Arabs may have found the arguments concerning self-determination – affirmed but then denied them by the League of Nations – overly theoretical, the Mufti had skilfully used the apparent threat to the Haram al Sharif as a powerful symbol of Palestinian identity. The Palestinian-Zionist contest spilt over into the religious domain, drawing in the Arab and Muslim worlds. It also blurred the distinction many Arabs had maintained hitherto between Zionist and non-Zionist Jews – hence the attacks on the older Jewish communities. Since then, the Haram al Sharif and the Wailing Wall have lost none of their emotive appeal for the protagonists.

The events of 1929 proved a turning point in the Palestinian national movement, and British punishment of some perpetrators of the massacres fuelled Arab nationalist opinion further. While Britain again refused a Palestinian demand for national government in 1930, it did agree to stop Jewish immigration and ban land transfers, but retreated from these undertakings the following year. Predictably, this vacillation merely heightened Jewish and Palestinian apprehensions concerning British policy.

Meanwhile, Jewish land purchase continued apace, exacerbating Palestinian disquiet. Land purchases up to the mid-1920s had tended to be from absentee landlords, living mainly outside Palestine. Peasants working on such land were usually evicted, sometimes with compensation, sometimes without.[17] Furthermore, land was purchased through the Jewish National Fund (JNF) which adhered to two vital principles: all land purchased by the JNF would remain inalienably Jewish and only Jews could work on it. As an official British report of 1930 inquiring into the causes of the 1929 massacres reported:

> The result of the purchase of land in Palestine by the Jewish National Fund has been that land has been extra-territorialized. It ceases to be land from which the Arab can gain any advantage either now or at any time in the future. Not only can he never hope to lease or to cultivate it, but by the stringent provisions of the lease of the JNF he is deprived for ever from employment on that land.[18]

But British efforts to protect Arab landholders were wholly ineffective. The Zionists, determined to acquire more land, got around each piece of legislation.[19] As the potential for land purchase from absentees diminished, so the JNF found local notables willing or compelled by changing economic circumstances to sell cultivated land.

From the early 1930s Jewish land acquisition policy shifted from being purely economic to being more geo-political, securing, for example, a strong foothold in eastern Galilee.[20] This was partly in response to the deteriorating situation for Jews in Europe. The Yishuv had grown from 8 per cent of the whole population in 1918 to only 17 per cent by 1931. But as immigrants arrived from Europe in the 1930s, this growth accelerated, reaching 33 per cent by 1940.

Given the general economic transformation in train in Palestine, Zionist land acquisition began to impinge far more directly on peasant consciousness. In 1936 peasants in the northern part of the country rose in an attempt to drive out both unwanted rulers and settlers. The revolt was most virulent in those areas where new Jewish settlement was greatest and around Haifa, to which much casual Arab labour had been attracted. It took British troops eighteen months to suppress the revolt. Notables, including the Mufti, lent their support because they felt they could not afford to remain on the sidelines.

It was this popular violence rather than the interventions of notables which finally persuaded Britain, in 1937, to establish the Royal (Peel) Commission to inquire into the causes of the rebellion, and to admit the incompatibility of its promises to indigenous Palestinian and Zionist settlers. The Peel Report proposed a partition of Palestine, which offered the Jews a coastal enclave running from south of Jaffa to the Lebanese border and all Galilee. A corridor including Jerusalem and running down to Jaffa would remain under permanent British control and the rest would remain Arab. Apart from Galilee, where the population was predominantly Arab, the Peel Partition Plan reflected the demographic pattern of Palestine a good deal more accurately than the partition eventually adopted.

However, publication of the Peel Report provoked a renewed outbreak of the Arab revolt, and this in turn led the authorities to reconsider the wisdom of partition, in consultation with Jewish and Arab representatives. The key demands of the Palestinian Arab were that Jewish immigration and land purchases be stopped; that Palestine become an independent state connected to Britain by treaty, as in the case of Iraq; that the ratio of Jews to the total population (approximately 30 per cent) not be surpassed, but that Jewish political and civil rights be safeguarded and Hebrew given the status of official second language in Jewish regions.[21]

The Jews were resolutely opposed to any halt in immigration or the abandonment of the idea of partition which Ben Gurion and other Zionists hailed as a critical step towards their goal, even if it gave them less of Palestine than Zionism demanded. Furthermore, the Arab revolt persuaded most Zionists, and certainly the most influential leaders, that reconciliation with the Arabs was no longer possible, and that possession of Palestine would fall to the stronger of the two parties. As the Palestinian Arabs fell into political and military disarray following the collapse of the revolt and the exile of its leaders, so the Jewish underground forces, the Haganah, began to grow in size, organization and military capability.

Britain, however, favoured a bi-national state solution, one less explicitly 'Arab' than the Arabs wanted but one in which, in response to Arab fears, Jews would not constitute more than one-third of the total population. It was therefore prepared to restrict Jewish immigration to a total of 75,000 over five years, and to indicate that as soon as conditions allowed it would begin to form a Palestine government that would eventually acquire sovereignty. This position was made clear in the government White Paper of 1939.[22] The following year, in order to protect Arab lands, Britain prohibited all further Jewish land purchase except in the coastal and Esdraelon plains.

In view of what was happening in Europe, the White Paper and land purchase restrictions triggered bitter and understandable Jewish opposition. To British dismay the Palestinian Arabs also rejected the White Paper, not because it did not go far enough on control of Jewish immigration, but because it did not include an explicit and cast-iron commitment to Palestinian independence at the end of the transitional period (now clearly defined by the oncoming war between Britain and Germany). The Palestinian Arab leaders believed that Britain would only promote an all-Palestinian government if the Zionists acquiesced, a most unlikely contingency. But even if the Palestinians had accepted the White Paper, the Jewish Holocaust in Europe and the eclipse of Britain by the United States would have changed everything. Neither they nor the British were able to resist the implications for Palestine. By this time the Palestinian Arabs were in a far weaker position than in 1936. Their guerrilla bands were smashed, and their political leaders, most notably the Mufti himself, in exile.

In the meantime the Yishuv was substantially stronger both militarily and politically. The Haganah, the Jewish defence force, had benefited from the commando training provided by British officers for the defence of Jewish settlements, 1936–9. Jewish brigades had served in the British army during the war. Finally, two urban guerrilla groups, Irgun and LEHI (Stern) were beginning campaigns of terror first against the British but subsequently against the Arab inhabitants of Palestine.

In the political sphere the Zionist leadership had anticipated the shift in power from Britain to the United States, and established a strong position for itself among American Jews and, as far as it could, among American policy-makers. An American Zionist conference at the Biltmore Hotel, New York, urged in 1942

> that the gates of Palestine be opened; that the Jewish Agency be vested with control of immigration into Palestine and with the necessary authority for upbuilding the country, including the development of its unoccupied and uncultivated lands; and that Palestine be established as a Jewish Commonwealth.[23]

In essence, such a declaration, adopted by the Jewish Agency Executive, amounted to the demand that Palestine be a Jewish State. Some Zionists rejected Biltmore, on the grounds that the call for a state at this juncture could only lead to partition. As in the Arab camp, deep disagreement existed between those pragmatists who wished to work within the framework of what could be achieved at a particular moment, and those who insisted on the fulfilment of principle. Up to 1967 the Jewish pragmatists largely prevailed, whereas in the Palestinian Arab camp the pragmatists were defeated by the Husayni faction.

With the extermination of European Jews and the desperate plight of Jewish survivors and refugees, the Western sense of guilt was heightened by unseemly British attempts to keep their undertaking to the Arabs by turning back illegal immigrant ships. In 1947 Britain decided it could no longer fulfil the promises it had made 30 years earlier, and asked the United Nations, as heir to the League of Nations, to terminate the Mandate, and take whatever steps it felt necessary to resolve the question of Palestine.

Partition

The United Nations Special Committee on Palestine (UNSCOP) recommended partition of Palestine into two states, Jewish and Arab, and an international zone including Jerusalem and Bethlehem (see map 2). It was envisaged that the whole should be in economic union. The Jewish Yishuv accepted the partition. The Palestinian Arabs rejected it, having already boycotted UNSCOP's inquiry prior to its recommendations. The argument of the former, broadly speaking, was that

Map 2   The partition of Palestine

recognition of a sovereign Jewish state in part of Palestine outweighed the fact that the proposed Jewish portion fell far short of the Zionist dream of 1919.

The Palestinian Arabs remained opposed in principle to any partition of Palestine and in practice to a partition which seemed intrinsically unfair. They did not see why the Jews should be awarded 54 per cent of the land area of Palestine while they constituted barely one-third of the population. Nor did they see why the Jewish State should be awarded the Naqab desert (or Negev as it became known) in disregard of over 90,000 Naqab bedouin compared with less than 600 Jewish settlers.[24] The plan implied a Jewish state with an Arab population of almost exactly 50 per cent owning three times as much land as the Jewish community, and an Arab state with a Jewish population of only 1.3 per cent.[25] It could reasonably be asked how the former state would be workable as a democracy, how the Palestinian Arabs could conceivably view the proposed partition as fair, or how economic union could work between two deeply opposed communities.

Such doubts were never put to the test. Fighting broke out between Jews and Arabs, and on 15 May, when Britain evacuated the last of its troops, neighbouring Arab states sent armies into Palestine ostensibly to help defeat the Jews. By this time, however, Jewish forces of the new Israeli state had captured sizeable parts of the area allocated for an Arab state and there were already over 300,000 Arab refugees from the areas under Jewish control on both sides of the partition line. During the subsequent fighting Israel continued to gain territory, and when an armistice was agreed in early 1949 it controlled 73 per cent of Palestine.

Altogether about 725,000 Palestinian Arabs lost their homes in the course of the war. In Lausanne in 1949 the United Nations Palestine Conciliation Commission (PCC) failed to persuade Israel and the Arab states to make peace or to reach a settlement concerning the refugees. The United Nations affirmed that

> the refugees wishing to return to their homes to live at peace with their neighbours should be permitted to do so at the earliest practicable date, and that compensation should be paid for the property of those not choosing to return and for the loss or damage to property which, under principles of international law or in equity, should be made good by the Governments or authorities responsible.[26]

Israel resolutely opposed this call.

1949–67: the failure to make peace

The remnants of Arab Palestine, what became known as the West Bank and the Gaza Strip, fell under Transjordanian and Egyptian administration respectively. Transjordan formally annexed the West Bank adopting a new name, Jordan. To the outside world the conflict became inter-statal, between Israel and neighbouring Arab states. The Palestinian dimension did not go beyond the future of the refugees.

In successive years Israel's borders were seldom quiet. Large numbers of Palestinians tried to creep back to their homes, and a few attempted violent revenge. Israel adopted a rigorous policy of exacting retribution for border violations and forays. Sometimes it struck back at the nearest village beyond the border, sometimes against government forces. Both sides accused the other of responsibility. In November 1956 Israel, acting in collusion with France and Britain, attacked Egypt and occupied Gaza and Sinai, but as a result of US pressure, was forced to withdraw in March 1957.

In 1966 tension grew between Israel and Syria. Syria was following Israel's example in exploiting the Jordan headwaters and was also allowing Palestinian guerrillas to operate from its territory. Israeli threats against Syria resulted in a defence pact between Syria and Egypt, making it almost inevitable that Egypt would be drawn into any Israeli-Syrian confrontation. In November 1966 a major Israeli reprisal against the village of Samu in the West Bank led to violent demonstrations and order was restored only with difficulty. To deflect internal criticism, King Husayn accused Egypt of a failure to match words with actions. Both in Israel and in the Arab states the more aggressively minded outmanoeuvred the proponents of restraint. In May 1967 Syria became convinced that Israel intended to implement recent threats against it. Egypt felt compelled to act, closing the Straits of Tiran to Israeli shipping (Israel's sole gain from its '56 campaign) and instructing the United Nations to remove its Emergency Force, deployed at Egypt's request following Israel's Sinai campaign a decade earlier. Egypt's action was acclaimed in the Arab world, encouraging a belligerent posture. On 30 May Egypt and Jordan signed a mutual defence pact, but it seems that Nasser had no wish for war but hoped to score a stunning diplomatic victory over Israel. It was a victory Israel was unwilling to allow and on 5 June 1967 it attacked Egypt. The speed with which it vanquished Egyptian, Jordanian and Syrian forces was sensational. By 11 June it had captured all Sinai, the rest of Arab

Palestine, and a portion of the Jawlan, or Golan as it now became known.

1967–73: the failure of war

Both sides hardened in their attitude. Israel, in its newly acquired ascendancy, annexed East Jerusalem, and began to establish settlements in the Jordan valley and Golan, ostensibly for defensive purposes. The Arab states, in their defeat, decided on four guiding principles: no peace with Israel, no recognition of Israel, no negotiations with Israel and action to safeguard the Palestinian people's right to their homeland.

At the United Nations, Israel's annexation of Jerusalem was condemned, and in November the Security Council approved Resolution 242, which emphasized 'the inadmissibility of the acquisition of territory by war and the need to work for a just and lasting peace'. Such a peace, it stated, should include 'Withdrawal of Israeli armed forces from territories occupied in the recent conflict; acknowledgement of the sovereignty, territorial integrity and political independence of every State in the area and their right to live in peace within secure and recognised boundaries'. It also affirmed the need 'For guaranteeing freedom of navigation through international waterways in the area; for achieving a just settlement of the refugee problem; for guaranteeing the territorial inviolability and political independence of every State in the area'. Finally, it called for a UN Special Representative 'to proceed to the Middle East to establish and maintain contacts with the States concerned to promote agreement . . . to achieve a peaceful and accepted settlement'. Egypt and Jordan accepted the resolution. Israel only accepted it under US pressure some three years later, with the reservation that it would not evacuate all the territory it had captured.

The United Nations Special Representative, Gunnar Jarring, accepted failure after years of effort. Israel insisted on direct bilateral negotiations with each Arab state, while the latter insisted on a general peace conference.

In the absence of progress, Egypt began a war of attrition to tire Israel and force it to withdraw from the Suez Canal. Israel responded with deep penetration raids, hitting both military and civilian targets. In 1969 Egypt installed Soviet missiles operated by Soviet personnel to thwart Israeli air attacks. Neither the United States nor the Soviet Union wished to be drawn into a direct conflict by their regional allies. As a result of superpower negotiations, US Secretary of State William

Rogers announced a peace plan in 1970, accepted by both Jordan and Egypt but which led to the break up of the Israeli cabinet, when Prime Minister Golda Meir bowed to US pressure. In due .course, Rogers' efforts, like those of Jarring, petered out.

In October 1973 Egypt and Syria broke the deadlock by launching a surprise attack on Israeli positions. Egyptian troops crossed the canal, and Israeli forces only recovered and took the initiative after substantial US assistance. On the Syrian front, the Israelis recovered ground and increased their hold on the Golan. United States Secretary of State Henry Kissinger put pressure on the parties to observe a cease-fire called for by UN Security Council Resolution 338, and agree to troop disengagements that permitted the Egyptians to reopen the Suez Canal. It made no progress, however, on Resolution 338's call for the immediate implementation of the requirements of Resolution 242.

The PLO years

Meanwhile, the loss of all Palestine had created the first real surge of Palestinian solidarity since 1948. Although the Arab states had created a Palestinian Liberation Organization in 1964, this was considered more a means of controlling Palestinian nationalism than allowing it free reign. Another group, Fatah, had begun pinprick raids on Israel in 1965, and stepped up its attacks after the dismal Arab showing of 1967. Palestinians everywhere felt that in view of the Arab failure, only they, the Palestinian people, could recover Palestine. Recruits quickly flocked to Fatah, particularly after its bloody but heroic stand against a strong Israeli reprisal on Karama, on the East Bank of Jordan in 1968. The following year, Fatah's leader, Yasser Arafat, became chairman of the PLO Executive Committee.

During the next twenty years the PLO became a central feature of the Middle East conflict. In Israel and the West it became best known for terrorism and, implicitly, as an obstruction to a negotiated peace. It was seen as violent and extremist in its aims. Its charter, formulated by the Palestine National Council (the Palestinians' parliament), pronounced armed struggle as the path to liberation, and called for an end to the Israeli State. Although PLO thinking changed, its charter did not, and this became a powerful argument against PLO legitimacy in the West.

In the Arab world, however, and particularly among the Palestinian diaspora, the PLO symbolized the refusal to accept defeat so humiliatingly inflicted on the regular armies of the Arab countries. Through its myriad social, economic and political activities the PLO gave Palestinians everywhere a vital sense of cohesion, one which no denial of the PLO by the West could shake.

Fatah came to dominate the PLO and remained easily the most popular constituent group since it appealed solely to the idea of 'the return' to Palestine. But most of the other member groups, notably the Popular Front for the Liberation of Palestine (PFLP) and the breakaway Democratic Front for the Liberation of Palestine (DFLP) were more revolutionary in ideology. They were leftist and Arab nationalist, seeing the recovery of Palestine as part of an Arab (rather than solely Palestinian) struggle for liberation. This liberation included the replacement of reactionary Arab regimes with progressive socialist ones. Fatah's simple creed, which begged no awkward questions about the kind of Palestine it envisaged, appealed to the masses in the camps. The more ideological guerrilla groups appealed often to those with more education, or to those who felt that only a vision of what was to be created gave any meaning to their endeavours to recover Palestine. Outside the region, however, these groups were seen as 'rejectionist', since they rejected any compromise with Israel.

Jordan became not only the main springboard for guerrilla attacks on Israeli targets, but also the immediate target of those groups which believed in the need for a new Arab political order. Tension between King Husayn and the guerrilla groups heightened during 1969–70, with rumours of the former's imminent overthrow. In 1970 the PFLP hijacked two international airliners, and destroyed them on a remote airstrip in the Jordanian desert. Husayn decided his regime might not survive another humiliation to his authority and committed his army to eliminating the guerrilla movement from Jordan. Some of the latter surrendered to Israeli troops on the river Jordan, rather than fall into the hands of Husayn's troops.

The focus for the Palestinian struggle now switched to the refugee camps of Lebanon, where the guerrilla movement painfully rebuilt itself. The commandos were immensely popular in the camps, which for the first time since 1948 were able to remove Lebanese secret police and begin to control their own affairs. The PLO was also initially popular with the Shiite community of south Lebanon, since they shared a common persecuted and downtrodden identity. Together, perhaps, they might liberate themselves from their powerful enemies.

Palestinian attacks on northern Israel, however, provoked reprisals not only against the refugee camps, but also against Shiite villages in the border areas, many of which harboured PLO guerrillas unwillingly. From 1973 to 1978 Israel turned much of the Shiite south into a wasteland, driving many poor villagers north to the slums of Beirut, and also driving a wedge between the PLO and its now much less welcoming host population.

The Palestinian movement gained world attention by spectacular acts of terrorism and air piracy, both in the Middle East and internationally. It began to wield influence beyond its military strength and this was recognized in the wake of the 1973 war. Meeting in Rabat in October 1974 the Arab states recognized the PLO as the sole legitimate representative of the Palestinian people, a phrase accepted in word rather than spirit by Jordan, which stood to lose by the implications. The following month Arafat was invited to address the United Nations General Assembly. Israel and the United States agreed in 1975 not to recognize or negotiate with the PLO, condemning it as a terrorist organization.

In Beirut and its surroundings, the presence of the PLO forces acted as a catalyst in the disintegration of the national consensus on which Lebanon had operated since 1943. In 1975 the PLO found itself ranged on the side of the Muslims and Leftists who were challenging the hegemony of a Lebanese élite, presided over by a Maronite president. These Muslims and Leftists wanted constitutional changes to secularize the confessional nature of Lebanese politics and make it more democratic. The Christian groups wanted to protect the character of the Lebanese State against what it perceived as an Arabist threat. Lebanon became divided into two. In March 1978 Israeli forces invaded south Lebanon with the intention of destroying the PLO and its installations, but without success. The US government supported the United Nations in calling for its immediate withdrawal, and the deployment of an interim force in Lebanon (UNIFIL), along its southern border. UNIFIL was unable to deploy as required because of the establishment of an Israeli surrogate, the South Lebanese Army, in part of this area, and was obliged to operate as best it could in vacant areas between the PLO and Israeli-directed Lebanese forces.

The consequences of the Egyptian peace

Meanwhile, dramatic political developments occurred when President Sadat of Egypt decided unilaterally to visit Jerusalem in a peace mission in November 1977. This mission derailed superpower efforts to reconvene the Geneva peace conference, which had last met briefly in 1973. Under United States brokership, Israel and Egypt signed a number of accords at Camp David in 1978, culminating in a formal peace agreement in 1979. Egypt was the first and – a decade later – only Arab state to make peace with Israel. Israel agreed to evacuate all Egyptian territory. With regard to the occupied territories, Israel agreed to a temporary suspension of its settlements and to introduce autonomy for the Palestinian inhabitants for a five year period but without any indication of what might then happen. Egypt was bitterly denounced by most Arab states, which formed a 'steadfastness front' to support those under occupation and also the frontline states, Syria and Jordan. The Palestinians themselves also condemned Egypt and the autonomy, which they believed could only be a fig leaf for continued Israeli control.

Peace with Egypt freed Israel's militant government, under Menachem Begin, to attack its enemies without fear from its southern front. In 1982 it sent its army into Lebanon, ostensibly to achieve peace for Galilee. However, its forces advanced well beyond the initial 40 km limit, and surrounded West Beirut in alliance with Christian Lebanese forces. Its motive was to destroy the PLO, and thereby to destroy the focus of loyalty and solidarity for the Palestinians under Israeli occupation. After a ten-week siege, the United States brokered the withdrawal of the PLO from Beirut but failed to protect Palestinian civilians as it had undertaken to do. When Lebanon's President-elect, Bashir Gemayel, was assassinated a few days later, Israeli forces broke their undertaking and entered the city, sending Christian militiamen into the Palestinian camp of Sabra/Shatila. The latter committed major massacres over a three day period before international reports and protests persuaded Israeli forces to intervene to prevent further killings. Israel slowly withdrew from Lebanon, leaving a residual force in the border area to support the South Lebanese Army in 1985.

In autumn 1982 three peace plans were proposed to avoid further convulsions in the region, one by US President Ronald Reagan, another by the Arab heads of state, meeting in Fez, and the third by the Soviet Union. The Arab states were careful not to reject either the United States' or Soviet proposals. The United States disliked the Arab call for Palestinian self-determination and ignored the Fez declaration. The Soviet plan was almost completely ignored except in the Arab states. Israel rejected all three peace plans.

Scattered to different Arab countries, the PLO's fortunes continued to plummet. In 1983 discontent over Arafat's agreement to withdraw from Beirut exploded into open rebellion among those PLO fighters in Syrian areas of control in Lebanon. With Syrian support, these moved on Arafat's last stronghold in Lebanon, the refugee camps on the northern edge of Tripoli. Once again, Arafat and his fighters had to negotiate their way out of the city, made possible because of the pressure applied by Arab states on Damascus.

Jordan and the PLO

Bereft of independent or military options, Arafat commenced talks with King Husayn of Jordan with a view to trying to break the diplomatic impasse. These talks intensified the schisms within the PLO, leading to the distancing of the PFLP, DFLP, and other factions from Yasser Arafat's leadership. But in February 1985 they also led to an agreement between Husayn and Arafat to 'march together toward a just, peaceful settlement of the Middle East issue'. The wording of the agreement was intended to open the way for PLO participation in peace negotiations under United States auspices, for both the PLO and Jordan believed that only the United States had the ability and credibility to act as broker. They therefore called for a comprehensive peace settlement based on: land in exchange for peace, all UN resolutions on the conflict, the Palestinian right to self-determination and a solution to the refugee problem in accordance with UN resolutions. It was envisaged that the PLO would be represented within a joint Jordanian–Palestinian delegation, and that if the negotiations were successful a Palestinian–Jordanian confederation would emerge.

These proposals were unacceptable to the United States without an explicit acceptance of Resolution 242, a recognition of Israel's right to exist, and a renunciation of violence by the PLO. Furthermore, the United States ruled out any possibility of Palestinian statehood. The issue of self-determination, rather than Resolution 242 lay at the heart of the failure of the PLO–Jordanian initiative. The PLO told the United States it would accept Resolution 242 *explicitly*, if the United States would explicitly recognize the Palestinian right to self-determination in return. This the United States was unwilling to do.[27]

The argument over Resolution 242 revealed that while the PLO was unwilling to accept it in isolation from other UN resolutions on Palestine, but would accept it within that corpus, the United States wished to exclude all resolutions on Palestine *except* 242, thus to deny the right to self-determination explicitly recognized in other resolutions.

In the meantime two terrorist outrages, in Larnaca harbour and on the pleasure ship *Achille Lauro* in the autumn of 1985, seriously weakened Arafat's credibility and angered public opinion in the United States. Either Arafat was responsible for these acts, or he had insufficient control over the PLO's constituent groups to be a credible negotiator. Israel bombed the PLO Headquarters in Tunis in retaliation. With the encouragement of the United States, Husayn formally broke with Arafat in March 1986.

Jordan began to co-operate with the United States policy of improving the conditions of life in the occupied territories, a policy aimed at satisfying local discontent while bolstering the position of Jordan and Israel as the two authorities with which the Palestinians had to deal.

The PLO, on the other hand, faced a gloomy prospect with no independent base, and still facing Syrian hostility and internal schism. In Lebanon refugee camps still supportive of Arafat came under repeated siege from Syria's surrogate Shiite militia, Amal. In the occupied territories the people began to feel the impact of Israel's tough new iron fist policy applied, it was believed, to crush any expectation of political progress.

The Palestinian resurgence

The following year, 1987, however, saw the beginning of a remarkable revival in PLO fortunes. Most years since its foundation, the governing body of the PLO, the Palestine National Council (PNC) had managed to meet somewhere in the Arab world to affirm PLO policy principles. The 17th PNC had met in Amman in November 1984, but had been boycotted by several important factions. In April 1987 the 18th Palestine National Congress met in Algiers, with representatives of the Damascus dissident groups, PFLP, DFLP, and the Communist Party in attendance. In the course of deliberations, most of the post-1982 schisms were brought to an end, as the PLO formally renounced the 1985 accord with Jordan, and reaffirmed its rejection of Resolution 242 in isolation.

The most important outcome of the 18th PNC, as it turned out, was the reconciliation of factions inside the occupied territories, making the political ground far more propitious for united action than it had been for many years. When Gaza exploded in anger and frustration on 9 December 1987, the underground political leaders were ready.

Part I
THE INTERNATIONAL CONTEXT

1
PALESTINE: THE INTERNATIONAL CONFLICT

As seen in the preceding chapter, the struggle between Jew and Arab for Palestine became largely an inter-statal one from 1948 onwards. Palestine disappeared from the map and Arab nationalism over the next twenty years emphasized the recovery of Palestine as the foremost duty of every Arab state. By 1967 even the refugees, the last vestige of things Palestinian to the outside world, had become a permanent and institutionalized presence under each host government, and half of them were by then Jordanian citizens.

With the passage of time and the growth of a network of relationships between the young nations of the region and the great powers outside, the conflict became far more complex. Palestine assumed the same level of international importance and sensitivity as the Balkans did in the nineteenth century.[1] Just as the weakening of the Ottoman hold on the Balkans had drawn the great powers into regional competition, so the weakening of Britain's hold on the Middle East, particularly Palestine, at the end of the Second World War drew the United States and the Soviet Union into the region, and also sucked neighbouring Arab states into the Palestine conflict. As a consequence the struggle for Palestine has been carried out on many levels, creating a complexity which even the participants have at times found difficult to follow.

The regional, local and global contests

At the regional level, Palestine became the focus for inter-Arab rivalries because of its potent position in the Arab consciousness. It was impossible to discuss the idea of Arab nationalism without mentioning Palestine, because the Arab political awakening occurred in the very years of Zionist settlement in Palestine in the first half of this century. Zionism was an alien presence in the Arab body politic. During the 1950s and 1960s the fate of Palestine gained in importance in Arab national thinking. The refugee presence in neighbouring countries made the Palestine question highly visible, while from an Arab perspective the creation of Israel could only be seen as a smack in the face of the Arab nation.

The Arab world, and especially Egypt, embarked upon a revolutionary process, shedding (or so they thought) the shackles of imperialism and colonialism, of which Israel remained the most striking example. Arab national consciousness was profoundly shaken by the ease with which the fledgeling State of Israel defied and defeated the Arab world in 1948. How could the strength of the Arab nation be vindicated except through its ability to evict this alien presence from Arab soil? The success of Arab nationalism was predicated upon the recovery of Palestine. It was a propagandist and political issue no Arab government could avoid. For any Arab regime to deny the centrality of Palestine was virtually to deny the Arab nation. Palestine remained a passionately felt issue by the Arab masses from the Atlantic seaboard to the Indian Ocean. There was no easier way of embarrassing another Arab state than to charge it with betrayal of the Palestinian cause.

Palestine was invoked repeatedly in regional struggles, in the first decade after 1948, between Arab nationalists and the Hashemites in their competition to control the Fertile Crescent, and in the competition between Iraq and Egypt for political leadership of the Arab world. Iraq was in an easier position concerning Palestine since it did not share a border with Israel. Once Egypt had established itself as undisputed leader, it was required to demonstrate its credentials in the context of Palestine. It was this pressure that led it into war in 1967.

Before the 1967 war Syria, Egypt and Jordan had all been concerned with the issues of Arab nationalism. Syria and Egypt had been intent on fulfilling the promise of this nationalism – the realization of Arab stature – while Jordan had sought to survive its revolutionary implications. After their defeat, each became primarily preoccupied with the recovery of the territory they had lost to Israel. In the case of Syria and Jordan there was the fear that if Egypt, easily the strongest of the three, negotiated separately with Israel, they would be too weak to recover their own lost territories. When those fears were fulfilled in 1978, Jordan and Syria condemned Egypt and refused to follow in its path.

Neither believed it could obtain its minimal requirements by negotiation.

After Egypt's semi-retirement from the conflict in 1978 and Iraq's growing conflict with Iran in 1979, Syria emerged as regional leader against Israel. Its programme necessarily went beyond the question of Palestine or the recovery of the Golan Heights, to the fulfilment of its regional ambitions. A contest was almost inevitable, regardless of the conflict over Palestine. Israel perceived its military supremacy as essential for its safety, while Syria regarded it as a mortal threat to its own interests. Ascendancy in geographical Syria – the region between the Taurus mountains and Sinai – remained an imperative for both.

The contest between Syria and Israel has evolved with increasing clarity since the 1967 war. Both have tried to wield their influence over Jordan and Lebanon, the two weaker states of geographical Syria, or at least deny the other's interference. For example, in 1958 Israel allowed the British and US forces to overfly its territory and use its facilities in their respective operations to safeguard the Hashemite monarchy in Jordan and the government in Lebanon, both then threatened by Arab radicalism. In 1970 Syria invaded Jordan in support of the Palestinian guerrillas, but promptly withdrew when Israel warned that it would intervene to protect Jordan. Israel secured its objective of preserving Jordan against the challenge of the PLO and Syria but, in so doing, left Jordan embarrassed in the Arab arena. Subsequently the Labour Party in Israel sought common ground with Jordan against Syria and the PLO, on the basis of some form of shared responsibility for the occupied territories. In Lebanon however, Syria defeated Israel. In the years 1982–5, it successfully defended its primacy in Lebanese affairs despite its rout on the battlefield in 1982.

Syria remained hostile to any political process which would leave it standing alone against Israel. It could not tolerate the possibility, in the years 1983–6, of Jordan and the accommodationist wing of the PLO negotiating a separate peace agreement, since this was bound to weaken its own regional position and destroy its primacy in the Arab struggle against Israel. It therefore did everything it could to shipwreck such a process. It remained determined to lead the Arabs in peace negotiations, hence its continued opposition to independent PLO action.

After 1967 Jordan hoped that it could recover the West Bank, and believed for some years that this would be possible. But the rise of the PLO made the whole issue more dangerous and complex, partly because it became unclear whether the majority of people in the West Bank wanted either Jordan or the PLO back, and partly because Jordan's East Bank population was 40 per cent Palestinian. Jordan's overriding objective continued to be survival, caught between the two regional powers, Syria and Israel, and between the imperatives of the Palestinian movement and its own interest in the West Bank. Any edging of the conflict either towards war between Syria and Israel or towards a peace settlement spelt danger for Jordan. However, it was also unable to run away from the peace process since the dangers of doing nothing were even greater. Because of its East Bank Palestinians, Jordan could not abdicate entirely from diplomatic attempts to regain the West Bank. Yet by 1986 it was clear that it could not live safely either with the West Bank re-incorporated into Jordan or with a Palestinian state in the West Bank. Both eventualities might create great tensions within the state and lead to its overthrow. On the other hand, failure to make any apparent headway towards regaining the West Bank threatened to weaken the regime domestically. Jordan therefore tried to foster the appearance of progress towards peace while fearing the dangers peace might actually bring.

Israel, in a position of comparative strength, remained unwilling to make any substantial concessions since it was under no costly duress to do so. It considered its gains in the 1967 war as vital to its regional security. As a matter of policy it kept its neighbours in a state of disarray and weakness, although it was frequently able to leave them to achieve this on their own – for example by Iraq's costly attack on Iran in 1980. It also consciously evolved a policy of fragmentation where possible, supporting distinct ethnic or religious communities to challenge the Arab environment in which they existed, for example with the Kurds in Iraq and the Maronites in Lebanon. When necessary, it was also willing to strike at perceived threats, for example Iraq's nuclear reactor in 1981.

Although obscured by the regional and global struggles surrounding it, the local struggle at the centre of the conflict remained the most explicit and the most inimical. Israel remained determined to retain military control if not sovereignty over all Eretz Israel/Palestine and to prevent the emergence of a Palestinian state. It perceived the Palestinian movement as an explicit challenge to its own legitimacy. Eretz Israel, it believed, was the home of only one national community and that was Jewish. Until 1988 it had been under virtually no pressure to modify its stance.

The PLO, for its part, remained determined to achieve a Palestinian state in part if not all of Palestine. Composed of differing strands of Palestinian nationalist thought, the PLO was weakened by internal disagreements over whether to parley with the enemy, and if so on what grounds. The refusal of Israel to countenance any diplomatic contact made the debate partly academic. But it radically affected PLO relations with other Arab states. One part of the PLO (Fatah) wished to work with Jordan towards a diplomatic solution. Another part (principally the PFLP and PFLP-General Command) felt closer to the rejectionist stance of Syria, and disliked the thought of any talks with the enemy unless they were based on equal or superior strength.

Because of the perceived strategic sensitivities of the region, the regional and local contestants – Syria, Jordan, Israel, Egypt and the PLO – were unable to conduct their struggles without the involvement of the superpowers. Support was welcomed, but except in the case of Israel and the United States, the relationships which evolved tended to be as frustrating as rewarding for all the contestants.

At the global level, both superpowers have been primarily concerned with their relationship with each other, a relationship marked more by rivalry than co-operation.[2] Normally the spirit of rivalry has prevailed. However, when both have felt threatened by developments in the Middle East they have demonstrated their ability to work together. Their ability to contain or manage the conflict when this has threatened to engulf them as well as the regional contestants, for example in 1967 and 1973, contrasts sharply with their inability to transact a peace process which transcends their own rivalry in order to resolve the conflict.

It must be borne in mind that there is a crucial distinction between crisis management and crisis resolution. Since any comprehensive peace implies a reduction of influence by, and local dependency on, the superpowers, it cannot be assumed that either superpower has a strong interest in a genuine peace, unless it is able to derive greater advantage from peace than it can from continued conflict. Consequently, the United States has tended to be most vociferous about a 'peace process' when this has excluded the Soviet Union, and promised a solution which would strengthen American influence in the region.

The interplay of such regional, local and superpower interests has led to a complex 'Balkan' situation in the Middle East. Two regional blocs have emerged: Israel supported by the United States, and against it certain Arab states supported in part by the Soviet Union. The superpowers have seen the conflict as a function of their own struggle, and seen regional contestants either as friends or as surrogates of the enemy. Accommodationist Arab states – termed 'moderate' in the West – have found themselves occupying a difficult position in relation to the rest of the Arab world and to the superpowers outside.

The development of alliances

Neither bloc was monolithic nor entirely predictable at the outset. In 1948 both the US and Soviet governments raced to recognize the new Jewish state. The United States saw the creation of the state as a way to remove the British from Palestine, but also feared that Jewish socialism, dominant in the Yishuv, might be a springboard for Soviet entry into a pro-Western but semi-feudal Arab world. In the end United States support swung behind the new Jewish state largely on the personal decision of President Truman, following his historic meeting with Chaim Weizmann.[3] Even so, US policy in the region remained relatively impartial until the early 1960s. For the first five years of Israel's existence the Soviet Union likewise took a noncommital stance between Israel and its neighbours. Israel was able to exploit the fears of both to its own advantage.[4]

However, Israeli leaders were driven inexorably into alignment with the West, particularly the United States.[5] The latter was not only unquestionably the most powerful state on earth, but it contained a large, wealthy and powerful Jewish community with which the new Jewish state could build a relationship. No similar possibility existed with the Soviet Jewish community, since it was only possible to have relations with the Soviet Union through its government. In January 1949 the United States provided Israel with a $100 million loan, while money poured in from private American Jewish sources.[6]

The Arab world had no historical relationship with the Soviet Union and was suspicious of communism. In the early 1950s, however, the Egyptian revolution and the widespread Arab nationalist sentiments which it fostered throughout the Arab world found expression in anti-Western sentiment. Egyptian non-alignment and its receipt of arms from Czechoslovakia was taken in the West to be dangerously pro-Soviet, and Britain and the United States expressed their disapproval by withdrawing their offer of substantial economic aid. A similar process happened with regard to US aid for Syria. In 1955 a major Israeli reprisal raid on Gaza persuaded Egypt that it must arm itself, and it found a ready supplier in the Soviet Union which was anxious to gain a foothold in the Middle East as part of its policy of making friends in the post-colonial Third World.

It was unnecessary for Israel to persuade the Western powers of the Soviet danger to the Middle East. In 1954 Britain had fostered the Baghdad Pact to create a band of friendly pro-Western states against the Soviet threat. In 1955 Egypt persuaded the Bandung Conference to denounce Iraq for joining the Pact. The following year Israel persuaded Britain and France to join in an attack on Egypt following the latter's nationalization of the Suez Canal. Although obliged to withdraw its troops from Sinai, Israel successfully advanced the polarization of the Middle East into a pro-Western and a pro-Soviet camp.

Israeli leaders had recognized for some time the need for a powerful outside backer. As Menachem Begin recalled 'Ben Gurion used to say that if you're pursuing a policy that may lead to war, it's vital to have a great power behind you.'[7] That great power was inevitably the United States, although the latter was initially reticent concerning Israeli advances. As Eisenhower stated in 1953 'The United States should . . . make clear that Israel will not, merely because of its Jewish population, receive preferential treatment over any Arab state . . . our policy toward Israel is limited to assisting Israel in becoming a viable state living in amity with the Arab states, and . . . our interest in the well-being of each of the Arab states corresponds substantially with our interest in Israel.'[8]

In fact the United States was already tilting towards Israel in order to prevent its economic collapse but intending to 'progressively reduce the amount of economic aid to Israel, so as to bring it into impartial relationship to aid to others in the area'.[9] Following the tumultuous events of 1958 – a revolution in Iraq, an attempted anti-Hashemite coup in Jordan and a short-lived civil war in Lebanon – the United States began to view Israel as its most stable friend in the region and a strategic asset against Soviet expansionism. But it was still resistant to an open alliance.[10]

However, when he assumed office in November 1963, President Johnson transformed the relationship with Israel. Within a month of his succession to Kennedy, Israeli newspapers were suggesting that 'President Johnson will be more responsive than his predecessor to appeals from sympathisers in the US.'[11] His liking for Israel was well known. He now had reasons beyond his own inclinations to support Israel because of what he saw as the growing global challenge by the Soviet Union, most immediately felt in Vietnam. Israel was a stable ally against that threat in the Middle East. The new relationship meant that the United States would support Israel against any regional adversary which was either an actual or potential ally of the Soviet Union. The provision of US assistance to Israel tells its own story. In the financial year 1964 (Kennedy's last) Israel received $40 million almost entirely for civil use. In 1965 it received $71 million, of which 20 per cent was for military use. In 1966 it received $130 million, of which 71 per cent was in military assistance, more in fact than the cumulative total of military assistance from 1948.[12] During the last days of May 1967 the United States reached an understanding with Israel, clearing the way for the latter's attack on Egypt on 5 June 1967.[13]

The perception of Israel as an anti-Soviet bastion has persisted. In 1970 President Nixon affirmed 'we are for Israel because Israel in our view is the only state in the Mideast which is pro-freedom and an effective opponent to Soviet expansion.'[14] A decade later President Reagan was making similar statements, speaking of Israel 'as perhaps the only remaining strategic asset in the region on which the United States can truly rely . . . Only by full appreciation of the critical role the State of Israel plays in our strategic calculus, can we build the foundation for thwarting Moscow's designs on territories and resources vital to our security and our national well-being.'[15]

America's alliance with Israel developed strongly after the 1967 war. This was partly due to the way in which Egypt, Syria and Israel adroitly drew their superpower sponsors into the struggle. Both the Soviet Union and the United States were now engaged in an open competition. Neither could allow its client to be vanquished. By the middle of 1967 Syria and Egypt had received arms from the Soviet Union well beyond the extent of their losses in 1967.[16] In response the United States supplied Israel with the superior A–4 Skyhawk long-range aircraft which, given Israel's new frontiers, made the main Arab capitals far more vulnerable. During 1968 the United States agreed to supply the F–4E Phantom which would, as *The New York Times* warned, 'set off a new round in the Middle East arms race'.[17]

In an attempt to change the balance, Egypt embarked upon a war of attrition, on the assumption that Israel could tolerate casualties less than Egypt. But Israel used its newly acquired Phantoms to strike at civilian targets deep inside Egypt. Egypt persuaded the Soviet Union that neither could afford another humiliating defeat. In April 1970 the Soviet Union commenced the shipment of 15,000 soldiers and missile crewmen, 80 SAM–3 missile launchers with 160 missiles, and 150 MiG–21s in order to protect Egypt adequately. By September there were at least 5,000 missiles deployed along the Suez Canal.[18] Israel lost overall air supremacy for the first time since 1948.

The October 1973 war was the result of Egyptian–Soviet efforts to change the balance in the Middle East, but it was the United States which became the prime beneficiary. The latter airlifted $2.2 billion worth of weaponry to prevent Israel's defeat but on condition that it did not press home a counter-attack. It was then able to negotiate a disengagement in Sinai which removed the Soviet Union from the field, granted Egypt the use of the Canal again, and guaranteed Israel its strategic and tactical support.

The United States' open support for Israel was formalized in 1975 in a joint memorandum of understanding whereby 'threats to the security and sovereignty of Israel by a world power would be seen with special severity by the United States government.'[19] It promised to consult with Israel during Middle Eastern emergencies in order to determine the degree of assistance that could be offered: 'the U.S. government will make every effort to be fully responsive . . . on an ongoing and long term basis to Israel's military equipment and other defense requirements, to its energy requirements and other economic needs.'[20] Furthermore, it 'will not join in and will seek to prevent efforts by others to bring about consideration of proposals which it and Israel agree are detrimental to the interests of Israel'.[21]

Ten years later, in 1984, President Reagan took co-operation further with the formation of a joint political-military group to strengthen the strategic alliance.[22] Reagan's presidency may prove to have been the high watermark of the US–Israeli alliance, combining an unprecedented commitment to military co-operation with an almost wholly uncritical view of Israel. 'Harking back to his career in Hollywood, he [Reagan] held a romantic view of Israel as a vibrant democracy.'[23] He also held a simplistic visionary view of Israel: 'You know, I turn back to your ancient prophets in the Old Testament, and the signs foretelling Armageddon, and I find myself wondering if, if we're in the generation that's going to see it come about. I don't know if you've noted any of the prophecies lately, but, believe me, they certainly describe the time we're going through.'[24]

The Soviet Union, for its part, tried to build relationships within the region in the hope that it could displace the Western powers on the tide of Arab nationalism.[25] Soviet support for the Arab world, however, proved weaker than America's for Israel for several reasons. The very weakness of the Arab states, economically, militarily and in terms of political stability, made it dangerous for the Soviet Union to support them unconditionally. In 1970 and 1982 the Soviets provided missiles and manpower to protect Egypt and Syria respectively from the devastating impact of an Israeli attack. On both occasions the Soviet Union made up for the extreme weakness of its client but, by providing the personnel to operate missile sites, it was consciously limiting the ways in which these missiles could be used against Israel.

Moreover, while the Soviet Union welcomed the chance to help Egypt and other revolutionary Arab states to evict their old colonial masters, it did not wish to make them strong enough to become independent of itself. Furthermore, it recognized that because it could not supply such high quality weaponry as the United States, and because communism did not commend itself to most Arab regimes,[26] the Soviet–Arab bond was bound to remain weaker than the American–Israeli one. The Soviet Union and the Arab states knew that the United States promised to remain a substantially stronger player in the region.

When the opportunity presented itself some Arab states, for example Egypt (which formally repudiated its treaty in 1976) and Iraq (1982–3), discarded or downgraded the Soviet Union in their foreign relations and cultivated the United States. Accommodationist states like Jordan and Kuwait only dealt with the Soviet Union because of favours withheld by the United States. Even the PLO, were it able to, would have put relations with the USA before those with Moscow. It was the United States' adamant policy with respect to the PLO that made the latter's relations with Moscow so robust.[27] By 1980 the Soviet Union was left with only two substantial associates in the region, Syria and the PLO, themselves uneasy allies against Israel.

By contrast, although there have been disagreements Israel's bond with the United States has been rock-solid, built upon agreement 'concerning the nature and extent of the Soviet threat to the region'.[28] It is also built upon shared cultural, religious and political values, which take the relationship beyond a governmental one – the only relationship possible between the Soviet and Arab governments – into the democratic constituency of both states. This cultural relationship is manifest in the pro-Israeli American lobby, composed both of Jewish American groups and non-Jewish Zionists. Such is its influence that no congressman can be strongly critical of Israel and hope to advance his political career.

Resolution 242 and the pursuit of peace

Alongside the rivalry which characterized foreign relations in the Middle East, most governments desired peace if they could achieve it without weakening their own position. After the dismemberment of Palestine and the failure of the Palestine Conciliation Commission at the Lausanne Conference in 1949, most governments concluded, however, that a negotiated peace agreement could not be achieved. They hoped that the division of Palestine into Israeli and Jordanian parts could become permanent and that in time the reasons for war would slowly fade away.

The 1967 war swept such optimistic assumptions aside. Israel wanted to keep some if not all of her gains. The Arab states, on the other hand, were devastated by the scale of their loss and this profoundly affected their political consciousness. Whereas before the 1967 war most of the bellicosity had been verbal, after 1967 it was expressed in greatly intensified rearming. The international community could no longer hope that the reasons for war would fade away.

Given the actual situation following the 1967 war, it was natural that the Security Council, in consultation with the belligerents themselves, should cast its prescriptive Resolution 242 of November 1967 in inter-statal terms: a return (more or less) to the pre-June 1967 frontiers, implying that the 1949 Armistice Line should now become a substantive and internationally recognized inter-state border, and an end to the state of war and full recognition for every state in the area. The only non-statal element was the call for 'a just settlement of the refugee problem'.

Resolution 242 became the corner-stone of almost every peace initiative that followed. UN Special Representative, Gunnar Jarring, and the US Secretary of State, William Rogers, both made it the foundation of their peace efforts before their failure led to the October 1973 war. This war, too, came to an end with a call (Resolution 338) for the immediate implementation of Resolution 242. The United States, the Soviet Union and other leading member states, all adhered to 242, disagreeing only over whether Israel should withdraw completely or could insist on minor border rectifications. The United States accepted the idea of minor border rectifications,[29] while the Soviet Union insisted on an absolute withdrawal. In subsequent initiatives US Secretaries of State Henry Kissinger, Cyrus Vance, and George Schultz all upheld the centrality of 242 in 'the peace process', a term used particularly in the Middle East conflict.

There are good reasons why insistence on Resolution 242 persisted. The 1949 Armistice Line is an internationally recognized benchmark in any solution. The territory captured by Israel was recognized by the whole international community as 'occupied' and therefore protected by the provisions of the 1949 (IVth) Geneva Convention. More than anyone else, the inhabitants of the occupied territories were anxious that this benchmark and the protection of the Convention should not be removed. Most UN member states shared that anxiety, and for that reason the preamble to Resolution 242 included an affirmation of the inadmissibility of acquiring territory by war.

The Security Council members wanted to reach arrangements with the existing states of the region. After the rise of the PLO and its acceptance by the Arab states as sole legitimate representative of the Palestinian people in 1974, there was still a natural reluctance, even among some Arab states, to accord it negotiating authority for the Palestinian people. Any non-governmental movement might be suspect in such circumstances, untried and lacking in those essential relationships and assets by which inter-state bargains can be struck. In the PLO's case this was compounded by its mercurial and ambiguous policy statements, and by the acts of terror committed by members of the Palestinian movement. Jordan, well-disposed to the West but with relations with the Soviet Union, seemed a more reliable front runner for striking a durable bargain with Israel. Finally, there was the fear that a solution based on any principle other than the 1949 Armistice Line would have destabilizing repercussions on Jordan and Israel.

Such considerations disregarded key factors in the conflict, above all the will of the Palestinians themselves. Since in 1967 no coherent Palestinian movement existed, it was natural that the international community did not accord Palestinian interests the consideration they deserved. Resolution 242 did not foresee the possibility of the Palestinian people acquiring their own voice, distinct from those of Jordan and Egypt which had governed so many of them. Yet even as 242 was being drafted, just such a voice was emerging. By 1974 the people of the occupied territories clearly did not wish to return to Jordanian or Egyptian control and wanted self-determination, something which 242 did not propose, as the PLO began to complain. Even the requirement of 'A just settlement of the refugee problem' begged the question of the 1949 Armistice Line as a practicable international border. Where would the refugees go? No one, apart from the Palestinians, seriously thought of a return to the (Israeli) part of Palestine from which they came. But it was unlikely that the Palestinians would accept anything else as a just settlement. Least noticeably but perhaps most dangerously, the Palestinians living inside the 1949 Armistice Line, barely 11 per cent of the Israeli population at the time, were nevertheless growing faster than the Jewish community and were expected to exceed 20 per cent by the end of the century.

The international community clung to Resolution 242 despite its growing obsolescence, as the only agreed basis for a solution. During the period 1967–73 the difficulty of finding sufficient common ground between the belligerents, even within the terms of 242, became glaringly apparent. As an ambiguous statement of that common ground

Resolution 242 was a triumph, but it was insufficient to bring the parties together. Israel demanded bilateral and direct negotiations. The defeated Arab states, fearful of being picked off one by one, insisted on indirect and collective negotiations.

Israel only accepted Resolution 242 without qualification in 1970, but acceptance did not reflect its true position for it was already opposed to the return of substantial territory in return for peace. When discussion of a reconvened Geneva conference was in the air in December 1973, the government stated that 'Israel will not return to the lines of June 4, 1967, which were a temptation to aggression.'[30] In the meantime, its decision to settle Jews in the occupied territories also brought the practical validity of the 1949 Armistice Line in any negotiated agreement into question.

From the outset, it was doubtful whether Israel could be persuaded to relinquish its gains. As early as September 1967 the US government had cabled its ambassador in Tel Aviv to make clear to Abba Eban, then foreign minister, that

> There is growing concern among governments friendly to Israel at indications Israeli objectives may be shifting from original position seeking peace with no repeat no territorial gains toward one of territorial expansionism. Israel's refusal to authorize the return of all refugees desiring to resume residence on the West Bank, reported breaking off of West Bank banking negotiations and statements by senior Israeli officials quoted in American press gives rise to impression that Israeli government may be moving toward policy of seeking security simply by retaining occupied areas rather than by achieving peaceful settlement with Arabs.[31]

Each act of Jewish settlement was a repudiation of 242 as understood by every member of the Security Council.

The United States told Israel that the establishment of Jewish settlements in the territories was a violation of the 1949 Geneva Convention. Yet it was incapable of acting with resolution. On 1 March 1980 it voted for Security Council Resolution 465 calling on Israel to dismantle its settlements (including East Jerusalem). Two days later, after pro-Israel lobby protests, it retracted calling its vote 'a mistake', a 'failure of communications'.[32] Neither the United States nor any other Western government which censured Israel took any effective action to stop the settlement process. None of Israel's Western friends considered its innovations sufficiently serious to require concrete preventive measures or penalties. They simply repeated their censure periodically while Israel continued to destroy almost every facet of Resolution 242's validity by land seizures, illegal settlements, and the annexation of both Jerusalem and the Golan Heights. They all felt constrained by Israel's proximity to the Western bloc, and this took precedence over the enforcement of the 1949 Geneva Convention.

Despite their far longer involvement in the Middle East, the members of the European Community felt inhibited from acting with more resolution than the United States. This was partly because of their sensitive relationship with Israel arising from the Jewish Holocaust in Europe. It was also partly because of a sense of loyalty to the United States as leader of the Western alliance. The Community followed a muted policy, based upon declaratory statements of principle rather than pro-active diplomacy. It agreed with the United States that Resolutions 242 and 338 were the benchmarks for a peaceful solution, but sharply disagreed over their interpretation. The primary area for disagreement lay in Europe's recognition of the 'legitimate rights of the Palestinians' first enunciated in 1973. But it also lay in the European view, at a time when Kissinger was hard at work with his piecemeal diplomacy, that a comprehensive approach rather than a step-by-step strategy was the essential road to peace.

Europe continued to follow where the United States led. It felt it could not oppose the Israeli-Egyptian peace treaty brokered by the United States in March 1979, but at the same time viewed it with ambivalence. On the one hand it expressed its unease, recalling the need for a comprehensive solution which 'must translate into fact the right of the Palestinian people to a homeland', but on the other hand certain members of the Community – Britain, Italy, the Netherlands and France – agreed to help implement the treaty militarily.[33]

Europe had a tendency to make bold forays but then retreat from them. In June 1980 its Venice Declaration advocated full self-determination for the Palestinian people and the involvement of the PLO in peace negotiations, given its acceptance of Resolutions 242 and 338. It was viewed as worthy but inadequate by the Arab world, as intrinsically hostile by Israel, and as dangerously wrong-headed by the United States.

Europe's failure stemmed from the dissonance between its relations with the Mediterranean world and its security dependence on the United States. Each European member was bound to find its own point of balance between these two concerns. However, since Europe's guiding principles for resolution of the Arab–Israeli conflict were closer to those of the Soviet Union than to those of the United States, the latter was bound to request Europe not to obstruct implementation of its own version of the peace process. During the 1980s Europe retreated even from its declaratory policy. The risks of peacemaking seemed too great. In part, this retreat reflected a natural contraction in foreign policy concerns by a number of members.

However, Europe made it clear that it would continue to defer to the leadership of the United States in the 'peace process', as it had done in the 1970s.

The limitations of power

From 1967 onwards, the United States and Israel enjoyed unassailable political and military strength in the region. It was inevitable that this strength, particularly when confronted by such weakness, generated the belief in both countries that they could transact a peace settlement which safeguarded their respective concerns. For the decade following the October 1973 war the United States conducted its policy (but for a brief moment in 1977) on the assumption that it could exclude the Soviet Union from the political process. At the time there seemed good reasons for this assumption, the United States being irreplaceable as mediator with Israel. In Sinai and on the Golan Heights, Henry Kissinger carried out his step-by-step disengagement plan. Kissinger's peace process eventually ran into the ground. Egypt's 1977 peace initiative and entry into direct negotiations with Israel brokered by the United States at Camp David reinforced perceptions of American influence in the region. Once again the United States seemed to be the arbiter of war and peace in the Middle East.

President Reagan came to power with greater hostility for the Soviets than any of his predecessors, and he quickly reached an understanding with Israel concerning those it saw as the Soviet Union's regional proxies, Syria and the PLO.[34] In June 1982 Israel's invasion of Lebanon provided an opportunity to destroy the PLO and mould a new Lebanese state free of Syrian, Palestinian and Soviet influence and by implication dependent on the United States. However, although the PLO was removed, the United States and Israel failed to remove either Syrian or Soviet influence from the country, still less to create a new pro-American Lebanese state. The Israeli-Lebanese Withdrawal Agreement of 17 May 1983, brokered by the United States, collapsed as soon as Syria refused to co-operate. The major US aid programme to restore the Lebanese economy and to rebuild the armed forces disintegrated in January 1984, with the collapse of the US military presence following suicide attacks on US Marine barracks and the collapse of the Phalangist government.

America's close association with Israel led to expectations that it enjoyed indirect control over the behaviour of the latter. Indeed, it had supported Israel in its wars of 1967 and 1982 in the belief that Israel could create a situation in which a peace settlement that met American and Israeli interests would be possible. This proved not to be the case, partly because the relationship between the two countries underwent a transformation in the period 1966–70. By the end of the period the United States had become as dependent upon Israel in its Middle East policy as Israel was dependent upon the United States. Also, the United States and Israel had different considerations for a settlement. While committed to a strong and secure Israel, the United States remained a consistent advocate of the return of virtually all the territories captured in 1967 in exchange for peace. This is how it understood Resolution 242.

Israel, strongly disagreeing with this interpretation, thwarted all American attempts at a diplomatic settlement. 'I ask Rabin to make concessions,' Henry Kissinger wrote in 1975, 'and he says he can't because Israel is weak. So I give him more arms and he says he doesn't need to make concessions because Israel is strong.'[35] Israel repeatedly and successfully obstructed America's will, at no particular cost to itself. It felt no difficulty in repudiating the Reagan Plan of 1982, nor of thwarting President Carter's understanding of the Camp David Accords by intensification of its settlement programme in the occupied territories two years earlier.

The United States' experience with its ally is not unique. One of the features of the conflict which has made its resolution so difficult has been the inability of any of the protagonists – internal or external, powerful or weak – to mould events or other players to its will, and the ability of even the weakest players to throw a spanner into the works of both allies and adversaries. Just as Israel at times has thwarted United States' regional objectives, so also the PLO has at times thwarted the policies of Jordan and Syria; Egypt has reneged on its commitment to the Soviet Union and a defeated Syria was able to destroy the Israeli-Lebanese Withdrawal Agreement virtually overnight.

Furthermore, repeated wars have demonstrated the inability of outsiders to contain the virulence of the conflict once they felt this was desirable, *except* when the superpowers were both agreed on the necessity to rein in their clients. The United States was unable to restrain Israel even when it felt it was necessary to do so against Syria in June 1967 and against Lebanon in 1982. Twelve years earlier, in 1970, the Soviet Union had been unable to restrain the PFLP from provoking a showdown with Jordan.

It has been assumed that the superpowers acting in unison can bring sufficient pressure to bear on their respective clients to enable peace negotiations. Events so far have not borne this out. When American diplomatic efforts included *détente* and co-operation with the Soviet Union, Israel skilfully used the human rights issue of Soviet Jewry as a jemmy to prise the superpowers apart in 1973 and 1977.[36] Nothing more clearly demonstrated the unreliability of this assumption than the Joint Soviet–American Statement of 1 October 1977. This was an attempt to secure the reconvening of the Geneva Conference on terms mutually agreeable to the superpowers, both of which intended to expose their clients to some pressure, but not at the cost of a damaging political reverse. The United States accepted for the first time the phrase 'legitimate rights of the Palestinian people' and called for the participation of the 'Palestinian people', a major concession to the Soviet Union, in return for Soviet retraction of its previous insistence on the participation of the PLO, the establishment of an independent Palestinian state, and the *total* withdrawal of Israeli forces to the 1949 Armistice Line. It seemed a reasonable bargain in which each superpower could exert restraint over its regional allies. However, within four days, Israel and its lobby in America had forced the US administration to backtrack, abandoning its entire policy.[37]

Israel has benefited more from competition than co-operation between the superpowers in the region. The key to Israel's success, and to a lesser extent Syria's, had been its ability to prey on the strategic anxieties of its superpower patron.

However, Israel discovered, just like the United States, that it too could be thwarted by the weaker and more vulnerable contestants in the conflict. In August–September 1982 it proved unable to clinch a peace treaty with its Maronite ally, having effectively installed it as the new Lebanese government. Most frustrating of all, Israel was unable to persuade the weakest contestants, the civilian population of the occupied territories, to comply with its own version of the Camp David autonomy plan.

Israel has proved highly successful at achieving regional predominance in association with the United States but this has been at the price of increasing economic and military dependence on its outside patron. It has placed its diplomatic future in the hands of one outside power, and this may eventually prove more dangerous than adopting a less aggressive policy towards its neighbours.

Arab weakness and Palestinian strength

A major reason for the failure of the peace process lies in the weakness of the Arab world. Ever since 1948, the Arabs have found it difficult to agree among themselves. The accommodationist states were inhibited by the rejectionist ones and were not strong enough militarily without the latter to be credible. As a result they have been weak in the diplomatic arena. The rejectionist states which have viewed Western, particularly American, influence in the region as an inherent part of the problem, have also been characterized by weakness.[38] All these regimes, accommodationist or rejectionist, have had one flaw in common. Not one of them has enjoyed internal political loyalty and they have therefore lacked the strength or authority to transact formal negotiations in which controversial concessions might have to be made.

At the heart of the conflict, the Palestinian people have been particularly familiar with political weakness. Following the June 1967 war the Palestine Liberation Organization replaced the Arab states as the focus for Palestinian hopes. However, like the Arab states the PLO was unable to establish sufficient military strength to threaten Israel, or even to obtain diplomatic recognition with the more influential Western powers. By the early 1980s 'PLO nationalism' was declining in credibility as Arab nationalism had done in the 1970s.

Yet the PLO enjoyed what every Arab regime lacked and needed most of all, the heartfelt loyalty of the people it represented. It remained the most powerful card the PLO had to play. Paradoxically the PLO and the Palestinian people have drawn strength from their military and political weakness. Particularly after 1982 they had no independent power base, no military forces of any consequence on Israel's borders, no diplomatic position in the West and no apparent way of halting Israel's integration of the occupied territories into the Israeli state. They had little more to lose. They preferred undisguised military occupation to self-administration and refused to co-operate with Israel's attempts to create an accommodationist Palestinian leadership in the territories.

Palestinian stubbornness has become a major stumbling block to the peace process as conceived by the United States. Jordan dare not move without PLO approval. As Prime Minister Peres ruefully remarked in 1986 'the Palestinians alone can prevent a solution.'[39] They have consistently refused to co-operate with any venture that has fallen short of the promise of self-determination. By the end of 1987 the furthest that they had gone was to accept 'non-PLO' Palestinians to represent them in a Jordanian–Palestinian delegation, but they drew the line at renouncing violence or recognizing Israel's right to exist. They claimed the right to liberate themselves by armed struggle and they saw any recognition of Israel's legitimacy as contingent on Israeli and American recognition of their own right to self-determination. Thus, the Palestinians, the weakest of all contenders, showed themselves able to render the peace process ineffectual until they were granted participation on acceptable terms.

The Palestinians have also successfully challenged America's assumption that it was pre-eminently qualified to act as peace broker, an assumption that had underscored US policy in the Middle East since 1967. President Reagan's claim that 'No other nation is in a position to deal with the key parties to the conflict on the basis of trust and reliability'[40] jarred with assessments in early 1982 that no more than 0.5 per cent of Palestinians in the West Bank considered the United States was 'helpful' to the Palestinians in the search for a solution, and only approximately 2 per cent in the territories believed the United States was serious about a peaceful solution to the Middle East.[41] Until 1988 there had been nothing to indicate an increase in Palestinian confidence in the United States. The collapse of repeated initiatives by Secretary of State George Schultz was welcomed by a growing number of Palestinians in the territories. The Uprising was primarily a rejection of Israeli rule and an affirmation of Palestinian identity, but it was also a rejection of American interference. Participation by the United States was recognized by Palestinians only as an unwelcome necessity. Only after the Uprising had established new political realities did the PLO feel strong enough to concede the demands made by Western nations – renouncing terrorism, accepting 242 and recognizing Israel more explicitly than before. Even so, the decision of the 19th Palestine National Council in November 1988 to take this highly accommodationist road was not an easy one, and was only possible because it had become apparent that the world now recognized that no substantive peace negotiations were likely to materialize without formal PLO participation. The PLO felt able to play what had been for fifteen years its 'last card' – recognition of Israel – because it had gained a stronger one through the Uprising.

The United States found the implications of these new political realities harder to accept than the rest of the international community, which had almost unanimously welcomed the PLO's clarified accommodationism. Indeed, it only recognized the PLO as a substantive interlocutor for the Palestinian people after world condemnation of its decision to bar Arafat from entry to the United States to address the United Nations in New York in December 1988, and after he had addressed its General Assembly in Geneva instead.

The United States decided that isolation with Israel from the consensus of the whole world community was too high a price to pay. In order to prove it was not composed of 'patsies', as Reagan put it, the United States insisted that Arafat repeat specifically worded concessions concerning terrorism and recognition of Israel, and when he failed to do so *verbatim*, it required him to repeat the authorized US version. These statements added little to what Arafat had already said but such casuistry, the decision to limit official contact with the PLO to the US embassy in Tunis, and the warning that any terrorist incident attributable to a PLO faction would render US recognition of the PLO void, suggested that the outgoing US administration had acted with considerable reluctance. Its expressed view, that the Uprising was part of that violence which the United States now wished the PLO to bring to an end, indicated it wished to eliminate the source of the new political reality, against which it had laboured so long through its preference for negotiations through Jordan.

In this way, the weakest contestants demonstrated that even they could influence the course of international diplomacy. But it remained uncertain whether they were strong enough to create conditions in which peace could be negotiated even on the most minimal of their terms.

A valid peace process?

No one can underestimate the difficulties implicit in achieving a negotiated settlement. Nevertheless, the lack of genuine progress toward peace in the region during the period 1967–88 casts doubt upon the validity of the peace process as it has been conceived. Has it in fact been a peace process at all? Its defenders claim that to create the impression of progress is in itself a vital part of crisis management. The justification for crisis management, to those who argue the case, lies in the self-evident desirability of avoiding instability or open war. The impression of diplomatic progress, so the argument runs, has a quietening effect on the region. However, it is ingenuous to suppose that peace process brokers do not have their strategic interests first and foremost in mind. Their 'peace process' is likely to be, primarily, an avenue for those strategic goals, and therefore remains an alternative method to war, whereby rivals may be worsted and allies strengthened.

This may seem a jaundiced view, but the evidence is disturbing. The United States crowned its greatest diplomatic triumph in the region, the peace treaty between Israel and Egypt, by distributing to both parties swords as well as ploughshares. With Egypt out of the fray, Israel and the United States felt stronger while Syria and the Soviet Union felt more threatened. In 1982 Israel invaded Lebanon with greater self-confidence than in any previous war, safe in the knowledge that the Egyptian front was quiescent. The United States saw this war as an opportunity to change things in the Middle East, and celebrated the Lebanese–Israeli Withdrawal Agreement by lifting its year-old ban on the sale of seventy-five F-16 jet fighters to Israel. The same day the US Senate approved the Administration's $251 million military and economic package for Lebanon.[42] Military supplies to Lebanon's Maronite government were seen by many Lebanese (as well as Syria) as a contribution to conflict, not to the restoration of order. Inevitably, US support for a Lebanon dominated by the Phalangists was violently challenged by other Lebanese groups. Just as inevitably, the Soviet Union and Syria both felt compelled to redouble their efforts to fortify their respective positions in the conflict, to offset the damage this agreement had done them. As in 1970 with Egypt, so after 1982 the Soviet Union gave Syria its most sophisticated air defence system and missile system, and tactical ballistic missiles capable of reaching Tel Aviv.[43]

The conclusion must be drawn that at the end of the period 1978–83, when America's peace process was at its height, the dangers for the Middle East, particularly Israel, had increased rather than receded. The same, of course had been true of the period of intensive 'peace efforts', 1967–73. Each round of war and 'peace process' drew the superpowers into yet more sophisticated rearming of their clients and increased the tactical and strategic threats to the participants. Superpower involvement has raised the stakes rather than lowered them.

Furthermore at the local level, although the international community still conversed 'in a dead language, the Latin of the Middle East: 242 and 338',[44] it was difficult to ignore the fact that the conflict was increasingly inter-communal, crossing the 1949 Armistice Line – with growing numbers of Israeli Palestinians to the west and Israeli Jewish settlers to the east of it. It was impossible to disregard the fact that King Husayn's renunciation of the West Bank in July 1988, too, undermined the inter-statal approach of Resolution 242, and emphasized the inter-communal aspect of the conflict inside Palestine.

In November 1988, the 19th Palestine National Council passed a resolution specifically recognizing 242, and all other relevant United Nations resolutions on Palestine. It did so as a gesture towards the United States, that it was now willing to accept this resolution as the basis of its participation in an international peace conference. By its declaration of Palestinian independence the PNC filled the inter-statal void left by Jordan's abdication of the West Bank, though it was doubtful that the United States would accept it as such.

Does PNC acceptance of Resolution 242 validate the latter as a basis for peace? One must be doubtful. Because of international insistence on it, Resolution 242 is undoubtedly the entry ticket to an international peace conference. To that extent it still has value. However – with the loss of Jordanian sovereignty – until the United States accepts the Palestinian claim to sovereignty over the occupied territories, Resolution 242 is bound to remain bereft of meaning, since there is no US-recognized state to which the West Bank and Gaza can be returned.

It must be remembered, too, that Resolution 242 was deliberately ambiguous. It recognized through its wording that the superpowers, the regional contestants and the local ones, had differing interpretations of what it meant. Did it mean a return to the 1949 Armistice Line? Did 'a just settlement of the refugee problem' imply implementation of Resolution 194 of 1948 (confirming the right of return), as an innocent might assume? The fact is that Israel, the Arab states, including the new State of Palestine, the United States and the Soviet Union have different interpretations. Resolution 242 may get them around the same table but it leaves the real bones of contention untouched. Furthermore it does not deal with the long-term inter-communal aspect – Israel's own growing Palestinian population (an issue discussed in chapters 6, 7 and 11). This ingredient is vital to the continued stability of the region.

If there is regret over the failure of Resolution 242 as a blueprint for peace, which had seemed so promising in 1967, there are grounds for even greater regret that the 1949 (IVth) Geneva Convention has not been vigorously upheld by those who claimed to be seeking a basis for peace. In November 1988 the new Likud-dominated government resumed the process of settling the territories with Jews, rendering the implementation of Resolution 242 more remote than ever.

In view of such evidence the peace process seems much less convincing than its proponents have suggested. That it has been 'the only game in town', as many have argued, has not meant that it has necessarily been worth following, either from an Israeli or a Palestinian view. As the Israeli writer, Amos Kenan, observed, 'The big powers need an arrangement, not peace. So we will get in the Middle East the kind of solution there is between East and West Germany, or North and South Korea . . . it rests on a kind of status quo, a state of expectation, until something happens or something dies, or something changes, and life goes on, that's all. It is not peace and not war; it is the modern solution.'[45] For Israelis and Palestinians such a solution is highly unsatisfactory.

The climate for peace

It is natural to ask what circumstances are desirable for an effective peace process to come into being. The idea that the superpowers are vital to the success of the peace process is based upon the influence they exert on the regional contestants, but in reality they have helped to perpetuate regional conflict and global competition in the area, with the encouragement of local clients.

The superpowers' activity has resulted from the importance they attach to the region. A decline in activity may now come about if both accord the region less strategic value than they have given it hitherto. Fifty years ago the region seemed critical to British imperial interests. Then Arab oil became the focus of Western concern, particularly following the 1973 war. In the 1980s the Iran–Iraq war demonstrated that the supply of oil to interested clients was possible in even the most threatening and unstable situations. Moreover, the threat to supplies brought the two superpowers closer together. The idea of one global power holding the other to ransom seems less credible now than it has done previously. There are grounds therefore for believing that superpower activity in the Middle East may now be in a phase of decline.

Furthermore, it is now becoming increasingly apparent that neither superpower can afford to sustain the level of economic and military aid that has been provided hitherto to allies and client states. The servicing of perceived strategic needs is outrunning economic capacity. This is clearly implicit in the major reforms introduced by President Gorbachev. The United States may also be approaching the same conclusion, for between 1980 and 1988 it moved from being the world's largest creditor to being its largest debtor. Although much of this is attributable to the tax cuts policy of the Reagan era, it also results from the military expenditure Reagan believed was consistent with his view of a strong America.

The greatest contribution outside powers can make in creating a climate for peace lies less in the field of diplomacy than in that of law observance. So far, the Western countries have shown far greater enthusiasm for applying law to international terrorism than for enforcement of the (IVth) Geneva Convention. Fulfilment of their legal obligation,[46] would send a powerful message to the contestants: to the Palestinians of the occupied territories that they can hope for protection, and to Israel that it cannot disobey international law with impunity. If the United States wishes to be an effective peace broker, it must accept the fundamental need for law enforcement, uphold the illegality of Israeli settlement and abandon its policy of appeasing its ally. The European Community has already made a modest start in this direction.[47]

At the regional and local levels, Israel has never been seriously challenged. Another prerequisite therefore may be a closer matching of political and military strength which would oblige Israel to think in new ways. This may now be taking place. No state in the region is now invulnerable to attack by another. Syria and Iraq have advanced rocketry systems and in the case of the latter – if not Syria also – a chemical and biological warfare capacity. Given Israel's inability to sustain large casualties this must be seen as a weapon of similarly fearsome proportions to Israel's own nuclear capacity.

On the conventional battlefield Syria's unprecedented programme of militarization may put pressure on Israel to reassess the respective costs of war and peace. If it chooses war it may deem it necessary to attack Syria before the latter becomes more powerful, but in doing so it risks incurring unacceptably high casualties. Or it may sit tight in the reasonable hope that either the economic strain proves too great and Syria's military strength is sapped by political and economic instability, or that Syria will dissipate its strength against its eastern adversary, Iraq. If the danger increases, Israel may seek an easing of tension with Syria by a new agreement based upon the abandonment of the Golan Heights on condition of permanent demilitarization. Currently this may seem unacceptable as well as unlikely, but may no longer be so if Israel itself experiences military and economic recession.

However, the most important ingredient missing hitherto from the peace process – international acceptance of the Palestinians' choice of representative – was dramatically fulfilled at the time of the first anniversary of the Uprising. This international acceptance was emphatically less the result of the peace process than of the Uprising. The United States, the most loquacious exponent of peace, had also been the most reluctant member of the international community to accept the PLO as representative for the Palestinians.

At the beginning of 1989 it remained uncertain whether this unenthusiastic recognition would survive the vicissitudes of negotiation. The United States required continuing evidence of PLO acceptance of Israel and repudiation of violence as the price for diplomatic contact, but it was unclear whether it was yet willing to encourage Palestinian accommodationist tendencies by granting the PLO anything more than a hearing. There was no evidence yet of the even-handedness necessary in a true peace-broker, for it did not demand of Israel recognition of the PLO, let alone recognition of the Palestinian right to self-determination, something the United States itself was not yet ready to concede. Nor did it demand that Israel, like the PLO, abandon the use of violence in its treatment of enemy civilians either inside or beyond the territories under its control. But a modest start had been made.

Only Israel continued to reject any recognition of the PLO, a position of isolation which was becoming decreasingly defensible. After all, one can only make peace with one's enemies. It is only when the United States persuades Israel that it cannot continue to deny the choice of representative that the Palestinian people have made – however reprehensible that representative may seem – that any meaningful international dialogue towards peace can take place. At the beginning of 1989 it remained a hope awaiting fulfilment, that the incoming Bush administration would undertake that role of persuasion which previous administrations had eschewed.

In the midst of such uncertainties one thing was clear. The dramatic political and diplomatic developments of 1988 – of more importance to the achievement of a substantive peace than anything else since 1967 – owed nothing to the peace process. They were a direct result of the Uprising. Furthermore, future international progress towards peace seemed likely to remain contingent on the strength and durability of the Uprising.

2

THE JORDANIAN DIMENSION

The fallacy, so long espoused by the United States, that any political settlement for the West Bank must primarily involve Jordan was sharply exposed by the Uprising. On 31 July 1988, after eight months of unrest in the territories, King Husayn formally relinquished his claim to the West Bank, and initiated the administrative steps necessary to sever all those links which implied sovereignty or responsibility for the fate of the territory.

For the Palestinians and the PLO, King Husayn's announcement was a tremendous victory, for he had formally renounced the claim he had refused to concede after Rabat in 1974. There was a bitter tinge to the triumph, however, for he neither warned nor consulted the PLO before his announcement. His precipitate action was clearly calculated to make life harder rather than easier for the PLO as he abandoned responsibility for civil servants in the West Bank. The suspicion remained that he might be hoping that the PLO would fail to meet the challenge, and consequent disaffection in the West Bank would lead perhaps to his eventual reinstatement. But such a calculation could only be a gamble. In the meantime Palestinians were exultant.

King Husayn's decision was a major blow for Israel's Labour Party. For it came barely three months before Israel's general election, in which the fate of the territories was the central issue. Labour had maintained ever since 1967 that the foundation of any settlement of the territories was an arrangement with Jordan. Husayn had now removed the central plank of Labour's electoral manifesto to the delight of Likud, which rejected negotiations with Jordan as irrelevant to the kind of autonomy it envisaged for Palestinians living in Eretz Israel.

The United States was similarly dismayed, for it still hoped for a Labour electoral victory and an eventual political settlement with

Jordan. In June 1988 Secretary of State Schultz was still discounting any idea of Palestinian independence, insisting that any Palestinian representation must be under Jordanian auspices.

Until the Uprising even the PLO leadership – albeit with a great deal of hesitation – was ready to accept the formula of a joint Jordanian and Palestinian delegation, it being understood that the Palestinian component, even though not PLO leaders themselves, would be a genuine and equal partner with the Jordanians.

In the West Bank and Gaza Strip, the two areas most immediately affected, this had been the subject of heated debate. In April 1983, for example, an opinion poll indicated that while 32 per cent favoured a joint team, 43 per cent considered the team should be solely Palestinian.[1] One year before the Uprising another poll indicated that only 6.3 per cent of the population would accept Jordanian sovereignty even on an interim basis.[2] A confederation between two sovereign states, Jordan and Palestine, might have been acceptable, but not a federation under King Husayn. This had been the position of the most accommodationist end of the PLO, led by Yasser Arafat.

In its anxiety to transact a settlement, the international community, particularly the United States, seriously misjudged Palestinian feelings towards the Hashemite monarchy. There was a tendency to ascribe residual ill-feeling to the East Bank civil war of 1970–1, and to the comparative neglect of the West Bank under Hashemite rule before 1967. Such explanations overlooked the history and depth of tension between the Hashemites and Palestinians, and ignored the continuing disparity of purpose between the two parties over the past half century.

The Amir Abdallah of Transjordan

This tension originated in the political ambitions of the first ruler of Transjordan, the Amir Abdallah, grandfather of King Husayn. Abdallah and his brother Faysal had hoped to benefit from the alliance made in 1915 between their father Husayn, Sharif of Mecca and ruler of the Hijaz, and the British. That alliance promised the prospect of a kingdom in the areas which they wrested from Ottoman control.[3]

Having led the Arab revolt, Faysal briefly became King of Syria before French forces expelled him in July 1920. He was compensated by Britain with Iraq. But Faysal's brother, Abdallah, advanced from the Hijaz through the territory east of the Jordan – under British nominal control but for which no political arrangements had been made – with the avowed intention of ejecting the French from Syria. Britain bought him off by offering him the sovereignty of this area, 'Transjordan'.

Abdallah never abandoned his ambition to rule Syria. Over his remaining thirty years of life he tried to fulfil the Hashemite ambition to rule the whole Arab Levant. With his brother in Iraq, a Hashemite-ruled Fertile Crescent remained a realistic objective. While France remained in Syria any hope of recovering it was pointless. But Palestine was a different matter since it was under British rule. Britain favoured the Hashemites and might consider Abdallah a suitable ruler in due course. The acquisition of Palestine would greatly increase his economic and political power, which was marginal given the poor resources of Transjordan. Palestine, even without the new Jewish settlers, was more populous and more advanced. As ruler of both banks of the Jordan Abdallah's position would be greatly enhanced.

Unlike the Arab inhabitants of Palestine, Abdallah welcomed the prospect of economic development which the Zionist programme promised. Palestinian nationalists became suspicious, since there were soon rumours that he was seeking recognition as Amir of Palestine in return for support of Zionist policy.[4]

By the early 1930s it was clear that Abdallah intended to develop friendly co-operation with the Jewish Agency.[5] In 1934 he proposed to it that Palestine and Transjordan should be united under his crown, the Arabs recognizing the Mandate, including Jewish rights, and each state keeping its own political status with the respective prime ministers reporting to Abdallah. He also suggested special terms for Jewish immigration and land purchase,[6] and told the Jewish Agency that he hoped Syria would later join this 'united kingdom'.

When the Palestinian revolt broke out in 1936, Abdallah secretly urged Britain to exile Palestinian leaders, and offered to work with the Jewish Agency to sabotage intervention by other Arab states. When the Peel Commission proposed partition in 1937, Abdallah was virtually alone in the Arab world in his support for it contingent, however, on the incorporation of the Arab portion into his Amirate.[7] 'I consider it my duty to strive to ward off the calamity by bringing about the union of Palestine and Transjordan', he told the Palestinians.[8]

The Zionists were interested in Abdallah's plans, partly because uniting Transjordan and Palestine might renew Zionist opportunities east of the Jordan. Ben Gurion had strongly favoured Abdallah's support of partition in 1937.[9] Britain, too, favoured the association of the proposed Arab state with Transjordan, but backtracked in the face of widespread hostility which made Abdallah unpopular throughout the Arab world.[10]

Abdallah nursed his ambitions for Palestine. Following the declaration of the Biltmore Programme in 1942, he approached the Zionists with the idea of a four state federation, Palestine (with proportional representation), Transjordan, Syria and Iraq, with the question of Jewish immigration being contingent not upon Palestinian Arab consent but upon the economic absorptive capacity of the country.[11] But the Zionists were not interested. They were gripped by anxiety over the fate of European Jewry.

Once Britain decided to relinquish the Palestine mandate, Abdallah, now king, renewed his work for partition. Along with every other Arab state he officially opposed the partition, but the others knew his intention was the opposite. In July 1947 he agreed with the Jewish Agency to support partition and the establishment of a Jewish state in return for Jewish financial help for Transjordan.[12]

A few days before the vote on partition in the UN General Assembly, Abdallah secretly met Jewish Agency officials. 'I am prepared for a partition that will not put me to shame before the Arabs' they reported him as saying, and he assured one of them, Golda Meir, 'that he would not attack the partitioned Jewish State but that he would annex [Arab] Palestine.' Golda Meir replied that 'if he was ready and willing to confront us and the world with a *fait accompli* [i.e. annexation of Arab Palestine] – the traditional friendship between us would continue and we would certainly find a common language in arranging matters of interest to both sides.'[13] This was confirmed in April 1948, when 'it was agreed that Abdallah would control Arab Palestine if he did not interfere with efforts to set up a Jewish State.' In March he had secured British assent for his plans. Britain then obtained United States agreement too.[14]

Palestinian nationalists remained opposed to Abdallah's plans but had few alternatives. If the proposed partition led to fighting, the Arabs who were bereft of any coherent leadership (the Mufti and other Palestinian leaders had been exiled since 1939), would depend wholly on the armies of their Arab neighbours, of which Abdallah's was not only unquestionably the best but also stood to capture most territory.

When the United States proposed a truce plan on 8 April 1948 to stop the fighting between Jews and Arabs, it was Abdallah who was most hostile to it.[15] He warned that even if the Arab League accepted the truce proposal, he would still send his army into Palestine after

15 May.[16] Syria, Egypt and the Palestinians were all, for different reasons, extremely uneasy. Syria feared this was the first step in his long-awaited Greater Syria project. Egypt feared the Hashemites intended to control the land from the Mediterranean across the Negev to the Gulf, and the Palestinians feared that foreign Arab armies spelt the end of Palestinian hopes to determine their own future.

Abdallah honoured his understandings with the Jewish Agency. On 14 May, on the eve of the Arab forces' entry into Palestine, he changed the invasion plan to prevent the Syrians from attacking south of the Sea of Galilee. This kept Syrian troops away from the West Bank area which Abdallah wished to incorporate into Transjordan, and undermined the Arab League plan to cut off east Galilee, which had been allocated to the Jewish State.[17]

On 15 May, the day after Britain's withdrawal, Transjordanian troops entered Palestine, taking up defensive positions around Jerusalem, the key to the central uplands. Here they fought bitterly with Jewish forces for control of the Jerusalem area, which had been allocated to neither side under the Partition Plan. Egypt, more concerned with countering Abdallah's ambitions in the Arab-designated areas than with defeating the Jews, moved its troops to Beersheba, Hebron and towards Jerusalem.

In the central sector, the Transjordanians abandoned two large towns, Lydda and Ramla, to their fate, in the belief that they were tactically indefensible.[18] The Jewish forces could hardly believe their good fortune.[19] To the Palestinians the loss of Lydda and Ramla remained symbols of Hashemite betrayal. Further south, Abdallah's troops quickly occupied Bethlehem and Hebron when the Jews pushed Egyptian forces out of the central southern sector in October. Their first act was to disarm all armed elements in the area, both Egyptians and those belonging to the Mufti's irregular forces, for Abdallah's chief aim was to remove Egyptian forces from Palestine,[20] and prevent any Palestinian entity emerging.

Abdallah was outmanoeuvred by the Zionists. He had served their purpose by supporting partition and keeping the Arab armies divided. He wanted to annex the West Bank formally and conclude an armistice with Israel.[21] But Israel resisted this until it was in a much stronger position by concluding one with Egypt in February 1949. It then adopted a far less conciliatory approach, demanding the evacuation of the small Transjordanian force from the Negev, access to the Wailing Wall and Mount Scopus in Jerusalem, and refusing to recognize Transjordanian sovereignty over the West Bank. In March Israeli troops outflanked Abdallah's forces in the Negev to capture the whole area and reach Eilat. His forces withdrew without firing a shot. Militarily stronger by ten to one, Israel made Abdallah agree to an armistice in April 1949 whereby he ceded thirty villages in and near Wadi Ara, in the area which became known inside Israel as the Little Triangle.[22]

In 1948 Abdallah had moved quickly to establish his legitimacy in those areas of Palestine under his control. In October he summoned to Amman the local notables favourable to his rule, where they asked him to put all Arab-occupied Palestine under his protection.[23] Two months later he convened a major conference in Jericho, choosing as its president the mayor of Hebron, Shaikh Muhammad Ali Ja'bari, his long standing supporter. This conference called for the unity of Palestine and Transjordan, and declared Abdallah king of all Palestine. Pro-Hashemite figures were quickly installed in key positions in what became known as 'the West Bank'.[24]

The Hashemite Kingdom of Jordan

Abdallah erased the identity of Palestine. In March 1949 the official name of his enlarged state became the Hashemite Kingdom of Jordan. When a Palestinian delegation asked to participate in the armistice negotiations, its request was rejected and the armistice was signed only by East Bankers.[25] In March 1950 Abdallah instructed that the word 'Palestine' be removed from all maps and official statements.[26]

Hashemite political control was established by division of the local administration of the West Bank and by incorporation of the local notable class. Jerusalem, which had become politically pre-eminent during the Mandate, receded in importance compared with Amman, to which all its government offices were transferred. The civil governor of each governorate, Nablus, Jerusalem and Hebron, was usually an East Bank Jordanian.[27] Popular participation even in local government was limited by the direct control of Amman through its governors, the local notable class, and through the low number of those eligible to vote.[28] The Jordanian Chamber of Deputies was now composed of forty deputies, twenty from each side of the river. In view of the over-whelming Palestinian demographic preponderance, this arrangement was a good deal less equitable than it at first seems. Most of the families which had supported Abdallah were represented.[29]

Many notables and landowners benefited from incorporation into Jordan. The increased demand for agricultural produce, not only for the refugee population but also for the new markets to the east, which replaced the previous west-facing economy, brought government in Amman and the landowners of the West Bank closer together. In order to market successfully across the river, West Bankers needed to work with associates in government in Amman, and with those able to transport and market goods on the East Bank. Notable families were better able to do this than small farmers.[30]

The Hashemite regime neglected the West Bank as a matter of deliberate policy. It did not want the political centre of gravity to shift across the river. Nor did it want the more advanced economic state of the West Bank, which was itself backward compared with the coastal areas of Palestine, to continue. The agriculture of small farmers remained undeveloped, while the industrial sector which was small but had considerable potential with the influx of the coastal refugee population received no single investment of more than about $28,000 in the whole period.[31] The East Bank was consistently preferred when it came to investment, for irrigation, land reclamation, electricity, transport and communications. Throughout the 1950s newspapers continued to report the complaints of West Bank traders at the economic stagnation which resulted. The chambers of commerce of West Bank towns complained of their inability to obtain import and export licences, let alone the capital they needed to develop both industrial and agricultural potential. By 1967 the industrial sector of the West Bank had not only shrunk from 12 per cent to 9 per cent of the gross domestic product, but was now smaller than in any neighbouring Arab area, and in particular in comparison with industry in the East Bank, which had been virtually non-existent before 1948.[32]

Annexation and the incorporation of both the indigenous and refugee Palestinians created a fundamental instability in the new kingdom. Jordan was now integrated into the Palestine conflict, with its regime controlling, rather than supporting, the Palestinian people. This has committed it to an inevitable struggle with the Palestinians for control of policy on the Palestine question and, by extension, for control of Jordan itself.

Before the 1948 war the population of Transjordan had been 430,000. After the war and the acquisition of the West Bank, the population rose to 1,280,000, of whom 850,000, or 66 per cent, were Palestinian. Of the Palestinian population a slight majority, 450,000, were refugees, while 400,000 were indigenous to the West Bank. Transjordan's capital, Amman, became predominantly Palestinian almost overnight. Today it is about 75 per cent Palestinian.

Inevitably the Hashemites faced an acute political difficulty. Widening political participation in the life of the new state risked the creation of a Palestinian opposition to Hashemite policy. While the regime tried to incorporate the notables into the ruling establishment, the refugee camps on both the West and East Banks became a focus for the activities of the Jordan Communist Party (the Arab rump of the Palestine Communist Party), the Muslim Brotherhood and the Islamic Liberation Party, all of which were hostile to a settlement with Israel unless it included the right of the refugees to return to their homeland.

King Abdallah was assassinated by a Palestinian in Jerusalem in July 1951. Following the accession of his grandson, Husayn, in 1953 (after his son Talal had abdicated on account of mental instability), anti-Hashemite demonstrations and riots broke out. These expressed hostility to Britain's pre-eminent position, the demand for greater democracy in the country, and a widely held belief that the Hashemites had an understanding with Israel not to attempt to recapture any of Israeli Palestine but to punish severely any Palestinian who violated the Armistice Line. The immediate cause was an Israeli reprisal raid in October 1953 on the village of Qibya in which 66 villagers were killed. Qibya symbolized the political as well as military failure of the Hashemites to uphold the Palestinian cause. Throughout 1954 there were a number of anti-Hashemite demonstrations, culminating in serious riots in Jerusalem, Ramallah and even Amman.[33]

In the mid-1950s there was a short-lived chance that Jordan would develop into a parliamentary democracy. Many young notables were attracted to the new ideologies then current in the Arab world, notably the Communist Party (the only party of any significance to have opposed the erasure of 'Palestine' from the Jordanian maps), and the Ba'ath. In 1956 a newly formed party, the National Socialists, who sought greater economic as well as political freedom, were able to form a coalition with the Ba'athists and Communists to assume government.[34]

Within a month the new government faced the political implications of the Suez campaign, and the vehement anti-Hashemite feelings it provoked. It abrogated the treaty with Britain, affirmed its support for Arab nationalism, and turned to other Arab regimes for the subsidies necessary for the Jordanian economy. King Husayn reluctantly gave the government his support. The crisis soon developed into open disagreement between government and king over their respective powers. In April 1957 Husayn sacked his prime minister. Three days later army elements, apparently with the knowledge of the outgoing government, attempted an unsuccessful *coup d'état*. Husayn suspended the constitution, declared martial law, banned all political parties and arrested hundreds of politicians. When Arab governments refused to provide the subsidies promised to the late government Husayn turned to the United States, which provided a $10 million emergency grant, and a further $30 million during the course of the year. Thus ended Jordan's brief experiment in democracy, with the country firmly within the United States' growing political orbit in the region.

For the next decade, until June 1967, the Palestinians watched with envy the triumphs of Arab nationalism under Nasser's leadership, but remained politically passive. Anyone who sought to translate their feelings into political activity soon found themselves in jail.

Jordan without its West Bank

The loss of the West Bank in the June 1967 war created an entirely new situation. About 300,000 Palestinians, largely though not exclusively 1948 refugees, crossed the river Jordan. While the loss of the West Bank reduced the demographic preponderance of the Palestinians in the state, the flight of so many eastwards and the drift of many to the economically more prosperous East Bank in previous years, left Jordan with at least 40 per cent of its population Palestinian. Furthermore, the convulsion of 1967 concentrated yet more Palestinians around the most sensitive parts of the kingdom, Amman itself and the towns running northwards to the Syrian border.

Jordan did not abandon its claim to the West Bank. During the months after its loss, it felt compelled to maintain solidarity with Egypt and Syria. However, the United States persuaded it to accept UN Security Council Resolution 242, giving an assurance that it would ensure that the critical wording 'withdrawal from territories captured' would mean no more than minor border rectifications.[35]

On the ground Husayn worked to maintain the loyalty of the municipal structure, which remained in place after Israel's occupation, through subsidies and through Israel's open bridge policy, which in addition to relieving the pressures on the West Bank population, gave him considerable control over a large proportion of that population. Since they held Jordanian passports, it followed that those wishing to work or travel outside the West Bank had to pass over the bridge. Only a fool or a very determined and principled Palestinian was ready to jeopardize that crossing by openly opposing Husayn's claim over the West Bank.

On the East Bank, King Husayn had a more immediate Palestinian threat to deal with in the meteoric rise of the Palestinian resistance movement. Although the mainstream group, Fatah, made clear that it ruled out any question of subverting the Hashemite regime, other groups, of which the PFLP was the most notable, made equally clear their view that the overthrow of the Hashemites was a necessary preliminary to the recovery of Palestine. Both Fatah and the more radical groups like the PFLP enjoyed widespread support in the camps on the East Bank. By its hijacking and destruction of Western civil airliners, the PFLP forced Husayn to move against the guerrilla groups in September 1970. The whole Palestinian resistance was evicted from Jordan within a year, amid widespread bloodshed in which perhaps as many as 3,000 refugees perished. It left people feeling deeply embittered.

This civil war had also created bitter feelings on the West Bank, but an eventual return to Jordanian rule was expected. As time passed, politicians began to hedge their bets, creating uncertainty both for Jordan and the PLO, which was not yet wholly accepted in the West Bank. In March 1972 King Husayn proposed a federation of Transjordan and the West Bank as a United Arab Kingdom. Pro-Jordanian leaders sought Israeli consent to form an assembly to negotiate a settlement on the basis of the king's federation scheme. It was probably the best chance for the 'Jordanian option', but Israel turned it down, and the United Arab Kingdom proposal died.

The October 1973 war changed the balance strongly in favour of the PLO in the West Bank, for Jordan's passivity reflected its weakness. At Rabat in October 1974 and a month later at the United Nations, the PLO routed Jordanian claims to represent the West Bank population. In practice Husayn did not accept its implications.[36]

The PLO's triumph both in the Arab arena and internationally was underestimated by Jordan and by Israel, which called for new municipal elections in 1976. These swept most of the old pro-Jordanian figures from office, and brought in younger more radical men who recognized the PLO as their national leadership. Jordan hoped to recover its position on the West Bank, paying subsidies for loyalty and continuing functional co-operation with Israel, as if the growth of political awareness in the area could not only be contained but diminished.

Jordan's hope of containing the PLO challenge lay in Washington's decision in 1975 not to recognize the PLO unless it accepted the legitimacy of Israel and Security Council Resolution 242. Since the PLO, composed of both accommodationist and rejectionist groups, could not accept either without damaging its internal unity, Jordan seemed pivotal to any settlement for the West Bank.

Recognition of this fact led Jordan and the PLO to co-operate despite frosty relations. Neither forgot that they co-operated as rivals rather than as potentially mutual beneficiaries of a settlement. They were driven closer together by President Sadat's political initiative of November 1977, and the subsequent peace negotiations between Egypt and Israel. The accommodationist states including Jordan, in order to satisfy domestic opinion – in Jordan's case its East Bank Palestinian population – felt obliged to move into a common 'steadfastness' stance with the more radical Arab states, most of which agreed to pay money into a Jordanian–PLO Joint Fund for Steadfastness. 'Steadfastness' meant helping the population of the occupied territories financially to stay put.

Despite PLO–Hashemite co-operation, Jordan did not abandon its claim to the West Bank. In 1983 the PLO seemed to be falling apart, following Syria's move against it in Lebanon. Husayn stated that if the PLO fell under Syrian domination there was a legitimate question as to whether it could continue to speak for the Palestinian people. In other words Jordan would have to act for the Palestinians. This idea was reiterated by US Secretary of State, George Schultz,[37] reflecting US determination that any settlement for the West Bank should exclude the PLO and restore Jordanian sovereignty, in theory if not in practice. As a result the Hashemite monarchy was confirmed in Palestinian minds as the chosen client and instrument of the United States.

The Palestinian need for Jordan seemed to be borne out during the years 1983–6 when the PLO lived on the edge of political extinction. King Husayn used this situation to persuade the PLO to embark upon its risky alliance with Jordan in pursuit of a peace solution, which finally collapsed in early 1986.

Husayn proceeded in the belief that he could discard the PLO, which was in a weaker condition than at any time since 1967. He hoped that the people of the occupied territories were so desperate for an end to Israeli rule that they would respond to his overtures. During spring 1986 his government arranged for a number of 'spontaneous' demonstrations of support in the West Bank, and a series of newspaper articles appeared confirming popular support for his efforts and denouncing the PLO's betrayal of an historic opportunity for peace.[38]

Such efforts merely demonstrated a lack of support for Husayn and the depth of commitment to the PLO despite its weakness. When the mayor of Nablus, Zafir al Masri, was assassinated in March 1986, his funeral turned into the largest pro-PLO demonstration the territories had seen for years. This was hardly surprising. A poll in 1982 had suggested that 72 per cent of the West Bank felt that Husayn in no way represented them. Only 17 per cent felt he was acceptable even as a co-representative.[39] A year later another poll suggested that 65 per cent of the population of the occupied territories considered him to be insincere and hostile to Palestinian interests.[40] By 1986 support for Husayn had fallen to 3.3 per cent.[41]

Despite such indications, Husayn pressed ahead with efforts to wean the West Bank away from the PLO. His long-term aim was to foster a new leadership which would be more sympathetic to Jordan. During the summer months of 1986 it became clear that this approach enjoyed strong backing from the United States and Britain.[42] He closed PLO offices in the East Bank, expelling Arafat's deputy, Abu Jihad. He also froze all West Bank funds in Jordanian banks, and suspended aid to West Bank institutions.[43] West Bank Palestinians crossing the bridge came under close scrutiny. Those known for PLO sympathy were interrogated, harassed or turned back. Some had their passports seized.[44] Husayn enjoyed the active support of the Israeli government, which proceeded to deport or detain activists identified not only with the left (who had been the target of stringent measures before), but also those of the mainstream PLO.

In June 1986 he unveiled a five year development programme for the occupied territories, proposing to spend $1,200 million, which depended upon funding from Jordan's Western friends, particularly the United States and the European Community, and was focused on the development of the rural and commercial sectors, the two areas deemed least supportive of the PLO. 'We need to consider how the economy of the West Bank can one day be integrated with that of the East Bank', declared Jordan's minister for the occupied territories, 'We are drawing up a West Bank five year development plan aimed at integrating what we do there with what we have here. Everyone must be made to remember that this is one country, the Hashemite Kingdom of Jordan.'[45] Israel welcomed the plan as a placebo to Palestinian restiveness, a subsidy to its own administration of the territories, and a useful accessory in Israel's own policy of reward and punishment. By the end of the year Husayn had only obtained a fraction of the funding he sought.

Husayn's efforts to persuade the West Bank to abandon the PLO proved counterproductive. Almost every action by Israel against Palestinians was attributed to 'Jordanian requests'.[46] In spring 1987 he suffered a further blow when the constituent members of the PLO – split since 1983 – were reconciled at the 18th PNC in Algiers, and formally renounced the 1985 accord with Jordan.

On the East Bank Husayn's moves against the PLO exacerbated existing tensions concerning how the state was run. In July 1986 violent demonstrations occurred at Yarmuk University in which thousands were arrested. Many were Palestinians. It had long been understood that, while the refugee camps of the East Bank had remained pro-PLO ever since the events of 1970–1, the wealthier Palestinians had incorporated themselves into the Jordanian establishment. While this was true for the adult population, Yarmuk indicated that the younger of the bourgeois Palestinian class felt deep unease over their identity.[47]

The fact that almost half his people in the East Bank are either pro-PLO or are ambivalent in their loyalties remains a crucial factor in Husayn's Palestine policy. His attempt to woo the West Bank has definitively failed. The Uprising has shown beyond all doubt that King Husayn cannot represent the Palestinian people. His concern now must be to protect what remains of his kingdom.

Husayn was aware of the dangers long before the Uprising. By 1986 it was clear that an actual return of the territories to Jordanian sovereignty would threaten his long term authority on the East as well as the West Bank. An independent Palestinian state, however, would increase restiveness among the Jordanian Palestinians of the East Bank. Husayn could only contemplate this option with equanimity if most of the Palestine refugees moved out of his territory – presumably back to Palestine, an issue considered in the next chapter. The third possibility of no solution, but a progressive deterioration in the territories remained the most dangerous. His greatest fear was that the intensifying cycle of Israeli repression and Palestinian unrest would encourage Israeli hardliners in their view that only expulsion of the Palestinians would solve the problem of the occupied territories. The Hashemite monarchy would be unlikely to survive this eventuality. While his involvement in the affairs of the West Bank, in co-operation with the PLO or with Israel, could prevent things boiling over, he had good reason to remain involved. By July 1988, however, the Uprising had reached a stage where he felt constrained to erect a constitutional (and physical) barrier to protect the East Bank of Jordan from what might happen.

After half a century, the Hashemite adventure in Palestine seems to be drawing to its close. Unless the Palestinians suffer a dramatic reverse Jordan cannot conceivably negotiate for them. It still has an important part to play but as a secondary negotiator, possibly as an underwriter to any arrangement Israel may reach with the Palestinians. A Palestinian state would depend vitally on good relations with Jordan. Even so, Jordan's importance in a peace settlement may now be secondary not only to the Palestinians, but also to Syria.

3

GOING HOME?
THE REFUGEE ISSUE

A key security problem facing Jordan's future is the presence of a large number of Palestine refugees, by 1988 numbering over 862,000 out of a total of 2.25 million UN-registered refugees. Although Resolution 242 affirmed the need for a just settlement of the refugee problem, few in the international arena believe that this will mean a return of refugees to the part of Palestine that became Israel. A contradiction exists between the pragmatic view that there will be no return, and the legalistic one calling almost yearly for repatriation or compensation of the refugees.[1]

There is, of course, no secret at all to this contradictory position. Technically, according to almost every human rights convention or legal instrument on refugees and displaced people, the Palestine refugees enjoy an unassailable moral right to return. However, Israel has consistently refused a return of refugees except within the framework of an overall settlement with neighbouring Arab states. It was, of course, linking two issues with no moral connection. The question of the refugees' return was a direct obligation of Israel towards the refugees, not towards the Arab states.[2]

Israel did not want the refugees to return because it desperately needed their land and villages to absorb Jewish immigrants. Nor did it want the return of a population that would dissent from the Zionist identity of the state and threaten it demographically. For a nation which had fought a costly war of survival and independence to invite back the very presence which threatened national existence was, and remained unthinkable.

At the time, many Israelis believed their government's explanation that the Arabs had left either of their own free will or at the behest of their leaders. Had they been given a more accurate picture of what was actually taking place, would they have reacted differently? Some Israelis

Table 1   The Palestine Refugees

Country	1950	1988[a]
Lebanon	127,600	286,000
Syrian Arab Republic	82,194	263,000[b]
Jordan	506,200	862,000[bc]
West Bank	—[d]	381,000
Gaza Strip	198,227	453,000
Total	914,221[e]	2,245,000

[a] UNRWA figures (rounded) for April 1988.

[b] These figures do not include a further 210,000 in Jordan and 125,000 in Syria not recognized as refugees, but who have remained displaced as a result of the 1967 war. It should be noted, however, that these two figures have not been revised since the 1970s, and their accuracy must therefore be in question.

[c] This figure includes 355,022 refugees and their descendants who were displaced from the West Bank or Gaza Strip during or after the 1967 war.

[d] The figure for Jordan in 1950 includes those in the West Bank, who were estimated at approximately 280,000 in 1948 and were probably more than 300,000 by 1950.

[e] This total excludes 45,800 persons who, although inside Israel, lost both their homes and their means of livelihood and who were the responsibility of UNRWA until June 1952.

believe that the adherents of Socialist Zionism would not have accepted the idea that Arabs *driven out*, either directly or by the pressures of circumstance, had no moral right to return. This may have been so. Most Labour Zionists were of German or at any rate European origin, and tended to be the better educated of the Jewish population in Palestine. A poll conducted among Jewish Israelis in 1949 indicated that 73 per cent opposed the return of the Arab refugees but 27 per cent did not. However, the poll revealed a sharp difference between German and Arab Jews. While 45 per cent of German Jews agreed to a return, Arab Jews were 100 per cent opposed. Furthermore, the lower the level of education, the more likely the respondent was to oppose the return of the refugees.[3] Possibly, then, Jewish Israelis with a fuller picture might have reacted differently. While this must remain conjecture, it should be remembered that 1949 was a critical juncture. Thereafter the chance of a refugee return became more remote.

The 1949 failure to solve the refugee question

The international community realized by the autumn of 1948 that most refugees would be unlikely to return home. Its call to Israel to facilitate repatriation or compensation was an affirmation of the human rights of the situation, but did not reflect the pragmatic expectation. Nevertheless, efforts were made to persuade Israel to accept back at least some of the refugees. Some of those in the Palestine Conciliation Commission (PCC) did recognize, like Mark Ethridge, the United States member, that 'the developing impasse over the refugees was lethal to any possibility of peace in the Middle East.'[4] Ethridge realized that both Israel and the Arab states were using the refugees as political pawns. He believed that a generous gesture by Israel to accept back a large number might break the impasse, and generate an atmosphere conducive to an overall settlement.

Under pressure from the PCC and the United States, Israel toyed with two possibilities. The first was to incorporate the Gaza Strip into Israel, including its refugee population who might possibly be returned to their original villages. In May 1949 Israel informed the PCC that it 'would be prepared to accept . . . all Arabs at present located in the Gaza area, whether inhabitants or refugees, as citizens of Israel'.[5] However, it retreated from this position, partly because it feared strong adverse reaction particularly from its political Right, and also because it had seriously underestimated the number of Arabs in Gaza, at 100,000–150,000 when it was nearer 280,000. While Israel retreated, Egypt also repudiated the proposal. It could not afford the political cost of conceding yet more Arab territory to the new Jewish state. So, on both Israeli and Egyptian sides the Gaza Plan died. Had it been accepted, Israel's population would be one-third Palestinian Arab today, with the prospect of being one-half Arab by the year 2020, and the Israeli government would already be facing a demographic crisis within the State of Israel which is currently still some thirty years away.

Under United States pressure also, Israel made one further offer in July, to accept the return of 100,000. But publication of this offer caused a major political explosion in Tel Aviv, even within Mapai (Labour) itself. Nor did it impress the Arab states, which pointed out that if Israel was able to absorb hundreds of thousands of Jews it could certainly absorb more than 100,000 Palestinian returnees; or the United States, which did not think the Israeli offer 'provide[d] a suitable basis for contributing to solution of Arab refugee question.'[6] With the failure of the 100,000 plan the chances of any kind of conciliation between Israel and the Arabs died.

Almost everyone, with the exception of the refugees themselves, accepted that a return was not feasible. It was felt that a political settlement involving agreed borders and arrangements for non-belligerency, a view later echoed by Resolution 242, was more important, since these issues affected the security of Israel and the Arab states more directly.

However, the Arab states also wished to escape the political impact of the refugee presence upon their own internal stability. This was no idle fear, for Palestine already had a potent effect on popular opinion throughout the Arab world. Quite naturally, therefore, each Arab government was guided by its own considerations rather than the best interests of the refugees. Syria secretly offered to resettle 300,000 refugees as part of a comprehensive settlement.[7]

As the Egyptian representative to the PCC told a leading representative of the Palestinian refugees at that time, Egypt was more interested in its own problems in the Sudan, in Suez, and in the receipt of American aid and arms. He also pointed out that the Nile, if it flooded, might well drown a greater number of people than all the refugees.[8] Egypt had already secretly proposed that Israel should set up a Palestine Liberation Committee to pursue a solution to the refugee problem in the form of a small Palestinian state in the Arab-held parts of Palestine.[9] In this Egypt not only wished to remove the refugee problem as a political issue, but also to encourage Israel to deny the West Bank to Jordan, Egypt's enemy over the fate of Palestine. Egypt had no great wish to hang onto Gaza and its refugee population. The granting of a Palestinian state in Gaza by Israel would protect Egypt from the ignominy of surrendering Gaza to Israeli sovereignty, its principle objection to Israel's Gaza plan offer. As for Transjordan, it indicated that the more occupied territory Israel was willing to cede, the more refugees Transjordan would be willing to absorb and resettle.[10]

In the end, all the Arab states dug their heels in and demanded refugee repatriation as an essential element to peace, thereby joining Israel in linking the refugee issue to an overall peace. In a sense they had little alternative on account of Israel's refusal to accept the return of the refugees and the refugees' own outright refusal of resettlement. As a result, the 1949 Lausanne conference was a failure.

In retrospect, this period offered the best chance for a settlement. The Arab states, with the exception of Lebanon and possibly Egypt, might well have resettled the bulk of the refugees, had Israel accepted the principle of the right of return by receiving back about one-quarter of them and had the international community generously funded resettlement.

A refugee delegation had proposed to Eliahu Sasson, the head of the Israeli Foreign Ministry's Middle East Department at Lausanne, that Israel should annex the Gaza Strip and also the area subsequently known as the West Bank, while granting these areas local autonomy and absorbing another 100,000 refugees from surrounding Arab countries. Had such a plan been feasible, it would have achieved the complete withdrawal of all Arab armies and preserved the integrity of Palestine. Sasson himself believed it would 'complete resolution of the Palestine question' and possibly hasten peace between Israel and the Arab states.[11] However, while most Arab states might have gone along with this (if only to worst Abdallah), it was clear that Jordan would not contemplate the loss of the gains for which it had gone to war.

With the end to any possibility of repatriation at the Lausanne conference, towards the end of 1949 the United Nations authorized the creation of a special agency, the United Nations Relief and Works Agency for Palestine Refugees in the Near East (UNRWA). This began operations in May 1950, taking over responsibilities from the Red Cross and from the American Friends Service Committee. It was still believed, or at any rate hoped, that the refugees would in due course come to terms with their situation and accept resettlement. In January 1952 the General Assembly endorsed a three year development programme for the refugees, 'without prejudice to the provisions', concerning their rights to repatriation or compensation. It was recognized that 'the absorption, even temporarily, of one million persons into a community of five and a half millions (excluding Egypt) requires a digestive capacity far beyond the economic possibilities of the area as they exist today', as UNRWA reported in 1953.[12]

In the mid-fifties UNRWA committed itself to two major development schemes which offered the prospect of resettling between 200,000 and 300,000 refugees. In Jordan, a Yarmuk–Jordan valley development proposal to irrigate 500,000 dunums and to generate hydro-electricity; in Sinai another irrigation project, this time using the Nile waters, promised self-supporting agriculture on desert land. Both were thwarted by political considerations.[13]

In any case, UNRWA's resettlement plan coincided with the rise of Nasserist Arabism, the desire for strength to defeat the pervasive influence of foreign powers in the Arab body politic, of which the existence of Israel was the most potent manifestation. Arab nationalism came within an ace of overthrowing King Husayn in Jordan, and the latter's acceptance of UNRWA's resettlement programme, which also implied agreement with Israel over the Jordan waters, might have tipped the scales against him.

UNRWA remained permanently compromised with the refugee population it served as a result of these resettlement efforts. Every time any rumour sprang up concerning some kind of resettlement at any refugee camp, it reawakened old suspicions that UNRWA was an accomplice in the liquidation of the problem.[14] In one way these fears were justified, for UNRWA had no will of its own but was the servant of the international community. There were grounds for believing that only fear of the consequences of dismantling UNRWA for the stability of the host governments guaranteed the perpetuation of its services, pending a solution to the refugee problem.

The principal and at times sole opponents of refugee resettlement were the refugees themselves. Committees sprang up in the refugee concentrations around Israel's new borders.[15] Of these the most important was the Ramallah Congress of Refugee Delegates, which provided relief services in the West Bank with help from the Red Cross and Jordanian authorities. Meeting in March 1949, these delegates demanded the return of the refugees 'without awaiting the ultimate settlement of the Palestine question' (i.e. a political settlement).[16] The Congress soon found its desire to implement a return, regardless of political considerations, opposed not only by Israel but by the Arab states, and even the Palestinian Arab Higher Committee itself, which did not welcome this challenge to their authority in the management of negotiations with the enemy.

At Lausanne, the Ramallah Congress delegation discovered that without a representative government the refugee community had no standing, except as the subject of the deliberations. Even so, it presented its case with such cogency that the other Arab delegations agreed to meet to co-ordinate presentation of the Palestinian Arab case to the PCC. It persuaded the Palestinian delegations (each Arab state marshalled its own Palestinian representation) to focus the debate on the refugee issue. Two options were to be put to the Arab states, the first was to make their demands to Israel concerning borders, the return of the refugees, and so on, on the basis of determination to prosecute the war if Israel did not comply. The alternative option, clearly the one it favoured, was 'to *accept Israel as it existed* on the condition that each refugee be allowed to return to his home, *whether it was under Arab or Israeli jurisdiction.*'[17]

The Ramallah Congress delegation argued 'it should first be decided to allow the refugees to return, and once that is decided their actual return should not be affected by the discussion on the border question . . . The refugees would necessarily be subject to whatever authority and jurisdiction control the area in which they live, be it in the Arab area or within Israel.'[18]

The Israeli representative at Lausanne knew this position, for a Ramallah delegate had proposed that Israel should agree to the repatriation of 400,000 refugees 'who would live in peace with Israel and act as a "peace bridge" between Israel and the Arab states'.[19] But such proposals had little chance. Israel did not want the refugees back under any conditions and Jordan did not want a refugee body acting independently.[20]

The hardening of attitudes

In 1967 many more lost their homes in Palestine. By December, 245,000 had fled from the West Bank and Gaza Strip across the Jordan, 116,000 had fled from the Golan further into Syria, and 11,000 had left Gaza for Egypt. Of these 145,000 were UNRWA refugees uprooted for the second time.[21] Many more left in the following months, either forcibly expelled by the occupying authorities or choosing not to live under Israeli military government. Over 300,000 probably left Palestine as a result of the 1967 war.[22] Most of these were 1948 refugees, but some were indigenous to the West Bank. Once again, Israel demonstrated its determination not to allow the refugees to return.[23] Until 1967 roughly half the Palestinian people had still been somewhere in Palestine. From 1967 onwards the majority was outside.

Before 1967 Israel assumed, as did many others, that since the Palestinian Arabs had not achieved nationhood they would soon assimilate into the Arab host countries neighbouring Israel, if the latter had half a mind to allow it to happen. Today that assumption no longer really exists, but it also no longer needs to. The increasingly accepted argument in Israel today is that Eretz Israel in any case belongs primarily to the Jews and that all the Palestinian Arabs, refugee or otherwise, have a lesser claim upon it.

This change of perception may be discernible in the hardening of attitudes since 1949. Polls in 1971 and 1974 suggested that between 60 and 70 per cent of Jewish Israelis were wholly hostile while a further 21 to 27 per cent were moderately unfavourable to any return of the 1948 refugees. Only about 10 per cent of respondents favoured a return.[24] Furthermore, 66 per cent of respondents were against the return of even the 1967 refugees. By 1980 only about 5 per cent seemed to be favourably disposed towards a return of the 1948 refugees,[25] and this may have declined to 3 per cent during the 1980s.[26]

Even among the more categorically accommodationist Jewish Israeli proponents of Palestinian self-determination, there is unwillingness to brook a return of the refugees. In his case for a Palestinian state Mark Heller explains why, even with the recognition of Palestinian rights to self-determination, the right of return is wholly unacceptable to Israel: 'The return of the Palestinians . . . is impossible . . . because their introduction into Israel would derange the basic character of Israeli society and thus negate one of the primary purposes of Israeli withdrawal from the West Bank and Gaza.'[27] For another accommodationist, General Aharon Yariv, Director of the Tel Aviv Centre for Strategic Studies, 'Palestinian refugees would not be repatriated to Israel . . . but would be dealt with during gradual implementation of self-determination, presumably within the Palestinian territory or in other Arab states.'[28] Similarly, the leftist politician, Meir Pa'il does not foresee a return in the sense intended in UN Resolution 194: 'Clearly, the mere establishment of a Palestinian state in the West Bank and the Gaza Strip would not provide a concrete solution for the problem of the Palestine refugees in Lebanon and perhaps not even for those in the Gaza Strip . . . Part of the refugee problem will be solved by granting them the right of return to Palestine (i.e. the West Bank and Gaza Strip) or to the Jordanian-Palestinian federation.' He proposes that the Lebanon refugees should be resettled in Syria.[29]

Because of Israel's rigid stance, even the most sympathetic international proposals for the refugees, for example those advanced by the American Friends Service Committee, see the West Bank and Gaza as the only Palestinian destination for the refugees. Even this would be conditional and limited: 'the right of these groups [refugees] to move to the West Bank and Gaza Strip would have to be established through negotiations . . . It is unrealistic to assume that all the Palestinians currently living in the Arab states, whether still in refugee camps or integrated into their host society, could or would want to return to a West Bank-Gaza Palestinian state.'[30]

Given such a broad international consensus, shared by the more accommodationist Israeli and Western liberals, it is hardly surprising that since 1974 the PLO has played down the refugee issue, and concentrated on the only acceptable diplomacy concerning a territorial return to the 1949 Armistice Line. The right of refugee return remained firmly part of the rhetoric but it was less clear whether it was still as firmly a part of policy. Everyone felt that even the attainment of a small portion of Palestine for the Palestinian Arabs would be a triumph. Furthermore, if such an event occurred, everyone recognized that the PLO would be under intense external pressure to sacrifice the refugee right of return.

Even if the PLO did waive refugee rights, it is questionable whether it would be able to maintain such a waiver. As in 1949 at Lausanne, so the probability is that many refugees would oppose any surrender of their claim and would continue to struggle for a solution which goes a substantial way towards meeting both their physical needs and their sense of grievance.

Imperatives for the 'Return'

Refugee feelings concerning the right of return are intense. This is a key aspect of the refugee question which has so far received inadequate attention. The issue is not so much whether or how far the sense of grievance or of legitimate right can be justified objectively but rather its potency as a force in the equation, just as an unwavering Jewish belief in the right to all Eretz Israel has proved indispensable to the achievements of Zionism. Not every Zionist or Palestinian needs to be a fervent believer in this kind of credo for it to have a force and tenacity which cannot be ignored.

There is a second equally important facet of the refugee question which has also been underrated. Quite apart from the question of the right of return, or even the strong feelings which this issue engenders, there are compelling physical and economic reasons for at least a partial return. This, too, has its mirror image in the Zionist experience, when Jews found themselves endangered in Europe. The scale may be different but the 'push factor', albeit less intense, is nevertheless persistent. Unless this is understood and addressed, it is difficult to see how a durable peace can be achieved.

Of all the host countries, there is the greatest possibility in Syria, as in 1949, that the Palestine refugee population could be resettled and persuaded to accept its lot as a permanent part of the host country. This is partly because of the tight political control exercised by the state, but also because in Syria refugees have always enjoyed equal rights with Syrian citizens while maintaining their own identity. They have been able to work in government service, even in the army, and there has been no need for work permits.[31] Even so, the refugees themselves are likely to resist any settlement unless it is forced upon them by the Syrian government itself.

Syria is in a strong position since the refugees number 258,000, only 2.5 per cent of its population. Although by the end of the century their numbers are likely to rise to approximately 350,000, their proportion to the whole Syrian population is unlikely to change. In theory Syria could resettle many more, including the refugees in Lebanon, which Meir Pa'il proposes it resettles in return for Israeli acquiescence in Syria's incorporation of Lebanon.[32] Such an idea is unlikely to commend itself to Israel (for strategic reasons), or Lebanon, Syria or the refugees themselves.

Syria will determine whether to accept any resettlement, or whether to continue its support of the refugee demand to return to Palestine, as a function of its own regional objectives. It remains determined to achieve regional parity with Israel in order to compel the latter to make peace on terms favourable to itself, including a return of the Golan and possibly the 1949 demilitarized zone along the eastern edge of the Sea of Galilee to allow access to its waters. So it is likely to use the right of return as a bargaining chip over territorial concessions, unless it believes it is strong enough to obtain both territory and a return. Either way, the issue remains an important component of any Israeli-Syrian settlement.

In Lebanon there can be no prospect of the refugees accepting permanent settlement, regardless of the political circumstances. By 1988 there were almost 300,000, just under 10 per cent of the estimated population of Lebanon. The size of their presence, even after any political recovery in Lebanon, is bound to affect the country's stability.

The relationship between Lebanon and its Palestinian guests has always been difficult. The refugees who arrived starving and thirsty in 1948 do not have happy memories of their reception. On the contrary, their recollection is embittered by the cruelty, exploitation and official oppression which they recall.[33]

With the rise of the Palestinian resistance movement following the 1967 war, refugee areas asserted their independence from the Lebanese state. In the short run the Palestinian revolution acted as a magnet for those Lebanese, mainly Muslims, who wanted to redefine Lebanon's identity in terms of pan-Arab nationalism and as a focus of hostility for those, mainly Maronite Christians, who feared just such a process. Polarization led to civil war, marked by major massacres in which the Palestinian refugees were the prime victims. The Palestinian movement also drew Israel onto Lebanese soil in response to guerrilla raids into Israel. These reprisals set out specifically and successfully to drive a wedge of animosity between the Palestinians and their increasingly resentful hosts in south Lebanon, the Shiite community. Following Israel's 1982 invasion, the latter began to assert itself, hoping to become the chief arbiter in Lebanon's future. Between 1985 and 1987 the leading Shiite militia, Amal, attacked the south Beirut refugee camps with the same ferocity which had characterized attacks by the Maronites in the preceding phase of civil war. Amal acted not only on its own behalf, but for its patron, Syria, which also wished to remove the PLO from Beirut. After the failure of Amal's assaults, Syria's own subordinate Palestinian units drove PLO forces out of its Beirut strongholds of Shatila and Burj al Barajna in May 1988.

The continued armed presence of Palestinians, defending the camp areas but also renewing their attacks on Israel's northern border, destroyed much of the remaining solidarity offered by the Sunni Muslim and Druze communities. In the years after 1982, these began to reassess the balance of Lebanese, sectarian and pan-Arab identities. By 1988 the majority in both these communities were moving back towards greater emphasis on Lebanese identity, albeit hoping for a new constitutional basis, and they increasingly viewed the Palestinian presence as an undesirable one. Only the small secular Lebanese parties, particularly the Communists, and also the visionary Shiite party, Hizballah, still expressed solidarity with the Palestinian movement on Lebanese soil.

During the period since 1975, Palestinians have fled from repeated assaults upon almost every refugee camp in Lebanon.[34] It is inconceivable that they can now have a secure future in Lebanon, whether or not state authority is restored. Any re-establishment of government authority, be it under the old confessional dispensation or under a new Syrian-sponsored one, would not be comfortable for the Palestine refugee community, which by the turn of the century will number roughly 390,000, given no significant population movements.

Consequently, these refugees are not merely attracted emotionally to return to Palestine but live under the pressure of a hostile environment which will continue to encourage them to leave Lebanon. The problem is sufficiently acute that its political implications cannot easily be ignored.

Even in the event of Israel's relinquishing the occupied territories this political problem is likely to continue, partly because the absorptive capacity of the West Bank is limited but also because the vast majority of refugees in Lebanon come from Galilee, Haifa and Acre, and consider these places to be home. If the West Bank could absorb them, these refugees might conceivably settle and call it home. But if the West Bank cannot accommodate them, will they accept a political settlement which does not allow at least a substantial proportion to return to Galilee? This is the kind of question which has no answer, since no difference between commitment and rhetoric will be discernible until refugees are faced with a real choice between some kind of a settlement falling short of the ideal and holding out for the ideal itself.

Jordan's stability is also threatened. It gives refuge to the largest single concentration of Palestinians, almost 900,000 of whom were registered with UNRWA in 1988, and about another 210,000 who were displaced across the Jordan river as a result of the 1967 war.[35] Given a number of unregistered refugees, the total of Palestinians on the East Bank is probably in the order of 1.1 to 1.2 million. These form just over 40 per cent of the East Bank population.[36]

The refugee presence in Jordan is two-edged. A comprehensive settlement, whether or not this encompassed the return of the refugee population, would leave Jordan marginalized in the Middle East. If its greatest danger lies in the Israeli threat to push yet more Palestinians across the river Jordan and in a consequent revolution, Jordan's greatest asset lies in the support it receives from the West, anxious to bolster Jordan as a 'moderate' in the Arab world so long as the Middle East conflict persists. If a comprehensive settlement included the repatriation of the refugees (admittedly a wholly inconceivable eventuality at present), Jordan would cease to have either economic or political importance, and would probably be absorbed eventually either by Syria or by the Palestinian state. If, on the other hand, following a political solution to the West Bank, Jordan were left with the current refugee population but without substantial Western support, its future economic and political stability would be in question. Unless they demonstrated their loyalty, Jordan would be keen to be rid of most of the refugees before they became a source of sedition.

Without substantial economic development, there is also little prospect that Jordan could offer a reasonable living for its refugee population. Currently a substantial proportion of Jordanian Palestinians seek a living as migrant workers elsewhere, overwhelmingly in the Gulf states. In the early 1980s an estimated 228,000 Jordanian nationals worked in the Gulf[37] and it must be assumed that East Bank Palestinians, with a large number of dependants on the East Bank, are a majority of these. But from 1983 opportunities in the Gulf were substantially reduced when the region experienced a severe economic downturn as a result of both an oil and a world-wide recession. Moreover the situation is likely to remain insecure, since in the longer term nationals of the Gulf countries will be preferred for better paid employment. Consequently, in spite of the currently tolerable situation, the outlook is economically unsatisfactory for East Bank Palestinians. This can be welcome neither to the Jordanian regime nor to themselves.

Such factors are to do with where the refugees currently find themselves, not with the urge to return to Palestine. This urge is not merely the nostalgic 'village patriotism' of a dwindling breed who remember Palestine before 1948, as is widely believed in Israel.[38] It is a yearning for Palestine which permeates the whole refugee community and is most ardently espoused by the younger refugees, for whom home exists only in the imagination. Virtually every camp, in Lebanon, Syria, Jordan, and also in the West Bank, is organized according to a refugee family's village or place of origin. The first thing a refugee child learns is the name of his or her home village in Palestine. The belief in 'return' is fervently held. It is worth reiterating that this yearning to return is a potent mirror image of Zionist belief and aspiration earlier in the century, and is likely to have the same tenacity. Like the Zionist experience too, this yearning is reinforced by repeated exposure to legal and physical vulnerability.

A proper understanding of all this is long overdue, for the blend of dream and necessity for a place in Palestine will not disappear. To suppose that Palestinians' emotions concerning their identity in exile have weakened, or will weaken, over the years ignores the way they have responded to exile even where this has been relatively comfortable. Almost anywhere where a substantial Palestinian community exists it has generated its own institutions for social, economic as well as political activity. Such institutions are the envy of many Arab countries for they reflect a commitment to national identity that one will seek in vain in most parts of the Arab world. Furthermore, there is a lively interest in events inside Palestine, creating its own political dangers for Lebanon, Jordan, and elsewhere in the Arab world.

The international consensus seems to be that any return will be only to the West Bank and Gaza Strip. Will such a return be adequate? The capacity of the occupied territories to absorb part or all of the refugee population will be considered in chapter 9.

Part II
THE CHALLENGE TODAY

4

THE OCCUPIED TERRITORIES: FROM CONTROL TO REVOLT

For many years before the Uprising a level of Palestinian protest in the territories had been normal, comprising occasional violent attacks on Jews, stone throwing and occasional shutdowns and demonstrations. During the mid-1980s there had been a decline of organized violence inspired by the PLO but an increase in individual acts, a register of growing popular frustration at the situation and, in retrospect, a register of the growing internal pressures.[1]

The most significant characteristic of this unrest, however, was the impression that it could be contained almost indefinitely by a skilful and manipulative military government. Normality consisted of permanent occupation, with the limitations and restrictions implicit in such a process, punctuated by occasional outbursts of anger. The Uprising destroyed this normality, and one must ask why it occurred, and why it occurred when it did, twenty years after the territories fell under Israeli rule.

When Israel captured the territories in 1967 it was unsure what to do with them. There was no national consensus except over East Jerusalem, which was annexed in July, and over the Golan Heights, which was also declared non-negotiable by the end of the year. Pending any agreement with the Arab states, particularly with Jordan which hoped to secure the return of its lost territory, Israel's Defence Minister, Moshe Dayan, established a pattern which remained the bedrock of Israel's occupation policy.

The creation of normality

Dayan determined to retain a strong but relatively invisible grip on the territories while also creating an impression of normality for the residents. Military forces were deployed mainly in the Jordan valley along the new frontier with Jordan, while the Arabic-speaking and mainly Druze Border Guards and the plain clothes General Security Service (Shin Bet) exercised control over the population through a large network of informers.[2] Both Dayan and the deputy prime minister, Yigal Allon, established *nahal* (agricultural/military) settlements along the floor of the Jordan valley, as a permanent presence. There was no intention ever to remove these, nor the few that were established on the central ridge dominating the West Bank.

Under Dayan, Israel took a series of measures to make its occupation permanent. It normalized daily life with access for the population across the 'open bridge' to Jordan. It refused to let back the 300,000 or so who crossed to the East Bank during or after the 1967 war, but it allowed 100,000 'summer visitors' to cross each year to maintain contact with their families.

In the administrative sphere it decided to operate through the traditional élites which had worked for the Jordanian government. It reactivated the municipalities and initiated a process of integration between Israel and its newly captured territories. This was intended to make Gaza and the West Bank wholly dependent on Israel and frustrate any efforts to build a community power base.

At the infrastructural level, the highways and transport system of Israel, Gaza and the West Bank were developed in such a way that it became increasingly easy to drive from Israel direct to one of the West Bank Jewish settlements without passing through Arab population centres. By the late 1980s the main arterial routes of the West Bank primarily reflected the transport and communications needs of the Israeli State and its settler population.[3] Even the main Arab towns, like Nablus and al Bira-Ramallah, were bypassed by these highways, which provided ready and quick access between the coastal plain and the new settlements high in the West Bank hills. These settlements were established on public and private land progressively seized by Israel from 1967 onwards, declared 'state land' and given over to Jewish rather than Palestinian use. By 1987 52 per cent of the West Bank and approximately 30 per cent of the Gaza Strip had been transferred to Jewish control.

Israel also took control of the water sources of the West Bank and integrated them into its national water system. It restricted the use of water by proclamation,[4] and introduced meters to ration water consumption for agricultural use at its pre-1967 level, thereby limiting the amount of expansion possible in the most important sector of the

The West Bank

- Israeli civilian settlements
- Israeli military settlements
- Refugee camps
- Major cities

ISRAEL
Jenin
Tulkarm
Nablus
Tel Aviv
Mediterranean Sea
River Jordan
JORDAN
Ramallah
Jericho
Jerusalem
Bethlehem
Dead Sea
Hebron
0 miles 10

Gaza Strip

- Israeli civilian settlements
- Israeli military settlements
- Refugee camps
- Major cities

Mediterranean Sea
Gaza
ISRAEL
Khan Yunis
Rafah
EGYPT
Sinai Peninsula
0 miles 5

Map 3   Jewish Settlement in the occupied territories by 1988

territories' economy. It also integrated the supply of electricity into the national grid curtailing and, in 1987, finally taking over the only independent Palestinian energy supplier, the Jerusalem Electricity Company. Thus, Israel took direct control of two vital ingredients of economic activity, water and electricity.

It also proceeded to control and use the people of the occupied territories economically by allowing them to work inside Israel. This policy had several advantages. It absorbed a number of otherwise unemployed Palestinians, thus reducing the potential for political ferment. By offering better wages in Israel it placed an obstacle in the way of local industry, which did not benefit from subsidies or other forms of assistance enjoyed by Israeli industry. In the absence of local employment alternatives which might otherwise have developed, it made between one-third and one-half of the Palestinian work-force dependent for its livelihood upon employment by Israeli enterprises.

This labour policy also gave Israel important economic and social benefits. Arab labour had none of the securities which Jewish labour enjoyed through its trade union federation, the Histadrut. Rather, it constituted an almost limitless pool of cheap labour which could be hired on a casual basis in response to the expansion or concentration of the economy. The influx of cheap Arab labour from the occupied territories allowed the Israeli economy to expand rapidly after 1967, pushing unskilled Jewish labour into higher grade work. The shift in the labour pattern significantly reduced the tensions between the European and non-European and largely unskilled Jewish elements in Israel which during the 1960s was becoming a serious social and political issue since the latter grew faster demographically than the former.[5]

Overall, Israel's absorption of over 100,000 Palestinians as casual labourers created a feeling of weakness and helplessness in the Palestinian community, and of success and power within the Israeli economy.

Since the territories were captive, Israel could develop them as its second largest export market (after the United States), with an export value of $800 million annually by 1986.[6] This amounted to 10.9 per cent of Israel's overall export of goods. The territories constituted an outlet for surplus or substandard production, with the same elasticity for the economy which Arab labour afforded.

At the strategic level of integrating the territories into the Israeli economy, the competitive edge of Israel's highly developed and heavily subsidized productive capacity in industry and agriculture destroyed the Palestinian sector almost in its entirety – although there was not an enormous amount to destroy because of the Jordanian legacy of economic neglect. Israel did not have to do much more than open the area to its own produce and place obstacles in the way of anyone trying to develop enterprises or co-operative ventures.

The struggle for control

Israel profited from Arab attitudes towards the political future of the territories. Arab regimes, particularly Jordan, welcomed Israel's reappointment of the old élite to provide municipal services, for it created the impression that the occupation was not permanent and that Jordanian authority was still recognized through the employment of its municipal and civil servants. While Israel's policy was directed towards the normalization of life under occupation, Jordan's prime preoccupation was to prevent political developments among the people of the West Bank which it would be unable to control.[7]

Israel allowed the old élite to travel to Amman freely so that, despite the loss of physical control of the territories, Jordan was still able to direct much of what happened. In Amman Jordan was able to remind these notables of the benefits of the Jordanian connection and their continued loyalty. It provided the West Bank mayors and notables with financial disbursements and economic favours. In 1968 Israel allowed Jordan to establish a Council of West Bank Chambers of Commerce, to facilitate the export of Palestinian goods across the open bridge. Jordan was able to exercise considerable control of the West Bank's agricultural economy through this Council.[8]

Jordan's nervousness concerning local initiatives was well founded. Immediately after the war the Muslim religious leadership and then the communists and leftists, as a National Guidance Committee, attempted to organize a political resistance together.[9] Both were cold-shouldered by Jordan and suppressed by Israel. Even Jordan's closest supporters were tempted by the opportunities which the Israeli occupation offered. The best known mayor of the time, Shaikh Muhammad Ali Ja'bari (who had led the West Bank notables to accept Hashemite rule in 1948), offered to act as an intermediary between the Israelis and Amman – a role which, as Amman was quick to perceive, greatly enhanced Ja'bari's standing as 'the leader' of the West Bank population. He secured the support of mayors south of Jerusalem, and clearly hoped to extend his influence northwards. He even sounded out the Israeli authorities on the chance for local autonomy, making (for him) the dramatic statement that 'Jordan is not authorised to decide the future of the Palestinian population on the West Bank'.[10] Evidently Jordan could not trust even its old clients, unless they were bound to the East Bank by powerful economic considerations.

For the first five years of occupation the PLO, too, feared that it would lose its modest foothold in the territories. Either Jordan would completely eliminate its influence, as seemed likely following the 1970–1 war in Jordan, or the West Bank élite might fill the leadership vacuum, or a local national liberation movement might develop over which it had no control. It had grounds for such fears, since it was struggling to legitimize itself as the Palestinian representative and did not wish this to be challenged by any independent local movement. Furthermore, it had been alarmed at local initiatives taken in the immediate aftermath of the June war. Of these the most dramatic had been taken by a Ramallah lawyer, Aziz Shehadeh, who had already demonstrated his independent thinking in 1948 as a leading spirit in the Ramallah Congress of Refugee Delegates (see above pp. 83–5). Within days of Israel's victory, Shehadeh had suggested to senior Israelis that they should permit the West Bank to declare an independent Palestinian state forthwith, without waiting for a political settlement with the rest of the Arab world. In Palestinian circles Shehadeh's proposal was highly controversial, since it dealt directly with the enemy, was implicitly ready to accept the reality of Israel and disregarded the pan-Arab dimension of the Palestine struggle.

Quite apart from any ideological objections it may have had, the PLO found such initiatives very threatening. It even opposed independent local attempts to send West Bank representatives to Arab countries to discuss political problems. It found itself in unanimity with Jordan in warning people like Ja'bari against any unauthorized initiative with the enemy.[11] This unanimity encouraged local leaders to abstain from political initiatives and to concentrate on local and day-to-day issues. It also encouraged them to resist any change whatever in local institutions or in elections for community representation, except with the specific approval of the Jordanian government and the PLO itself.[12] The duty of the people of the West Bank was to await liberation through armed struggle.

As a result, the concerns of the outside contestants, Israel, Jordan and the PLO, ran along parallel lines. Israel's immediate reappointment of the mayors and municipal structure was a deliberate measure not only to ensure normality but also to thwart the emergence of any all-West Bank leadership.[13] Had West Bank society been industrialized, with the social transformation this implies, the Israelis would have had difficulty preventing these mayors from producing a united national leadership.

West Bank political, economic and social life had been notable throughout the period since 1920 for its localism. Whatever Ja'bari's strength in the area south of Jerusalem, it was probable that any growth in his power would be strenuously opposed in, say, Ramallah, Nablus or Tulkarm. This suited Israel, Jordan and the PLO.

The lack of national coherence also suited the old élite. By and large they fell in happily with the exhortations they received from the Arab world not to take any unauthorized political initiatives. They were encouraged to believe that external agents would tackle the problem of a territorial settlement. They were free to pursue their localist goals unhindered, while making strong-sounding nationalist statements which authenticated their leadership among the local community where they had economic or family status.

This posture of nationalistic utterances but pursuit of only localist goals was natural in the Arab nationalist atmosphere of the late 1960s and early 1970s. Palestine was still an all-Arab question and few believed that it would be recovered save through the united endeavours of the Arab states.

PLO attitudes changed following Husayn's defeat of its forces, his announcement of a United Arab Kingdom plan in March 1972 (which challenged PLO ambitions) and the outcome of the municipal elections of April 1972. These elections, the first to be called since 1963, had been opposed by both the PLO and Jordan, but neither had sufficient influence to ensure an effective boycott. However, the electoral result largely reinstated the existing mayors, effectively a victory for Jordan, which accorded most of them post facto recognition.[14]

In order to win West Bank allegiance in the face of Israeli and Jordanian competition, the PLO had to find a local partner. In 1973 it confirmed its support of the Palestine Patriotic Front (successor to the short-lived National Guidance Committee), which had been etablished by the Palestine (previously Jordan) Communist Party. It was not a natural choice for the PLO, but its options were very limited. Only the Communists and radicals, who had been outlawed in pre-1967 days, had the established underground networks through which to operate.

At first relations between the PLO outside and the Patriotic Front inside were cordial, but as time went by the PLO leadership became increasingly uneasy about the Patriotic Front taking its own initiatives. While PLO constituents, Fatah, the DFLP and independents, were given representation in the Patriotic Front, the PLO refused to reciprocate by granting the Communist Party representation on the PLO executive.[15] In the end the PLO tried to replace the Patriotic Front with a right-wing alternative of its own.[16]

Despite this tension the Patriotic Front and the PLO had a deeply politicizing effect on the inhabitants of the territories during the period 1973–5. Although they privately felt that they themselves should properly decide the fate of the territories, even the most conservative mayors began to acknowledge the PLO.[17] The PLO, dominated by Fatah, reaped the fruits while the Patriotic Front fell apart as a result of the undermining effect of the Palestinian right, the enormous surge in PLO power following the Rabat summit of October 1974 and Arafat's address to the General Assembly of the United Nations the following month.

The PLO's capture of the hearts and minds of those under occupation was the first great blow to Israel's policy of normalization. In December 1975, during an upsurge of national feeling in the territories, the defence minister, Shimon Peres, ordered new municipal elections to take place in April 1976. With a substantial widening of the franchise, Peres hoped to head off what he saw as PLO-inspired recalcitrance and allow the accommodationist vote to prevail. One must doubt whether it was the Israeli 'government's intention to introduce into the West Bank the Israeli norm of democratic elections'[18] since the authorities deeply regretted the outcome, and did not repeat the experiment. The accommodationist vote proved to be largely imaginary, and radical new candidates swept away most of the old guard, to become mayors of most of the West Bank's towns.

The PLO's victory removed neither Jordan nor the traditional élite. from the scene. The new mayors were summoned to Amman and reminded of the value of good relations for marketing agricultural produce to Jordan. Each was helped to assess the balance of loyalty by the offer of financial assistance to his municipality.[19]

Although the new mayors tended to be younger men, they did not represent a new class of people. They were, almost without exception, young scions of old notable families of the towns they now represented, persuaded by their families to stand for election in order to maintain the family interest.[20] Many of these families carefully weighed the balance of pro-PLO and pro-Jordanian sympathy locally, and chose from their ranks a suitable candidate to reflect opinion in the voting population. In this way what appeared as politically radical to the outside world, was perceived locally as social traditionalism.[21] The most radical of these new mayors, like Bassam Shak'a of Nablus and Karim Khalaf of Ramallah, found themselves facing almost as much difficulty from Jordan and the PLO leadership as they did from the Israeli authorities.[22]

The autonomy plan for the occupied territories embodied within the Camp David Accords of 1978, however, brought the different strands within the West Bank and Gaza leaderships together. Autonomy was seen in the occupied territories as a denial of the demand for self-determination, not a step towards it. There was also unease that an implicit judicial separation from Jordan implied a change in the status of the territories. They would cease to be 'occupied' and therefore cease to enjoy the legal protection of the 1949 (IVth) Geneva Convention and the withdrawal requirement in Resolution 242.

To confront these dangers, the mayors and other leading individuals established a new National Guidance Committee (NGC). Their attempt to create effective liaison and co-operation with the PLO leadership outside, however, led to unease when the latter called for restraint since the Camp David accords were 'under serious scrutiny and assessment'.[23] In the view of the NGC, the PLO did not appreciate either the seriousness of the Camp David threat or the strength of feeling in the territories. The scale of demonstrations throughout the territories quickly persuaded the PLO to reject the autonomy plan.

Once again, as in 1973–5, a serious debate arose concerning local or external control. Within the PLO leadership the dominant group, Fatah, wanted to retain a firm external hold on local activity. Its rivals, the PFLP and DFLP, wanted to allow local leaders to oppose the autonomy plan as they thought best.[24] Like the NGC, the PFLP and DFLP suspected that Fatah was toying with the peace process.[25]

It was not long before disagreements emerged between Fatah and the NGC, particularly once the radical mayors Shak'a and Khalaf emerged as leaders of the NGC, to the detriment of a more accommodationist tendency.[26] When Israel decided to expel Shak'a in 1979, the PLO cautioned against a mass resignation of mayors proposed by the NGC. In the event thirteen mayors submitted their resignation to the Israelis, totally rejecting the PLO directive. As Mayor Muhammad Milhem of Halhoul, himself no radical, remarked: 'We have the true picture. Our friends outside do not.'[27] The radical Palestinian factions outside supported the NGC in its decision, partly to reduce Fatah influence in the West Bank.

Fatah now feared that the NGC and the radical factions would wrest leadership of the Palestinian movement in the territories completely from its grasp. Tensions increased when the NGC sought the right to disburse steadfastness money instead of the Jordanian–PLO Joint Committee set up in Amman. This was money voted by the Arab states in Baghdad in 1978 to confront the implications of Camp David and assist the inhabitants of the territories to stay put and be 'steadfast'.

It was not long before the Joint Committee began to starve the NGC and associated radical elements of financial support, while fostering rival groups and individuals. Fatah and the Jordanian authorities started to work co-operatively against the common threat of radical nationalism in the territories. The Jordanians opened passport offices to bypass mayors who had previously renewed travel documents, and established co-operative associations in the villages around Nablus for the marketing of agricultural produce to Jordan.[28] Fatah was not particularly regretful when the Israeli authorities finally closed the NGC down in 1982.

The struggle between the NGC and the PLO leadership was one of several important developments which persuaded the people in the West Bank and Gaza that neither the Arab states nor the PLO were capable of liberating them militarily or diplomatically and that it was pointless to continue to hope for a solution from the outside.

It proved a painful lesson. First, there were the Camp David accords which promised an autonomy they neither wanted nor received. Israel began to integrate elements of the military government into its own civil ministries, proving that the kind of autonomy it had in mind implied less rather than more Palestinian control over their affairs. It also set up Village Leagues, an attempt to create a co-operative Palestinian structure in the less politically active villages of the West Bank.[29] In 1982 Israel invaded Lebanon to remove the PLO from the battlefield. The following year the PLO fell apart, under attack from Syria as well as its own dissidents.

Inside the territories the NGC was dismembered by Israel, its leaders expelled, imprisoned or confined to their home town. Elements of both the Jordanian government and the PLO seemed undismayed by the expulsion or detention of leftist or independently-minded members of the NGC. From 1984 to 1986 the people of the territories watched uneasily as the mainstream PLO tried to recover its position by uniting with Jordan in an initiative intended to rescue the territories from occupation. Many people in the territories felt that Arafat was sailing too close to the wind and were relieved by the collapse of his accord with King Husayn.

The collapse of the Husayn–Arafat accord led to a new phase of co-operation between Israel, the United States and Jordan aimed at objectives similar to those of the early seventies: the erosion of support for the PLO in the territories, the reinforcement of the normality of occupation by a programme to improve 'the quality of life', a term coined in this context by US Secretary of State George Schultz. The United States announced the availability of increased USAID funds to develop the occupied territories. Israel made it clear that such development would be primarily in social and welfare spheres, and would not include any kind of economic development which ran contrary to its interests. Jordan also announced its $1.2 billion development plan.

In the autumn of 1986 Jordan and Israel demonstrated their practical co-operation with the opening of the Cairo-Amman Bank branch in Nablus, and the appointment of jointly selected mayors for Hebron, Ramallah and al Bira.

Proposals to improve the quality of life coincided with the tenure of the National Unity Government under the initial premiership of Shimon Peres, widely regarded outside the territories as the most promising Israeli proponent of a peace settlement. However, the return to partial Labour rule did not usher in a period of optimistic progress towards a settlement. The emollient international posture of Prime Minister Peres contrasted sharply with the toughest crackdown the West Bank and Gaza Strip had experienced since the period 1969–72. From 1985 there were demolitions of homes, arrests and expulsions on a scale unsurpassed during the more explicitly doctrinaire tenure of Likud, 1977–84.[30]

For Palestinians this was not surprising. Labour implemented a more repressive policy on the ground than Likud while pretending to greater moderation in the international domain. In its control of the territories, it had been more interfering and manipulative with Palestinian social institutions, recognizing that *all* social institutions, even kindergartens, were potential bases for community solidarity and resistance.

The final blow in a decade of reverses, 1977–87, was the apparent abandonment of the Palestine cause by the Arab world. In November 1987 the heads of most Arab states met in Amman for a summit conference. Their most pressing concern was the seven-year-old Iran–Iraq war, and the Palestine question was pushed to the bottom of the list of priorities for the first time in the history of the Arab League. Arafat was snubbed by his host, King Husayn, while Syria tried but failed to achieve a conference resolution which omitted the PLO as a participant in a future international peace conference. For the people of the territories it was a reminder that Jordan, Egypt and Syria were all more concerned with their own national and regional priorities than with the recovery of Palestine.

By the closing weeks of 1987 the population of the occupied territories had concluded that they faced not only the prevarication of Israel and Jordan but also the acquiescence of the other Arab states. They also saw that, bereft of a power base or allies, the PLO was powerless. After twenty years of struggle it seemed less likely to liberate any part of Palestine than it had in 1967. The people could look for deliverance to no one but themselves.

The sinews of solidarity

Developments inside Palestinian society in the territories over the same decade had been less obvious but more significant. Without them it is questionable whether the Uprising would have happened and if it had, whether it could either have embraced the total population or sustained itself for so long.

These developments stemmed from the growing awareness among political cadres, intellectuals and development workers from 1978 onward that the community under occupation had to learn to take power into its own hands. Fundamental to the thinking of this comparatively small group of people was the ease and skill with which Israel had been able to exert its will, control dissent, and remove local leadership as soon as its challenge to the authorities necessitated this. It had happened repeatedly, from the short-lived first National Guidance Committee of 1967 to the second NGC established in response to Camp David and suppressed by Ariel Sharon in early 1982. The harsh lesson was that visible leaders, even journalists, were an easy target for either the Israeli or Jordanian authorities whose interest in containing Palestinian radicalism coincided.

Palestinian activism began to spread institutionally, through various strands of society. A profound transformation took place, one which was far from obvious to the casual outside observer. Crudely put, authority and leadership began to move from traditional leaders, be they the old pro-Jordanian élite or the post-1976 pro-PLO mayors (most of whom had been eliminated by the authorities), into new but less visible hands.[31]

The new leadership proved more diffuse – beyond the narrow confines of the traditional élite and professional classes – and younger. The constituent groups of the PLO, Fatah, PFLP, DFLP and the Communist Party, all had their cadres in the territories which maintained their outward anonymity to avoid arrest. These built up their strength through youth organizations, clubs and activity centres in the refugee camps and towns. These youth centres increasingly became targets of Israeli harassment and closure.

After the outbreak of the Uprising there was considerable discussion of its youthfulness, as if this itself was a revolution in Palestinian society. In part it undeniably was, for younger Palestinians displaced traditionally older leaders, and young women participated more fully than ever before. But it also reflected the demographic composition of

Palestinian society. Sixty five per cent of Palestinians were under twenty, genuinely 'children of the occupation'. Almost 80 per cent were under the age of thirty. It was natural that the youth, who grew up with the failure of the Arab world and of their elders (and social superiors) to recover Palestine, should become a leading political force in the country. Only six months before the Uprising a leading Palestinian journalist presciently noted

These young people who have grown up under Israeli occupation take a much more radical approach than the PLO leadership. Having grown up under the nose of the Israeli war machine, young Palestinians have come to the conclusion that, in the world they inhabit, might is right and the only way to survive and flourish is to be strong and violent. Diplomatic missions and political initiatives don't mean anything to these young people who have seen only more oppression as Israel speaks of peace. Although for the present time this generation has strong feelings for the PLO and its chairman, Yasser Arafat, they have grown impatient with the niceties of political diplomacy.[32]

As a result of the youthfulness of society, higher education institutions became a barometer of political currents. By 1985 there were eight colleges and universities in the territories, and four UNRWA vocational training centres. Both on and off campus students demonstrated against Israeli and Jordanian interference and fought bitter internal representative elections which were closely followed by the community, since they reflected the moods and internal conflicts which so fragmented society. These contests were between the various components of the formal Palestinian movement, Fatah, the DFLP, the PFLP, the Communist Party, and also the Islamic Tendency, which was strong in Hebron and Gaza and enjoyed substantial support elsewhere.

A fierce struggle developed between NGC and Fatah supporters in the period 1978–82. In elections at Birzeit University in December 1980, Fatah in association with an Islamic Bloc (see below) began to reduce the overall power of the radicals, taking one-third of the seats on the student council. In those at Hebron and Nablus in mid-1981 the Fatah/Islamic Bloc coalition actually won a majority over the NGC supporters.[33] The struggle between these groups reflected events outside Palestine as well as within. Following the great unity forged in adversity in 1982, fragmentation of the PLO the following year triggered bitter feuds on every college campus. After four years of strife reconciliation of the PLO factions in Algiers in April 1987 was reflected on the ground, as the various groups found it easier to accept their differences and to agree on the importance of national unity. As one Palestinian remarked: 'Many splits of the past few years have already been forgotten. Certain labour unions belonging to the PFLP, the DFLP or the Communist Party, have joined ranks with the Fatah labour unions. As much as you Israelis are split between Likud and Labour, we Palestinians in the territories have become united during the past two months, more united than ever before.'[34]

The geographical pattern of political loyalty in the West Bank had also changed. During the early 1970s Palestinian nationalism had affected villages less than the urban areas. After 1976 both Jordan and Israel made conscious efforts to detach rural society from the leadership offered by local towns, the former through the landlords and merchants who controlled agricultural marketing, the latter through its Village Leagues, a network aimed at maintaining dependency and destroying the credibility of the nationalist urban leadership.

The Village Leagues posed a serious threat since they affected many West Bank villages. Jordan warned Village League followers that they risked the charge of treason. The PLO supported Jordan against the Village Leagues, since its own legitimacy was directly challenged by them. Jordan and the PLO defeated the Leagues, and in the process made the villages more politically aware.[35] The PLO rather than Jordan reaped the fruit, so much so that after the collapse of the Jordanian–PLO accord in 1986 many Village Leaguers were rehabilitated in Jordanian eyes. By the end of 1987 West Bank villagers were hardly less politically aware than their urban counterparts. The significant difference was that in rural areas Fatah tended to rule alone, whereas in the camps and towns, the radicals posed a strong challenge.

Israeli land seizure also politicized the rural population. This was not merely through the intrinsic loss but also because family status and honour were intimately linked to possession of land.[36] The spread of nationalism into rural areas also reflected the economic transformation that had taken place since 1967. The shift from the main traditional occupation, agriculture, to unskilled labour, was considerable. Three-quarters of village income by the mid-1980s was earned outside, either elsewhere in the West Bank, or more usually in Israel, which might account for 60 per cent of village income.[37] The transformation of the peasantry into a rural proletariat weakened *hamula* (patrilineal extended family) ties, and strengthened class ones. One clear sign was the growing rejection of village headmen, or *mukhtars*, as village leaders. The appointment of a *mukhtar*, introduced by the Ottomans for taxation and conscription purposes, had reinforced family power. Britain and Israel both used the system. It was inevitable that with the unpopularity of Israeli rule, the use of *mukhtars* to enforce unwelcome regulations and the exposure of the village workforce to a less traditional culture in their place of work, the system lost credibility. By the mid-1980s *mukhtars* were frequently considered collaborationist.

It was natural that this growing rural proletariat should turn to trade unions for support. Those who worked legally inside Israel paid compulsory dues to the Israeli union, the Histadrut, but received no benefits or support from it. As a result, Palestinian migrant workers routinely earned a fraction of what their Israeli counterparts were paid inside Israel.[38] Some workers turned to Palestinian unions, although these had had a chequered career. Six small unions in Gaza had been closed down by Israel in 1967, and only allowed to re-open in 1979, on condition they neither held fresh elections nor recruited new members. As one unionist remarked, 'they gave us the key, but forbade us to open the door.' In the West Bank there had been twenty-six unions in 1967, belonging to a West Bank federation. These grew in number, many existing solely on paper, but remained weak. Their services were modest, and collective written agreements with employers remained exceptional.[39]

Towards the end of the 1970s these unions began to revive, in response both to labour needs and to frustration at the failure of the conventional political process. Some unions, and union blocs, reflected the political outlook of component groups of the PLO. It was not long before the authorities began to harass the unions, and to maintain an aura of fear to keep their membership dormant.[40] Organizations with a political outlook, such as the Workers' Unity Bloc, the Progressive Workers' Bloc and the Workers' Youth Movement all became targets for harassment.[41]

In the mid-1980s Israeli control of the unions began to fail. In 1986 when young activists decided to revive the six Gaza unions, the leaders were arrested and the unions temporarily closed down. Early the following year, however, two of these unions defied Israeli bans and organized new elections.[42] Despite further arrests, defiance of Israeli authority had an electrifying effect on labourers throughout the territories. Although membership remained low, only about 20 per cent of the West Bank labour force, the resurgence of the union movement symbolized a new national populism which the authorities seemed unable to stifle. Trade unionism became a key element in national solidarity and social education.

The Islamic revival

A more controversial element in popular feeling was the religious one. Open Islamic expression began to revive from 1978. Islam traditionally held an important place on the political stage of the West Bank.[43] However, religious identity had taken second place to secular nationalism for a whole generation. This was partly because of the idea of national unity between Muslim and Christian Palestinians, but also because the Muslim dimension was masked during the heyday of Arab nationalism, from the 1950s until the mid-1970s.[44]

With the decline of secular Arabism as a credible ideology in the late 1970s, some Palestinians began to affirm their religious loyalties. For many there was a substantial overlap between religious and national identity.[45] Moreover, there were long-standing and intimate links between the Muslim Brotherhood and Fatah.[46] In Gaza there was an old relationship between poor Palestinians and the Muslim Brotherhood in Egypt.[47] Islam was firmly woven into the warp of Gazan life. In the twenty years 1967–87, for example, the number of mosques in Gaza doubled from 75 to 150.[48]

Like the secular movements, the Islamic tendency was expressed in university life. In the 1978 student elections at Birzeit the Islamic bloc won only 3 per cent of the vote but a year later, inspired by Khomeini's victory, it won 43 per cent. At al Najah and Hebron universities, it won the 1981 elections in association with Fatah. In 1987 it won 27 per cent of the Birzeit student vote, 85 per cent of the Hebron University vote, and over 40 per cent of the vote at al Najah, where the threat of violence between secular and religious students provoked the voluntary closure of the university until feelings had sufficiently abated.

Many Palestinians found the Muslim revival shocking. Growing up in the more liberal atmosphere of secularist nationalism in the 1950s and 1960s, it was easy to forget the vigour of Islam. As secularists, they saw the Islamic resurgence as retrograde, leading away from the kind of society they hoped to create. For Christians it defined a national identity from which they were excluded. Israel exploited the tension between secular nationalism and Muslim fundamentalism as far as it was able.[49]

There was also a tendency to treat the Muslim revival as a single extremist development. In fact it had diversities similar to those in secular nationalism. There was a large conservative establishment of senior Muslim divines in the territories, which had tried to fill the political vacuum in June 1967. In Hebron Sheikh Ja'bari established a Centre for Islamic Studies (later, Hebron University) in 1971 but his motive was less religious than political. He established it as an alternative power base in Hebron as his mayoral leadership came under increasing challenge from secular nationalists.

The Muslim Brotherhood was less concerned with the liberation of Palestine than with the establishment of an Islamic state by peaceful means, possibly as a part of Jordan where its activities were tolerated by the authorities.

The Brotherhood provided the moral climate in which more strident cultures could flourish. Some were small but violent, like Islamic Jihad, which had broken from the Muslim Brotherhood in the 1960s. Inspired by the Iranian revolution, Islamic Jihad launched attacks on the Israeli occupation. Although it remained small, its attacks – the murder of two Israeli taxi drivers in Gaza Market in October 1986, a hand-grenade attack on troops at the Wailing Wall the same month, and the murder of IDF Captain Ron Tal in September 1987 – attracted attention. In October 1987 the army clashed with an armed group in Gaza and later arrested over fifty Islamic Jihad suspects and uncovered a large arms cache.[50]

Other non-violent groups, like al Mujama'a (The Community) which commanded a large following in the refugee camps of Gaza and the Islamic Association inside Israel (see p. 152), posed a different kind of challenge to the authorities. By 1988 al Mujama'a had an active following of about 2,000 working mainly in the refugee camps.[51] As a movement for social organization and mobilization, it threatened Israel's long-term hold on the territories more than isolated attacks by guerrilla cells. This potential danger became apparent with the emergence eight months after the beginning of the Uprising of a new group, the Islamic Resistance Movement, better known by its acronym, *Hamas* (zeal). *Hamas* was widely believed to draw its inspiration from the spiritual leaders of Mujama'a in the Gaza Strip. In any case it soon demonstrated its reluctance to accept the discipline of the Unified National Leadership of the Uprising, by organizing a major strike on the twentieth anniversary of the arson attack on the al Aqsa Mosque in Jerusalem on 21 August. It also declared its own political position in a thirty-nine page charter which stated: 'Initiatives, peace proposals and international conferences to solve the Palestine problem run counter to the principles of the Islamic Resistance Movement, since giving up part of Palestine is like giving up part of our religion.'[52]

The rise of the popular movement

Of far greater significance than the Islamic resurgence, however, was the rise of 'the popular movement'. This movement was a direct response by intellectuals, both men and women, to the failure of the community under occupation to translate *sumud*, the idea of steadfastness, into a more active concept of taking control of as many areas of human existence as possible under occupation. Student activity and the resurgence of trade unionism, already discussed, were obvious facets of this new version of steadfastness.

In part the popular movement was a response to the damaging effect of external assistance, in particular the money which entered the territories from outside. This had generally taken three forms, of which the largest was remittances to their families by the large number of Palestinians from the territories working in the Gulf and elsewhere. It was not unusual for a West Bank or Gaza household with one or two family members abroad to receive as much as $10,000 annually.[53] There was also steadfastness funding from the Jordanian–PLO Joint Fund. And thirdly, international funding through international, governmental and non-governmental agencies.

All these forms of economic assistance encouraged passivity and unconsciously shifted people's priorities away from the quality of human resources to the quantity of financial ones. Family remittances led to a massive increase in conspicuous consumption, largely in the form of modern villas and expensive cars rather than investment in local economic activity. The Joint Committee gave millions of dollars to various institutions, and this soon acquired a political and moral significance. In Amman, Jordanian and largely right-wing PLO representatives controlled these funds. The latter agreed that the Jordanian secret service should screen potential recipient institutions and individuals. As a result left-wing groups or those hostile or dangerous to Jordanian influence in the territories were starved of funding, while groups which co-operated with Amman (both the government and the PLO officials there), were rewarded. In this way the chambers of commerce, co-operatives, trade unions and other structures felt the corrosive, divisive and corrupting effect of money which, far from strengthening resolve to resist the occupation, was used to advance one political viewpoint over another.[54]

In the aid field also, the sheer quantity of funds in search of development projects had a distorting effect, encouraging dependence on outside help. A substantial proportion of the population, the refugees, had been dependent on international help since 1949. The services provided by UNRWA in health, education and relief, were in many ways superior to what was available to non-refugees. However, the manner in which these services were administered by largely non-camp refugees of higher social status and supervised by an international cadre had already created a profoundly damaging sense of dependency. Refugee recipients had very little say in the administration of services and were insufficiently encouraged to do so. Furthermore, there was a tendency for many decisions to be made not in proximity to the camps but in UNRWA's headquarters in Vienna.[55]

Other UN agencies started to throw money at the problems of the territories, for example both Unicef and UNDP provided money for activities selected and overseen by the Israeli authorities, thus – however innocent the intention – allowing aid to become an instrument of control rather than support for independent development.[56] Likewise, USAID funding was routed to American non-governmental organizations, *via* the Israeli authorities and subject to their approval.

The comparatively large sums involved conferred on all these agencies a substantial power of patronage over recipient institutions. Even the most well-intentioned and politically sensitive non-governmental organizations found themselves supporting projects which in the long term strengthened individuals rather than communities, unrealistically raised expectations or created unintended dependency relationships.

A fierce debate arose among those trying to respond to the unfavourable economic and social effects of occupation. Broadly speaking, one argument asserted that any improvement in the adverse conditions of life was inherently desirable and should not be withheld from a needy community. It believed politics should be kept out of aid work and that any relief of suffering was beneficial. The other point of view was that the origin *and* route of funding, whether it be via Jordanian or Israeli authorities, or from an external funding agency – even Palestinian nationalist sources – necessarily implied a kind of patronage which was bound to strengthen external control over the community. This, they argued, was the antithesis of their definition of development, the process whereby a community learns to stand on its own feet. Furthermore, this argument continued, the quantities of money available corrupted expectations and encouraged people to think development was essentially material advancement rather than community organization. It was natural that the latter point of view was associated with leftist thinking. The argument came to a head in 1986 following the US Secretary of State's programme to 'improve the quality of life', when a number of American agencies receiving USAID funding began to be shunned by many Palestinian development workers.

The damaging effects of external assistance were, ironically, best documented in the case of Zubaydat, a poor village in the Jordan valley, where two foreign agencies most anxious to avoid such eventualities had introduced drip irrigation in order to increase village productivity and to demonstrate the value of modern intermediate technology methods. One unforeseen result was the expectation on the part of the recipient villagers that foreign funds would continue to provide capital, repair costs, and so on. Individual villagers remained unwilling or unable to co-operate to raise necessary communal funds between them, for example to repair a broken pump.[57]

The case of Zubaydat revealed other problems which had until then received scant attention. Although the villagers of Zubaydat significantly increased their productivity through the introduction of drip irrigation, they quickly found that their real problem lay with marketing. Their difficulties stemmed from three sources. Israel, in order to guarantee the occupied territories as a captive market for its own agricultural production, had started in 1984 to apply strict limits to Palestinian produce.[58] It made the marketing of Palestinian goods inside Israel subject to a licence that in practice was only given for produce, like olives, which was not produced by Jews in commercial quantities. It would not allow Palestinian goods to be exported westwards to compete against its own produce in the European market. Palestinians therefore had to compete with subsidized Israeli produce in the home market while being denied access to the Israeli one.

Through the open bridge policy Israel had skilfully encouraged the export of Palestinian agricultural produce to the Arab world. This too, had major problems. Apart from the paperwork and delays incurred on both sides of the bridge, exporters found themselves exposed to political pressures and a declining market, as Jordan developed its own agricultural potential on the east side of the Jordan valley.

However, it was increasingly recognized that the most significant obstacle to development lay within Palestinian society itself. Most Jordan valley farmers are sharecroppers, normally giving 50 per cent of their produce to their landlord. In most cases the landlord is also the commission agent who purchases produce wholesale and either auctions it in the local market or arranges for it to be boxed and exported to Amman, an operation which requires friendly relations with the authorities in Amman. Since the landlords/commission agents are also the main dealers in seed, fertilizers and equipment, it is virtually impossible for individual farmers to resist them. Two landlords/ commission agents control virtually the whole produce of the Jordan valley. While a farmer might sell a 14 kg box of tomatoes for two shekels, the same tomatoes would retail in Jerusalem at two shekels per kg, indicating a fourteen-fold profit for middleman and retailer. It was not surprising that a growing number of small farmers in the West Bank viewed the commission agents not only as too closely connected with Amman politically, but also as parasites upon their labour.

As a result, a number of Palestinian intellectuals and development workers began arguing that liberation from Israel was only part of a broader process and indeed unless that broader process, which implied radical economic change, took place no liberation from Israel was likely.

Similar questions were being asked in the social sphere, notably with regard to health and to the role of women in society. Those who examined the health conditions of the occupied territories quickly discovered a conflict between the claims by Israel of a steady improvement in health services and the reality. For example, it was claimed that the military government had reduced the infant mortality rate to between 24 and 30 per thousand in the West Bank and 30 per thousand in Gaza, comparing very favourably with the rate, 22 per thousand, for Palestinians in Israel.[59] Such claims were contradicted by research which indicated that the true level might be about 70 per thousand.[60] Significantly, it was found that overall the infant mortality rate was slipping behind those of Jordan and Syria as well as Israel.

Furthermore it was discovered not only that the ratio of physician to population was substantially worse than for Israel or Jordan but that owing to insufficient funding and planning, 280 doctors were actually unemployed in the territories and another 120 were employed on low salaries under a local professional union's absorption programme.[61] At the same time physicians in government clinics in Gaza examined an impossibly large number of patients – on average 100 patients per day, while in UNRWA clinics a doctor would examine between 70 and 120 patients daily.[62] The provision of hospital beds was in decline, having been 2.2 per thousand in 1974 it had fallen to 1.6 per thousand by 1985, due to both hospital cuts and to natural increase. Malnutrition and parasite infestation were high, reflecting the generally low health status of the population. For example, in a rural locality close to Jerusalem, 34 per cent of children under three showed signs of malnutrition.[63]

There was little surprising in such findings. Governmental expenditure on health services in the occupied territories amounted to US$30 per person compared with US$350 per person inside the State of Israel.[64] Furthermore, while 70 per cent of the population lived in rural (village or refugee camp) localities, almost all health facilities were located in towns. Less than one-third of inhabited localities had basic mother and child health facilities, a fundamental health requirement. Only a fraction of the population could afford the cost of the government health insurance scheme which replaced the low cost health service previously available.[65] There existed severe imbalances in terms of expenditure which favoured hospitals over primary health care centres, towns over rural locations, the more affluent central area over the far south and far north of the West Bank, and between the rich and poor, male and female. Research showed that both infant mortality rates and malnutrition tended to be higher among girls than boys, a fact which could not conceivably be ascribed to the occupation but reflected traditional attitudes that damaged the health of the community.[66]

To a growing number of health professionals it was self-evident that Israel's priority was the application of a system which ensured dependence and control rather than the good health of the community. Consequently, when a handful of practitioners came together in 1979, it did so with a single guiding principle: 'the real measure of development is the ability of a people to build its own comprehensive and complimentary and independent infrastructure that is capable of dealing with its own problems, needs and aspirations.'[67]

Many health professionals were strongly attracted to the idea because it put them in touch with the community in a quite different way from their private clinics or hospital services. Some health professionals even argued that they learnt more from the process than did the 'recipient' villagers. Consequently, the movement rapidly grew, forming the Union of Palestinian Medical Relief Committees (UPMRC) in 1982. By 1988 the Union had over 700 health professionals giving their free time voluntarily, providing services to 50,000 patients, and reaching over one-quarter of the populated localities of the territories. It did not intend, it said, to replace any existing service but to complement them by providing services where there were none. But it operated in an entirely different way from the older service already operating.

The Union's guiding principle was the need for the local community itself to take charge of the process whereby health priorities were set and met. Previous experience, following WHO health manuals, had failed because insufficient attention was paid to the political, clan, class and gender divisions within communities. The Union made its assistance conditional on each community creating its own managerial committee. It also insisted that each committee must recruit candidates to be trained by the Union to act as local health workers.

In this way the Union successfully mobilized the population to take control in a way it had never done before, and to identify and overcome both health and social problems which had not previously been tackled. Obvious as such an approach may seem, it was a concept with revolutionary implications. The dynamic effect of the Union's work mobilized the communities directly affected, while many more communities heard about it and wished to participate. If the Union had made a significant contribution to solving health problems, it had also unquestionably played a more significant role in awakening community action.[68]

In the women's movement, too, a significant revolution took place over the same decade. Four networks, reflecting the ideologies of the four major Palestinian parties, Fatah, the DFLP, PFLP and the Communist Party, established committees all over the occupied territories to advance women's affairs, run kindergartens and literacy classes, assist with income-generating projects, and provide legal advice and support in such matters as employment.

These activities were not new. They had been provided for many years by the YWCA, and other urban based and normally middle class-run charitable societies dispensing relief and assistance. Part of the impetus had been the growing frustration felt by women in the voluntary work committees that they and the issues which concerned them tended to be elbowed aside by men. It also resulted from the sense of injustice, that women fared even worse than men in employment and domestic life. Such women decided they could only begin to tackle their problems through their own women's networks.

The revolutionary aspect of the new women's committees, as with the new medical work, was the transmission of power to the lowest community level by a network of committees in a large number of localities. The difficulty the women's committees discovered, however, was that social programmes with no nationalist content failed to attract women, while nationalist programmes quickly triggered wasteful competitive conflicts between the four committee networks for 'control' of a locality. This competition was exacerbated by the factionalism of the PLO during the years 1983–6. Following the formal reconciliation of PLO factions in April 1987, progress was made to achieve better harmony and co-ordination between these groups, and to find a happier balance between the twin goals of national and social justice, a process which fortuitously prepared the committees for the challenge posed by the Uprising.

The initiators of these popular committees were well aware of the way in which Israel had lopped off the leadership of previous political, labour and social movements. Consequently, part of their strategy was to diffuse the leadership of the movement as widely as possible. Each committee was aware of the dangers of individual or mass arrest, and contingency plans were made for the automatic replacement of committee members should they be arrested. It was an almost perfect system, for it implied that if Israel wished to dismantle the women's committees it would have to imprison the entire membership.[69]

In agriculture, the popular movement began to respond to the kind of difficulties that farmers like those in Zubaydat had encountered. Agriculture, despite its declining base, was still the primary element in the West Bank's economy. An agricultural relief committee was established in 1983 by a handful of young agricultural engineers, some of whom had already been working with 'the voluntary work committees', a network of skilled and unskilled workers which had been operating since the mid-1970s. As in the case of popular health work, these professionals were struck by the absence of applied research and extension services, particularly for poor farmers who stood in greatest need of such assistance. Apart from the continued seizure of cultivable land by the authorities, the main problems faced by farmers were the severe limitations on water use, unfavourable marketing conditions, production quotas, restrictions on the planting of fruit trees, and poor access to credit facilities.

Behind these problems lay not only the difficulties inherent in the occupation, but also the socio-economic realities of Palestinian society. Of these the overwhelming one was the fact that the peasant farmer suffered most from the effects of the occupation, while the large landowners seemed, comparatively at any rate, to benefit from the system of occupation. It was felt that they enjoyed the support of both Israel and Jordan, neither of which welcomed a growth in the economic power of an increasingly politicized peasantry. By 1986 over sixty agricultural professionals and 400 farmers were active members of the Palestinian Agricultural Relief Committees (PARCs), seeking strategies for overcoming such problems through research and education, pest control campaigns, the supply of competitively priced vegetable and olive tree seedlings, and most important of all, research into the characteristics of marketing.

In the longer term the Palestinian Agricultural Relief Committees tried to help individual farmers to eke out an adequate living, encourage the organization of small farmers at the village level, and foster the growth of a farming structure better able to stand up to the rigours of occupation than the present one in which middlemen and large landowners dominated agriculture. Central to Agricultural Relief, as with the other elements of the popular movement, remained the belief that the community had to set the agenda of priorities and participate in seeking solutions.

Self-reliance was also promoted in other economic spheres, albeit modestly. Until Palestinians learnt to rely upon themselves and their own productivity, implying a withdrawal of both custom and labour from the Israeli sector, there could be no hope of liberation. This, at any rate, was the ideology. In its purest form, the doctrine advocated a return to subsistence economy but on a less individualistic and more communal basis. Voluntary Work Committees worked hard to encourage *iqtisad bayti*, or household production, a concept pioneered by Agricultural Relief[70] with activities such as chicken farming, market gardening and food processing. During 1987 a women's household production network (in fact inspired and organized by a foreign worker) also began to produce pickled vegetables for retail in grocery stores in the West Bank, to displace Israeli produce. By the time of the Uprising such ventures had not gone beyond examples of what theoretically could be done. Among some development workers this utopian view of development caused unease.

The reason for this unease lay in the doubtful practicability of total self-sufficiency. The trend of things had been for agricultural land to go out of production because it was easier to earn a living working in Israel. This was not a new development resulting from the occupation. Rather, if one considered the nineteen years of Jordanian rule to be an interruption in the physical integrity of Palestine, it could be argued that ever since the beginning of the century an increasing proportion of the agricultural labour force of the Palestinian uplands provided seasonal labour on the coastal plain for Jewish, Arab and other industrial and agricultural enterprises. Nevertheless, the ideal was there, and its symbolism and potential were important.

Uprising: the power of the people

The popular movement did not produce the Uprising, but its proven *modus operandi* was found to be essential to its success. By the end of 1987 not only had large numbers of people participated in community activities but many others were aware of the model. Furthermore, through the trade unions and the women's committees, the major political organizations were well aware of the potential political importance of the popular movement. Thus, while the health, agricultural and voluntary work committees remained social rather than political in their programmes, they blazed a trail that others widened into a national highway. As a result, almost as soon as Israel tried to suppress the Uprising with curfews, blockades and violent policing, the community organized itself along the lines the popular movement had already prescribed.

In virtually every locality in the occupied territories, popular neighbourhood committees established themselves, assuming responsibility for public hygiene, health, education (after schools were closed), maintaining a watch on the streets for the approach of Israeli troops or settlers, organizing household production, distributing agricultural produce to the needy and reclaiming land. The spontaneity and autonomy of these committees within 'the national consensus' were striking features. The Unified Leadership (UNLU) claimed these 'are more than temporary committees which will operate for a limited period of time. They will represent a permanent structural change in the form of organisation of Palestinian society . . . These structures are not explicitly political. They function as democratic structures of local organisation.'[71]

The rise of the committees implied disengagement from Israel. UNLU repeatedly stressed the need for police and tax officials to resign, for people to refuse tax demands, to boycott Israeli goods, to avoid labouring in Israel and to be as self-reliant and self-sufficient as possible. When Israel proclaimed the committees illegal, accusing them of receiving 'PLO money', UNLU answered:

> The reality is that the popular committees are not being funded by anyone . . . rather they are responding to the lack of funding of the community services [i.e. by the authorities] by trying to organise their own. The conditions which have initiated and sustained the Uprising have been characterised not by subversive money but by a lack of money . . . The real irony is that if Israel continues to systematically close all community service institutions, while the government sector has all but collapsed, then the people will be left with no option but to organise things for themselves . . . in the end only the popular committees will be left.[72]

It was easy to assume, in the euphoria of this new found self-reliance which Israel found so difficult to break, that the occupied territories were on the road to political freedom. The achievements of the first nine months of the Uprising were impressive. The most obvious of these had been to bring the fate of the occupied territories onto centre stage internationally, persuading George Schultz to renew his peace mediation efforts. It had also wrought a fundamental shift in power between the PLO and the Arab world, and within the Palestinian community between the PLO and the people of the territories. Although it had been obscured by the emphasis put on the military and diplomatic struggles within the Arab world and in the international arena ever since 1967, the centrality of the people under occupation in the national struggle could no longer be disregarded.

A critical relationship had already developed between the PLO and the Palestinians of the territories. The latter, whilst loyal to the PLO leadership, were among its sharpest critics. At the time of the 18th PNC in April 1987, when the different PLO factions were reconciled, the Jerusalem *al Fajr English Weekly* commented on the lack of effective leadership:

> we will not be satisfied by the PLO leaders simply kissing and making up. A lot of hard work needs to be done. To begin with, the Palestinian leadership must conduct an honest and tough critique of the events of the past, of our position at present, and where we want to go from here.[73]

There was also unease at the PLO's propensity to act against local opinion, witnessed in its treatment of the home-grown NGC in the late 1970s, its abuse of Joint Committee funds for politically corrupt purposes, and in Arafat's flirtation with Husayn in the mid-1980s.

It was feared that Arafat was so desperate to achieve diplomatic action in the early months of the Uprising that he might betray its purpose by a renewal of the PLO–Jordanian alliance. Ever since 1983 the general mood in the territories had been consistently against Jordanian representation of the Palestinians, even as part of a joint team.[74] Most people in the territories feared the PLO was in danger of rushing into some unsatisfactory settlement rather than holding out for the right conditions.[75] Warning of the growing impatience of the *shabab*, the youth, one journalist wrote 'if they [the *shabab*] see that the PLO's political initiatives are producing no results, they will force the PLO into a more radical posture or else they will go looking for a more radical leadership within the PLO.'[76]

After the Uprising, UNLU was not afraid to criticize the PLO openly. When Husayn ceded sovereignty over the West Bank in July 1988, UNLU publicly warned the leadership 'the PLO outside the occupied territories should not "fill the gap" left by Jordan by duplicating its work, which was based on the principle of patronage through corruption. The challenge is to find ways to support the existing popular structures so that they can better continue their struggle.'[77] UNLU would not have given such a warning had it not feared how the PLO outside might behave. When Arafat met with King Husayn and President Mubarak in Aqaba in October 1988 amid reports of negotiations on a Palestinian–Jordanian confederation, UNLU was quick to condemn the idea and express its own concern: 'when the Palestine National Movement is increasingly united around clear, unambiguous political proposals, rumors of confederation negotiations are worrying and confusing.'[78]

It was also feared that the PLO would instruct 'acceptable Palestinians' to meet George Schultz. For this reason UNLU cautioned it to boycott Schultz, through the strikes and demonstrations it was able to organize during his visit to Israel, 3–5 June. This, too, indicated how UNLU now led, and the PLO followed. Some felt it was the way things should always have been.

It was inevitable that the shift of leadership from the PLO outside to UNLU should give rise to thoughts of a split in Palestinian ranks, between the 'inside' and 'outside'. UNLU communiqués, however, were emphatic not only in their recognition of the PLO, but also that the PLO represented all Palestinian people, both outside and inside Palestine. Despite the setbacks before the Uprising there had been growing recognition of PLO leadership in the territories. In 1986, for example, a poll suggested that 95 per cent of the population recognized the PLO as their sole legitimate representative, a 9 per cent increase in support since 1982.[79]

Nevertheless, differences did exist between the outside and inside view. In 1986 one poll suggested that one-quarter of the population found the PLO leadership too accommodationist.[80] There was considerable ambivalence, too, about a final two state solution implicit in the Arafat–Husayn initiative and the 1983 Fez plan.[81] The dream of a democratic secular state in all Palestine, viewed as an unrealistic non-starter by virtually all the international community and probably by most of the PLO leadership, enjoyed growing support according to opinion polls, 58 per cent in 1983, rising to 77.9 per cent in 1986.[82] Even as an interim objective, the idea of a West Bank and Gaza state apparently enjoyed the support of only 50.1 per cent of respondents, while 43.6 per cent preferred to continue the struggle for all Palestine.[83] Although such polls should be treated with caution, it is not surprising in view of such opinions that the vast majority of the occupied territories population, 80.6 per cent, also rejected Resolution 242.[84]

It was difficult to be sure where this left the objectives of the Uprising. Repeated UNLU communiqués called for recognition of the PLO, the refugees' right of return, and the right to self-determination and the establishment of a Palestinian state. They stressed UNLU's moderate demands, calling for a two state solution, mutual recognition, direct Israeli-PLO negotiations, concluding 'the Palestinians are calling for no more than peace with a reasonable measure of justice.'[85] Such calls were similar to the known PLO position.

However, there clearly were differences between the PLO leadership and UNLU but more, perhaps, of tone than of political content. The PLO leadership seemed readier to compromise and accommodate Israel, Jordan, the United States and the Arab League than were the people under occupation. By contrast opinion in the occupied territories concerning these other players was hardening rather than softening. There were now clearer limitations to what the PLO could do without provoking open protest from its constituents in the occupied territories. The implication for Israel and the international community was that it might have been easier to transact a deal with the PLO before the Uprising than after it.

People in the popular movement had a different kind of disquiet with the leadership of the PLO. It is important to frame this disquiet in the correct context. There was no question of the popular movement, even the most radical in it, actually rejecting the PLO's political and institutional leadership. The anxiety was more one of style, about its bureaucracy, its lack of enthusiasm for social and economic change and its susceptibility to venality and materialism (most clearly expressed in its use of Joint Fund money). Among many activists there was a feeling that the PLO leadership had become the property of the Palestinian middle classes in the diaspora and that many of the leadership led relatively luxurious lives, insulated from the realities of nation building as these were experienced under occupation.

The tension persists in a number of spheres. Where the popular committees are devoted to encouraging the development of self-reliance and local power through co-operative activity in different fields, it is

feared that Fatah, the dominant component of the PLO, has little vision
of social and economic change. On the contrary, many in the popular
movement believe that Fatah has more interest, as one activist put it, in
hospitals than in mobile health clinics, in bureaucracy than in local
control, and in co-operation with the economic and political notables
than with grass-roots movements.

Suspicion of outside money, even from the PLO, remained deep.
Some leading exponents of the popular movement believed that if large
quantities of money were sent to support the Uprising they would,
instead, destroy it by creating political jealousies and deflecting the
Uprising from the central theme of self-reliance.

Some, particularly within the popular movement, feared a sudden
political settlement in which the PLO leadership might be installed as
the government of Palestine. Some preferred to suffer occupation for
longer, than to achieve freedom before local institutions were robust
enough to ensure that they were not swept aside by a newly installed
government of 'outsiders'. They feared that the community-based social
and political work directed towards a more democratic and egalitarian
society than currently existed would be undone by an influx of
'bourgeois' values and money. In view of the prominent part taken by
the women's movement and of the general position of women in
society, it was not surprising that women felt particularly strongly on
such issues.[86]

Many Palestinians also feared that the PLO leadership would not
welcome the kind of lively debate and democracy which the popular
movement had fostered, but would wish to be authoritarian in its
government. This fear was well expressed by one long-serving member
of the popular movement, 'the PLO will be keen to control. Insiders will
be crushed by the PLO military, there is bound to be conflict between
insiders and outsiders. The PLO failed as a leadership, not as an idea.
Unfortunately the PLO remains obsessed with its own survival
problems.'[87] But it is important to bear in mind that such misgivings are
made privately. There is no question of the popular movement rejecting
the PLO. On the contrary, its support is total. It merely wants the PLO
to learn, as the members of the popular movement themselves have
learnt, that the strength of the national movement lies in the philosophy
which has taken root so strongly in the territories over the 1977–87
decade.

5

THE ISRAELI PALESTINIANS: HOW THEY ARE CONTROLLED

Solving the dispute over the occupied territories may seem daunting for Israel, yet it is straightforward when compared with the question of its own Arab citizens. To suggest this line of argument can be unwelcome. There are people on the Left of Israeli politics who argue that it raises fears of Palestinian Israeli irredentism, and plays into the hands of the Right in Israel.[1] But only a small minority of Palestinian Israelis currently reject the idea of working within the democratic and parliamentary framework of the state. These fears will only become a reality if the problem of the status of Palestinians remains unaddressed.

Israel's proclamation of independence declared that the state 'will maintain complete equality of social and political rights for all citizens, without distinction of creed, race or sex.' Technically, therefore, Palestinian and Jewish citizens of the State of Israel are equal in the eyes of the law. Both have equal rights in elections to the Israeli parliament, the Knesset. In theory the law does not discriminate, except in three explicit areas: the Law of Return (1950) accords any Jew the automatic right to settle in Israel – contrasting with the denial of any return for the country's refugees; the Law of Citizenship (1952) accords any Jewish immigrant *automatic* citizenship, whereas even for those Palestinians still in what became Israel in 1948, citizenship was not automatic; finally a Knesset law defines Israel as 'the State of the Jewish people', a definition whereby Palestinians feel explicitly excluded. 'When we say "Jewish independence" or a "Jewish State",' Ben Gurion had declared in 1945, 'we mean Jewish country, Jewish soil, we mean Jewish labour, we mean Jewish economy, Jewish agriculture, Jewish industry, Jewish sea.'[2] How, Palestinians ask, can they possibly be equal in such a state?

In practice, as this chapter describes, the Palestinian citizens of Israel have always been subject to systematic and widespread discrimination. To argue, as some dovish Israelis do, that this discrimination is a social and economic issue, ignores the fact that it is fundamentally political. It is about power.

The majority of Palestinian Israelis have yet to commit themselves unambiguously either to irredentism – the desire to reforge Arab Palestine – or to espousal of the state. The choice made between these two extremes, or more moderate positions between them, will depend upon two critical and interdependent issues: the outcome of the dispute over the occupied territories (and the time span in which this dispute is resolved); and the choice made by the state, and implicitly by Jewish Israeli society, whether or not to embrace, enrich and promote the Palestinian dimension of Israeli national life alongside its already highly developed Jewish dimension.

The failure to deal satisfactorily with the occupied territories is bound to increase Palestinian alienation inside Israel. It is also likely to deepen Jewish prejudice against Palestinian co-nationals. The sooner the occupied territories dispute is settled, the greater will be the chance for a happier Jewish–Palestinian relationship within Israel, at state and popular levels. It should be noted, however, that not every Jewish or Palestinian Israeli desires a happier relationship within the state as currently constituted. Some Jews wish to expel Palestinian Israelis, some Palestinians may well reciprocate that sentiment, while others wish to replace the Zionist State with a secular democratic one for all Palestine.

If the Palestinian population inside Israel were declining proportionately (if not numerically), a discussion of its future in the Jewish State would be an academic exercise. However, the Palestinians are increasing as a proportion of the Israeli population, albeit not at the pace feared by many Israelis.[3] In 1949, immediately after the war, the Palestinian population stood at 15 per cent, but was reduced to barely 11 per cent by 1951 as a result of Jewish immigration. Between 1967 and 1980 the Palestinians (including those resident in Arab East Jerusalem, annexed in 1967) slowly crept back to 15 per cent of the Israeli population, and accounted for 18 per cent by 1988; by 2005 they could reach approximately 25 per cent.[4] In the long term, therefore, Jewish Israelis cannot afford to ignore the growing say of Palestinian Israelis, nor the implications of this for the identity of the Jewish State.

The ominous (or exciting) prospects for the future will be determined by how Palestinians feel about their position in Israeli national life. This can only be properly understood in the light of the way in which the state has controlled its Arab minority.

Military government, 1948–66

When the armistice was signed between Israel and its neighbours in early 1949 approximately 156,000 Palestinian Arabs remained inside the new Jewish State. Almost all lived in the countryside, since the vast majority of the urban Arab population had fled or been expelled. The highest concentrations were in Galilee, but others lived in the 'Little Triangle', a strip of land ceded by Transjordan in the armistice negotiation, running along the western edge of the West Bank from Qalqilya northwards to Wadi Ara just outside the north-west tip of the West Bank. In the south there were 11,000 bedouin mainly in the northern part of the Negev desert. Most of these Palestinian Arabs were illiterate subsistence farmers and sharecroppers whose social, political and economic world hardly extended beyond the ancestral village. Bereft of any political, intellectual or financial leadership, they were particularly vulnerable to manipulation.

Israel was created with fundamental Zionist objectives, primarily to gather in the Jewish people from all corners of the world and to redeem the Land of Israel. The former implied massive immigration of Jews and this occurred, nearly destroying the economy of the fledgeling state. In 1948 there were 650,000 Jews in Israel, but during the years 1948–60 another one million arrived. Most came in the first three years, so that by the end of 1951 the Jewish Israeli population had doubled. The state had to receive, house and employ this massive influx, and through their employment create a productive infrastructure. Redemption of the land had two immediate implications. The Land of Israel had to be secured by a physical Jewish presence – in the border areas against the Arab enemy without and in other areas to take control of the land from Arabs still within the state. Prime Minister David Ben Gurion spoke of a 'closely linked chain of settlements' in areas of strategic importance.[5] The other was the need to establish control of those Arabs in the Jewish State.

In order to provide a framework for the implementation of these objectives, a military government was established in the Arab-populated areas of the state.[6] It enjoyed virtually absolute powers over approximately 80 per cent of Israel's Palestinians, able to restrict freedom of movement, detain or expel inhabitants, designate any lands required for military or other purposes as 'closed areas', and control the issue of travel permits, a precondition to employment outside the village.[7] Its practices, inaugurated under the provisions of the British

Mandate Defence (Emergency) Regulations 1945,[8] invalidated the state's commitment to the equality of all its citizens under the law. The theory that Palestinians enjoyed equal rights and opportunities has remained a fiction to the present day.

The primary means whereby the state fulfilled its objectives lay in the transfer of previously Arab-held lands into state ownership and control. Myriad laws were employed to effect this transfer in a legal manner. The primary instrument was the Absentee Property Law of 1950 which declared all property 'abandoned' – in other words, from which Arabs may have temporarily fled – to be under the custodianship of the state. This land was reallocated for Jewish use. The total quantity of 'absentee' property amounted to some 300 abandoned or semi-abandoned villages with over 16 million dunums of land.[9] State seizures included virtually all the property of the *waqf*, the Islamic institution of religious endowments, the principal property owner in Palestine.[10]

Through its powers to close areas to unauthorized persons the military government was able to prevent many internally displaced Palestinians from returning to their village, even when they were encamped close at hand. In many cases the inhabitants had been moved out of their village after the cessation of hostilities, only to discover it closed when they tried to return. In other cases summary regulations were invoked in order to expel. At least one-quarter of the Palestinian population remained internally displaced.[11] The best known expulsion cases were of two Christian villages near the Lebanese border, Kafr Bir'am and Iqrit. In both the villagers won court orders entitling them to return to their villages. To prevent this actually happening troops destroyed their homes before they were able to return. By 1988 the villagers had still not obtained government implementation of the court ruling.[12]

In other cases Palestinian farmers were denied access to their lands by various legal and administrative instruments so that they were unable to cultivate their fields. Lands uncultivated for three successive years could be handed over by the Ministry of Agriculture to another party to cultivate.[13] An estimated 40 per cent of the land owned by legal residents of Israel was confiscated by the state under the Absentee Property Law,[14] but if one takes into account land acquisitions by other legal or quasi-legal means the total is probably in excess of 50 per cent.

Having wrested Arab lands from their owners, Israel determined to prevent their return in perpetuity. Responsibility for virtually all sequestered lands was effectively given to the Jewish National Fund (JNF). In November 1947 the JNF's landholdings amounted to only 6 per cent of Palestine, or 14 per cent of its cultivable land. Virtually overnight in 1948 it became the single most powerful national institution. It acquired control of all state lands, through the creation of the Israel Land Administration (jointly administered by the JNF and the Ministry of Agriculture) and the Land Development Authority (for which the JNF had exclusive responsibility). Today, these two bodies still develop, lease and administer 92 per cent of Israel's land area. Even where the JNF does not exercise direct control its Zionist principle of inalienability (from the Jewish people) is applied to all state landholdings.[15] By this means, the designation 'state land' ceases to mean Israeli national land, in the sense that all Israel's citizens can in theory benefit, and becomes Jewish national land, in the sense that all Jews who come to Israel, even those coming for their retirement from another country, may benefit while Palestinian Israelis may not.

The military government came to an end in 1966, because it had outlived its usefulness. It was expected that its end would allow the Palestinians to play a fuller, more integrated part in national life. This, however, did not happen because of the overriding motive for liberalization. Expansion of the economy, partly due to the influx of capital in the form of German war reparations, had led to the upward movement of Afro-Asian Jewish immigrants into skilled or semi-skilled employment, leaving a vacuum below. This vacuum was filled by Arabs, previously debarred from the Jewish sector.[16] Free movement of Arab labour had become an economic imperative. There was no question of liberalization meaning the extension of equal rights or opportunities.

Israel's 1967 victory, resulting in the acquisition of the rest of Palestine, gave rise to serious new demographic and ideological problems. If Israel viewed the area now under its rule as Eretz Israel, it was clear that Palestinians viewed the same area as still Palestine. There was the danger that Palestinians would abandon their political passivity. This posed dangers particularly for Galilee and the Little Triangle, where irredentism could lead to attempts to secede and unite with Palestinians of the West Bank. Since both areas had been set aside by the United Nations to be part of an Arab state, such fears were well grounded.

Consequently, its efforts to bring Arab-held land into state ownership were renewed. Few Arab villages escaped this new drive to 'judaize' Galilee and the Little Triangle, as it was infelicitously described.[17] In 1966 most Palestinian villages had already lost about half their land, but by the mid-1970s they had lost two-thirds.[18] State seizure of Arab land continues, with the construction of new housing but with increasing difficulty in attracting Jewish settlers.[19]

The system of control

Segmentation

When military government came to an end in 1966 the Palestinians remained astonishingly acquiescent. In his classic study, *Arabs in the Jewish State* (Austin, 1980), Ian Lustick identified three components to the state's continuing ability to control its Palestinian population – segmentation, dependence, and co-optation. Both collectively and individually, these components imply exclusion from power, from the benefits of citizenship and from social or economic well-being.

From the outset, the state segmented its Palestinians in a number of ways. It kept them separated from Jews socially, politically and administratively. It did not want Jews and Arabs to fraternize. Most Palestinians lived in exclusively Arab villages, but in 1951 some 12 per cent still lived in what were once in part or in whole Arab cities and towns: Haifa, Acre, Jaffa, Lydda and Ramla. These became 'mixed cities', with a Jewish majority. Contrary to normal patterns of development and urbanization, Palestinians were not drawn into these cities from the villages. Instead, the proportion of Palestinians who lived in these towns (exclusive of Arab East Jerusalem annexed in 1967) fell to 9 per cent by 1976.

Acre exemplifies state efforts to reduce the Palestinian proportion in mixed cities. When Acre city council initiated a Greater Acre Renovation Programme, the old Arab quarter – with a population of 8,000 – was excluded, on the grounds that the funding for refurbishment came from Jewish agencies. In fact more than two-thirds of the money made available for this renewal programme came from public rather than specifically Jewish sources.[20] Even if such sources were Jewish, the city council had already turned down attempts by the Muslim *waqf* to fund housing improvements in Acre, as well as Palestinian inhabitants' requests for housing in Acre New Town to cope with their population increase.[21] Although thousands of housing units were built in Acre New Town, by 1973 only forty of these had been assigned to Palestinians.[22]

Despite being refused alternative accommodation in Acre New Town, inhabitants of the Old Quarter were forbidden to undertake the repair of the seriously delapidated buildings they continued to inhabit. They concluded that the city council wished them to evacuate the picturesque old quarter and turn it from an Arab city into a 'living museum', controlled and exploited by Jews,[23] that it wished to remove from the centre of the city a population with a record of strong Palestinian feeling,[24] and that it wanted to make Acre an overwhelmingly Jewish city.

A master-plan drawn up in 1971 proposed to establish an Arab quarter on an unspecified site outside Acre, foreseeing 'merely 4,000 Arabs within the present boundaries of the city in 1985 . . . the Arab population would be thus reduced from more than a quarter in 1971 to about 6 per cent in 1985.'[25] At first the Arab population did indeed fall, from 9,100 to 8,600 between 1973 and 1976, as inhabitants were relocated to al Makr, a rural township 8 km east of Acre. Despite such efforts, the Palestinian population of Acre was still 8,000, or 22 per cent of total population in 1985, suggesting that it was more difficult to reduce the Arab component of mixed cities than had been expected. However, the policy has persisted.[26]

Even in these mixed cities, Jews and Arabs live in distinct and separate quarters. Palestinians trying to move closer to their place of work find it almost impossible to move to Jewish residential areas. Government and Histadrut housing companies are reluctant to sell or rent their apartments to Palestinians even though some of these housing units have been empty for several years. Even where Palestinians have been able to rent apartments privately, they run the gauntlet of local hostility, backed by members of the establishment. When a Palestinian recently attempted to buy an apartment in the Jewish settlement of Nevi Yacov in East Jerusalem the Chief Rabbi, Mordechai Eliayahu, pronounced: 'It is forbidden to sell apartments in the Land of Israel to Gentiles.'[27] Jewish hostility, in the words of the police minister, is a problem 'far wider and deeper than many realise'.[28]

Palestinians are also segregated from Jews administratively. Almost every government ministry has a separate Arab department, whereby Arabs can be treated differently from Jews. The heads of these Arab departments have almost invariably been Jewish.

The Palestinians have also been excluded from the institutional sources of power. The army is the foundation for adulthood in Israel. Army service has a direct effect on future employment and career prospects. Many jobs and sometimes housing are available only to army veterans, as are many state benefits. In 1970 the Discharged Soldiers Act (Return to Work) of 1949 was amended to entitle the children of soldiers and of their immediate kin (spouse, parents, or children) to special benefits, including welfare grants, and kindergarten, housing and job training entitlements. In practice beneficiaries include children of Jewish Israelis who have not served in the forces. In effect 'Service in the army was . . . used to distinguish, crudely but seemingly innocently, between Jews and Arabs, since it rewarded Jews who had not served in the army at all.'[29] Since Palestinians, with the exception of the Druzes and some bedouin, do not serve in the army, they are excluded from these benefits.

Israel's powerful umbrella trade union, the Histadrut, finally accepted Arab members in 1959. But it created a special Arab department. Although the Histadrut controls one-quarter of Israel's productive capacity, it did not establish a single factory or firm in a Palestinian population area. In contrast with Jewish areas, it was also reluctant to build health clinics in Palestinian areas, although health benefit was a key reason why Palestinians joined the Histadrut. The original justification for a separate Arab department was a linguistic one, but by the late 1960s the Palestinian work-force spoke Hebrew. Maintenance of an Arab department, as in government, is part of a broad policy of segregation and exclusion.

The Palestinian Arabs are excluded institutionally from many of the benefits received by Jews. The existence of para-statal funding organizations, the Jewish Agency, the World Zionist Organization and the JNF, provided a structure whereby the Jewish community could benefit while the Palestinians could be excluded, without the state itself implementing openly discriminatory policies. According to Ian Lustick, the resources of the Jewish Agency – responsible for the social and economic establishment of immigrants – are so great that its development expenditure in Israel has at times exceeded the development budget of the state.[30] Thus Jews have automatically received housing, agricultural assistance, the provision of infrastructure, and so on, where the Palestinians have not.

Palestinian villages are themselves physically separated from national life. Most of them lie well off the main arteries of the country, down ill-maintained roads, largely invisible to the casual passer-by. During the years of military government the travel restrictions imposed intensified this sense of separation. A Palestinian could not even visit a neighbouring village without declaring his purpose. Each village was kept as isolated as possible from others.[31]

Segmentation was intensified by the deliberate attempt to intersperse Arab villages – seen as a strategic danger – with Jewish settlements, part of Ben Gurion's 'closely-linked chain'. Large numbers of Jewish immigrants were sent to these areas, particularly Galilee. In the words of the then Deputy Minister of Defence, Shimon Peres, himself a keen advocate of military government:

Galilee without any Jewish settlements . . . may well give rise to a movement similar to the 'Italia Irredenta' movement of 1879. In Galilee today there are hundreds of thousands of dunums of unsettled land, and these areas are earmarked for programmed settlement. But there has been an attempt at unlicensed settlement [*sic*]; hundreds of [Arab] houses have been built on the hills of Galilee without permits. If we are agreed that settlement has a far reaching political import, we must prevent the creation of a *fait accompli* incompatible both with the Zionist concept of the State of Israel and the law.[32]

The presence of the settlers had another purpose, to ensure that there could be no serious discussion of returning any of these lands earmarked for an Arab state by the United Nations to Arab control. By 1964 there were over 200 Jewish settlements in the Northern District. Within Galilee proper, two settlements formed regional Jewish 'capitals', Nazaret Illit or Upper Nazareth, established in 1956, overlooking the Arab city and designed to control it strategically, and Carmiel further north, built on Arab village lands in 1962.[33] Through intensive settlement Jews, who had still been a minority in Galilee in 1949, outnumbered Palestinians by a ratio of three to two by the beginning of 1964.[34] As already mentioned, after 1967 there were renewed efforts to judaize Galilee. Furthermore, in keeping with the policy of segmentation social contacts between Palestinians across the Armistice Line, particularly marriages, were vigorously discouraged.

The state also segmented its Arabs along religious and cultural lines. In the religious sphere, the Arab population had been defined as either Muslim or Christian under British rule. The majority of both religions resisted Israeli attempts to displace geographical identity (Palestine) with the religious one. While official government documents referred to the Muslim and Christian communities, the community itself defined itself either as Arab or Palestinian.

However, Israel was more successful with the Druze community, a schismatic sect which had broken away from Islam in the eleventh century AD. Its idiosyncratic beliefs existed on the very fringe of Islam, hardly conforming to even the most rudimentary Muslim beliefs. Druzes were considered by most Muslims to have abandoned Islam. Like many minority sects in the Near East, the Druzes practised dissimulation in situations where they were vulnerable to the Muslim majority. In Lebanon and in south Syria the Druzes achieved sufficient strength to enjoy a degree of autonomy as Druzes. In Palestine, however, the smaller number of Druze villages never achieved this level of local strength, and endeavoured to remain inconspicuous and to avoid disputes with their Muslim neighbours and with the government. Most Druze villages were sited either on the Mount Carmel range, overlooking Haifa, or in northern Galilee.[35] In spite of their instinctive reluctance to be drawn into the struggle for Palestine, the Druzes were unable to remain neutral. In the Arab revolt, 1936–9, the rebels sought the support of Druze villages and when this was not forthcoming they took reprisals. The Druzes retaliated, implicitly aligning themselves with the Jewish community.[36] In 1948 the Druzes allied themselves openly with the Jewish forces, both they and Palestinian nationalists bitterly recalling their feud in 1936–9.

The emergence of the Jewish State encouraged the Druzes to abandon their traditional policy of remaining inconspicuous. State desire to cultivate them as 'co-operative Arabs' harmonized with their desire to exercise their particularism in a way that had not been possible before. The state cultivated the traditional secular and religious leadership of the Druze community, recognizing the exceptionally strong ties of communal solidarity which this leadership controlled. In 1956 Druze leaders and the government agreed that Druzes should perform military service, like Jewish citizens but unlike the other Arab citizens of the state. In 1957 the Druzes were recognized as a separate and autonomous community, and a law established specifically Druze judiciary organs. Four years later the nationality (as opposed to citizenship) was changed from 'Arab' to 'Druze' on all ID cards carried by Druzes. In 1967 the Druzes no longer came under the Arab departments established in most government ministries for the administration of the Arab community. In 1976 the education of Druze children was segregated from Arab education, 'to emphasize Druze tradition and history'. The state and community leaders shared an interest in the progressive separation of the Druzes from the Palestinian Arab community, and the investment of the Druzes with their own separate status and nationality.[37] Nevertheless, the Druzes did not escape land seizure on the same scale as other Palestinians.[38]

The state also intensified the cultural and geographical separation of bedouin from sedentary Palestinians, both in the Galilee and the main bedouin area, the Negev. By 1948 about 15,000 bedouin lived in Galilee, while another 90,000 lived in the Negev.[39] The latter category had brought virtually all the Negev which was cultivable without irrigation under cultivation, totalling about 2 million dunams.[40] Although the bedouin were organized socially into ninety-five tribes, these operated politically in three or four larger confederations.

By the early 1950s there were only about 11,000 of these 90,000 Negev bedouin left, representing only nineteen of the previous ninety-five tribes, but all belonging to the Tiyaha confederation.[41] In 1951 the new Israeli government temporarily relocated eleven of these nineteen tribes in a closed area north-east of Beersheba, but giving assurances that their lands would be safeguarded for them.[42] Until 1966 those living in the closed area were not allowed out, except in special circumstances or to attend market day in Beersheba on certain days.[43] This ensured that they had no access to the outside world, or to other Palestinian Arabs. Furthermore, bedouin of one tribe were forbidden to visit the area of another without permission. In this way the state was able to destroy the old political solidarity of the Tiyaha confederation and establish individual relations with each tribe.[44] As in the case of Kafr Bir'am and Iqrit, those tribes temporarily moved discovered that relocation was permanent, with their ancestral lands being delcared 'absentee' (since they were not living on them, but were in the closed areas), or that their lands were required for development or security purposes.[45]

It was true that much sequestered Arab land was needed to settle Jewish immigrants and that the Negev was designated for this purpose. Nevertheless, no account was made of traditional bedouin landholdings. Having stripped the bedouin of the lands they had cultivated, the Israel Lands Administration established the practice of leasing some sequestered lands, under certain principles: that land cannot ever be leased to the original landholder; that no individual may rent the same plot of land for more than nine months; and that no trees may be planted on the plot. By contrast, Jewish farmers in the Negev were allowed to lease land in the Negev for forty-nine years.[46]

State policy with regard to the bedouin was aimed at preventing any bedouin attachment to specific lands, either previously owned or presently cultivated. It had two other effects, to cause tension between erstwhile owners and present tillers of particular plots, and by the brevity of tenure to ensure that plots are overworked rather than developed, increasing bedouin segmentation and dependency. Political segmentation between sedentary and bedouin Palestinians was reinforced by the government's decision to allow the latter to volunteer for military service.

Among the sedentary Palestinian population, as among the bedouin, the state revived and manipulated the dying traditional social structures. Each Palestinian village was organized traditionally according to the *hamula*, the patrilineal extended family. Most villages had several *hamulas* but by 1948 these were in decay. Among the bedouin the system of tribal shaikhs was also in decay, as life was organized within the larger confederation framework. In both cases, by creating local councils in Arab localities in which each *hamula* was represented, the state successfully emphasized the *hamula* as a political as well as social unit. By the offer, or refusal, of benefits, travel permits, work permits, house building permits and so forth, it was able to play one *hamula* off against another. It was not difficult to use this segmentation politically in national elections, through the offer of privileges to *hamula* heads who promised to ensure the votes of the family or the village to Labour or another Zionist party. But Palestinians were not allowed to play a part in party life. Each Zionist party tended to create an 'affiliated Arab list' of candidates for whom Palestinians could vote. This provided the Zionist parties, primarily Labour, with votes, but it offered the Palestinians no political power whatever.

Dependence

The loss of so much agricultural land, and the burden of dependent refugees in almost every surviving village, made the Palestinian community acutely dependent on the Jewish sector for employment. At first there was large-scale unemployment, and only some Palestinians were able to obtain work. Those who did so frequently found themselves hired to labour in fields which had been their own until 1948.

The strict control on Palestinian labour was primarily intended to ensure priority of employment for Jewish immigrants. Inevitably a black market grew in Arab labour desperate enough to be willing to work at a fraction of the wage paid to equivalent Jewish labourers.[47] In return for 'loyalty', *hamula* heads were able to provide work permits within the extended family.

The inability of Jewish labour to fill Israel's increased economic capacity brought military government to an end. The Jewish economy benefited from the large pool of Arab labour, particularly since this labour could serve it according to the ebb and flow of labour demand. As in the case of labour from the occupied territories this cushioned Jewish labour from the full impact of recessions, and left the Palestinian work-force dependent on the Jewish sector. The latter remained subject to the dictates of the Jewish economy but did not fall into line with national employment patterns.

Although agricultural employment was already in decline it was still the major sector of Palestinian employment in 1966. But there were deliberate efforts to reduce Palestinian agriculture, because it implied economic autonomy. When Carmiel was established the authorities seized cultivated land on which to build it, although the three Palestinian villages losing the land offered to provide alternative less productive areas. They were informed, however, that since those losing their livelihood would find work opportunities in Carmiel, the villages no longer needed those cultivated lands.[48]

Despite the degree of land seizure those still with land continued to till it, while a substantial number of others continued to find work on lands taken from them, frequently on land sublet in breach of official regulations. The war of 1967, with its new demographic implications for Israel, reawakened fears that the Arabs were creeping back onto the land. The Agricultural Settlement Law of August 1967 prohibited Palestinians who in the late 1950s and early 1960s had returned to their former lands as agricultural workers, lessees or sharecroppers, from working on JNF owned or controlled lands, effectively all the land expropriated during the preceding nineteen years.[49] The impact of this new legislation was severe. In 1966, 39.1 per cent (25,600 jobs) of the Palestinian work-force had been employed in agriculture. By 1974 the proportion had declined to 14.5 per cent (14,800 jobs), and by 1984 had dropped to only 9 per cent.[50]

The state shifted Palestinian workers from relatively autonomous agriculture to more dependent forms of employment. The decline in agricultural employment was complemented by increased employment in the construction industry, from 8 per cent in 1954 to 24 per cent by 1974. In the 1980s a recession in construction activity led to a shift to manufacturing industries – textile and clothing manufacture, basic metal and metal products, food, beverages and tobacco industries – which by 1985 employed 22 per cent of the Palestinian work-force.[51] All these industries dovetailed into a larger, Jewish-controlled economy. Usually 'textile and clothing manufacture' implied no more than low paid piece-work by Palestinian women in the villages. Employment in heavy machinery, electrical and electronic, or transport equipment remained minimal 'for security reasons', at 6 per cent compared with a level of 33 per cent of the work-force nationally.[52] Employment in services, essentially in restaurants, cafés and hotels increased from 6 per cent in 1954 to 16 per cent by 1985.

In all these sectors, Palestinians were to be found mainly in the lowest paid and most menial occupations, the very jobs most responsive to booms and slumps in the national economy. By the mid-1980s the largest single occupational category for Palestinian labour remained 'non-specified unskilled workers'.[53] The gap between Arab and Jewish labour patterns had grown. While the national distribution of labour shifted from 37 per cent white collar and 63 per cent blue collar in 1954 to 54 per cent and 46 per cent respectively in 1984, distribution of Palestinian labour shifted from 16 per cent white collar and 84 per cent blue collar in 1954 to 26 per cent and 74 per cent respectively in 1984.[54] Palestinian participation in the labour force remains below the national rate.[55] When recession occurs, as in 1966–7 and from 1984 onwards, Palestinian unemployment outstrips the national rate.[56]

As a result of such factors, Palestinian per capita income by 1982 was only 46 per cent of average Jewish per capita income.[57] In theory a Jew and a Palestinian receive the same pay for the same job, but the official statistics belie this. Even between unskilled workers, in 1982 the net average income of a Palestinian household was 80 per cent of a Jewish one.[58]

One of the characteristics which betrays dependence on the Jewish sector is the high level of physical mobility of Palestinian labour. In 1984 78,000 workers, almost half the Palestinian work-force, regularly left their towns and villages to work in Jewish economic areas, a pattern established in the late 1950s. Institutional, political and social barriers already mentioned have prevented Palestinians moving closer to their place of work.

State policy of avoiding investment in Palestinian economic develop-ment to prevent the emergence of Palestinian-owned centres of economic power remains in operation, as Prime Minister Shimon Peres confirmed at the beginning of 1986.[59] In recent years, particularly during the 1980s, the government has offered modest encouragement for the establishment of certain light industries such as textiles and clothes manufacture in Palestinian areas. These are almost invariably either Jewish-owned or joint Jewish–Arab owned factories taking advantage of cheap industrial premises and low labour costs, and tending to serve the Jewish economy, but doing little to develop local economic potential.

All Israeli capitalists, both Jewish and Arab, are aware of state policy. For this reason private investment in the Palestinian sector is low. Only the most dedicated investor is likely to support the growth of Palestinian enterprises which confer economic power on the Palestinian community. They know that their investment efforts will almost certainly fail as the state excludes such endeavours from the support, markets and outlets on which they are likely to depend.

It is on account of the absence of state support and the lack of private or public investment that the standard reasons given for Palestinian economic backwardness, a 'traditional mentality' and a 'lack of initiative' are unconvincing. Traditionalism and lack of initiative may be factors, but they can only be put to the test if Palestinian industrialists and businessmen enjoy the same access to state subsidies and private investment as Jewish Israelis do.

The state has deliberately maintained a condition of dependency in civic and social matters, too, by denying Palestinian localities the benefits granted to Jewish ones. There are only three Palestinian municipalities in Israel, two of which, Nazareth and Shafa Amr, already enjoyed this status before 1948. Israel has conferred municipal status on only one Palestinian locality, Umm al Fahm, a village of 3,000 in 1948 but by 1985 – when it was given municipal status – a bustling town of 25,000 inhabitants.

The remaining Palestinians live in what are misleadingly described as 'urbanized' localities, but which have the status of villages. Since many of these villages have a population of 7,000 or more they are effectively towns, denied the status, characteristics or infrastructural advantages they would enjoy if so designated. None of them, for example, has a sewage system. By 1987 only 56 out of 137 Palestinian towns and villages actually had an elected local authority, leaving one-quarter of the Palestinian population without local or municipal services.[60] The bedouin resettlement towns, like Rahat with a population of over 14,000, are administered by government appointees headed by a Jewish Israeli. It is argued that bedouin society is too strife-torn to be capable of running its own affairs,[61] an unconvincing argument since almost 100,000 bedouin had organized their communal existence satisfactorily until 1948. The real reason for strife among the bedouin more probably lies in the policy of segmentation.

Where they exist, most local councils are no longer controlled or influenced by the state as they were at first. In fact they have in large part become the vehicle, at local level, for Palestinian protest and campaigning to obtain a fairer share of the national cake. Nevertheless their scope and powers are limited because they remain dependent on central government in certain key respects.

In 1965 the state required all local authorities to produce a master-plan for the development of their area. Approval, provided to all Jewish councils, empowers a local council to issue building permits according to the master-plan without further reference to central government. In its absence, the local authority must apply on a case-by-case basis to central government for approval for any construction. Despite the submission of master-plans over the past twenty years, barely a single Palestinian local authority has received approval for its plan. In Majd al Kurum, for example, a village in western Galilee, work on a master-plan began in 1966 and was completed, despite setbacks, in 1978. In the twenty years from 1966 its population had grown from 4,000 to 6,700, but no extra land had been authorized for building.[62] Majd al Kurum still awaits approval, but even if this were granted it would have to rework its master-plan in view of the unplanned consequences of population increase. It contrasts, like other neighbouring villages, with the tall buildings, wide avenues and orderly layout of Carmiel, 5 km away. State reluctance to give approval is partly because it disputes the status of much of the land involved in these plans, and also because through the provision or denial of building permits, the state can exert power over the Palestinian community, rewarding co-operative Arabs and punishing recalcitrant ones.[63]

Palestinian local authorities are caught between the conflicting imperatives of obeying state directives and of responding to the pressure of population increase. Since the population has increased fourfold since 1948, and since few building permits have been granted, Palestinians have been compelled to build unlicensed homes. Where possible they have been added onto existing homes, or within the built-up areas. However, there has also been considerable spillage onto state land, land originally belonging to the locality in question. No one knows for certain how many illegal homes have been built over the years, but it certainly runs into several thousands.[64] In the Negev the problem is compounded by the tenacity of some bedouin tribes to remain on their ancestral lands. Whole encampments, usually shanties, are illegal and liable to demolition.[65]

There is a financial aspect to the withholding of permits. Local authorities may not levy local taxes on unlicensed buildings and they are themselves unable to raise perhaps as much as 35 per cent of their local tax base. The longer building permits are not issued, the greater the tax loss for Palestinian localities. Local authorities face bankruptcy because of their declining finance base.

For many years the state has authorized the demolition of illegal buildings. Although many homes have been demolished, a more usual practice has been either to fine the occupants, or to leave houses unlicensed, and therefore liable to demolition *sine die*. This gives the state the opportunity to secure co-operation from the family involved.

Illegal housing has relieved some of the pressure but overcrowding in most villages is acute. A survey conducted in the early 1980s concluded that 72 per cent of Palestinians suffer from overcrowding compared with only 22 per cent of Jews.[66] On average there are two persons per room in a Palestinian house, compared with an average of one person per room in a Jewish one.[67] The average Palestinian household contains 5.72 inhabitants compared with the Jewish average of 3.39.[68] With the continued higher birthrate, and larger average families in the Palestinian sector, the problem of overcrowding will deteriorate further.

The government has taken no steps to accommodate this increase, apart from the construction of a few hundred apartments in Nazareth. The policy of neglect stretches beyond the official state apparatus to quasi-state institutions. Despite Arab membership of the Histadrut, not one of the 150,000 apartments constructed by the Histadrut since 1948 has been allocated on completion to a Palestinian family.,[69]

Being determined to prevent any kind of autonomous growth, the state denies the Palestinian community economic development benefits extended on a regional or local basis. By its development law the country has been demarcated into three zones, two of which qualify for development assistance.[70] Under this law generous incentives are offered in priority areas, 'Zone A', for industrial projects, including reduced rent on industrial buildings and low-interest loans (for the construction of buildings, for working capital and grants for industrial site development, for on-the-job training of workers and for the transfer of existing enterprises).[71] Similar incentives are offered in secondary areas, 'Zone B', but at lower rates.

The most undeveloped areas of the state – which are Palestinian – have been largely excluded from these benefits. Zone A includes upper and eastern Galilee, the areas of Jewish numerical predominance, but excludes western Galilee which is predominantly Palestinian. Part of western Galilee is defined as Zone B, but here the line has been drawn to include Nazaret Illit, Carmiel, Ma'alot but to exclude Palestinian centres, notably Arab Nazareth (despite its proximity to Nazaret Illit), Shafa Amr, and Kfar Yasif, just outside Acre. The Palestinian villages of the Little Triangle fall outside either development zone, even though the 100,000 or so Palestinians living there have no industry of their own.

In the south of the country Zone A includes all the Negev except for the area immediately around Beersheba, where Israel's bedouin population is settled. They fall in Zone B. A comparison between Rahat, a bedouin resettlement town, and Arad, a Jewish development town, each with an official population of roughly 14,000, demonstrates the disparity between bedouin and Jewish localities. Rahat has no sewage system, no public parks or playgrounds, and no sidewalks for pedestrians. Some areas, despite the town's official status, still had no electricity in 1987. Only 110 inhabitants are employed locally and there are only three doctors, none of whom were available out of office hours until 1986. By comparison, Arad has one doctor for every 950 residents. It also has two swimming pools, tennis courts, two sports grounds, five public gardens, a cultural centre and a museum.[72]

Central government provides funds for the infrastructural development needs on a discriminatory basis. On a per capita basis, an average Palestinian locality receives only 10 per cent of an equivalent Jewish locality.[73] Regarding ordinary (as opposed to development) budgets, purely Palestinian localities receive only 3.3 per cent of central funding, although these localities contain 12 per cent of the Israeli population.[74]

Although the provision of electricity, water and sewage facilities are an obvious necessity for any kind of local economic development, the government provided the first Palestinian village, Tayiba, with electricity in 1955 and had electrified only five other villages by 1961.[75] Electrification came to most Palestinian villages only after Israel's twentieth anniversary, and then more often than not as a result of local effort and expenditure rather than the state's.[76]

There has always been a marked disparity in state policy towards Jewish and Palestinian local councils. In 1973 an official (Jirisi) commission publicized a discrepancy between comparably sized Palestinian and Jewish local councils, ranging from fourfold to as much as eight or ninefold in the Jewish favour.[77] However, because in absolute terms per capita taxes in Palestinian villages are substantially lower than in Jewish ones (reflecting the lower earning situation of Palestinians), Palestinian councils are less able than Jewish ones to qualify for matching funds for various development projects. The state bases its grant giving on the absolute rather than proportionate level of tax revenue.

Israel's dependency policy extends even into the field of health. Only basic medical facilities exist in Palestinian villages. In the early years of the state the infant mortality rate (IMR) was nearly the same for both the indigenous Arab and immigrant Jewish population.[78] Over the years the rate among both communities fell dramatically. By 1983 the Palestinian IMR fell as low as 20.6 per thousand, comparing favourably with rates in the occupied territories, and neighbouring countries.[79] It was a comparison that demonstrated the material benefits of life in the Jewish State. A comparison with Jewish citizens, however, reflected a substantial inequality of benefit, for the Jewish Israeli IMR in 1983, 10.3 per thousand, was exactly half the Palestinian rate.[80] There is a tendency to ascribe the differences in mortality and morbidity to the less hygienic lifestyle of Arabs, but this remains a highly questionable theory. Since roughly half Israel's Jews are of African or Asian origin, it is difficult to argue that Arabs are naturally 'dirtier' or 'less healthy' than Jewish immigrants arriving from less healthy environments. The real reason lies in the meagre health services in Palestinian areas. Apart from three small and inadequate private hospitals in Nazareth, all other hospitals are found either in exclusively or predominantly Jewish population centres.[81]

The absence of public sanitation facilities is the most serious aspect of Palestinian community health. Most Palestinian villages received piped water during the 1960s and 1970s, leading to a tenfold increase in water consumption, from 10–15 litres per person per day to 100–150 litres per person per day, as villagers obtained flush toilets, showers and washing machines.[82] In the absence of any overall master-plan and with no planning or funding for sewage systems, villagers converted their old rain-water catchment cisterns into cess pits, or dug new sewage tanks. The considerable expense of emptying septic tanks regularly has led to a state of semi-permanent overflow of raw sewage into the streets of many Palestinian villages and towns.

An unforeseen consequence has been the pollution of western Galilee ground water.[83] Pollution occurs both to drinking water and also to the environment more generally. Sewage corrodes drinking water pipes, leading to an estimated 30 per cent loss of water piped to some villages. When water pipes are repaired the negative pressure created by the interruption in supply results in sewage or sewage-soaked earth being sucked into the piping, and has led to major cholera epidemics.[84] The obvious solution would be the installation of central sewage systems as exist for virtually every Jewish settlement of 5,000 persons, and for many smaller ones. The financing of such systems has so far proved an insuperable problem for Palestinian village and town councils.[85] Jewish councils do not face the same difficulties, either at planning or construction stages, since they can and do obtain sufficient funding from para-statal sources like the Jewish Agency.[86]

The Palestinian community is bound to suffer most from the growing health hazard, exacerbated by overcrowding and population increase. In the longer term, however, the Jewish community will also suffer. A study of water resources in the Northern District in 1979–82 revealed a 14.6 per cent level of pollution, more than twice the national average.[87]

There is a contradiction between state policy which encourages on the one hand reverence for the Land of Israel and, on the other, the pollution of it.

The retention of poor health facilities for the Palestinian sector is one of the more contradictory aspects of state dependency policy. While the infant mortality rate remains substantially higher among Palestinians than among Jews, Palestinians are bound to continue to have larger families. By its policy the state unwittingly accelerates the growth of its unwanted minority.

Palestinians fare worse than Jews in terms of welfare and social services. In the 1960s government relief work for unemployed workers was given at a rate of thirty-five work days per unemployed Palestinian compared with one hundred days for an unemployed Jewish Israeli.[88] Until 1970 government welfare payments to poverty-stricken Palestinians were, as a matter of policy, usually only 60 per cent of payments made to Jews on account of their generally lower standard of living.[89]

The most damaging area of exclusion and dependency lies in the field of education, since it is only by education that the Palestinian community has any chance of playing a fuller role in the life of the state.[90] Yet education for Palestinians has remained underfunded, closely controlled, and segregated from Hebrew education.[91] Since it is compulsory, state education has reached a substantially increased number of Palestinian children since 1949.[92] In the 6–13 age group enrolment is almost as high among Palestinians as among Jews. In the age group 14–17, however, there is a considerable discrepancy reflecting the pressures on young Palestinians to begin earning, and their low prospects of better employment opportunities following secondary education.[93]

Palestinian children generally receive only one-third of the national average per capita allocation.[94] As a result, the provision of teachers, buildings and equipment is inadequate both in quality and quantity. As the Committee on Arab Education reports 'if the standards of education in the Jewish sector were applied to the Arab establishments, then the latter would be in need of 11,740 teachers rather than the 7,600 actually present today.'[95] At primary level the pupil/teacher ratio is 28:1 compared with 20:1 for Jews. At secondary level the ratio is 16:1 compared with 8:1 for Jews.[96] The average number of pupils in a Palestinian class is 32 compared with 27 in a Jewish one.[97] Classes with 35 students or more account for one-quarter of the Jewish sector, but 40 per cent of the Palestinian sector.[98]

Palestinian school buildings lack the facilities normally found in Jewish schools. Proportionately, twice as many Jewish children at secondary level have access to physics, chemistry or biology laboratories as Palestinian children in the same category.[99] Palestinian school libraries have on average five books per student, while Jewish ones have an average of fifteen books per student.[100]

Although there is an increasing shortfall in trained teachers for the Palestinian sector and although teaching is virtually the only profession open to Palestinian graduates, the government halved the vacancies for training between 1975 and the early 1980s.[101] While there are forty-one teacher training institutes for Hebrew education there are only two for the Palestinian sector. While 11,600 students were enrolled in the former in 1985/6, there were only 420 Palestinian students in the latter,[102] despite the fact that Palestinian children constituted over 20 per cent of the total category of schoolchildren, and despite the fact that more than one-quarter of those teaching in Palestinian primary schools were still unqualified during the early 1980s.[103]

The education curriculum subordinates Arab, let alone Palestinian, identity to the Jewishness of the state. While Palestinians are required to study Hebrew, Jews are not required to study Arabic, even though this is the second official language of the state, spoken by an increasing proportion of its citizens. While Palestinians must study Jewish history and religion, Jewish children are not required to study the Koran, the Gospels or Arab history.[104] The Arab history and culture studied by Palestinians avoids issues of Arab or Palestinian nationalism. Their 'culture' is set in the early years of the Arab empire or areas bereft of dangerous ideas of identity.[105] Jewish children barely study any Arab history at all.

The contradiction between daily reality and the ruler's version given in school brings the education system, and the Palestinians who work as teachers, into disrepute with the children it is designed to serve. These children learn more from the environment in which they live, and from their community and its experience of Zionism since before 1948. The reluctance to discuss Arab and Palestinian history and nationalism openly in schools leads to anger, alienation and frustration. It cannot, by any stretch of the imagination, contribute to the tranquillity of the state.

Co-optation and exclusion

The state, dominated during the period of military government by Mapai (subsequently the Labour party) also skilfully co-opted the Palestinian community into serving state interests. Its police and the

Shin Bet were able to create a network of agents and informers which penetrated virtually every *hamula*, or patrilineal extended family, in the country.[106]

It also worked through the *mukhtars*, or village headmen. Those willing to act as *mukhtar* for the authorities, be they Ottoman, British or Israeli, tended to be reactionary and politically submissive to external authority regardless of the latter's character. In return for their loyalty such people received favours, for example travel permits for themselves and their families, and were able to extend these favours. For many years, no teacher or civil servant could hope to be appointed without enjoying the favour of such agents of the state.[107]

The military government ensured that municipal councils were composed of those willing to serve its interests. It prepared lists of approved candidates for council elections and used pressure to obtain the required result. It also ensured that Arab members of Mapai were elected in Knesset elections, even though Mapai's policy was so clearly inimical to the Palestinian community.[108] The most striking proof of Mapai's success was in the Knesset elections of 1951 and 1955, when Mapai's Arab list obtained 67 and 64 per cent of the Arab vote respectively, proportionately twice as many votes as Mapai obtained from the Jewish electorate.[109] Such was the subservience of Mapai's elected Arab Knesset members that they voted even against abolition of the military government in 1962–3.[110] The abuse of the electoral process by Mapai led to conflict with other parties, and to the end of military government.

Co-optation of the Palestinians fell into disrepute in the 1970s, as Labour lost the proportion of votes it had previously enjoyed and as it became harder to use employment opportunities to co-opt educated Palestinians. Co-optation only continues to any degree among the Druzes, and to a lesser extent among the bedouin shaikhs.

Today co-optation is no longer widespread, but it does not need to be. The effects of segmentation and dependency keep most Palestinian Arabs busily concerned with the problems of day-to-day living. Those Palestinians who take more interest in political issues, notably those who go to university, are still relatively small in number. At some stage the continued economic and social decline of the Palestinians will trigger a more widespread political response to their treatment by the state.

The policy of excluding Palestinians from virtually every aspect of control or authority in national life, forged by Labour and followed by Likud, qualifies the notion of Israeli democracy. It remains a central tenet of the state, even though Palestinians have increased from one-tenth to one-fifth of the total population since the early 1960s.

Palestinians have never shared political power and have no prospect in the foreseeable future of doing so. Although some have played a role as co-opted members of Zionist political parties, they have never been given ministerial authority or party power.[111] Their role has been token, to give credibility to the claim on Arab votes and to the impression of a fully fledged democracy. For Palestinians it has been a democracy bereft of substance. The longer they remain out of sight and disempowered, the greater will be the social and political danger once they openly assert themselves in public life.

6

PALESTINIAN RESPONSES TO THE JEWISH STATE

How Palestinian Israelis should respond to their experience raises formidable and dangerous challenges. While they strive to obtain recognition as a national minority and rectification of the long years of discrimination, they must also avoid fuelling the Jewish Israeli belief that their intentions are inimical to the safety of Jewish inhabitants of the land.

After forty years, they are still astonishingly ambivalent in their attitudes to the state, partly because experience has made them apprehensive, but also because of the strength of Israeli culture, which genuinely divides them from other Palestinians even in the occupied territories.

The most striking feature of this ambivalence is the durability of the 'accommodationist' vote. In the 1950s and 1960s Mapai (Labour) was able to win the majority of votes, through its effective manipulation of the *hamula*, despite a major massacre of Palestinians in the village of Kafr Qasim in 1956, the end of military government in 1966, the 1967 war and contact with the West Bank. It even survived the rise of the Palestinian national consciousness in the 1970s and Israel's destruction of life and property in the refugee camps of Lebanon in 1982. The erosion of the accommodationist vote has come about slowly, as the *hamula* system slowly disintegrates, and Palestinian nationalism takes an increasing hold upon the community inside Israel. Its disintegration has probably been accelerated by the Uprising, but may take many more years to die.

Those Palestinians rejecting such docility fall into two broad categories, those who are prepared to recognize the legitimacy of the state – and are consequently willing to work within its institutions to achieve full equality – and those who are not. Neither category has yet achieved even a fraction of their objectives, and yet their endeavours suggest that the political potential of the Palestinian community has scarcely begun to be realized, either within the state's political institutions, or outside them.

Palestinians of 'loyal dissent'

The first category, which may be described as one of 'loyal dissent', goes back to the foundation of the state, when the Communist Party opposed state repression of the Palestinian community in the country. This party, including the Arab membership, had supported partition in 1947. During the 1950s its popularity among Palestinians soared, as the only party prepared to stand up for their interests, and reached a zenith in the years 1955–8, when international communism seemed to be supporting the Arab nationalist movement against Western imperialism. In 1955 it attracted 4.5 per cent of the national vote in the Knesset elections, a feat it did not repeat for twenty years. In 1958 the quarrel in the Arab world between nationalists, led by Nasser, and communists seriously undermined the support Palestinians gave the Israeli Communist Party and it only won three seats in the 1959 election.[1]

In 1965 the Communist Party split and one of the two groups, Rakah, became the only party in which Palestinians were able genuinely and effectively to participate. It was anti-Zionist in advocating a state in which all citizens could enjoy equality of rights and opportunities, irrespective of their ethnic identity. It clawed back some of the voters lost in 1959, but remained a party of protest supported almost solely by Palestinians (even though its central committee was 50 per cent Jewish) and almost completely excluded from mainstream Israeli political life. From 1965–88 it continued to win between three and five seats in the Knesset, reflecting its inability to attract more than about 4.5 per cent of the national vote and roughly one-third of the Palestinian vote.[2]

Rakah's difficulty reflects both the solidity and tardy decline of the accommodationist vote, and also the reluctance of many Palestinians to accept it as *the* party representing the Palestinian interest. Over the years it has done much: resisting land expropriation; improving employment, wages, and local council budgets and powers; providing help to prisoners' families and opposition to demolition of homes; and organizing Palestinian civil and economic rights. An important foundation to party loyalty has been its scholarship programme for able young

Palestinians to continue their training in Eastern Bloc countries when denied access to higher education in Israel.

Several groups, none of which belong specifically to it, owe their existence to Rakah. These include the Committee for the Defence of Arab Lands which, although a one-issue group, enjoys the whole-hearted support of about 80 per cent of the Palestinian community.[3] The committee was formed in 1975 with the specific aim of inhibiting state appropriation of land, and demonstrated its success on 'Land Day', 30 March 1976 when the level of popular protest, in which troops shot dead six people, forced the state to proceed more circumspectly. By the late 1980s the committee's restraining effect on Israel's land policy was the most effective area of Palestinian resistance to state encroachment.

One other group which owes much to Rakah's support is the Committee of Heads of Local Councils. This was originally formed in 1974 with government encouragement, to uphold the position of the docile councils of the time against the political dissidents. But in a surprise electoral upset in 1975, Rakah captured the municipality of Nazareth, the 'capital' of Palestinian Israel, and in subsequent local elections it acquired a majority hold on the committee, supporting its efforts to get a greater share of Israel's local government budget.

Despite such endeavours, Rakah's authoritarian and doctrinaire behaviour and its apparent subservience to the dictates of Moscow created deep opposition. Its reluctance to co-operate with other political groups that disagreed with its ideology but shared some of its practical aims, its expulsion or removal from office of party workers who disagreed with some of its actions, and its outward socialism alienated many who might otherwise have felt happy in its ranks.

One example of such alienation is among the Druze community. In the 1970s Rakah fostered a group known as 'al Mubadira' (The Committee for the Druze Initiative), intended to wean young Druzes away from very effective state co-optation among older Druzes. By the mid-1970s it seemed as if al Mubadira was making serious inroads, partly because of the charismatic impact of the young Druze poet, Samih al Qasim, who was an active member of Rakah. However, expectations remained unfulfilled. By the late 1970s membership was claimed to exceed 6,000, or 10 per cent of the Druze community, but this declined by half during the 1980s. The reason for this failure seems to have been Rakah's desire to incorporate al Mubadira into the party. While many Druze no longer shared the enthusiasm of the older generation to serve the state, they did not feel attracted to Rakah's socialism, nor to the way it wished to downplay Druze distinctiveness. Druze particularist attitudes are so deeply rooted that al Mubadira, or a similar oppositional group, is unlikely to become a serious force unless its inspiration, organization and control remain firmly within the Druze community.

In 1984 many Palestinians who repudiated Rakah supported an entirely new party, the Progressive List for Peace (PLP). This party had been established by two radical Zionists, Uri Avnery and Reserve General Matti Peled, in the words of the former 'to create for the first time, a real integrated Jewish–Arab movement in Israel, based on an agreed peace programme'.[4]

Its prime purpose was to achieve 'co-existence of Israel and a Palestinian state (this to be set up in the occupied territories); complete equality of all Israeli citizens irrespective of nationality, religion, community or sex,' a manifesto for which it had the explicit support of Yasser Arafat.[5] Arafat, like Avnery and Peled, believed that the prime purpose of the new party was to change Jewish opinion and for this reason suggested that a Jew should head the list. However, according to Avnery, 'Sadly, our Arab friends in Israel did not grasp this point, and insisted that one of their members be number one on the list.'[6] The new party was headed by Muhammad Miari, who had once been a member of an outlawed Arab nationalist movement in Israel, al Ard (The Land). As a result the PLP attracted few Jews but many Palestinians. Some had not previously voted in Knesset elections, others were accommodationists who switched to the PLP after Labour's credibility had been damaged by its defeats in 1977 and 1981.

The PLP provided a non-ideological platform for Palestinians who wanted a fairer share of national life but did not like Rakah. It was the kind of party to which those in the occupied territories and the diaspora who supported Fatah might give their assent. But it found itself in immediate and bitter conflict with Rakah. This stemmed from the similarity of programme and the belief in Rakah that this new group was challenging, as indeed it was, Rakah's hard-earned leadership in the struggle for equality inside Israel.

In the 1984 election the PLP gained about 20 per cent of the Arab vote, winning two seats compared with four for 'Hadash', the leftist coalition dominated by Rakah. However, partly as a result of state hostility, but also because it lacked Rakah's kind of roots in the community, it had failed to advance any of the objectives it had set itself by the time of the Knesset elections in 1988 and was reduced to one seat.

The dissidents

Beyond the two parties of loyal dissent are those Palestinians who reject the legitimacy of the Israeli State, and are consequently unwilling to work within the parliamentary system. They repudiate the legitimacy of the United Nations partition of 1947, and the inclusion in Israel of Galilee (by war) and the Little Triangle (by armistice with Jordan). They also resort to extra-parliamentary activity because of the treatment meted out by the state. Almost all these dissidents, who reject even the description 'Israeli Palestinians', seek the creation of one democratic Palestine for Jews and Arabs.

The first 'dissident' group of significance was al Ard, a group of nationalists who split from the Communists in 1959, and began to produce a weekly paper of that name which the authorities quickly closed down.[7] In 1964 al Ard took its fight for existence to the Supreme Court, but it was unsuccessful and several of its leaders were imprisoned. It had argued for a programme 'to achieve complete equality and social justice for all classes of people in Israel' and 'to find a just solution for the Palestine problem as a whole, and as an indivisible unit.'[8]

Al Ard's experience indicated the limitations of state tolerance. A number of conclusions were drawn: that no challenge to Israel *as the Jewish State* would be tolerated, that Palestinian political expression would be suppressed and that the Israeli establishment considered it vital to keep the Palestinian vote split between different parties. Many Palestinians believed that Rakah would have been crushed, despite its recognition of the state, had it only had Palestinian membership. It was only its Jewish membership which protected it. When the PLP was born in 1984 certain Israeli politicians tried to stifle it, because it threatened to increase the specifically Palestinian vote, and because it recognized the PLO and enjoyed its blessing.

When a number of young Palestinian intellectuals formed a new nationalist movement, Abna al Balad (The Sons of the Homeland), in the mid-1970s, they rejected the idea of working within Israel's parliamentary institution. Instead, they formed a network of local groups which hoped to achieve power within the community through local council elections and popular activities. Its programme was reminiscent of al Ard's: self-determination for Palestinians inside Israel; rejection of alliances with most left-wing Jewish groups; explicit support for the PLO as representative of the Palestinians; eventual establishment of a single democratic state in Palestine.[9] It condemned those parties which allied themselves to *hamulas* in order to ensure success in elections. While this clearly included Zionist parties, Abna al Balad's chief target was Rakah, which it considered had betrayed its own socialist principles in the pursuit of political power.

Abna al Balad achieved a considerable following in the mid-1970s, when Palestinian national identity attracted many younger Palestinians. It has continued to influence student groups in the different universities, although support declined from an estimated 18 per cent of the community in the 1970s to less than 10 per cent in the 1980s.[10] This decline resulted from the apparent fruitlessness of taking such a stance against the Likud government, and also from the surge in Rakah's perceived effectiveness from 1975 onwards.[11]

In 1984 Abna al Balad was split by serious internal disagreement, over whether to vote in the Knesset election or not. A breakaway group, calling itself al Ansar, decided to vote and, against the plea of Abna al Balad, instructed its membership to support the PLP. Al Ansar's decision to vote may have been in response to Arafat's condemnation of those Israeli Palestinians who boycotted the elections.[12] In any case, by 1987 al Ansar had dwindled to a small group, having suffered further fragmentation subsequently.[13]

Abna al Balad, which at the time had seemed to be the greater loser, started to claw back its position in the Palestinian community. It did this despite its opposition to Arafat's two state approach. A major factor in Abna al Balad's recovery was its ability to mobilize Israeli Palestinians in support of the Uprising in the occupied territories at the end of 1987. The Uprising vindicated Abna al Balad's insistence on the Palestinian identity of Israel's Arabs, a definition which both the PLP and Rakah had been far more hesitant to use.

The second dissident category is Islamic. Devout Muslims, repudiating secularist politics, found both Rakah and Abna al Balad unattractive. This was partly because of traditional Muslim hostility to leftist politics, with its atheistic or at least secularist connotations. In the case of Rakah, this unease was increased by the predominance of Greek Orthodox Palestinians.

As in the occupied territories, the Islamic revival is widely perceived as a threat, particularly by Christians and secularists (see page 108). The revival is real enough. In September 1987, Umm al Fahm's local newspaper reported an opinion poll claiming that 63 per cent of its secondary students favoured participation of the Muslim Youth Movement in local elections, compared with only 30 per cent supporting

Rakah.[14] Whatever the dubious reliability of such a poll, the Islamic revival in Palestinian towns and villages during the 1980s is unmistakable.

As elsewhere, the revival received a fillip from the Iranian revolution of 1979, but there were also special factors in Israel's case. As one shaikh recalled, 'After the Six Day War, we were united with our culture.'[15] After twenty years of isolation, Israeli Muslims had access to other Muslim centres, Jerusalem, Nablus, Hebron and Gaza. Following the peace treaty with Egypt, they were also able to visit al Azhar, the capital of Arab Muslim learning.

The Islamic revivalists have created a substantial following through the Islamic Association (al Rabita al Islamiyya), a network of chapters in many villages providing a range of social and welfare facilities. The most visible feature had been the mushrooming of mosques.[16] Of greater significance are the youth and other groups which built the mosques, kindergartens, clinics and roads. Such achievements have influenced even the traditionally unreligious bedouin communities in the Negev and Galilee. In an environment where unemployment and poverty are widespread, the Islamic Association demonstrates the capacity of the Muslim community to overcome difficulties, providing services the government has failed to supply.[17]

Whether the Islamic revival will displace Rakah, the PLP and Abna al Balad as the central platform of Israeli Palestinian expression must remain doubtful. In 1988 the Islamic Association supported participation in the parliamentary process, encouraging Muslims to vote for a 'non-Zionist' party. Its future as a political – as opposed to moral – force will depend upon the success or failure of these parties to secure concessions from the state in the struggle for equality in Israel and for self-determination for the occupied territories.

It should also be remembered that the Israeli Palestinian community is becoming increasingly Muslim in composition. In 1950 only two-thirds were Muslim, but by 1995 the proportion will have risen to three-quarters. In the same period the Christian community, growing less quickly, is shrinking from one-fifth to only one-tenth, while the Druzes remain just under one-tenth.

Popular Palestinian perceptions

While the majority of Palestinians reject the Jewish–Zionist framework of the state, the different opposition groups indicate a very substantial degree of disagreement on how to respond. This has made it far easier for the state to control the community. As long as Rakah, the PLP and Abna al Balad view each other with suspicion or hostility it will not be difficult for the state, despite the eclipse of the accommodationist vote, to avoid a strong Palestinian challenge to its control system.

However, certain political characteristics have been developing among the Palestinians which are likely to prove more durable and significant in the long run than present party affiliations. The first is the steady growth of Palestinian identity since the mid-1970s. In 1976, according to surveys by the Jewish Israeli, Dr Sammy Smooha, only 46 per cent described their identity in Palestinian terms, whereas by 1980 the proportion had risen to 55 per cent.[18] The significance of these figures is in the relative growth of this Palestinian sense of identity, rather than the actual percentage, for many would have been cautious in affirming Palestinian identity to Haifa University interviewers.

In 1982 a Palestinian psychologist, Nadim Rouhana, found that 74 per cent of his sample of adults defined their identity in Palestinian terms. Among young adults (18–25) the figure rose to 80 per cent.[19] Furthermore, while most described themselves as Palestinian–Arab, among those who chose alternative descriptions more opted for the identity 'Palestinian' than 'Arab'. Only 18 per cent, according to Rouhana, identify themselves as Israeli Arab, compared with 38 per cent in the 1980 Smooha survey.[20]

What precisely does being an Israeli Palestinian Arab mean? The answer provided by the Rouhana survey indicates that out of eight categories – homeland, Palestinian people, Arab nation, Arabs in Israel, class, religion, family and Israel – attachment to the 'homeland' (meaning Palestine) outweighs all others, even attachment to the Palestinian people. Moreover, identity with class and religion, both significantly weaker than that with land and community, is still twice as strong as identity with Israel, which is very weak.[21] If the Israeli establishment wishes to forge Palestinian loyalty to the state it faces an enormous task.

Israeli Palestinian feelings about Israel indicate that the sense of alienation after forty years remains substantial but inconsistent. In 1980 59 per cent accepted its right to exist, compared with 50 per cent in 1976.[22] However, a large majority, 70 per cent, feel that Palestinians cannot be equal citizens in a Zionist state.[23] When asked their view of Zionism, 64 per cent considered it racist, while an additional 25 per cent questioned its morality. Ninety per cent favoured a repeal of the Law of Return, which embodies the automatic right of Jews anywhere 'to return' to Israel, or an amendment, presumably to extend the right to Palestinian refugees.[24] Since the Law of Return is a foundation stone of the Jewish State, it follows that nine out of ten Palestinians challenge the Zionist basis of the state. In 1985 another survey by Dr Smooha revealed that 89 per cent of Israeli Palestinians in varying degrees opposed the status quo.[25] Of these, 50 per cent support parties or groups committed to ending Israel's Zionist identity, e.g. Rakah, the PLP or dissident groups. Probably a far larger group would welcome this if they thought it was a practicable objective.

However, while a sense of Palestinian political identity has grown since the 1970s, so also has an Israeli cultural identity. At least half the Palestinian community is now bilingual and bicultural. This is a result of deliberate education policy, and the dependence on Jewish Israeli employers. More Palestinians read the Hebrew than the Arabic press. One of Israel's most elegant Hebrew writers is the Palestinian Anton Shammas. This cultural identity is a factor towards seeking solutions within the state context rather than outside it. It retards and limits the sense of affinity with Palestinians elsewhere. The degree of biculturalism is bound to be limited, however, by the extent to which Palestinians are accepted in Israeli society. So far acceptance has been minimal and reluctant.

One issue on which the community has strong and united feelings is the right to operate its own institutions. It has already achieved this to a degree in local government, even though this sector is starved of resources by the state. About 80 per cent of Palestinians believe they should be allowed to control their own education system and create new institutions, for example a university using Arabic as the language of instruction, a radio or television station, and an economic development body for their sector. There are strong feelings concerning such issues, and equally strong opposition from the state and from Jewish Israelis who in similar numbers, over 80 per cent, oppose any increase in Palestinian autonomy within the state.[26]

In such circumstances there is a very low expectation, among both Palestinians and Jews, that parliamentary politics can effect substantial changes. Consequently, 64 per cent of Palestinians in 1980 favoured the use of legal extra-parliamentary means, strikes, boycotts, and so on, in order to achieve changes in the system. A further 18 per cent favoured the use of illegal means.[27]

Nevertheless, about 60 per cent of Palestinians, those who voted for Rakah or the PLP in 1984, are still committed to an objective of Israeli pluralism in which the Palestinian minority is separate but equal.[28]

Rakah has consistently emphasized reconciliation between Jews and Palestinians, repudiating the radicalism of dissident groups. These might appear areas of common interest with the state, but the latter has viewed Rakah as anti-Israeli and extremist, rather than as a moderating force in Palestinian politics.[29]

In a situation where a solid minority favours secession from, or the overthrow of, the state, Jewish establishment policy towards Rakah and the PLP seems reckless. In 1984, for example, instead of uniting with Likud, Shimon Peres could have formed a narrowly based government of his own 'if he had been ready to rely on the votes of our [the PLP] list and the Communists . . . even after we told the President . . . that we were ready to support such a government without joining it, if it were based on a minimum programme of peace and equality.'[30]

Furthermore, since the loss of land and the denial of Palestinian institutions are the greatest causes of grievance and radicalization, it could be argued that the state's best policy for retaining Palestinian acquiescence is to return some lands and to allow a specifically Palestinian party to be represented in national life.[31] With the growth and crystallization of dissident ranks, the policy of denial runs the risk of encouraging the more dissident to turn to extra-legal political action.

Across the Armistice Line

Nothing imperils the security and stability of the Jewish State more than the chemistry between Palestinians in the West Bank and those in Israel itself. Until 1987 only a minority of Israelis understood that *de facto* abolition of the Armistice Line would threaten the fundamental identity of the Jewish State almost as much as its *de jure* abolition. Most Jewish Israelis viewed the incorporation of Judea, Samaria and Gaza as an enlargement of the Jewish patrimony. Likewise, few Palestinians on either side of the Armistice Line looked beyond the question of self-determination for the occupied territories or the question of greater equality for Israeli Palestinians, to the long term implications of the *de facto* removal of intervening borders.

This was partly because the international debate, framing a just and durable peace in terms of Resolution 242, ignored the cross-border dimension. Palestinians under occupation saw little mileage in pursing grandiose territorial plans. Those living inside Israel adopted a hard-headed pragmatism, that they had troubles enough without inviting a return to military government which pan-Palestinian utterances might encourage.

It was also because, after nineteen years of separation (1948–67) the Arabs of the two parts of Palestine belong to two different cultures, a fact immediately apparent to anyone moving from one side of the Armistice Line to the other. Israeli Palestinians find this difference uncomfortable, for they are painfully aware that they belong to a hybrid culture, living as half-castes between Israel and the Arab world. Many feel they belong nowhere, feeling like an Israeli in Nablus, and like an Arab in Tel Aviv.[32] This painful dilemma is felt most acutely by the younger Palestinian Israelis who have been educated in Hebrew and use it daily in their work place. Their linguistic and cultural integration has been so successfully fostered by the state education system, that they can express themselves less easily on paper in Arabic than in Hebrew. This has had a powerful psychological effect on the sense of identity.

The sense of difference is mutual. West Bank and Gaza Palestinians find the comparatively brusque and abrasive manner of Israeli Palestinians alien and reminiscent of their common rulers. It creates an unease of which both sides are aware, and which acts as a disincentive to much social contact. The absence of a relaxed cultural atmosphere means that the level of social interchange across the Armistice Line is sufficiently low that it is not difficult for the state security apparatus to monitor those who do cross the line regularly for social rather than economic reasons, particularly among the more educated Palestinians. Only the more determined are prepared to brave the attention they attract.

As a result, contacts between Palestinians on either side of the line have tended to be more declaratory than substantive.[33] In cultural terms the gulf between the two communities is growing not narrowing. Nevertheless, there has been an unmistakable growth in mutual recognition as to the nature of their respective predicaments and the policies of the state. While the cultural gap grows, the sense of political identity narrows.[34]

At first, in 1967, Israeli Palestinians were shocked to discover how little their compatriots had progressed under Jordanian rule, and West Bank Palestinians were shocked to see the effects of the Jewish State's apparently insatiable appetite for land.

Perhaps naïvely, some Israeli leaders hoped that their own Palestinians would have a moderating effect on the West Bank population and show them by example how to accommodate themselves to the strictures of the Israeli State. As early as January 1968, however, the Prime Minister's Adviser on Arab Affairs, Shmuel Toledano, suggested that the flow of influence would be predominantly in the other direction, and that the Arabs whom Israel had so successfully cowed for nineteen years would fall under the negative influence of the territories.[35] This assessment was shared by diaspora Palestinians, possibly more as a result of wishful thinking than established fact.[36] Toledano was correct in his assessment, and the 'negative influence' to which he referred undoubtedly increased over the years. The longer the occupied territories remained under Israeli rule, the greater was the impact on Israeli Palestinian attitudes to the state.

Nothing served to bring the two Palestinian communities together politically more than the question of land. The immediate catalyst was the resumption of land seizures in Galilee and the acceleration of land expropriations in the West Bank in the mid-1970s. In response to the new campaign to judaize the Galilee through renewed expropriations, the first Land Day protest by Israeli Palestinians against state expropriation, on 30 March 1976, coincided with a wave of protests in the West Bank. Land Day, and the death of six Israeli Palestinians in the demonstrations, became a symbol of the struggle for the land more enthusiastically taken up each subsequent anniversary in the West Bank than in Israel.

The relationship with the occupied territories heightened the sense of Palestinian identity among Israeli Palestinians. From the 1973 October War and more noticeably from Land Day onwards, Israeli Arabs began to emphasize their Palestinian-ness with increasing clarity. When PLO candidates won the 1976 West Bank municipal elections they were hailed enthusiastically by Israeli Palestinians in a way that would have been unlikely in 1967 or 1968. On 28 September 1976 a strike by municipalities in Galilee, the Triangle, the West Bank and the Gaza Strip (in protest against the controversial Koenig report on the Galilee Arabs, see below p. 231) demonstrated how far the process had come. It was the first-ever joint strike, and set a precedent to be repeated in future years.

Inside Israel Land Day resulted in a split between Rakah, which was committed to a two state solution and therefore had major reservations about the West Bank's involvement, and Abna al Balad, committed as it was to one democratic Palestine. The latter saw the land issue, equality, the refugee question and the occupation as 'a comprehensive, integral and indivisible whole'.[37]

Rakah found itself in a difficult position. Since 1947 the Communists had consistently favoured a two state solution to the Palestine question. In 1967 Rakah called for Israeli withdrawal from the occupied territories, but condemned the idea of an independent Palestinian state there.[38] At that time it was committed to Jordanian sovereignty in the West Bank. Although in the early 1970s it embraced the idea of Palestinian self-determination in the occupied territories, it resolutely maintained that the political destiny of the Israeli Arabs was different from that of the people of the West Bank.

Years of endeavour had borne fruit for Rakah when it assumed power in Nazareth municipality in 1975 and became the engine room of popular Palestinian protest against state policies, particularly with regard to land. But as the tumultuous events of spring 1976 (protest demonstrations in the West Bank and Gaza in February, Land Day in March, and the West Bank municipal elections of April) caught the public imagination in Galilee and the Triangle, it was also clear that Rakah was riding a tiger. Public enthusiasm for such political developments could easily lead to calls for secession from the Israeli State.

Rakah steered a skilful course, remaining insistent on a two state solution but beginning to express a Palestinian (as opposed to Israeli Arab or Jordanian) identity more clearly. In April 1976 its organ, *al Ittihad* enthusiastically hailed the election of pro-PLO candidates in the West Bank as a victory for the Palestinian people. A fortnight later, the Rakah Mayor of Nazareth, Tawfiq Zayyad, speaking of the future of Israel's Arab community declared 'From now on there will be no communities and religious groups but only a single Arab minority, part of the Palestinian nation.'[39] This was a significant new development, even if it still foresaw separate political futures for Israel and the occupied territories. Since that time Rakah has continued to uphold the two state solution, and to base its own programme on the right to equality for the 'national minority' in Israel.

The national excitement generated in the mid-1970s did not last. The Camp David Accords, the 1982 invasion of Lebanon and the subsequent schisms in the PLO brought about a lapse of self-confidence among Palestinians, including those in Israel. Abna al Balad lost ground as it seemed to be further and further away from reality. People in the West Bank were not really concerned with the fate of Israeli Palestinians. They wanted self-determination, and most of them thought, certainly in 1980, that they would get it for the West Bank and Gaza Strip by the end of the decade.

The absence of any political progress in the early 1980s has encouraged reassessment. While Abna al Balad lost ground in the early

1980s in its campaign for a binational state, there has been no evidence of Rakah or PLP progress on the issue of equality. On the contrary, the indication is that the social and economic gap is widening. If Israeli Palestinians cease to believe that Rakah's programme can make any progress against state obduracy, and if there is no prospect of Israel relinquishing its hold on the occupied territories, they may become increasingly convinced that their political future will lie in association with West Bank Palestinians.

It is with this possibility in mind that the Israeli choice, whether or not to abandon the occupied territories, must be considered. If Israel continues to control the West Bank the belief in a common Palestinian political destiny is bound to broaden on both sides of the Armistice Line. There has been a popular inclination since 1986, when the prediction was first widely broadcast, to suggest that the year 2010 (in fact probably sooner than this), when the Jewish and Arab populations of geographical Palestine will be evenly matched, will be critical for the future of Israel. It is difficult to see why this should be so since two-thirds of the Palestinians, living in the West Bank and Gaza Strip, will presumably remain disenfranchised as long as Israeli rule persists. It is not the question of numbers which is at issue (for this is relevant only inside Israel where Palestinians are enfranchised), but the mental and material effect the West Bank and Gaza populations can have upon both Jewish and Palestinian Israelis.

Over the past twenty years the West Bank and Gaza Palestinians have given both practical and intellectual leadership to their Israeli Palestinian compatriots. In the 1970s it was largely provided by the mayors, and then by the National Guidance Committee's resistance to the Camp David Accords. In the mid-1980s the revival of contacts was partly cultural, for example the activities of al Hakawati theatre, the Arab Heritage Centre in Tayiba and the Arab Studies Society in Jerusalem. In 1987 the first Palestinian trade fair was held in Nazareth, attracting more West Bank than Israeli Palestinian entrepreneurs. But such things only affected a small number of intellectuals and businessmen.

Cross-border bonds have also been strengthened at a more popular level. In 1986, for the first time since 1948, a substantial number of Arabic readers all over geographical Palestine were able to read the same freely distributed weekly newspapers. Since these are funded by advertising they have contained only limited news and editorial matter. *Al Sinara* (The Fish-hook) quickly became the most important of these, distributed by grocery stores throughout predominantly Arab parts of

Palestine. From its establishment in 1986 until September 1987 its circulation soared from 5,000 to 65,000 copies, easily surpassing the circulation figures of all Arabic papers and periodicals and rivalling a number of Hebrew ones.[40] With editors in East Jerusalem and in Nazareth, *al Sinara* provided a careful blend of loyal (PLP) dissent in Israel and centrist nationalism for the occupied territories. Its significance, however, lies less in the ideas it propagates than in its role as an intellectual bridge between two communities. With the Uprising another significant but temporary bridge was created by Radio al Quds, operating out of south Lebanon or Syria, providing information and nationalist propaganda, and reaching all northern Israel as well as the West Bank.

Indeed, the Uprising nurtures the idea of a common political destiny. The strong Palestinian reaction inside Israel is a response, however, less to the PLO than to the firm popular basis of events in the occupied territories. Herein lies a threatening message for the Israeli State. It is one thing to thwart the machinations of the PLO. It will prove far harder to prize the Palestinian communities of Israel and the West Bank apart if they become committed to each other. Since Israel's continued control of the territories is bound to increase the haemorrhage of political ideas from the West Bank into the Galilee and the Triangle, it is difficult to imagine what steps the government can take if it is unwilling to slough off the territories. Even if sealing the Armistice Line for Palestinians were a feasible proposition, the knowledge that both sides remained under Israeli control would be enough to encourage a common bond of circumstance and fate. As Yehezkel Landau, spokesman of the small dovish religious group Oz v'Shalom, observed 'the realpolitik of the situation says that if you don't allow Palestinian nationalism some kind of expression in the West Bank and Gaza – Judea, Samaria and Gaza – you'll find it in Galilee within ten or fifteen years, all the stronger, and you'll have a secessionist movement there.'[41]

If Israeli Palestinians conclude that their political destiny is with their compatriots in the West Bank, a conclusion they are likely to draw if no settlement for the occupied territories occurs in the next decade, it is possible that they will cease to participate in Israeli electoral politics altogether. If this happens it will be a vindication and triumph for dissident groups like Abna al Balad and the Islamic Association. Conversely, the prospect of indefinite occupation of the territories is deeply threatening for Rakah and the PLP (or any successor party). Their position of loyalty to the Israeli State would be undermined, as Palestinian voters cease to believe that such loyalty has any credibility.

Rakah's whole stance since 1947 has been on Jewish–Arab socialist solidarity and since 1949 this has been defined as within but not beyond the Armistice Line. Almost half a century on, Rakah might be forced to redefine its political aim as Jewish–Arab socialist solidarity in all Palestine and seek union with the Palestine Communist Party. In short, Rakah might only be able to prevent the loss of its constituency and its position in local government by abandoning its identity of loyal dissent and becoming a dissident party outside national electoral politics.

However much they may be thorns in its side, the Israeli establishment must prefer Rakah and the PLP to operate within the national institutions than outside them. For if it fails to persuade its Palestinians to persist within its institutional framework, it is bound to face a secessionist movement. Allowing Rakah, therefore, some success in its struggle for equality is more than merely giving in to Arab demands. It may prove an essential tactic in keeping Israeli and West Bank Palestinians divided on their political objectives.

Failure to keep Palestinians of the two areas apart, failure to respond to the demand for Arab–Jewish equality, and failure to improve the conditions of life in Galilee and the Triangle tempts an explosion, possibly similar to the one which occurred in Gaza in December 1987. An uprising on both sides of the Armistice Line might prove containable in the short run but would also put the state's economic and military resources under great stress with no feasible long-term solution short of mass expulsion.

In such circumstances sloughing off the territories might seem the obviously safer course for Israel. The argument advanced by some Jewish Israeli Leftists is that once Palestinian political aspirations are achieved in the occupied territories, Israeli Palestinians will be far more reconciled to their lot inside Israel. This may be so, but it must be borne in mind that it is possible to make peace with the PLO and Palestinians in the occupied territories, with Jordan, Syria and even with Hizballah in Lebanon and still not enjoy satisfactory majority–minority relations within the state.

In that near miraculous condition of regional tranquillity, the whole focus would shift to the unresolved aspect of the Palestine question, the Israeli Palestinians. Resolution of the future of the occupied territories may stimulate renewed efforts by Israeli Palestinians for greater control over their own affairs. Some might be temped to seek secession for predominantly Arab areas of Israel. Others, for example Abna al Balad, might repudiate this in favour of the ultimate 'liberation' of all Palestine. A majority would probably reconcile itself to continued incorporation within the Israeli State but demand genuine equality and look wistfully across the newly re-established border at the progress made at both community and individual level in the West Bank.

Thus while in terms of external security getting rid of the occupied territories in exchange for agreements with neighbouring states may seem a self-evidently desirable objective, in terms of internal security getting rid of the territories may be nearly as perilous as hanging on to them, unless major efforts are made to empower Palestinian citizens to the same extent as the Jews of Israel.

At the conclusion of his study of state control of its minority, *Arabs in the Jewish State*, Ian Lustick points both to failures and imperatives for Israel. So far, he writes, the state has failed 'to enunciate or guide the implementation of a clear over-arching policy towards the Arab minority,' or to come to terms with the 'eroding structural foundations of effective control'.[42] The failure to 'develop a coherent, explicit and comprehensive approach' to the Palestinian community has, as he foresaw almost a decade ago, inexorably drawn in higher level decision-makers than the relatively junior officials who had so successfully administered the non-Jewish sector until the end of the 1970s. Three cabinet ministers had special responsibility for Arab affairs under the National Unity Government, 1984–8. When Israeli Palestinians demonstrated solidarity with the Uprising on 21 December 1987 the highest officers of the state, the president, prime minister and defence minister all felt constrained to warn the minority publicly against disobedience. The minority question is impinging increasingly upon Israeli consciousness. It is only masked by the more immediate demands of the Uprising across the Armistice Line.

Only when the linkage between Palestinian thinking on each side of the Armistice Line is properly recognized will adequate strategies, either for control or empowerment, be evolved by the state. A decade ago Ian Lustick estimated that no great strain would be placed upon the state by its minority for ten to fifteen years. Today his forecast is being fulfilled, accelerated by the political haemorrhage from the occupied territories, of which the demonstration of 21 December 1987 was the first serious indication. How long the process may now take is impossible to say. It may be the end of the century before the situation becomes as explosive in Galilee and the Triangle as it is today in the West Bank. But for a future – and hypothetical – government wishing to give its Palestinian citizens some reason for loyalty, there will be no time to lose.

7
DILEMMAS OF THE JEWISH STATE

The Uprising has brought into sharper focus problems of great magnitude and complexity now facing the State of Israel. By comparison, the problems the Palestinian people face may be great but they are comparatively simple. They desire self-determination for those already in Palestine, and the opportunity to return for those who live outside. They must either persuade Israel to yield to their demands or they must abandon their own identity. Having little to concede, the choice is straightforward. In his book, *The New Diplomacy* (London, 1983) Abba Eban placed responsibility for the fate of the occupied territories firmly in the Palestinian lap. 'In the final resort,' he wrote, 'the Arab cause in the West Bank and Gaza will stand or fall by the decision of the Palestinian Arabs.'[1] In view of the actual circumstances now facing Israel, such a verdict must be in doubt. It is Israel which must now decide what to do on account of its refusal to talk with the PLO and its continued retention of the occupied territories.

Today's Jewish Israelis no longer enjoy the simple verities that carried them forward in 1948, and which carry the Palestinians of the territories forward today. They are painfully circumscribed by the contradictions between Zionist ideology and growing realities, and by the fundamental choices that they must make to determine the fate of Palestine and its inhabitants. It is an unenviable position. No decisions can be made concerning the Palestinian Arabs which are not also to do with Israel's self-perception and the future of Zionism.

Zionism was the driving force of Israel's creation, the belief that the return of the Jews from the Diaspora would rescue them from the perils of Gentile rule, anti-semitism and assimilation, and that it would provide the opportunity to create for the first time in 2,000 years a society which was wholly Jewish in ethos and characteristics. The critical push factor had been the pogroms and anti-semitic policies of tsarist Russia, which caused 3 million Jews to migrate westwards during the years 1882–1914. Most of these went to the New World, some went to central or western Europe, and only a tiny fraction went to Palestine. Those who opted to build the Yishuv were secularists, motivated not by Judaism but by the climate of nineteenth-century European nationalism, fulfilling 'the quest for self-determination and liberation under the modern conditions of secularisation and liberalism.'[2]

Early Zionists believed that the Jewish nation should be based upon solidarity rather than territory, but the pogroms of 1881 changed such thinking into ambitions for a Jewish State in Palestine.[3] This was the dream of Theodor Herzl, the 'father' of modern Zionism, whose great achievement was to make the Zionist dream central to Jewish political thought.

It was inevitable that the vision of building a new all-Jewish society which would wipe away the odious caricatures associated with the Jews of Europe, attracted Jewish socialists of various hues, all of whom broadly subscribed to the idea of emancipation through labour. For some socialist thinkers, for example those who shared the views of Ber Borochov,[4] this was in part a matter of class war. For others, like the visionary Ahad Ha'am, it was more a matter of universal socialist redemption, but for most Labour Zionists it was 'an attempt to create an economic infrastructure for a Jewish community in Palestine founded on the Jews' own labour'.[5] The greatest practitioner of this outlook was David Ben Gurion, who saw Jewish economic independence as the essential precondition to political independence. The Zionist Labour movement dramatically achieved this precondition in Palestine during the Mandate period 1920–48.

The need for a Jewish majority

From the outset Zionism was predicated upon certain principles, of which the idea of creating a Jewish majority in Palestine was among the most important.[6] As a minority in Palestine the Jewish community would lose its meaning and be like Jewish communities in the Diaspora. The achievement of a majority was politically necessary – 'the establishment of a Jewish community large enough to give the Arabs a permanent feeling of respect' as Ben Gurion's colleague, Moshe Sharett put it.[7] Virtually all Zionists considered a Jewish majority 'an absolute prerequisite to Zionism,'[8] regardless of differences over how to deal with the Arab presence in Eretz Israel.

Today, however, the achievement of this majority is in jeopardy. Demographic statistics indicate that by 1993 the Jews will be no more than 60 per cent of the entire population in Eretz Israel (all Palestine), no more than 56 per cent by the end of the century, and no longer a majority by 2010 or thereabouts. Of those under the age of eight, Palestinians already outnumber Jews. If the claim that the population of the occupied territories has been seriously underestimated is valid, then the Jewish population is already less than 60 per cent and will probably cease to be a majority before 2005.[9] Inside the 1949 Armistice Line, too, the Jewish majority is being eroded, albeit more slowly.

What can the Jewish people do to retain the central Zionist principle of a Jewish majority in the land? The higher Arab birth rate has been a matter for recurrent comment and discussion in Zionist circles for over half a century, especially at times of low *aliyah*, or immigration. As early as 1924 Chaim Weizmann recognized the enormity of the challenge it posed. 'Only today,' he wrote to a friend 'I received the health statistics from Palestine. The natural increase in the Arab population amounts to about 15,000 a year. The Jews brought in last year 10,000. How can people possibly speak of ever forming a majority . . . if they don't throw every ounce of energy which they possess . . . to give us a proper position in Palestine?'[10] As the fate of Palestine approached the moment of crisis, in 1943, Ben Gurion called on parents to fulfil their 'demographic duty', stressing that 2.2 children per family was insufficient and that the Jewish population in Palestine was in a state of demographic decay.[11]

After the 1948 war, with the departure of almost all the Arabs and with massive immigration, the problem of the birth rate seemed less acute. Even so, Ben Gurion initiated an award scheme in 1949 for mothers bearing their tenth child. This was terminated ten years later since the object was contradicted by the number of Palestinian mothers claiming the award.[12] In the 1950s and early 1960s there were renewed concerns over natality rates. In 1966 Professor Roberto Bacchi reported to the cabinet that by the end of the century there would be 4.2 million Jews and 1.6 million Arabs in Israel. Partly as a result of his report, a government demographic centre was established in 1967 because 'an increase in natality in Israel is crucial for the future of the whole Jewish people.'[13]

This increase has not come about, despite repeated calls by politicians and the worry expressed, for example, by Golda Meir over the number of Arab babies born in Eretz Israel. During the years of intense immigration, 1950–3 the Jewish birth rate was 3.5 per cent, but by the early 1970s it had declined to 3 per cent and by the end of the 1970s it had fallen to 2.8 per cent. This level is substantially higher than the rate of 2.2 per cent in Western industrialized countries, but it did not compare with Arab birth rates of just over 4 per cent. At the end of 1985 the Likud Knesset Member (MK) Meir Cohen Avidor called for a year of internal *aliyah*, a euphemism for more babies: 'we should aim at 100,000 additional births in Israel next year,' he said, 'that would be more than the number of *olim* (immigrants) in a decade.'[14]

Exhortations to breed more babies are not confined to Israel's Right. On 11 May 1986 the National Unity Government met specifically to discuss the demographic situation. By that time 60,000 Palestinian Arab babies were being born annually in Palestine/Eretz Israel as against 50,000 Jewish ones. Speaking on Israel Radio, Prime Minister Peres appealed to mothers to have at least four children, and reiterated the essential imperative for Jews to remain a majority.[15]

The alternative and primary source of Jews for the Jewish State has been the Diaspora. The ingathering of world Jewry was another central principle of Zionism, the final objective after a Jewish majority had been established in the land. It came to be believed by many Zionists that those who failed to make the *aliyah* – literally meaning 'ascent' – remained unfulfilled as Jews. Even Dr Nahum Goldmann, who disagreed with the widely held Zionist view that the Diaspora would cease to exist by dint of the immigration of all Jews to Palestine, clearly stated 'Palestine and the Diaspora are two forms of Jewish existence, Palestine the higher, the purer, the more harmonious; the Diaspora the more difficult, the more problematic and specific; but the Jewish people form a unity existing in two spheres.'[16]

Immigration depended upon two factors, the driving force of Jewish refugee crises and the attraction Israel offered of a new future. In 1949 immigration almost overwhelmed Israel, but it was not destined to last. From 1948 until 1960 870,000 Jews came to live in Israel. During the next decade, 1961–71, 338,000 arrived, and in the period 1972–82, the number halved again to 178,000.

In order to hold the ratio between Jews and Arabs in all Palestine, and in the absence of any rise in the Jewish birth rate, Israel now needs a net immigration of 60,000 Jews annually. However, the 1980s reveal the worst immigration levels in Israel's history. In the United States, where almost six million Jews – two-thirds of Diaspora Jewry or just under half the total world Jewry – reside, a 1982 survey revealed that

80 per cent of Jewish Americans denied ever giving any serious consideration to settling in Israel.[17] In 1984 there were 19,000 Jewish immigrants to Israel, but this was exceptional. Even so, 10,000 also emigrated.[18] The next year was the worst on record, with only 12,000 immigrants and almost 17,000 emigrants, a net loss of 4,700.[19] In 1987 there was another net loss of 4,500 emigrants.[20] Much emigration represents the loss of substantial investment in the young: 25,000 children left Israel with their parents in the years 1981–5;[21] out of 110,000 Israelis who had obtained United States citizenship up to 1986, 78 per cent matriculated from Israeli high schools.[22]

Emigration is a sensitive issue.[23] It was at its highest in the early 1950s during the period of highest immigration, and took place almost entirely among the recently arrived in Israel who did not like what they found. The level stabilized but began to increase again after 1973. Emigration today, however, occurs mainly among *sabras*, native Jewish Israelis, suggesting that the Zionist solidarity of the state is weakening, perhaps under the cumulative economic and military burden of the Arab–Israeli conflict.[24] Since 1967, 546,000 Jews have migrated to Israel, but during the same period it is estimated that about 350,000, or 10 per cent of Jewish Israelis, have left permanently, a figure predicted to double by the end of the century.[25] One survey indicated that of the 18–29 age group, the group most likely to emigrate, 20 per cent were considering doing so. Among high school pupils the figure was even higher, 27 per cent. While the vast majority of Jewish Israelis consider emigration as harmful to the country, the danger is that a growing number of Jews 'will prefer to live with Christian European neighbours to living in this unstable state with Muslim neighbours'.[26] For a hardened warrior like Yitzhak Rabin such emigration may be 'the fallout of weaklings',[27] but his cabinet colleagues did not view emigration with the same equanimity. In 1986 the government offered 17,500 Israelis who had left in 1985 financial inducements to return.[28]

There has been a significant change in the kind of Jew choosing to migrate to Israel. Between 1948 and 1967, whatever their motives, most immigrants did not make the *aliyah* for religious or messianic reasons. By the 1980s, however, 80 per cent of immigrants were practising Orthodox Jews, and a high proportion were from the United States.[29] It is symptomatic of their outlook that half the recent immigrants from the United States have chosen to live in settlements in the occupied territories. New immigrants make up 20 per cent of the settler population and inevitably influence state policy with regard to the occupied territories.

An Israeli withdrawal from the territories would be a strong discouragement to *aliyah*, a fact recognized since the early 1970s.[30] It would send a message to Diaspora Jewry contradicting two principal Zionist credos, that the Jewish State had retreated from redemption of the whole Land of Israel, and that the ingathering of the Jewish people had ceased to be a prime Israeli objective.

On the other hand, it is likely that the continued failure to resolve the fate of the occupied territories, and the issue of demographic and political rights between Jews and Arabs, will also discourage further immigration. As Ben Gurion remarked sixty years ago, 'the feeling that Jews are sitting on a volcano could undermine the whole Zionist movement. Jews will see the country not as a haven but as a battlefield.'[31] Even discounting the Uprising, the lack of a solution to the occupied territories will encourage an increasing number of Israeli Jews to emigrate. It is a double bind.

In attracting more Jews to make the *aliyah*, Israel faces two difficulties. The only Jews who wish to come to Israel are religiously motivated or refugees. Apart from the Falashas, persuaded to make the journey from Ethiopia in 1983–4, there are currently few Jewish refugees. Israel faces the reluctance 'of almost all those Jewish communities in distress (South African, Persian, Argentinian and Russian) to look upon Israel as a new home . . . Clearly something very fundamental has gone awry.'[32] The problem was summed up succinctly in an article entitled 'Israel's national schizophrenia' which argued that 'Israel, which presents itself as the defender of world Jewry, is a complete anomaly in the international community, and its protracted conflict – which it makes almost no effort to end – menaces Jewish communities throughout the world. They are threatened not by any hostility from the people among whom they themselves live, but rather by the protracted conflict between Israel and its neighbours.'[33]

The claim of 400,000 Soviet Jews wishing to make *aliyah* hardly stands up to scrutiny.[34] Of those wishing to leave the Soviet Union, 80 per cent in recent years have generally chosen to abandon their exit visa destination of Israel in favour of the United States or another Western country. Indeed, during the mid-1980s an acrimonious debate grew between American Jewish organizations who helped Soviet Jews in Vienna and Rome to travel to the United States rather than Israel, and Israeli Zionists who maintained that they had an obligation to travel to Israel.[35] Nevertheless, the ingathering of Russian Jews has remained an objective, and Israel has continued to endeavour to block off Soviet Jewish 'escape routes' to the West by seeking Soviet agreement to route emigrants via Bucharest rather than through Rome or Vienna where Jews can jump ship.[36]

The failure to gather in the Diaspora is overshadowed by a far greater problem: the overall decline of world Jewry. As a result of the loss of an estimated 6 million Jews in the Nazi Holocaust, the world Jewish population stood at 11 million in 1945. It grew to a peak of 13 million in 1970 but by 1987 had declined to 12.8 million as a result of a Diaspora birth rate of 1.2 per cent, well below the replenishment level (2.1 per cent).[37] Diaspora Jewry currently numbering 9.3 million will decline to an estimated 8 million or below by the end of the century, and more rapidly thereafter.[38] The natural increase in Israel, although higher than that of most industrialized countries, will be insufficient to offset this decline.[39] Not surprisingly, in view of such dismal prognostications, a World Foundation to Promote Jewish Population Policies was established in Jerusalem in October 1987 to raise money for programmes to convince Jews to have more children.[40]

Just under half of world Jewry lives in the United States, characterized by a low birth rate and a high assimilation rate, of about 4 per 1,000 per annum.[41] As a result, the present American Jewish community of 6 million is expected to fall to about 4.6 million by the end of the century.

Partly as a result of numerical decline and also as a result of unease concerning the occupied territories, Israel also faces the prospect of a political and financial decline in support from American Jewry. In the words of the public relations director of the Jewish National Fund 'the constituency of Zionism is shrinking.'[43] American Jewish support seems to have been weakening slowly since the early 1970s and more rapidly in the 1980s.[44] There is increasing ambivalence on the part of American Jewry towards Israel.[45] Probably about two-thirds of American Jews favour a homeland for the Palestinian people in the occupied territories, an increase of about 30 per cent since 1983.[46] For Israel the loss of American Jewish financial support would not be as serious as a loss of political support, for 'the most effective sanction that the American Jewish community can employ is to refrain from lobbying for continued US economic aid.'[47]

One important factor in American Jewish attitudes is the growth in Orthodox support of Israel and the decline in that of Reform and Conservative Jews. A far higher proportion of American Orthodox Jews visit Israel than Reform or Conservative Jews.[48] There is an increasing awareness of the conflict between Orthodoxy and secularism in Israel which, in the words of the president of the United Jewish Appeal, 'has the effect of dampening enthusiasm for the Jewish State'.[49]

Religion and the New Zionism

Central to this conflict is the question of who is a Jew, one which was deliberately left unresolved in 1948 but which goes right to the heart of the identity of the Jewish State. The desire of the Orthodox camp in Israel to recast the Law of Return (automatically guaranteeing Israeli citizenship to any Jew) to deny Jewish identity to Reform and Conservative Jews, the majority in the United States, has serious implications.[50] The Labour Party resisted right-wing religious moves to make observance of the Orthodox *Halacha* (religious law) the essential definition of Jewishness lest it transform the secular basis of the state and alienate the wealthy and influential American community who would fall outside the definition. The Orthodox and the secular Right have endeavoured to amend the Law of Return in the Knesset on several occasions.[51] At the 31st Zionist Congress, in December 1987, a broad coalition of Jewish organizations, backed by the United Jewish Appeal, warned the Israeli establishment that capitulation to the Orthodox establishment on the issue would cause a severe rift with the Diaspora and would torpedo fund-raising efforts for the Jewish Agency and the World Zionist Organization.[52] It was a similar warning from American Jewry which persuaded Likud to form a new government, after the November 1988 election, with Labour rather than the religious and extreme rightist parties.

The struggle over Jewish identity draws attention to a political ideology not yet discussed. This is Messianic Zionism, which has been growing in strength over the past twenty years, and commands between 10 and 15 per cent of the Jewish vote. It claims Eretz Israel neither on the basis of the secular nationalism of Revisionist followers of Jabotinsky (who appealed to history and the use of force) nor the creed of Labour Zionism (which would possess the land by building it). Instead, it appeals purely to divine authority, tracing its inspiration back to the first Ashkenazi Chief Rabbi of the Yishuv, Abraham Yitzhak Kook.[53] Kook made the first systematic attempt to reconcile and integrate the centrality of the Land of Israel in political Zionism with religious Judaic tradition. His own dream was not one of national religious domination, though he did believe that only by the reintegration of the Torah, the People and the Land, both physically and spiritually, would 'all civilisations of the world' be 'renewed by the renaissance of our spirit.'[54] Kook attracted only a small following, viewed as somewhat eccentric by mainstream Zionists.

Kook's son, Rabbi Zvi Yehudah Kook, took this thinking concerning the land significantly further:

> We find ourselves here by virtue of the legacy of our ancestors, the basis of the Bible and history, and no one can change this fact. What does it resemble? A man left his house and others came and invaded it. This is exactly what happened to us. Some argue that there are Arab lands here. It is all a lie and a fraud! There are absolutely no Arab lands here.[55]

Shortly before the June 1967 war he delivered a sermon to *yeshiva* (religious seminary) students bewailing the partition of Eretz Israel and 'prophesying' that the Land would soon be one again.[56] For such students the June war was a fulfilment of prophecy. For secular Jews, too, who had never entered a synagogue in their lives, the capture of Jerusalem was an almost mystical experience, and they lined up in their thousands at the Wailing Wall to pray.[57] Many religious Jews throughout Israel were persuaded that the whole of Eretz Israel must now be possessed through settlement and the imposition of Israeli sovereignty. Gush Emunim is the most obvious manifestation of this outlook, but it is the tip of an iceberg.[58]

It was natural that such religious 'Whole Land of Israel' Zionists should make common cause with the more secular rightist Likud coalition. From this common cause a 'New Zionism' has emerged, one which places far greater emphasis than previous mainstream Zionism on *acting in religious faith* to fulfil God's covenant: 'Behold, I have set the land before you: go in and possess the land which the Lord sware unto your fathers, Abraham, Isaac and Jacob, to give unto them and their seed after them.'[59] The supposition that this view was gaining ground was confirmed in the 1988 election when the religious parties increased their Knesset representation from twelve to eighteen seats.

For Jews of the religious Right and for some of the secular Right the Palestinian Arab inhabitants are either usurpers or tolerated 'strangers' sojourning on the Land. It is a cast of mind accurately foreseen by Herzl. In 1902 he published his novel *Altneuland* (The Old New Land), which expressed his vision of utopian socialism, universal suffrage, and a welfare state in Palestine. Palestinian Arabs were to belong to and benefit from the new utopia established by Jewish settlers. Then a bigoted rabbi appears who seeks to limit membership of this utopia to Jews only. In the fiction of *Altneuland* the rabbi is worsted, rationalism and tolerance triumph.[60] In the reality of today's Land of Israel no such outcome is assured.

The decline of Labour Zionism

By contrast with this New Zionism, the traditional vision – certainly that of the mainstream Zionist movement of the Mandate period – is now in decay. Ben Gurion's agnostic vision was of physical, rather than religious, development and redemption of the land. He saw those areas outside Israel's coastal heartland as the scene of this redemptive work, in particular in the Negev desert. His views of Jewish title to the land rested on the idea of labour 'since the only right by which a people can claim to possess a land indefinitely is the right conferred by willingness to work.'[61]

Ben Gurion hoped to settle 1 million Jews in the Negev, but by 1988 only 240,000, one-quarter of his target, actually lived there. Of these no fewer than 198,000 live in towns, over half of them in Beersheba, on the northern edge of the desert. Israel's first development town, Yeroham, was established in 1951, 35 km south east of Beersheba. By 1965 it had 6,500 inhabitants, the size of the average Arab village. Twenty years later it was struggling to maintain this level. As the mayor of another Negev development town observed in 1984, 'The Negev is facing disaster in terms of population growth. Many settlements will be destroyed.'[62] Apart from Beersheba itself, there are few more Jewish settlers than bedouin.

The permanency of the Jewish presence in the development areas is far from assured. Economic recession tends to hit the development towns of Galilee and the Negev harder than the richer central coastal area.[63] During 1986 many development towns in Galilee decreased in population, the result of the drying up of investment in new high-technology plants, financial difficulties of agricultural settlements, absence of jobs for young people and lack of entertainment facilities.[64]

This decline is partly a result of New Zionism's priority of redemption of the occupied territories. Between 1968 and 1985 $2 billion was invested in these settlements, at an annual rate by 1985 of $200–250 million.[65] The 1984/85 public housing budget allocation indicates the low priority of the Negev and Galilee: the West Bank 29.4 per cent; central Israel 25.6 per cent; Jerusalem 23.1 per cent; Negev 7.9 per cent; Haifa 7.2 per cent; Galilee 6.8 per cent.[66] If one looks at government per capita support for regional councils, those in the occupied territories fare far better than those within Israel's own designated development areas: West Bank settlements, Gush Etzion $230, Mateh Benyamin $245, Jordan valley $408, Samaria $357; State of Israel development areas, Sha'ar Hanegev $126, Upper Galilee $97.[67] Only 38 per cent of development towns inside the state are granted highest incentive status for industrial development, while all eighteen industrial parks in the West Bank settlements enjoy this status.[68] Redemption of the occupied territories is being achieved at the cost of eroding the Jewish economic and demographic hold on the Galilee and the Negev.

Ben Gurion's maxim that possession of the Land of Israel would come about by dint of working the land, is also now in question. During the Mandate Ben Gurion argued that the Yishuv, the Jewish community in Palestine, must not be dependent on non-Jewish labour, otherwise it would be little different from the condition of Diaspora Jewry. Unless it ceased to depend upon the labour of others and upon remittances from abroad, it would be doomed to lose its political independence as well. Today the importance of non-Jewish labour and of regular US government funding is a measure of the distance Israel has travelled away from the ideals of the Yishuv.

The labour question is particularly apparent in agriculture. The basis of Israel's agriculture is the *moshav* and *kibbutz* movements, accounting for 90 per cent of the country's agricultural production. The *moshavim* are smallholdings which benefit from co-operative membership for the purchase of necessities and the sale of produce. The better known *kibbutzim* are socialist collectives, closely identified with Labour Zionism.[69] The state, conscious of the centrality of agriculture to its ideology, subsidizes the farming sector of the economy heavily. Nevertheless, both *moshavim* and *kibbutzim* have employed an increasing proportion of Palestinian Arab labour in order to remain economically viable. Ten years ago the secretary of the Moshav Movement saw 'the increase of hired labour in all its forms, including organized and unorganized Arab labour, as portending inestimable dangers to the state and the moshav'.[70] Insufficient Jews were willing to work for the low wages, and he considered the only solution was 'to introduce new and appropriate mechanization'. However, increased mechanization has produced a crisis for the *moshavim*. By 1987 Israel was suffering 'a farm crisis so complicated and enormous it would make Iowans stand up and take notice'.[71] By 1987 the *moshav* debt of $1.2 billion exceeded its annual productive value of $1.1 billion. Over the next decade the number of *moshavim* is likely to reduce from 420 (providing a livelihood to 27,000 families) to only 100.[72] Even so, the survivors are likely to remain dependent on cheaper Palestinian labour.

In 1935, while trying to persuade fellow Jews of the importance of expanding the Yishuv into Galilee and the Negev, Ben Gurion warned what happened to nations without a social and economic infrastructure rooted in the country:

> World history recalls one frightening example which should be a lesson to us . . . Hannibal . . . was one of the greatest military leaders of all times . . . Against him was pitted a large Roman army, larger than his own, and he defeated them time and again.
>
> Yet ultimately all his heroism and all his military and political genius did not sustain him . . . Eventually he was defeated, despite the fact that his adversaries were rather mediocre generals with no talent . . . For Carthage was a *city-state*, whereas Rome was a village-state, and in the desperate conflict between a city-people and a village-people, the village-people proved victorious . . . Hannibal's heroism was broken by the obstinate warfare of the Roman peasants. These peasants were not taken aback by the successive defeats inflicted on them – because they were integrated into their soil and tied to their land. And they overcame Carthage and wiped it off the face of the earth without leaving a trace.[73]

Ben Gurion, of course, had in mind the creation of a Jewish village-state, but it is impossible to dismiss today's reality of the Jewish city-state and the Arab village one. Was he correct, then, in his interpretation of history and if so, is it relevant to modern Israel? For Labour Zionists this is a painful question, for were he still alive Ben Gurion would see the decline of Jewish settlement, the spread of the Palestinian presence in Eretz Israel – by its demographic growth, its village-based society and its role in agricultural labour – as the most profound threat to the security of the Jewish State. As General Harkabi writes, 'it is precisely the backwardness of Arab societies that gives them the ability to endure, because one expression of underdevelopment is the decentralization of society – in a multiplicity of cells which are not strongly integrated.'[74]

The failing vision

In his conclusion to *The Making of Modern Zionism* Shlomo Avineri argues that 'the State of Israel put the public, normative dimension back into Jewish life. Without that having ever been defined or decided upon, it is a fact that to be Jewish today means, in one way or another, feeling some link with Israel . . . it is the State of Israel that united more Jewish people all over the world than any other factor in Jewish life.'[75] Unlike the Diaspora communities, Israel is much more than an aggregate of its population. It is a symbol of collective Jewish identity. Today that identity, which in Avineri's view came closest to the Labour Zionist ideal in the Yishuv of 1948, is in crisis. The exigences of statehood and the conflict with the indigenous people of Palestine contradict the moral values expected by world Jewry. Somehow Israel must still embody a spiritual dimension. 'If Israel becomes only a mirror image of Diaspora life,' Avineri argues, 'if it becomes, for example, just another Western consumer society, then it will lose its unique identification for World Jewry.'[76]

The danger, as the 1988 election indicated, is that the spiritual dimension takes Israel towards theocracy. New Zionism has offered one way forward, but it is one which leaves old-fashioned Zionists deeply troubled. Whether cast in religious or secular terms, those who dissent most strongly do so largely on moral grounds. They believe New Zionism destroys democracy, equality and respect for all mankind – Jew and Gentile alike.

While New Zionism traces its lineage from Kook and Jabotinsky, the peace movement which grew in the 1970s traces its descent from spiritual leaders like Ahad Ha'am and Yitzhak Epstein at the beginning of the century and from binationalists like Judah Magnes and Martin Buber during the Mandate period. Judah Magnes, rector of the Hebrew University, defined the moral position of spiritual Zionism after the 1929 Hebron massacre:

What is Zionism? What does Palestine mean for us? . . . I can answer for myself in almost the same terms that I have been in the habit of using for many years: Immigration . . . Settlement of the Land . . . Hebrew Life and Culture . . . If you can guarantee these for me, I should be willing to yield the Jewish State and the Jewish majority . . . What I am driving at is to distinguish between two policies. The one maintains that we can establish a Jewish home here through the suppression of the political aspirations of the Arabs, and therefore a home necessarily established on bayonets over a long period. . . . The other policy holds that we can establish a home here only if we are true to ourselves as democrats and internationalists . . . and intelligently and sincerely . . . work to find a modus vivendi et operandi.[77]

For Yeshayahu Leibowitz, the present spiritual mentor of the peace movement, Israel's physical survival remains contingent on its moral survival. Thus 'the real black day was the seventh day of the Six Day War. That day we had to decide retroactively whether we had fought a defensive war or a war of conquest, and we ruled that it had been a war of conquest. Israel's decline and fall dates from that day.'[78]

Reconciliation is implicit in this outlook and the peace movement pursued this by seeking 'to prove to both Israelis and Palestinians that Zionism is compatible with Israeli-Palestinian peace and that dialogue between Zionists and PLO representatives is possible.'[79] The peace movement has discovered, however, that while the PLO is willing to talk, the Israeli establishment is not. The peace movement, with its myriad smaller components, has remained marginal, commanding no more than 10 per cent of the Jewish vote.

The broader coalition, Peace Now, has marshalled larger numbers, over 20 per cent of the electorate including many Labour Knesset members. In so doing, however, it has remained fatally compromised. When Labour joined the National Unity Government in 1984, Peace Now protested neither its continued occupation of a security belt of territory inside Lebanon, nor yet its Iron Fist policy in the territories in 1985. Only after the PLO's explicit recognition of Resolution 242 in November 1988 did Peace Now call on the government to negotiate directly with the PLO. On both Right and Left, however, it is still dismissed for fudging or avoiding the issues.

The idea of democracy

One of the essential ideas of Zionism was the revival of the Hebrew culture. In his book, *The Tragedy of Zionism*, Bernard Avishai makes an interesting argument, that 'Hebrew is so ancient that, to anyone raised in it to the exclusion of other languages, it cannot fail to convey archaic ways of thinking about politics.'[80] 'Herut', he continues, the biblical word meaning freedom, implies national rather than individual freedom, and contrasts with European-derived words such as *democratia*. Avishai's thesis is that *herut* has a far stronger hold on Israeli Jews than *democratia*. The latter 'has seemed an added luxury free people enjoy, not a synonym for freedom'.[81]

As a result democracy in Israel is predicated on a Jewish (national) majority. This definition was explicitly stated in 1986 by Peres as Prime Minister, when urging increased natality: 'That which guarantees the

Jewish character of the State of Israel is first and foremost its democratic character: the necessity to remain a majority.'[82] This is a long-standing feature of Labour Zionism. Half a century ago Chaim Weizmann dismissed the idea that democracy was appropriate for the Palestinian Arabs: 'They are too primitive . . . and too much under the influence of Bolshevik, Catholic agitation . . . to understand what we are bringing them.'[83] In 1986 Peres perceived that anti-democratic influence as terrorist, Soviet or Islamic fundamentalist.[84]

The idea of a Jewish majority is implicit in the position of Peace Now. When it demonstrated in favour of a negotiated settlement for the occupied territories on 23 January 1988, one of its slogans was 'Yes to a democratic country with a Jewish majority and an Arab minority with equal rights.'[85] As Avishai points out, the idea of a Jewish majority is even implicit in the policies of the leftist secularist parties like Mapam and the Citizens Rights Movement, for otherwise it would be rational to call for a binational state – embracing both the Jewish and Palestinian Arab nations – in all Eretz Israel/Palestine (the PLO's ideal solution) or join Rakah and the PLP in advocating a secular state in which neither ethnic group enjoyed special status.[86] Advocacy of Palestinian self-determination in the occupied territories implies that Mapam and CRM are anxious to preserve the Jewish character of the state, a character which would be lost if Jews ceased to be the majority.

No one has challenged the validity of this view more strongly than the right-wing politician Rabbi Meir Kahane. When his party, Kach, was banned from the 1988 election he observed,

> Western democracy calls for full political rights for all people, no matter who they are, Jews or Gentiles. If the Arabs were to be a majority here, then they have the right to plan the sort of state they want. Zionism states that this is nonsense. It says that this country was created as a Jewish State and a Jewish State means Jewish sovereignty, and that non-Jews can never be allowed to have sovereignty. There is a basic contradiction. That's why when we speak of giving the Arabs equal rights, that's a lie, a fraud.[87]

In view of the overwhelming appeal of a 'Jewish democracy', even to left Zionist parties, it is not surprising that only 31.5 per cent of high school pupils think that Arabs should have the right to vote in the event of annexation of the territories.[88] Up to 1984, according to Avishai, poll after poll disclosed that about 90 per cent of Israeli Jewish youth described themselves as democratic. However, polls in 1984 and 1987 indicate that 60 per cent would curtail the rights of Israeli Palestinians.[89] Furthermore, 40 per cent specifically opposed the Palestinian right to vote in Knesset elections.[90] Whether or not one subscribes to Avishai's thesis (and there must be some caution concerning how accurately youthful attitudes reflect either more general adult ones, or indeed whether youths will maintain such attitudes as they mature), there can be little doubt that the idea of democracy is under threat as Jewish opinion moves further to the right.

The threat is not solely to Arab rights. The 1982 war in Lebanon marked a substantial increase in popular disapproval of press freedom, and of criticism of government defence and foreign policy, from roughly half to two-thirds of the electorate. Furthermore, the indication was that 17 per cent explicitly preferred a non-democratic government, while another 17 per cent did not care.[91] In 1986 a survey of adults reported growing political intolerance towards those straying outside the national consensus.[92] Twenty-four per cent of Jewish Israelis wished to deny Israeli Palestinians the vote in Knesset elections. Fifty-seven per cent wished to disenfranchise Zionist Jews (i.e. Mapam and CRM) favouring a Palestinian state in the West Bank and Gaza Strip, and 70 per cent would disenfranchise all non-Zionist Jews favouring a Palestinian state (i.e. Jewish supporters of Rakah and the PLP). Furthermore, '68 per cent of the Jews interviewed in the survey oppose an election list running for seats in the Knesset if it "accepts the rules of democracy and recognizes Israel's right to exist but objects to the State's Jewish-Zionist character."' This would deny the two parties for which Palestinian Israelis vote, Rakah and PLP, any parliamentary legitimacy, and thereby make the vote of most Palestinians meaningless. A Tel Aviv University poll in 1988 revealed that 45 per cent of the electorate considered the country was 'too democratic'.[93]

One of the interesting findings of the poll of young Israelis in 1987 was that while journalists and Knesset members were among the least trusted elements of society, combat soldiers and army officers enjoyed the highest confidence and respect.[94] Because of its centrality in national life, the outlook of the army is an important register in the shift of attitudes nationally. For the first twenty-five years of the state, the army was fairly solidly supportive of the Labour Alignment. After the October 1973 war, presumably as a result of the Labour government's unreadiness and Sharon's inspiring generalship, most voted for Likud.[95] In the 1984 election 45 per cent of the army vote went to Likud, or to parties to the right of it, Tehiya and Kach. Another 15 per cent of the army vote went to messianic religous parties, giving the New Zionist

Right 60 per cent of the army vote. In 1988 over 50 per cent of the vote went to Likud and parties of the Right, and the vote for religious parties increased also.[96]

Since the foundation of the state the military encroachment into the political domain has increased at an institutional level. This was, perhaps, inevitable for a country permanently at war, but it became more so after 1967 when the army found itself governing the occupied territories, with all the political decisions implicit in this responsibility, for it was given free rein in the least democratic domain of state activity. In 1978 for the first time an army Chief of Staff, Raphael Eitan, publicly expressed his own views on the ideological and political as well as security considerations regarding the occupied territories.[97] Previously the army had acted almost exclusively at the state level, and specific relations with individual political parties, with the exception to some extent of Labour, had not really existed. The period of Eitan's tenure, and his explicit encouragement of Gush Emunim settlers, brought this to an end.

Since 1978 the army's scope of activity has extended into many spheres of national life, and by the early 1980s it was 'easy to name army generals who support or identify with the Labour Movement, or with Likud or with other parties'.[98] The army's increasingly open ideological stance indicated a growing confidence that its political enterprises, particularly with regard to the territories, had assumed a legitimacy that need not remain hidden.[99]

In general, the army has remained satisfied with the way in which the civilian government has governed. One reason for this is the existence of a military-civil establishment which wields major influence not only in the political but also the economic sphere. There has been a strong military flavour to the government, with a high percentage of retired officers. Since 1967 all lieutenant-generals (Yitzhak Rabin, Haim Bar Lev, Mordechai Gur, Raphael Eitan) have achieved key political roles. So have some major-generals, for example Ezer Weizman and Ariel Sharon.[100] Many others move on retirement from the forces into the arms industry, which employs 25 per cent of the work-force, and accounts for 16 per cent of Israel's industrial exports. Even Shimon Peres, who has never served in the forces, has been closely involved in the defence establishment since the foundation of the state.

One may imagine that this military-industrial system would have a very strong point of view indeed regarding any policy evolved by a future Israeli government which cut across its own interests. For example, a peace policy which embarked upon a major run-down of arms manufacture could be faced with strong opposition not only from this military-industrial system but also from the Histadrut, anxious not to lose jobs. Military spending, it must be remembered, went up rather than down after both the 1967 and 1973 wars.

Yet the reduction of arms expenditure is an important prerequisite to any Israeli substantial economic recovery, for its economic fortunes can be directly related to the burden of war. During the years 1950–66 defence expenditure averaged 9 per cent of the annual gross national product. During this same period annual GNP growth was 10 per cent, investment accounting for 32 per cent of GNP. From 1967 to 1986 defence spending averaged 27 per cent of the GNP, and GNP growth steeply declined. Since 1980 GNP growth has been 1.5 per cent, and investment accounts now for only 22 per cent of the GNP.[101] By 1986 $500 million was being spent on military research and development compared with $100 million allocated for civil research and development.[102]

The importance of the military-industrial system was evident in the protracted struggle over the scrapping of the Lavi jet fighter. Neither Likud nor Labour was able to break the deadlock in government until the United States decided to withhold further funding in 1987. In an article on the conflict between Israel's civil and military needs, the economist Simha Bahiri claims that the whole Lebanon war, 1982–5, cost an estimated $5 billion, the amount needed to finance the total housing, infrastructure and jobs investment for 200,000 people, precisely the scale of settlement envisaged in the Ministry of the Interior's 1985–95 plan for Galilee.[103] By an irony, many of those who form the vanguard of the military-industrial system, like Ariel Sharon who was defence minister during the invasion of Lebanon, are also leading advocates of settlement in Palestinian population areas. The contradiction between military investment and economic development, whether or not this is seen in terms of judaizing the Land of Israel, has yet to be resolved.

So far the army, backed by the military-industrial system has played a major role in the running of the state, but it has not openly taken over the role of government from the elected one. However, no area of the state's activity is more liable to precipitate military intervention than the question of what to do about the occupied territories and their rebellious inhabitants. Furthermore, it is by no means certain whether, if it did intervene, it would do so on considerations purely of the strategic defence of the state or in order to take the helm in the event of a collapse of national consensus.

This raises another issue painfully well known in Israel. Since 1948 no political party has been able to form a government without taking other parties into coalition. This results from the almost absolute proportional representation system which allows any party attracting 1 per cent of the vote to be represented in the Knesset. No party has ever taken more than 38 per cent of the vote. While this may be admirable as an exercise in democracy, it has left every single administration compromised on questions of policy. Even at the height of Israel's power in 1968, the senior cabinet minister Yigal Allon concluded 'the Government contained such divergent viewpoints that every position was cancelled out from within; it was a paralysed government.'[104]

The weakness implicit in each administration reached a climax in 1984 when neither Labour nor Likud could form a government without being heavily compromised between constituent ideologies and with only the narrowest of majorities in the Knesset. In the event the rivals found it easier to form a national coalition, which brought absolute power in the Knesset but resulted in a government unable to agree on much. In the view of one leading commentator, 'the national unity government has turned Israel from a flourishing, often rowdy democracy into something akin to a one party state in several areas of our national life . . . the vitality of Israel's democratic system, which so impressed visitors and commentators from the West during the first decades of the State's existence has been stifled.'[105]

The 1988 election brought further polarization but no improvement in the electoral outcome. It took the largest party, Likud, seven weeks of hard negotiation before it was able to form a new coalition government, proving 'the total failure of proportional representation in Israel.'[106] There is little sign that this fundamental weakness in Israel's political life will change unless Israelis brace themselves for an acrimonious reform of the electoral system which will raise the voting threshold or introduce a constituency scheme. Previous efforts at electoral reform to produce stronger governments failed in 1977–8.[107] In a situation where coalition negates strong government policy, one cannot be sanguine about the ability of Israel to respond to the growing Palestinian challenge.

Part III
LOOKING TO THE FUTURE

8
THE PAST
REVISITED

The preceding chapters indicate the major challenges both Palestinian Arabs and Israeli Jews must face. Finding common ground on which Palestine/Eretz Israel may be equitably shared demands a willingness to compromise. This may only be possible if the demonology of the past is abandoned. That requires revisiting the past more critically than has generally been done, even if this concedes vital territory in the battle for historical legitimacy.

The radically different Arab and Zionist views of what has taken place in Palestine over the past century constitute a major obstacle to the negotiation of any settlement. Only when the two adversarial communities, or at any rate their leaderships, face what really happened and why, will they be able to make the mental concessions upon which subsequent material concessions may be based. Three areas of conflict have had a particularly damaging effect on Arab–Jewish perceptions: Zionist attitudes and Palestinian reactions; the events and issues of 1948; and the use of violence and rhetoric.

Zionist attitudes to the Palestinian Arabs

'The Palestine which will be the Jewish National Home,' Israel Zangwill wrote in 1919, 'will not be the Palestine now overrun by the Arabs . . . The whole country, to whose ruin Arab fecklessness has contributed as much as Turkish tyranny, will have to be re-created . . . there is no Arab people living in intimate fusion with the country: there is at best an Arab encampment.'[1] It was a sentiment typical of a dismissive attitude towards the inhabitants of Palestine.

It was a Zionist proposition that the Arabs of Palestine 'arrived' from

Arabia in the seventh century AD, long after Palestine had been the land of the Jews, ignoring the common sense probability that Palestine was Arab by culture but that its people might be largely indigenous and might even pre-date Jewish settlement in Biblical times.

For many Zionists there seemed little reason why the Arabs should stay. 'They have all Arabia with its million square miles – not to mention the vast new area freed from the Turk between Syria and Mesopotamia – and Israel has not a square inch' exclaimed Zangwill in 1917; 'There is no particular reason for the Arabs to cling to these few kilometres. "To fold their tents", and "silently steal away" is their proverbial habit: let them exemplify it now.'[2]

The idea that the Arabs could make room for a Jewish State was fundamental to Zionism and has persisted ever since. The Arabs of Palestine, Ben Gurion wrote in 1929, are 'but one droplet of the Arab people' and Palestine is a 'small parcel of a tremendous giant territory settled by Arabs.'[3] In 1958, Abba Eban argued:

> it [the Arab nation] has realised ambitions beyond the wildest expectations of recent years. Is the world really asking too much if it demands of this vast empire that it live in peace and harmony with the little State, established in the cradle of its birth, sustaining its life within the narrowest territory in which its national purposes can ever be fulfilled? To live in peace with Israel, as she is today, imposes no sacrifice, inflicts no injury, incurs no grievance for the Arab people in this golden age of its emancipation.[4]

More recently he wrote 'all the gains of Arab nationalism in twenty states outside Palestine were taken for granted as though they had no effect on the balance of equity between the rights of the Arabs and the Jewish peoples to independence.'[5]

In the early years Zionists were deliberately evasive both with the Ottoman government and with Arab leaders in Palestine concerning their intentions. At the first Zionist Congress in Basle in 1897, it was resolved to 'create for the Jewish people a home in Palestine secured by public law', and by this its authors had in mind an eventual Jewish State although they were careful to use the word *heimstatte* (homestead) so as not to alert the Ottoman authorities to their true intentions. 'It [the term *heimstatte*] was equivocal', Max Nordau wrote twenty-three years later, 'but we all understood what it meant . . . to us it signified "Judenstaat" and it signifies the same now.'[6]

Different Zionists came out with contradictory beliefs and ambitions, sometimes the same Zionist contradicted himself as he addressed different audiences. This was partly tactical, but it also reflected genuine disagreements within Zionist ranks about both the moral right and feasibility implicit in Zionism. Several Zionists made honourable if naïve attempts to accommodate the interests of the Jewish settlers and those of the native inhabitants. One basic view was that Jewish settlers would be beneficial to the Arab inhabitants, liberating them from their oppressive landlord class and helping them with education, technology and science to be free of the dark ignorance in which they lived. This was the view expressed in Herzl's *Altneuland*, written following a visit to Palestine. It envisaged a Jewish society in which the Arabs would benefit, enjoying equal rights, although implicitly under a Jewish system of values.[7]

When Herzl was writing, the die was already cast. Ahad Ha'am (Asher Ginsberg) writing as early as 1891 was well aware of growing Palestinian Arab apprehensions, and stated that 'The Arabs, and especially the city dwellers, understand very well what we want and what we do in the country . . . when the day will come in which the life of our people in the Land of Israel will develop to such a degree that they will push aside the local population by little or much, then it will not easily give up its place.'[8] He rebuked his fellow Jewish settlers for their hostile and cruel behaviour towards the Arab peasantry. Other Zionists, too, sounded a warning note. In 1907 Yitzhak Epstein (who had arrived in 1886) warned the 7th Zionist Congress that disregard of Arab feelings would lead inevitably to national conflict: 'there resides in our treasured land', he wrote, 'an entire people which has clung to it for hundreds of years and has never considered leaving it . . . we are making a flagrant psychological mistake with regard to a strong, resolute, and zealous people. While we harbour fierce sentiments towards the land of our fathers, we forget that the nation now living there is also endowed with a sensitive heart and loving soul. The Arab, like other men, is strongly attached to his homeland.'[9]

In 1914 Ahad Ha'am repeated earlier warnings: 'they [Zionist leaders] find it unpleasant to recall and are incensed at those who remind them, that there is a nation in Palestine which is already settled there and has no intention of leaving.'[10] Two years later, in 1916, another voice warned 'Jewish settlement in Palestine is built upon the ruin of the Arabs. Who are these Arabs? They are the established inhabitants of Palestine, who have lived there for hundreds of years before the arrival of Zionist settlers.'[11]

It was impossible for Jewish settlers to be unaware of Arab hostility from 1910 onwards. Settlements were sporadically attacked, two principal Arabic newspapers were both explicitly anti-Zionist and the threat of Zionism had become a major political issue.

In spite of such warnings, leading Zionists continued to be either evasive or deliberately contradictory in their statements. The most notable was Chaim Weizmann. In May 1918 he addressed Muslim, Christian and Jewish community leaders in Jaffa: 'I have come specially to remove the misunderstanding that has arisen . . . It is not our object to seize control of the higher policy of the province of Palestine. Nor has it ever been our objective to turn anyone out of his property.'[12] Less than a year later at the Paris Peace Conference, he was demanding circumstances in which it would be 'possible to send into Palestine 70,000 to 80,000 Jews annually . . . to build up gradually a nationality which would be as Jewish as the French nation was French and the British nation British. Later on, when the Jews formed the large majority, they would be ripe to establish such a Government as would answer to the state of the development of the country and to their ideals.'[13] Lord Curzon concluded that Weizmann 'contemplates a Jewish State, a Jewish nation, a subordinate population of Arabs etc, ruled by Jews; the Jews in possession of the fat of the land, and directing the administration.'[14]

Ben Gurion recognized that Zionism could only be realized against the will of the host population. He was candid about this from 1910 until 1917. After the Balfour Declaration he began to deny that any conflict existed or that such conflict as did exist might be solved by social revolution. He hoped that solidarity between Jewish and Arab workers would overcome inter-communal conflict but, in contradiction to this hope he was quite clear in his own mind that Zionist objectives came before socialist ones. After the Wailing Wall and Hebron riots of 1929 he again accepted openly that a fundamental conflict existed, but it was only after the Arab revolt of 1936 that he declared that reconciliation was impossible.[15]

Treating the Palestinian Arabs as indistinguishable from the mass of Arabs, Ben Gurion could also argue 'there is no conflict between Jewish and Palestinian nationalist because the Jewish nation is not in Palestine (*yet*) and the Palestinians are not a nation.'[16] It was understandable that Europeans with strong ideas of nation-state should think of Arabs without any such political framework as bereft of a sense of territorial identity. But it was an utterly mistaken view to take. Those who did recognize that Palestinian Arabs might have national sentiments belonged to two extremes. One of these, the 'integrationists', like Epstein and Sappir, and the later binationalists like Judah Magnes and Martin Buber, hoped that Jew and Arab could live together on equal and mutually beneficial terms. At the other extreme were the Revisionists, led by Vladimir Jabotinsky, who wished to 'revise' the borders of Palestine to include Transjordan. Jabotinsky believed that 'a voluntary agreement between us and the Arabs of Palestine is inconceivable, now or in the foreseeable future,' quite simply because both Jew and Arab harboured national ambitions; 'they [the Palestinians] are not a mob but *a living nation*' [emphasis added] who would only surrender Palestine as a result of the armed might of the Jews.[17]

Most Zionists, however, were reluctant to admit any Palestinian national identity, since that would beg the question of self-determination. Ben Gurion was usually careful to refer to the 'Jewish people (or nation)' on the one hand, and Palestinian 'Arabs' on the other. The former had a collective identity, the latter remained individuals owing their political allegiance and identity to an Arab power further east, Transjordan. Such attitudes disregarded Palestinian national conscious-ness which was in evidence before the First World War. Even if it did not yet conform to European national norms, the Zionists were mistaken to deny it.[18] Even after the beginning of the Uprising, until King Husayn relinquished the West Bank formally, Labour continued to disregard Palestinian nationhood, insisting on talking with Jordan. While it denied Jordanian sovereignty over the West Bank, it insisted that its inhabitants were Jordanian by nationality.[19] Inside Israel the Palestinians still have no community status and are only considered as individuals, the very status in Eastern Europe from which Jews fled at the turn of the century.

Palestinian reactions

Nevertheless, there has been a Palestinian tendency to exaggerate national solidarity against Zionism when it was actually divided by family, geography and class, particularly on how to react to Zionism. Some Palestinian landlords quietly sold land to Jews while protesting their commitment to the nationalist position. A minority was placatory, believing that it was better to accommodate to the inevitable in the hope that the impact could be lessened. A number of Palestinian leaders tried to reach deals with the Zionists which would not necessarily have pleased the Mufti and his associates. In 1934 a member of the eminent

Jerusalem Khalidi family proposed the division of Palestine into two autonomous cantons, Arab and Jewish, under British superintendence. At a time when Jews were still less than a quarter of the population this was a substantial offer, but Ben Gurion would not react unless it was endorsed by the Mufti, Hajj Amin himself, and in consequence the proposal died.[20] Hajj Amin had a reputation as an inflexible, stubborn and bigoted man, bereft of political judgement, but even he was not quite as rejectionist as he appeared. In late 1935, before the outbreak of the Arab revolt, both he and his colleague Musa Alami were prepared to compromise on Jewish immigration and hoped to strike a deal with Ben Gurion to allow the Jewish population of Palestine to become up to 44 per cent of the whole (it was barely 25 per cent Jewish at the time), provided that the Arab majority was guaranteed.[21]

There has also been a reluctance to recognize that the Palestinian national leadership, both the Arab Executive and its successor Higher Arab Committee, had poor political judgement and provided poor leadership. The tendency to cleave to principle even when there was little hope that it would be implemented proved politically disastrous. This had happened in 1923 over the proposed Legislative Council. Co-operation, it was felt, would be no more than a whitewash to British and Zionist policy for Palestine. In 1939, the Higher Arab Committee made another disastrous error of judgement in rejecting the British White Paper. This promised most of what the Arabs wanted, restricting Jewish immigration to ensure the Arabs remained the majority and the promise of an eventual Palestinian government that would in due course acquire sovereignty. The latter provision required the assent of both communities so had questionable value, but it was better than nothing. Had the Palestinian leadership demonstrated publicly that it could accept something less than perfect it might have erased the still widely held impression that it is only capable of rejecting whatever is on offer.

There has also been a tendency to exaggerate the impact of Jewish settlement. The number of peasants driven off the land by the Jews during the Mandate did not reach cataclysmic proportions. Only 14 per cent of cultivable Palestine was in Jewish ownership by 1947, not all the peasants were evicted and, in some cases, they received generous compensation. The effect on those who were evicted was inevitably heightened by the general economic transformation from a subsistence economy to a capital-based one. Zionist settlement may have been the main stimulus but it was not the only one. Sixty per cent of the industrial enterprises established in the period 1918–28 were in fact Arab, even if they were far smaller than Jewish enterprises.

Furthermore, whatever the Zionist doctrine, the Jewish and Arab economies did interact – until 1936 at any rate – and many members of one community worked with members of the other. By 1928 Jewish enterprises, accounting for 75 per cent of the industrial work-force, employed a good many Arabs.[22] The economic development of the coastal area by both Jew and Arab served as a magnet for the almost exclusively Arab hinterland.[23] However, the economic penetration of Palestine by the Zionists, their political ambition, their openly stated intention of creating a purely Jewish economy, and their unmistakably growing control of the economy of Palestine was bound to heighten the sense of ethnic take-over by Jews in an Arab society.

The United Nations Partition Plan

By far the most important areas for passionate disagreement in the struggle for Palestine, however, surround the UN Partition Plan of 1947 and the subsequent war in which Israel established itself but which also left over half the Arab inhabitants of Palestine homeless refugees. The Arab case is that the Partition Plan ignored majority views in Palestine and thus violated the UN Charter (which affirms the right to self-determination), and that they were therefore justified in rejecting it on democratic and also legal grounds.[24] The Jews, they claim, then embarked upon a campaign of terror and evictions to drive the Arab inhabitants out of all the areas which they could seize. The Jewish case is that they accepted the Partition Plan and were willing to abide by it, but that the Arabs having rejected it launched a war of annihilation against them, with Arab armies invading Israel as soon as Britain withdrew. Furthermore, the Arabs fled from their homes either from needless panic or because they were ordered to leave by their leaders.

Recent scholarship, particularly concerning the events of 1947–9, has now discredited much of the 'authorised versions'. Scholars, most notably Avi Shlaim, Simha Flapan, Benny Morris, Tom Segev and Charles Kamen have examined the Zionist archives to see what really happened and why.[25] As the distance with the past becomes greater, both Israeli and Palestinian scholars are able to look more dispassionately at what happened in the crucial years leading up to 1948.

Whether the Palestinian Arabs were wrong to oppose partition must remain debatable. They had very good grounds for their position: that they still constituted two-thirds of the population of Palestine and should have had the right to decide on partition or otherwise by a democratic vote; that even in the proposed Jewish State Arabs would be approximately half the total population; that Jews owned only 7 per cent of the land area; that the basis of partition which awarded the Jewish State more than half of Palestine, and the better parts at that, was intrinsically unjust; and that partition would have dangerous repercussions on the Arab states surrounding Palestine, in particular Jordan, Egypt and Syria. On the other hand, whether it was wise to oppose partition once the United Nations General Assembly had voted is more doubtful. To the last minute there was a good chance that the partition decision might be overturned or at least reconsidered. So Arab, and particularly Palestinian, hopes that by vigorous opposition partition could at least be staved off were not unrealistic. To the end Britain felt that partition was a mistake but it was suspected by the United States of merely wishing to hang on to Palestine. Yet even the United States, having done more than any other state to push through the resolution, had major last minute misgivings.[26]

Certainly the decision to allow any form of armed opposition to partition, made largely by the Palestinian leadership in exile, was a fatal mistake. It failed to take into account either the weakness of the Arabs compared with Jewish forces in Palestine or the potential damage that might be wrought by ill-disciplined volunteers entering Palestine. Most important of all, it failed to take into account the fact that most Palestinians had no intention of opposing partition by force. Only 3,000 at the most ever responded to the Mufti's call to arms.[27]

The Zionist leadership knew very well that the Palestinians were reluctant to fight.[28] On 14 March 1948 Ben Gurion wrote 'It is now clear, without the slightest doubt, that were we to face the Palestinians alone, everything would be alright. They, the decisive majority of them, do not want to fight us, and all of them together are unable to stand up to us, even at the present stage of our organisation and equipment.'[29] In many parts of the country Palestinians made non-aggression pacts with nearby Jewish settlements.[30]

Nor were the Palestinians alone in their reluctance to fight. In January 1948 the Syrian leader of the Arab volunteers, Fawzi al Qawukji, offered to negotiate a partition scheme with the Jewish Agency before he joined the fighting.[31] The Arab states harboured a similar reluctance to fight, as some Palestinians realized.[32] When the United States tried to negotiate a truce on the eve of partition by way of a trusteeship proposal, all the Arab states wanted to accept it and avoid war with the exception of Transjordan. The latter, like the Jewish Agency, rejected any truce since they both stood to gain from

Palestine's dismemberment.[33] The other Arab states knew that a truce would deprive Abdallah of the pretext to seize Arab Palestine. But if he chose to invade alone, they would appear as betrayers of the Arab cause and would be leaving Abdallah a free hand in Palestine. The stance of Abdallah and Ben Gurion prevented the Arab states from adopting a truce.[34]

Although the Jewish Agency accepted the partition plan, it did not accept the proposed borders as final and Israel's declaration of independence avoided the mention of any boundaries. A state in part of Palestine was seen as a stage towards a larger state when opportunity allowed. Although the borders were 'bad from a military and political point of view,' Ben Gurion urged fellow Jews to accept the UN Partition Plan, pointing out that arrangements are never final, 'not with regard to the regime, not with regard to borders, and not with regard to international agreements'.[35] The idea of partition being a temporary expedient dated back to the Peel Partition proposal of 1937. When the Zionist Congress had rejected partition on the grounds that the Jews had an inalienable right to settle anywhere in Palestine, Ben Gurion had argued in favour of acceptance, 'I see in the realisation of this plan practically the decisive stage in the beginning of full redemption and the most wonderful lever for the gradual conquest of all of Palestine.'[36]

The refugees: fled or driven?

Ben Gurion, like many of his colleagues, was concerned that the presence of a large number of Arabs in the proposed Jewish State 'does not provide a stable basis for a Jewish state. This fact must be seen in all of its clarity and acuteness. Such a composition does not even give us absolute assurance that control will remain in the hands of the Jewish majority.'[37] When Jewish forces implemented their offensive in March 1948 to secure Jewish populated areas and also strategic communications, the Haganah's Plan Dalet allowed for the 'expulsion over the borders of the local Arab population in the event of opposition to our attacks'.[38]

The refugee issue is the most sensitive area of the debate between Jews and Arabs, yet it is vital that the truth of the matter is clarified since Israel's claim that the refugees have no right to return hangs on the events of 1948–9. What has never been in doubt is that both expulsion and flight were already under way in March 1948, before the end of the Mandate and before the entry into Palestine of Arab regular armies. The Haganah's offensives in April precipitated mass flight. Early that month Ben Gurion seems to have given his first explicit sanction to expel Arabs from a whole area of Palestine.[39] Expulsion and destruction of the habitations from which the Arabs had fled or been expelled became systematic.

By 14 May, the formal end of the British Mandate, there were 200,000–300,000 refugees, 70 per cent of whom fled as a direct result of Jewish military or paramilitary action.[40] During the summer months, after initial skirmishes between Jewish and Arab farmers, a decision was taken to prevent Arab villagers, both in the forward battle area and behind Jewish lines, from harvesting their summer and winter crops in 1948. The denial of traditional food sources 'effectively deepened the psychological and physical separation of the Arab fellah and tenant farmer from his lands and home, reinforcing his sense of, and existence as, an exile. In the Negev, still largely in Arab hands, the prevention by fire and sword of Arab harvesting was one direct cause of the Palestinian exodus.'[41] In the case of Lydda and Ramla up to 70,000 inhabitants were expelled, almost 10 per cent of the total number of Palestinians made refugee during the war.[42] In Jaffa, too, Irgun forces attacked in late April, with the specific intention of creating mass flight.[43]

Many Arabs fled because they were terrified. On 9 April a major atrocity took place at Deir Yassin outside Jerusalem in which 254 villagers were killed by members of Menachem Begin's IZL (Irgun) gang. Some of the men from the village were paraded through Jerusalem before being killed.[44] Deir Yassin was a 'decisive accelerating factor'[45] in the flight elsewhere, and in Menachem Begin's words, 'Arabs throughout the country, induced to believe wild tales of "Irgun butchery", were seized with limitless panic and started to flee for their lives. This mass flight soon developed into a maddened, uncontrollable stampede.'[46] Indeed, the abandonment of Haifa and Jaffa, the two largest flights during the course of the war, took place later that month, in the shadow of Deir Yassin.

As the war continued many others left, some fearing that they would be the victims of atrocities. There were grounds for such fear. During the expulsion from Lydda on 12 July there had occurred what 'amounted to a largescale massacre'.[47] Expulsions became increasingly frequent in the cleaning-up operations from late summer onwards, both in Galilee and in southern Palestine, and there were more excesses.[48]

How many atrocities were committed may never be known, but they were on a sufficient scale to move the Minister of Agriculture, Aharon Cizling, to say 'Now Jews too have behaved like Nazis and my entire being has been shaken . . . Obviously we have to conceal these actions from the public, and I agree that we should not reveal that we are investigating them. But they must be investigated.'[49]

There was no overt order from the Zionist leadership to expel the Arabs yet it was generally understood by most junior commanders that this was to be done. Ben Gurion allowed Joseph Weitz, director of the Jewish National Fund Land Division and long-standing advocate of expulsion,[50] to form a 'Transfer Committee' in early summer to remove Arabs from certain areas on the coastal plain, in Galilee and around Baysan in the north Jordan valley. The policy of clearing the land of Palestinian Arabs was discernible before the formal end of the British Mandate. As one Mapam party member protested 'There is reason to assume that what is being done . . . [is being done] out of certain political aims and not only out of military necessity . . . In fact, what is called a "transfer" of the Arabs out of the area of the Jewish state is what is being done.'[51] Ben Gurion himself was careful to avoid giving any explicit orders, oral or written to Weitz and his colleagues. He wanted Weitz to get on with things without attributable or official authority.[52] Benny Morris, the leading authority on the origins of the refugee problem, concludes that in spite of the absence of any overt expulsion order at the most senior level, nevertheless 'it was a coalition government whose policy, albeit undeclared and indirect, was to reduce as much as possible the Arab minority which would be left in the country and to make sure that as few refugees as possible would return.'[53]

The decision not to allow any return had already taken shape before 14 May. Three weeks earlier Moshe Sharett (Israel's first foreign minister), cabled from New York, 'suggest consider issue warning Arabs now evacuating [that they] cannot be assured of return.'[54] On 1 June this became a formal decision. As Sharett said, 'They will not return. [That] is our policy. They are not returning.'[55] When the UN mediator raised the question of the return of the refugees with Sharett a few days later, he found Sharett 'as hard as rock'.[56]

The Israeli public generally believed the official version of events, that the Arab flight was 'a tactic of war on the part of the Arabs who directed the war against the Jews'.[57] This version, concocted by none other than the Transfer Committee in its report of November 1948, 'formulated the main line and arguments of Israeli propaganda in the following decades. It denied any Israeli culpability or responsibility for the Arab exodus – denied, in fact, its own members' roles in various areas and contexts. It also strongly advised against any return of the refugees.'[58]

The idea of transfer

In the course of war refugee situations frequently occur and there is little reason to believe that, had Arab rather than Jewish arms prevailed, the Jews of the Yishuv would not have suffered a similar or possibly worse fate. One of the more unsettling aspects of the refugee problem, however, was that in spite of all denials, the declared intention to remove the Palestinian Arabs was not new.

Although the evidence is not and probably never shall be conclusive, advocacy of the transfer of the native population is a thread running through Zionist thought. One need not take very seriously the recommendations of Theodor Herzl himself 'to spirit the penniless population across the border by procuring employment for it in transit countries, while denying it employment in our own country,'[59] nor yet his proposal to the Ottoman authorities in 1901 that Jews should have the right to transfer the native population.[60] Colonial powers in the nineteenth century had moved indigenous populations or liquidated them, as occasion demanded, for example in North America, Australia and Algeria. It is perhaps more remarkable that having visited Palestine for himself, Herzl revised his ideas and thought in terms of Jews and Arabs living in a new utopia.

Rather more significant, however, is the fact that such ideas of transfer were still being expressed by Zionists once it was perfectly well known that the people of Palestine, already numbering over half a million, were deeply opposed to Zionist settlement. Arthur Ruppin proposed a limited population transfer in 1911,[61] and Zangwill proposed a more general one in 1919.[62] Weizmann believed transfer was crucial to the Zionist programme and, although he avoided stating his views publicly, was persuaded of its feasibility by the population transfer between Greece and Turkey at the end of the First World War.[63] In 1930 he suggested to the British government the resettlement of Palestinian Arabs in Transjordan,[64] although transfer was still a controversial and minority idea in Zionist ranks.[65]

When the Arab rebellion of 1936 persuaded lingering Zionist doubters that peaceful co-existence with the Palestinian Arabs was wishful thinking, the idea of transfer took a much stronger hold. The Jewish Agency discreetly sowed the idea of an Arab population transfer to the

Peel Commission in 1937, and its partition proposal consequently included a 'population exchange' of 225,000 Palestinian Arabs from the coastal plain, the vale of Esdraelon, and the Jordan valley to Transjordan in exchange for only 1,250 Jews from Arab designated areas.[66] That the idea of transfer had been formally proposed by Britain made it much easier for Zionists to accept it publicly. As Ben Gurion wrote at the time, 'as the British propose to give the Arabs a part of the country they promised to us, it is only fair that the Arabs in our state should be transferred to the Arab part,'[67] a kind of 'heads I win, tails you lose' philosophy. Along with Weizmann, Ben Gurion emerged as one of the keenest advocates of transfer during the intense debate in Zionist ranks during 1936–7.[68] His views received strong support from another future Israeli prime minister, Golda Meir.[69] By June 1938, in spite of previous statements he had made concerning the rights of the Arabs, Ben Gurion pronounced 'I am for compulsory transfer; I don't see anything immoral in it . . . There are two central issues – sovereignty, and a reduction of the number of Arabs in the Jewish State, and we must insist on both of them.'[70] Exactly ten years later the idea of transfer came to fruition. Between November 1948 and the end of 1951 between 20,000 and 30,000 more Palestinians were expelled, and more might have been had international opinion not been so hostile.[71]

Inevitably the acquisition of the West Bank and Gaza Strip with its sizeable Arab population reawakened thoughts of transfer. Two weeks after the 1967 war the cabinet met to consider the difficult demographic implications of their conquests. An option recommended by two cabinet members was the demolition of the Palestine refugee camps, and the resettlement of the refugees themselves in Sinai. Two others favoured resettlement of these refugees in Syria and Iraq.[72] A resettlement plan was adopted and a special unit was charged with 'encouraging' the departure of Palestinians for foreign shores.[73] Not everyone was content merely with encouragement of this kind. An opinion poll three weeks after the 1967 victory revealed that 28 per cent of the Jewish electorate favoured expulsion of the Israeli Palestinians, and 22 per cent favoured it for the Palestinians of the occupied territories.[74] When Yitzhak Rabin became prime minister in 1974 he hoped to 'create in the course of the next ten or twenty years conditions which would attract natural and voluntary migration of the refugees from the Gaza Strip and West Bank of Jordan. To achieve this we have to come to an agreement with King Hussein and not with Yasir Arafat.'[75] Ideas of transferring the Palestinian Arab population are so deeply rooted that there can be little hope that they will disappear.

Did Israel really want peace?

There is a widely held belief in the West that Israel wanted peace with its neighbours in the period 1948–9 but was unable to get it. This was not really so, according to the Israeli scholar Simha Flapan.[76] Apart from its unwillingness to accept the United States proposal for a truce in March–April 1948, Israel did not respond seriously to the peace overtures of Egypt and Syria once these two countries recognized that further conflict would be disastrous.

Egypt approached Israel in September 1948, during a period of truce when it still controlled southern Palestine, with a view to a peace agreement.[77] Both feared that King Abdallah would allow the British to establish bases in the Negev if he acquired control of it, as proposed by the UN mediator. Egypt offered to hand over to Israel all those areas still in Egyptian hands designated by the Partition Plan for the Jewish State (i.e. practically all the Negev, except part abutting Egypt and Gaza, as demarcated in the Partition Plan). Against this, Egypt asked for cast-iron guarantees against Israeli expansion beyond agreed borders.[78] On 11 October 1948 senior officials from both sides went to Geneva to continue exploratory discussions. Four days later Israel attacked Egyptian positions in the Negev, taking control of the whole area except for the Gaza Strip. Having achieved its objective it concluded an armistice. In spite of specific undertakings, it expelled the remaining Arab inhabitants of Falluja, Beersheba and other areas.[79]

Syria also recognized its own weakness and wanted to make peace. In January 1949 it informed the United States of its wish to end the war so as to concentrate on economic development.[80] In return for a peace settlement it sought self-determination for the Palestinian Arabs and an alteration of the international frontier through the Sea of Galilee in order to protect the traditional fishing rights of Syrian peasants. A few days later Israel rebuffed a direct Syrian approach. It did not want the former to obtain a share of the precious Jordan river water resources.[81] Two months later a *coup d'état* brought Husni Za'im to power for a short-lived dictatorship of four and a half months. Within a week of assuming power, Za'im instructed the army to open armistice negotiations with Israel, and himself offered to meet Ben Gurion to discuss a formal peace agreement.[82] Za'im proposed to absorb and resettle 300,000 refugees in the potentially rich wheatlands of the Jazira region of north east Syria. But Ben Gurion was unwilling, in Flapan's words, 'to consider any meeting or ceasefire until all the Syrian bridgeheads in Palestine were, abolished and Syrian troops withdrawn to the international border.'[83] According to Avi Shlaim, 'During his brief tenure of power [Za'im] gave Israel every opportunity to bury the hatchet and lay the foundations for peaceful co-existence in the long term. If his overtures were spurned, if his constructive proposals were not put to the test, and if a historic opportunity was frittered away . . . the fault must be sought not with Za'im but on the Israeli side.'[84] In the end Syria withdrew to the international border, leaving the vacated area as a demilitarized zone to which civilians were to be allowed to return to live. Once again Israel made the area virtually uninhabitable and, from 1949 into the early 1950s, its 2,000 or so inhabitants were pressured into leaving.[85]

Jordan also wanted peace and made this clear in May 1949, soon after signing the armistice agreement. But Israel was reluctant to conclude an agreement.[86] It knew the weakness of its neighbours and did not wish to bargain if it did not have to. As Israel's own representative at the Lausanne Conciliation Conference observed, 'The Jews believe it is possible to obtain peace without [paying] any price, maximal or minimal. They want to achieve (a) Arab surrender of all the areas occupied today by Israel, (b) Arab agreement to absorb all the refugees in neighbouring (Arab) states, (c) Arab agreement to rectification of the present frontiers in the centre, south and Jerusalem area in favour of Israel only . . . etc, etc.'[87]

Israel did not get peace but only a grudging set of armistice arrangements which suited it and, in fact, the Arab states better. The latter, uncertain of their own stability, could claim devotion to the Arab destiny. In the long run the leaders of Syria, Egypt and Transjordan may have been relieved that Israel spurned their offers. An unpopular peace agreement might have toppled them.

When Sharett succeeded Ben Gurion as prime minister in December 1953, he initiated a secret peace diplomacy with the new Egyptian ruler, Gemal Abdul Nasser. In early 1954 Nasser, faced with overwhelming economic problems, was amenable to a settlement. Secret meetings took place later that year, but these were deliberately undermined by government colleagues -- Pinchas Lavon (Minister of Defence) and Moshe Dayan (Chief of Staff) – at the instigation of Ben Gurion.[88] During 1954 and 1955 the IDF mounted 'a series of operations, some of which were carried out without Sharett's knowledge and with the conscious aim of foiling his conciliatory diplomacy.'[89] In spring 1954 United States diplomats in the area were convinced that Israel was deliberately undermining UN truce arrangements to secure a better position.[90]

Sharett's efforts were foiled. Egypt and Syria became firmly convinced that Israel was determined to conduct a fundamentally bellicose policy towards them and armed accordingly. In a report on the Lavon Affair (an Israeli attempt in 1954 to bomb British and French installations in Egypt to damage their relations with Cairo), the director of the CIA wrote 'He [Sharett] attached major importance to this channel [his quiet diplomacy] through which he hoped to negotiate a lasting peace between Arabs and Jews . . . The disillusioned Nasser, believing [the Lavon group] had been used to deceive him, ordered a discontinuation of all contacts with the Israelis.'[91]

There were plenty of border violations from the Arab side during this period, mostly unauthorized guerrilla raids. Nevertheless, by 1964 US diplomats in the region still cabled Washington that Arab governments were averse to open conflict with Israel:

> Arabs concerned selves basically with preservation situation envisioned in [the UN armistice agreements] while Israel consistently sought gain full control. Even this aspect struggle visibly cooling during past eight years, with Israel emerging victorious largely because UN never able oppose aggressive and armed Israeli occupation and assertion actual control over such [demilitarised] areas, and Arab neighbours not really prepared for required fighting . . . Most UN observers accord certain amount credit to Syrians for restraint over long period in face Israel seizure control in D/Z's [the demilitarised zone] by force or constant threat of using it.[92]

In Egypt's case, even as late as 1965, the head of Mossad, Israel's intelligence service, believed Nasser wanted an *entente* with Israel. But like Sharett a decade earlier, Prime Minister Levi Eshkol was thwarted by the Israeli military chiefs.[93]

The uses of violence and rhetoric

From 1948 onwards, being far stronger, it was in Israel's interest to perpetuate a state of turmoil on its borders whereby it could improve its position. Arab governments were not blameless, though on the whole they did try to act with restraint. But they could not necessarily control either Palestinian raiders (or would-be returnees) or trigger-happy soldiers.[94]

However, it was undeniable that from the outset of Zionist settlement, Arabs had reacted violently. The first major outbreak of inter-communal violence, which left 200 Jews and 120 Arabs dead, resulted from an Arab explosion of anger in Jaffa in 1921. Both sides behaved with frenzy and savagery, and the Medical Officer for Jaffa was 'struck with the number of wounds on each body and the ferocity of the wounds'.[95] In 1929 Arabs attacked and killed 133 Jews in Jerusalem, and massacred another fifty-nine men, women and children in Hebron. During the 1936 Arab revolt many more attacks occurred against Jewish civilians, of which the most deliberate perhaps was the killing of nineteen men, women and children in Tiberias in October 1938.[96]

After 1967, the Palestinians took upon themselves the task of liberating their country in the belief that no one else would do it for them. In its National Charter, the Palestine National Council enshrined armed struggle as the only way to liberate Palestine.[97] During the following years constituent members of the PLO and splinter groups conducted a number of attacks upon Israeli, Jewish and international targets in order to advance this aim. When infiltration through Israeli lines into Palestine became increasingly difficult, Palestinian groups resorted to terrorist attacks and hijackings.

Of these groups, the Popular Front for the Liberation of Palestine (PFLP) was the most active and the most explicit. In the words of its leader, George Habash, 'We believe that to kill a Jew far away from the battlefield has more effect than killing a hundred of them in battle; it attracts more attention.'[98] Furthermore, he justified it on the grounds that 'the fact that the enemy relies on a worldwide Zionist movement means that it is the legitimate right of the Palestinian revolution to strike blows at the enemy outside Palestine.'[99]

'The assumption that by striking boldly in the international arena . . . the Palestinians could call world attention to the Palestinian political problem'[100] was fundamentally correct. The international community did react, though not to address the political problem but to crush the terrorists. In 1970 the PFLP's hijack and destruction of two civil airliners provoked the Jordanian authorities into crushing the PLO armed presence in the country. In 1972 Black September, born out of the events in Jordan, infiltrated the Olympic village at Munich and killed eight Israeli athletes. Under the eye of television cameras, it achieved massive publicity, but of a wholly adverse kind. Worldwide horror was intensified by Black September utterances, 'The Palestinian guards his identity only by bravery and action . . . it was necessary to revive . . . the spirit of the revolution . . . One of the objectives of the [Olympics] operation was to return the Palestinian to the source of his strength. The resistance says to the Palestinian: you have nothing except what you can obtain through your heroism.'[101]

Nothing more clearly demonstrated the counter-productivity of violence against civilians than the DFLP's attack on the northern Israeli town of Ma'alot in 1974. In many ways the DFLP offered the most realistic approach to a solution and had, like Fatah, rejected striking at targets outside Israel. In March 1974 DFLP's leader, Na'if Hawatma produced a statement published in the Hebrew *Yediot Aharonot*, which spelt out the DFLP's understanding of a 'national authority' as the creation of an independent Palestinian state in the West Bank and Gaza, a definition not formally adopted by the PLO until 1977.[102] For Israeli leftists such a statement, which included reference to 'the Israeli people', was immensely encouraging as promising a constructive and peaceful dialogue with elements of the PLO. But two months later the DFLP mounted an attack on Ma'alot, in which twenty-four Israelis, mainly hostage schoolchildren, were killed when Israeli paratroopers stormed the DFLP position.[103] It is only possible to understand the destructive effect of this episode or Munich in the prospects for peace by listening to Israelis speak about it. For them Munich and Ma'alot exemplify a hatred for the Jewish people which is of a piece with the Holocaust.

Although in terms of quantity Palestinian terrorism was less than 5 per cent of all international terrorism over the period 1967–87, Palestinians have established their pre-eminence as exponents and practitioners of terrorism by the use of sensational tactics.[104] Those who sent their men to commit such acts underestimated the impact these events would have and that, since they implied the vulnerability of ordinary civilians everywhere, especially in Europe and the United States, they were bound to have deeper negative impact than Israel's bombing of refugee camps, which remained psychologically distant and anonymous from Israeli and Western opinion. This impact was heightened by the skilful propaganda use made of them by Israel compared with the ineptitude of the Arabs and particularly the Palestinian armed factions.

The more conventional armed struggle launched first from Jordan and then from south Lebanon cannot be described as successful either. It did not persuade Israel to negotiate and it did no more than negligible material damage. It could almost be described as convenient since it justified Israel's refusal to talk with the PLO and its sympathizers and gave it the opportunity to drive a wedge between the latter and the host government. In Lebanon, the Palestinian armed struggle found itself in a quagmire of conflict with the Maronites, the Shiites and the Syrians.

The Uprising has demonstrated the greater efficacy of civil disobedience and protest in the Palestinian context. The people of the occupied territories have achieved much more in the liberation struggle than the PLO has achieved in twenty years of violence. It is still unclear whether the PLO has understood that violent acts have a long-term damaging impact on its efforts to secure a political dialogue with Western countries, let alone with Israel itself.

It must be said, too, that codification of PLO ideology in the Palestine National Charter was also unhelpful to the struggle. Article 6 of the Charter is particularly controversial. It reads 'The Jews who had normally resided in Palestine until the beginning of the Zionist invasion will be considered Palestinians.' It was natural that Zionists took this to mean that the Charter denied all Jewish Israelis the right to live in Palestine and did, indeed, intend 'to drive the Jews into the sea'. In fact this is not what Article 6 says and it could equally be understood to mean that the rights of Zionist Jews were contingent on recognizing Palestinian Arab rights, most importantly the right of the refugees to return.

When he addressed the United Nations General Assembly in November 1974 it was clear that Arafat did not interpret Article 6 as Zionists had done, for he said 'When we speak of our common hopes for the Palestine of the future we include in our perspective all Jews now living in Palestine who choose to live with us there in peace and without discrimination . . . that we might live together in a framework of a just peace in our democratic Palestine.' Israelis and many others preferred to believe their own inference from Article 6 and argued that only the revocation of the Palestinian National Charter would convince them that the PLO *might* have changed its objective of liquidating Jewish Israelis. Some Palestinians who recognized its damage argued that Article 6 should be expunged, but they were opposed.[105] Politically, the PLO felt it could not tear up its charter, however embarrassing certain aspects of it might have become. It simply referred to it less and less.

Although the Palestinians acquired an unrivalled reputation in their violence and extreme rhetoric, Israel's words and acts were barely less extreme. It denied the Palestinians national identity or the right to determine their own future. Its atrocities against Arabs did not end in 1948–9. In its reprisals it often deliberately destroyed civilians as well as combatants, for example at Qibya in 1953.[106] But there were more serious cases. In October 1956 troops deliberately shot forty-nine inhabitants of an Israeli Arab village, Kafr Qasim, for breaking a curfew of which they had not been informed. News of the massacre was at first suppressed and questions asked by a Communist Knesset Member were expunged from the records.[107] A few days later troops occupying the Gaza Strip during the Sinai campaign massacred many, possibly hundreds, of Palestinians in Khan Yunis and Rafah.[108] After the 1967 war troops on the Jordan river apparently routinely shot civilians trying to slip back home.[109] In 1982 in West Beirut Israeli forces were implicated in the Sabra/Shatila massacre, 16–18 September.[110]

Can the lessons be learnt?

There is no value in a catalogue of past atrocities if nothing is learnt from them. For both Palestinians and Jews these excesses have so far been an incentive for hate rather than a warning for the future. Both communities have demonstrated their ability to commit terrible acts. If the question of Palestine/Israel is not settled peaceably, past atrocities will probably be eclipsed by future ones.

Neither Jewish Israelis nor Palestinian Arabs have yet shown much propensity for a critical re-assessment of the past. Yet as General Yehoshafat Harkabi, one-time director of Israeli military intelligence and an inveterate critic of the PLO and its charter, pleads 'self criticism is imperative in order to counterbalance the tendencies to self-righteousness that stem from basic Jewish attitudes . . . No factor endangers Israel's future more than self-righteousness.'[111] In Israel few have responded to the uncomfortable truths raised by Harkabi, or other Israeli scholars.

So far, Palestinian leaders do not seem to have been significantly more receptive than Israeli ones to such warnings. In 1987 one of the more potent Palestinian myth-breakers, the cartoonist Naji al Ali, was assassinated, probably by Palestinian leaders who have been the target of his satire. As ordinary Palestinians knew best, Naji al Ali brought a ring of truth to the Palestinian scene, revealing the corruption and sterility implicit in much of the overly hallowed 'struggle'. A Palestinian scholar, Hisham Sharabi, recounted in late 1987 what a friend had told him on his return from a holiday in his birthplace, Tarshiha in western Galilee. 'And how do they [Israeli Palestinians] feel about the Arab regimes and the PLO?' Sharabi asked. 'They express nothing but ridicule of both' was the reply.[112] Earlier in the year Sabri Jiryis, director of the PLO Research Centre, had attracted hostility by his published criticisms of the PLO: 'In its present form – and in terms of man-power, organisation, administration, level of thinking – [the PLO] is unable to deal with the various aspects of the Palestine question; it cannot achieve more than what it has already done so far, which is not sufficient. What is now required is to change or transform it – by fair means if possible, by any means if necessary.'[113] Jiryis predicted the danger of a serious break between those in Palestine and those outside. Seven months later the Uprising took place. Palestinian 'myths' are being broken by the growth in stature and self-confidence that result from the Uprising and the self-criticism this growth has inevitably fostered.

The more impressive Israeli and Palestinian critics of the conduct of their respective national affairs, seem more able to share analysis of the conflict with each other than with the more adversarial of their own co-nationals. They may not agree on much, but even acceptance of the need for an impartial analysis of beliefs, myths, events and policies by both sides is a vital precondition to any progress towards peace. That, in itself, is an immensely important task barely begun.

9
THE OCCUPIED TERRITORIES: THE PROSPECTS

The objective of the Uprising is the achievement of freedom from those, be they Jewish or Arab, who wish to keep the Palestinian inhabitants enchained. This not only means freedom from Israel or from Jordan but also freedom from the handful of 'bosses' within Palestinian society itself. This has already, to some extent, occurred. The establishment of the Unified National Leadership of the Uprising, the creation of neighbourhood committees, and the authority of the *shabab* (young men) in ensuring that committee decisions are implemented, already indicates a sea change in the way Palestinian society operates. The *mukhtars*, the *hamula* or clan heads, the large landlords and the city merchants have all found their position weakened by the Uprising. They have either co-operated, or gone to ground. Even if the Uprising is suppressed, it is unlikely that such 'bosses' will recover their previous power. The Uprising, in this regard, has already achieved a substantial change on the ground, a change that works in favour of the cause of independence and against the interests of Israel and, if it still harbours any, those of Jordan.

There is a more profound sense in which the people of the occupied territories have already achieved freedom through the Uprising, and the question now is whether this new-found freedom can be retained. This is freedom of mind and spirit, the discovery of dignity and self-respect after decades of helplessness, frustration and dependence. This is the most important outcome of the Uprising. However, fundamental though the rediscovery of dignity and self-respect may be, it will obviously not satisfy those who have risen against the occupation.

The critical political question must be: can the Uprising wrest the occupied territories from Israel's grasp? If so can it be sustained for as long as proves necessary, even if that means another generation? In spring 1988 when it was clear that Israel had no hope of bringing the Uprising to an early end, the idea that the occupation was irreversible was strongly challenged by Palestinian commentators. 'I think,' said the Birzeit sociologist, Salim Tamari, 'the uprising has defeated the notion that the physical, economic and infrastructural integration of the West Bank and Gaza into the body of the state of Israel creates irreversible facts. This has been the position of the school of thought associated with Meron Benvenisti, and on the Palestinian side with people like Sari Nuseibeh. Integration has proceeded too far, they said. The best we can hope for now is a fight for civic equality, for enfranchisement. It is quite remarkable that it took Palestinian children just a few days of street rage to demolish this bizarre argument.'[1] Yet this refutation ignored the fact that even if the Palestinians achieved a semi-permanent state of ferment, withdrew a substantial proportion of their labour from Israel and dramatically reduced their dependence on Israeli goods, even with all these demonstrations of the solidarity and durability of the Uprising, Israel might still feel under no real duress to leave the territories.

Whether Israel can bear the cost of the Uprising cannot yet be assessed with any certainty. From July 1988 some of these costs were becoming clearer. Reserve military service had been increased from thirty-one to sixty-two days, implying added defence, economic (in days reservists were absent from work), and moral costs (in terms of the unpopularity of duty in the territories). The United States embassy estimated the monthly military and police bill at $120 million, plus a further $38 million in indirect costs.[2]

Furthermore, there were the first admissions of damage to the national economy. In early July official figures indicated that compared with the first quarter, exports in the second quarter of 1988 had declined by 12 per cent. 'July is the first month in which increase in exports has totally stopped. But signs of this decline have already been showing since April. Now it has been proved that it is a continuing phenomenon as a result of the current situation.'[3] One bank reported in September that the Uprising was responsible for a 2 per cent drop in national income, with the decline particularly marked in tourism (30 per cent down), and in Arab employment areas, textiles, cement and construction industries (15 per cent down).[4] In Jerusalem the municipal income was 4 per cent below budget requirement as a result of the Uprising.[5] But would such dents in Israel's economy be sufficient to break its hold? Would the Uprising find itself waging a war with no apparent outcome, except a bitter and costly stalemate?

This is the serious dilemma which the Palestinians under occupation face. Is there any point in sustaining the Uprising even when the initial euphoria has dissipated and still there is no glimmer of political freedom at the end of the tunnel? If the answer is yes, then it must be because the freedom of spirit already discovered is in itself a worthwhile gain that must not be relinquished. The success of the Uprising depends on the maintenance of that spirit, but it does not guarantee that Israel will give up the territories.

The unity achieved by the Uprising has been unprecedented, but a large number of Palestinians understandably fear that something may yet destroy it. One obvious possibility is that the authorities will, ultimately, crush the Uprising and re-establish the networks of informers through which the differences of opinion within the ranks of the Palestinian national movement can again be skilfully exploited, as they were previously. If the Uprising began to flag, might some elements be tempted to settle for less than self-determination?

A decision by Israel to negotiate with the PLO (or a provisional government) would imply great opportunities for the Palestinian people. The PLO would secure a legitimacy which has eluded it hitherto. If, indeed, Israel decided (as Labour implies it has decided) a negotiated settlement is unavoidable, then Israel would eventually be bound to recognize the PLO and negotiate with it. Any other position, as a number of Israelis have already observed, lacks credibility.

In fact an Israeli approach of this kind would be fraught with peril for the PLO. Bearing in mind the leadership's initial ambivalence concerning the autonomy proposals of the Camp David Accord, and its co-operation with Jordan, there is bound to be a fear in the territories that it may be persuaded to settle for less than they themselves are prepared to accept. Possibly the greatest threat to the Uprising is 'the potential of major differences between Palestinians over a specific plan for a political settlement of the conflict. If the PLO leadership is divided on this issue, division is likely to creep into the occupied territories as well and thus weaken the determination to sustain the Uprising . . . Internal differences among the groups comprising the leadership or between it and the Islamic movement could put an end to the national consensus and lead to the Uprising's demise.'[6] Such thoughts can only be speculative, but one can anticipate that the PLO, as a movement, may endure greater internal stress when it finally reaches the negotiating table, than it has done so far. This was precisely the experience of the Zionist movement, when it had to face the ideological and tactical implications of the decision to partition Palestine in 1947. The Revisionists rejected partition but were too weak to resist it, and the religious parties were cajoled into accepting a fudged definition of the Jewish State.[7]

The PLO leadership's willingness to negotiate with Israel and to fly controversial kites has been indicated on a number of occasions. In summer 1988 Arafat's adviser, Bassam Abu Sharif, accepted a two state solution unequivocally and indicated that Arafat would welcome a meeting with Israel's prime minister. There had been such indications earlier, as Shimon Peres acknowledged at the end of 1987. For example, Arafat had sought direct talks with Peres without international mediation in summer 1986.[8] However, the people of the territories have been far less willing to replace statements of principle with ploys to call Israel's bluff.[9] Palestinians under occupation do not trust unorthodox approaches to political problems, and remain uneasy about the PLO leadership's apparent propensity for departure from 'the national consensus'. If it comes to negotiations with the PLO, Israel will probably try to drive a wedge between the people of the territories and the PLO.

In November 1988 the Palestine National Council declared independence of the Palestinian state according to the Partition Resolution 181 of 1947, and formally accepted Resolution 242 as a basis for negotiations, implicitly recognizing Israel. In view of this declaration, any agenda for negotiations will have to be based on the demand for self-determination rather than self-rule, and on the borders in which the Palestinian state would be permitted to exist. Nothing else is likely to bring the Palestinians to the negotiating table. Undoubtedly many Palestinians hope that the declaration of independence will also supersede the damaging phraseology of the Palestine National Charter. If a provisional government were appointed, this would legitimize the popular committees.

The demographic and refugee challenge to Israel

For Israel the immediate challenge of the Uprising is to its authority, but the longer-term challenge is to its political skill. Israel may suppress the present Uprising, but future and increasingly desperate revolts are probably inevitable if this one fails, because of the growing demographic pressures.

The population of the occupied territories will increase substantially by the end of the century. Official estimates indicate populations of about 1,211,000 and 865,000 for the West Bank and Gaza by the year 2002, compared with 1985 figures of 813,400 and 525,500, increases of 48 per cent and 64 per cent respectively.[10] It is possible that a fall in natural increase or a rise in emigration will reduce this figure. But it is more likely that the estimate will be exceeded. For the government has admitted that while it includes in its statistics Israelis who have been absent from Israel for under a year, it omits to count Palestinians absent for a similar time span. It seems that has already led to a subtantial underestimation of the population of the West Bank and Gaza. If Palestinians were counted on the same basis as Jews there were probably, at the beginning of 1988, 1,090,000 (rather than 860,000) Palestinians in the West Bank, and 650,000 (rather than 560,000) in the Gaza Strip, indicating an underestimation of 27 per cent in the former and 16 per cent in the latter case.[11] This would probably mean a population in 2002 of 1.5 million in the West Bank and just over a million in the Gaza Strip.

Much significance has been given to the year in which Arabs outnumber Jews in Palestine, but the watershed is essentially psychological. If Israel has not relinquished the occupied territories by that time, it is hardly likely to enfranchise its population. Without electoral power, the growing Palestinian population will define its power in terms of economic strength and civil disobedience.

Popular unrest will be fuelled by the conditions of life. The harder these are, the more determined people will be. It is possible that by 2000 AD the West Bank could have successfully withdrawn most of both its labour and custom from the Israeli market. It is less likely in the case of Gaza, which has so few resources of its own. Account must be taken of the pressures of population growth, for example the annual increase of about 7,000 in the work-force. Unless the economy expands to employ new entrants (as well as to draw migrant labour back from Israel) there will be a growing pool of economically discontented young people in the towns, camps and villages of the territories. These may be driven to seek employment in Israel, thereby undermining the current drive of the Uprising, or they may take to the streets.

Population growth in the next decade will create severe social strains.[12] Housing is a good example. In 1983 49 per cent of the population in the West Bank and 45 per cent in the Gaza Strip lived at a density of seven persons per household.[13] This, of course, implies an even distribution, whereas in fact 32 per cent of the population lived in one-room dwellings and 46 per cent in two-room dwellings.[14] Between

1967 and 1987 39,000 new dwellings were built, providing only one housing unit for an increase of every nine people.[15] Merely to cater for the projected population increase between 1988 and the end of the century on the basis of seven persons per housing unit (i.e. mainten- ance of the present housing density) will require the construction of 90,000 new homes.

The refugee communities present in more than one way the most serious security problem for Israel. The refugee camps are the most overcrowded parts of the territories, and are therefore the hardest parts to control. In addition, because the refugees may not accept their sojourn in the territories as an indefinite one, Israel faces greater long- term danger from the refugees than it does from the indigenous inhabitants.

Forty-four per cent of the West Bank population and 70 per cent of the Gaza Strip population are refugees. Indigenous and refugee Palestinians have forty years' experience of living together in adverse conditions, welding them together powerfully in pursuit of political objectives. Their political solidarity has been convincingly expressed in the Uprising. The Unified Leadership (UNLU) has taken great care to stress in its comminiqués that its objectives include not only freedom for the occupied territories but also the refugee right of return. Indeed, some communiqués have placed the return of the refugees as the first demand.[16]

It is not yet clear what UNLU means precisely by the return of the refugees, and it probably does not yet wish to be specific. It will be anxious to support the PLO, if negotiations take place, in obtaining the optimum terms. It may be thought that the right of return, starting out as a maximalist one, will be bargained down to the widely accepted view that the 'return' can only be to the occupied territories. Such a possibility must be considered in the light of how it would affect the indigenous inhabitants and refugees, both those already in the territories and those outside.

Understandably both refugees and non-refugees are reluctant to voice any differences publicly, and little research has been done on their respective attitudes. However, the widespread assumption that the refugees are, or could be an integral part of West Bank and Gaza society must be questioned.

Differences between the two categories exist. In Gaza the refugee population was poorer but less traditional than the host community in 1948. Some refugees still feel a tension: 'I can't help feeling differently towards the town people . . . I grew up in the poverty and clutter of the camp . . . I look at the town people as people apart from us. They've grown up with relatively secure roots, relatively peacefully . . . They do OK under the occupation.'[17] Have the rigours of forty years of foreign rule largely obscured the sense of difference in Gaza? Without careful research it would be difficult to say.

In the West Bank, however, available evidence suggests that tensions do exist. All Palestinian families have a strong sense of honour, a sense closely associated with protection of land. The study of one particular village near Ramallah reveals that 'Most villagers have an extremely negative opinion of these refugees because of their dishonourable behaviour [in abandoning their land] . . . [That most refugees did not own their own land but cultivated it for absentee landlords] does not justify their shameful conduct to West Bankers.'[18] For the refugees, on the other hand, 'As non-property owners, the most critical element of honour for them was that of women's chastity. Hence, from their perspective they fled to better defend their honour.'[19] As a result of these quite different views on self-respect and honour, there is very little social interaction between villagers and refugees, regardless of whether the latter are in camps or in villages and towns.[20]

It is with this social dimension in mind that the future must be considered. In the year 2002 out of the total population (which one must assume will be substantially over the official projection of 1.2 million in the West Bank and 865,000 in Gaza), at least 533,000 and 605,000 respectively will be refugees.[21] Bearing in mind that even at present the absence of any real economic infrastructure makes the whole population highly dependent upon employment outside the territories, rapid population growth is bound to create enormous economic and social strain. Without land of their own, the refugees are likely to remain poorer than the indigenous population until industrial employment can be generated.

If a Palestinian state were created by 2002, one that had not secured any refugee return to Israel, the difference between the current population burden and what it will be by 2002 presents an immense challenge in itself. Such a state would almost certainly be unable to begin to consider any return of refugees from outside Palestine before it had been able to create a rudimentary and expanding economic infrastructure. Its first challenge would be to satisfy the resident refugees sufficiently, particularly those of Gaza, so that they would not destabilize the state in its early critical years.

In view of the appallingly impoverished and overcrowded conditions of the Gaza Strip the acquiescence of the resident refugees, even in a provisional settlement which did not relieve population pressure, must remain doubtful. Because of the refugee presence, the population density of Gaza is 4,000 persons per square mile (rivalling Hong Kong as the world's highest population density), instead of the 1,400 persons per square mile it would have been without the refugee presence. By the end of the century population density will be about 7,000 persons per square mile. The two largest Gaza camps, Jabaliya and Rafah, give some idea of the local problems involved. By 1988 each had just over 50,000 inhabitants. By the end of the century they are likely to house over 80,000 people each, without the attributes or amenities of a city, and without any planned increase in area or housing provision.

Any development programme would take years merely to accommodate most residents in productive employment. Unlike Israel in 1949, there would be no abandoned villages and lands on which to develop the state. The task would be formidable and success could not be assured. It is difficult to imagine the Gaza Strip being a stable political entity under such conditions.

Such are the challenges for the West Bank and Gaza Strip *before* contemplating a return to the occupied territories of any of the refugees who currently live outside Palestine. They are, in themselves, powerful reasons for non-refugees to wish that even those refugees already in the territories could return to their place of origin.[22]

These are solid reasons why the current idea in international fora, of resettling most refugees in their present host countries and bringing a minority to the West Bank and Gaza Strip, seems unlikely to prove workable in a comprehensive solution. Even with a partial return to the West Bank and the Gaza Strip, the economic strain might well cause everyone, indigenous inhabitants, refugee residents and refugee returnees, to repudiate any political settlement already reached until better terms could be secured. For example, if one were to assume that Lebanon's refugees (probably numbering about 390,000 by 2002) but not those of Syria or Jordan, would return, the West Bank population could be over 1.9 million by 2002. In the imaginary event of all those of Syria and Jordan also returning, the West Bank would have a population of 3 million in all. In neither case would absorption be easy since there is no industrial infrastructure, even of the kind Israel enjoyed in 1948, to build upon.

Israel's reasons for hanging on

The foregoing might seem to present an overwhelmingly persuasive case for Israel to get out of the territories as quickly as possible. However, it has powerful reasons for hanging on. A wide consensus exists in Israel that the territories are strategically essential as a military defensible zone in which any future Arab attack could be absorbed and repulsed, and for the early warning facilities which can be deployed on the eastern escarpment of the West Bank. The acquisition of long-range rocketry and space and aerial surveillance technology render the territories less significant militarily, but their psychological importance remains undiminished.

There is also a wide consensus that control of the territories' water resources is vital to Israel's well-being. About 475 million cu.m., one-quarter of Israel's annual water potential, originates in the West Bank. The annual potential of the West Bank aquifers is 600 million cu.m. of which Palestinian inhabitants are only allowed to use 20 million cu.m., less than 4 per cent of the total potential.[23] The rest is used by Israel or its West Bank settlements. In Gaza, too, in spite of its arid conditions, water is pumped to support Jewish agricultural activity not only in the Gaza Strip but also in the Negev.[24] It is inconceivable that Israel will willingly abandon water resources it considers essential to national safety.

With over 150,000 Jews settled in the 1967 territories, mainly around Jerusalem and areas within commuting distance of the coastal plain, Israel has another substantial reason for hanging on. To consider removing so large a number of people, it will have to be under far greater pressure than the Uprising has so far created.

After one year of Uprising no sign appeared of any great change in Israeli public opinion, which seemed solidly behind government policy of stringent treatment and, if it dissented at all, thought that the government had been too lenient. Commentators reported a shift to the right in public opinion, confirmed by the November 1988 election.[25]

The relative stability of Israeli public opinion, and its proximity to government policy is noteworthy. Over the past twenty years there have been no significant divergencies between society and government policy towards Arabs nor have there been massive fluctuations in public opinion, except in the case of the Sadat initiative. Even in that case government policy and public opinion remained closely in line.[26]

Attitudes with regard to the occupied territories have remained reasonably consistent and have fluctuated little. Compare, for example, public opinion of the government's handling of the Uprising in January 1988 with that expressed during June 1967 when harsh measures were used to establish control. In 1967 47 per cent thought army treatment of the inhabitants 'just right', while 51 per cent felt it was 'too good'.[27] A poll in January 1988 revealed that 46 per cent of the electorate approved of government handling of the Uprising, while 40 per cent thought it too lenient. Only 7 per cent considered it had been too harsh.[28]

There has also been relative stability in attitudes over the fate of the occupied territories since 1967. Immediately after the June war a poll reported that 47 per cent of Jewish Israelis wanted the territories and their inhabitants to remain under Israeli control, 22 per cent wanted the inhabitants to depart (while implicitly hanging on to the territories) and only 21 per cent favoured granting the inhabitants a state of their own.[29] Broadly speaking, until the 1980s between one-half and two-thirds of the electorate wished to retain the territories.[30]

The possibility of returning part of the territories in return for peace, however, indicates a less rigid posture. A poll in 1984 suggested that while 44 per cent opposed giving up any of the West Bank, 34 per cent were willing to give up parts. Only 18 per cent favoured giving up all except East Jerusalem.[31] Another poll attempted to measure the changes of opinion from March 1983 to July 1985, a period during which the PLO seemed weak but also desperate to find a diplomatic path to peace negotiations. With the exception of 7 per cent favouring the establishment of a Palestinian state, attitudes hardened slightly: one-third favoured continuing the status quo, one-third favoured giving up most of the occupied territories while the remaining third favoured annexation. More significantly, when denied the option of the status quo and faced with a choice between annexation or abandonment, 70 per cent of those who had favoured the status quo now favoured annexation, and only 23 per cent or so opted for giving up most of the territories.[32]

The general stability of these findings was confirmed by a subsequent poll, 1985–7, monitoring Jewish attitudes regarding the surrender of all or part of the territories to Jordan in return for a peace settlement.[33] Those unwilling to concede anything fluctuated between 49 and 44 per cent; those willing to forego parts of the territories between 36 and 32 per cent; those willing to evacuate all except East Jerusalem fluctuated around 15 per cent, while those willing to evacuate everything acquired in 1967 hovered around 4 per cent.[34] Following the Uprising there was a decline of 6 per cent in those refusing to cede any territory and a 5 per cent increase in those favouring a partial surrender of territory. Those willing to abandon all the territories except Jerusalem increased by only 1.6 per cent.[35]

Two points should be made about these opinion polls. They all presupposed that the territories would be surrendered to Jordan or to 'the Arabs', and not to the PLO, and they virtually all show that roughly half the Jewish electorate is agreed that there should be no territorial concessions. Polls carried out in 1986 and 1988 suggest that public opinion favouring annexation rose from 54 to 57 per cent, reflecting the relative solidity of this unyielding majority.[36] The balance remains divided and weakened between a majority who support the surrender of part of the territories and the minority, a miniscule 4 per cent if one includes East Jerusalem, who are ready to withdraw almost completely.

At no time has a majority favoured returning the territories to Arab control. At no time, either, has the Jewish electorate achieved anything like consensus over what to do with the territories and this naturally discourages any government, even a relatively strong one, from departing too far from a position on which it could expect majority, or nearly majority support.

Furthermore there has been a persistent majority of 60 per cent or more favouring the retention or expansion of the Jewish settlements in the occupied territories.[37] Forty-seven per cent of Labour voters and 80 per cent of Likud voters would oppose any dismantling of the settlements.[38]

Jerusalem

The fate of Jerusalem is, naturally, the most difficult area for discussion. On account of the holy places, and their historic links with the site, no more than 4 per cent of Jewish Israelis are willing to relinquish those areas captured in 1967, not even members of the Citizens' Rights Movement, the Zionist party (apart from Mapam) closest in sympathy to Palestinian national aspirations.

Yet the Uprising demonstrated conclusively that cities are essentially communities of people rather than buildings of stone, and that in this particular case, the two communities are as deeply divided as ever. While Israel's annexation demonstrated the ideological view of virtually the whole Jewish Israeli spectrum, the city's 130,000 Palestinian inhabitants have rejected the fact of union. Since 1967 the Palestinian population has grown from 26 to 28 per cent of Greater Jerusalem. The growth is slow and slight but, as minorities go, the Jerusalem Arabs are large enough to cause permanent tension in the city. (It should not be inferred that Arabs are the only ones to cause tension, since most of the violence in the Old City in recent years has arisen from the enthusiasm of yeshiva students (all of them newcomers to the Old City) to drive the Arab population away from certain areas which they consider particularly their own. Palestinians hold the view that the security forces have been rigorous against Palestinian violence, but a good deal less so with such students.)

Jewish population growth in Jerusalem is inflated by the higher birth rate of ultra-orthodox Jews, and this raises an issue going on within Jewish Jerusalem, one that has some bearing on Arab–Jewish relations in the city. This is between Zionists subscribing to the legitimacy of Israel conceived as a secular state and those whose loyalty is ambivalent or who believe that 'Zionism is diplomatic tourism', as one hoarding in the ultra-orthodox quarter of Mea Shearim puts it. Ultra-orthodox opposition to the state is predicated on the belief that any attempt to hasten the divine timetable for the Messiah's return is necessarily a blasphemy. One or two anti-Zionist commentators have been tempted to suggest that these ultra-orthodox Jews will work with the Palestinians against the Israeli State. In spite of recognition of the PLO and advocacy of a secular Palestinian government, Naturei Karta (as some of these ultra-orthodox are known) are too eccentric to be thought of in terms of a political alliance. They have no natural political allies among the Palestinian community, neither with leftists who recognize that their cast of mind is not dissimilar to that of Islamic fundamentalists, nor with the fundamentalists themselves who, like Naturei Karta, have a narrow agenda confined within the bounds of their own Holy Writ.

Nevertheless, the ultra-orthodox do have significance in this question, since their high birth rate makes them the fastest growing Jewish community in the city. In 1972 they were 22 per cent and by 1985 were estimated at 26 per cent of the city's Jewish population.[39] Ultra-orthodox Jews and Palestinian Arabs together form approximately 45 per cent of the city population, and may become a majority by 2010. It is unlikely that this will outweigh Israel's emotional commitment to the control of all Jerusalem, but it does affect the perception of Jerusalem as capital of the Jewish State. Whether Israel would consider abandoning control of the Arab part of the city, though possibly settling for some kind of joint or international administration of the Old City must remain doubtful. It is only likely to do so if it needs peace badly enough and can get this no other way.

Jewish views of the PLO and a Palestinian state

There are two other issues, perhaps not as sensitive as Jerusalem, which are central to any negotiated settlement and which attract vehement views: negotiations with the PLO, and allowing the establishment of a Palestinian state.

There has been greater vehemence but less stability on these issues than on other questions. In 1974 three-quarters of Jewish Israelis considered the concept of 'a Palestinian Arab people' an artificial one.[40] Three-quarters of the Jewish public also believed that the real Palestinian intention was to destroy Israel, a view justified by the high level of terrorism during the previous three years and by the PLO objective of replacing Israel with a binational state in all Palestine. Sixty-nine per cent of the Jewish public opposed any Palestinian representation in Geneva in 1974.[41] A similar percentage supported the government's decision not to negotiate with the PLO. To the very end of the 1970s between two-thirds and three-quarters remained hostile to any negotiation with the PLO or to the establishment of a Palestinian state.[42] In early 1978, during the euphoria of the Sadat initiative, this hostility reached a crescendo, when 87 per cent opposed negotiations with the PLO, and 91 per cent of a poll opposed a Palestinian state.[43]

Compared with the 1970s, the 1980s have seen a shift in opinion. Despite the small proportion, 7 per cent, advocating a Palestinian state for the West Bank and Gaza,[44] about 40 per cent of the Jewish electorate is now willing to consider negotiations with the PLO if the latter rejects violence and recognizes Israel's right to exist. However, opinions on this issue seem to be volatile and inconsistent.[45] In 1988 the Uprising seemed to have increased the proportion willing to negotiate with the PLO to nearly 50 per cent,[46] presumably that portion of the electorate willing to consider ceding part but not all of the territories.

The opinions expressed by respondent Jews do not solely reflect the need for security, nor the fear that the PLO and the Palestinians intend to destroy Israel, substantial though these fears may be. They also reflect a growing sense of proprietorial rights over the territories, particularly among the younger generation. An estimated 60 per cent of 15–18 year olds in 1987 considered that Jews had full rights to the occupied territories. Conversely, only 30 per cent considered that the Palestinian inhabitants had *almost* full rights, and only 10 per cent considered that Jews had minor or no rights in the territories, as opposed to roughly one-third who considered that the Palestinians had no rights in these territories.[47]

It is easy to attach too much importance or accuracy to such opinion polls. Nevertheless, there can be little doubt that successive Israeli governments have decided upon their policies very much with the popular mood in mind. During the Sadat initiative, the government stayed closely in step with popular attitudes. In September 1982 it had no hesitation in rejecting President Reagan's peace plan since over two-thirds of the electorate were opposed to it.[48] In practice no Israeli government has ever strayed far from the public consensus. How this affects the choices Israel must make will be considered in the final chapter.

10
ISRAELI
PALESTINIANS:
THE PROSPECTS

If there were some evidence of a fundamental change in state policies towards Israel's Palestinian minority, it might be possible to envisage a gradual process of reconciliation of the latter to the state. Virtually no such evidence exists. Only the short-lived incumbency of Ezer Weizman (1984–6) as minister responsible for Arab affairs has so far suggested any possibility of change. His were modest gestures, but they gave hope. He broke with past practice by calling for talks with all Arab local councils, including those controlled by Rakah which had previously been boycotted.[1] In the face of Jewish protests he accorded five Palestinian border villages financially beneficial front-line status (which allows extra funding to support villages liable to attack from Lebanon). He also caused a furore in the cabinet in August 1986 by pushing through the release of 12,000 dunums (1 dunum = 1,000 sq.m. or approximately ¼ acre) of the 65,000 dunum area known as 'Area Nine', in central Galilee, a zone originally appropriated by the British in 1944. The argument concerned less the release of land, than the allocation of 2,500 dunums of the area to its original (Palestinian) owners. For Palestinians a significant feature was that the lion's share, 9,500 dunums, was designated 'state land' and was thereby incorporated into the national patrimony, land available to Jews rather than Arabs.[2] If this balance of the share of national assets is indicative of what a more benign future may hold, most Palestinians would probably admit it is better than hitherto but nowhere near the balance necessary to avert a clash of interests between the Jewish State and the growing minority.

Palestinian demography: the national implications

There are still Jewish Israelis who believe that while social and economic problems exist, the problem is not a political one, nor is it one which directly challenges the viability or identity of the Jewish State. Take, for example, the words of an elder statesman and one of the more dovish members of the Labour Party, Abba Eban. He recognizes more readily than most of his party colleagues the need for the occupied territories to determine their own future and that putting off the moment for negotiations with the PLO is foolish. Yet on the question of Israel's own Palestinians Eban believes 'Israel can certainly define itself as a "Jewish State" even if there is a non-Jewish minority of 25 per cent. My own impression is that if we refrain from adding large new populations to the existing area of Israeli sovereignty the Arab population will scarcely exceed 20 per cent since its own rate of natural increase will decline in the measure that economic prosperity increases.'[3]

This statement, from a man who has taken an active interest and constructive concern in Arab–Jewish relations inside Israel, raises a number of critical points about population growth and the distribution of wealth in Israel. The most significant is the demographic prognosis. This is a large area in which some Israeli Jews have tended to exaggerate the demographic 'problem' while others have tried to minimize it as if, once it was ignored, dangerous rightist attitudes towards the Palestinian minority would begin to dissipate.[4]

Looking back at the twenty year period since 1967, there is a clear difference between the growth of Israel's Palestinian and Jewish populations. The former has doubled in the twenty year period 1967–87 (including the population of East Jerusalem for both dates), almost exclusively as a consequence of a high natural birth rate. The Jewish population, on the other hand, has increased by 50 per cent, but of this increase a substantial proportion resulted from immigration. Without immigration, it has increased by approximately 29 per cent, a high figure compared with most industrialized countries, but no competitor for the Palestinian rate.[5]

The view that the Palestinian minority 'will scarcely exceed 20 per cent' cannot be substantiated. It will reach this level in 1993 and over 24 per cent by the year 2005, when Israel's total population will be 5.7 million of whom some 4.3 million will be Jewish and 1.35 million

Palestinian.[6] The Palestinian birth rate, as Eban states, has fallen and is falling rapidly, although this is a recent phenomenon. But it is still far higher than the Jewish rate, 3.6 compared with 2.6 live births per mother.[7] Even if it tails off further, as is likely, it is highly probable that the Palestinian proportion of Israel's population will rise to exceed 30 per cent within the foreseeable future, probably between the years 2015–2020.

The portents of Palestinian demographic growth are already apparent. In 1985 the Palestinian proportion of Israel's under-twenty-year olds was almost 24 per cent. By the year 2005 this proportion will be 31 per cent.[8] Unless the birth rate of Palestinians in this age group falls to one equal with their Jewish counterparts at that time, one may expect the proportion of Palestinians in the Jewish State to increase still further. Young Muslim Palestinians are likely to continue to have a higher birth rate than their Jewish counterparts for some time to come.

There is another factor besides the falling birth rate on which predictions must be made. Today the Palestinian population of Israel is significantly younger than the Jewish one. In 1985 44.5 per cent of Palestinians were under the age of fifteen, compared with 30 per cent of Jews in the same category.[9] The age pattern of the former has already begun to move into conformity with the latter. Over the twenty year period 1965–85 the percentage of Jews under fifteen years of age fell only marginally, from 32 per cent to 30 per cent by 1970 – a level at which it seems (misleadingly) to have stabilized. Among Palestinians, however, 50 per cent were under fifteen until 1975 when the proportion started to fall slightly, but with accelerating speed, to 47 per cent in 1980 and 44.5 per cent in 1985.[10]

However, there will still be a substantial difference in age structure between the Palestinian and Jewish communities in 2005. Even over a fifteen year period, 1990–2005, while the Jewish population increasingly conforms to a pattern characteristic (except for the impact of immigration waves) of industrialized countries, the Palestinian population at the end of this period will still exhibit the youthful characteristics of a developing country. Indeed, while the proportion of Palestinians under the age of fifteen will continue to fall (to 42.6 per cent in 1990, 41.8 per cent in 1995, 39.4 per cent in 2000 and 37.6 per cent in 2005), the Jewish pattern will also change. By 1990 the proportion of Jews under fifteen will have dropped slightly to 27.9 per cent, but by 2005 it will have dropped to 25 per cent.[11] In other words, the *gap* between the respective proportion of Jew and Palestinian in this vital age group will have changed only slightly.

It is reasonable to assume it will take at least until 2020 and possibly beyond, before the Jewish and Palestinian Israeli age structure patterns correspond. By that time it seems that, even with a continued fall in birth rate, the proportion of Palestinians under twenty are likely to be 35 per cent or more of the age group nationally, with the distinct possibility of reaching 40 per cent or more by the middle of the twenty-first century.

Such a prognosis ignores changes in migration balance and other factors, such as the growing need for Palestinian women to work (and therefore have fewer babies), and the acute overcrowding of Palestinian living units which discourages large families. The likelihood is that both communities will experience a slow-down in population growth, although whether this will be more marked among the Palestinians or Jews is, at this juncture, difficult to say.

There is unlikely to be any significantly increased Jewish immigration in the future, certainly not on a scale to affect the demographic balance in the Jewish favour. There was a substantial decline in the level of immigration from 1980 to 1985 and the indications from 1985 onwards were that immigration is falling below the least optimistic official assessment. Furthermore, the tensions arising from the Palestinian demographic challenge and the state's response, may encourage an increasing number of Jewish Israelis in the 20–40 age band to emigrate.

When the Palestinian proportion of Israel exceeds 30 per cent, the majority of Jewish Israelis will probably cease to believe in the Jewish State as presently constituted. For it will have already become an Arab-Jewish state, and may hold the prospect of becoming as Arab as Jewish in the second half of the twenty-first century.

Since most of the Palestinian population is so young, its electoral potential is still largely masked. Whilst being over 17 per cent of the Israeli population overall, it constituted only 12 per cent of the adult (and voting) population of Israel in 1985. By the year 2000 this voting percentage will have increased to almost 20 per cent. Although in 1987 there were only six Palestinian Knesset members as a result of segmented voting, there could be sixteen or more in the year 2000. Unless there is a radical change in Israel's treatment of its Palestinian minority, the Palestinian vote is likely to consolidate, as Palestinians become increasingly aware of their voting potential. They are likely to use this potential to protest against discriminatory state policies. The first indications of such a consolidation came after the 1988 election in which the three anti-Zionist parties, Rakah/Hadash, PLP and the Arab Democratic Party, forfeited two Knesset seats by their refusal to pool surplus votes. After the election Rakah/Hadash joined the PLP in calling for an electoral bloc in future elections.

This would probably heighten the sense of political confrontation between Jew and Arab, creating further polarization within the Jewish electorate. Labour might be caught in a particularly difficult position. It might not be able to move to the left in case this led to a substantial electoral loss. Parties to its left are committed to Palestinian rights in the occupied territories, and to economic and social equality for Israel's own Palestinians. Labour's own inability or unreadiness to grant Palestinians social or economic equality has already cost it dearly. It has been losing its Arab vote over a number of years. In the 1950s and 1960s, Labour enjoyed over 50 per cent and sometimes over 60 per cent of the Arab vote, double the proportion it obtained from the Jewish electorate. In 1981 it obtained only 41 per cent of the Arab vote (29 per cent directly and 12 per cent from affiliated Arab lists), but in 1984 it dropped to 23 per cent.[12] The loss of this vote is now crucial. If Labour enjoyed the level of support in 1984 it had enjoyed from Palestinian voters thirty years earlier, it would have been able to govern without Likud. Had it received fewer Arab votes than it actually did in 1984 it would have been unable to participate with Likud in government, which is more or less what happened in 1988. Because of Labour's response to the Uprising its Arab Knesset member, Abd al Wahhab Darawsha, resigned in January 1988, to form his own Arab Democratic Party. Other erstwhile Palestinian supporters of Labour voted for the Citizens' Rights Movement instead. These two factors reduced the Arab vote for Labour in the 1988 election to only 16 per cent, despite one of the highest Arab electoral turnouts ever.[13]

It is unlikely that Labour can win back Arab votes without undermining Jewish support. In order to increase its Jewish vote it must demonstrate resolution and confidence that it can implement a solution which will solve Israel's problems and meet its security needs. It is unlikely this can be done without alienating either Palestinian or Jewish voters.

Labour and Likud have a common objective in thwarting the emergence of any coalition or party which threatens the Jewish State. Both parties have demonstrated their determination on this issue. In 1964–5 Labour crushed al Ard because, although it was committed to 'safeguard the rights of the Arab and Jewish peoples', it refused to recognize the State of Israel.[14] Twenty years later Likud tried to prevent the emergence of the new Progressive List for Peace when it registered for the Knesset elections of 1984.[15] It was primarily concerned with the opportunity the PLP offered for non-radical Jews (who did not wish to vote for Hadash/Rakah) to recognize the PLO. Although it failed in its efforts, Likud published a communiqué referring to its leaders' 'subversive intentions' and 'identification with enemies of the State' (a reference to its call for direct negotiations with the PLO). In fact while the PLP failed to draw many Jewish voters, it did attract many Arabs who had either not voted before or had previously voted Labour. As a result the Arab participation in 1984 was 68 per cent higher than it had been in the 1981 election.[16] The new National Unity government proceeded to make life as hard as possible for the new party.[17]

On 31 July 1985, one year after the elections, the Knesset amended the electoral law (Basic Law: the Knesset, Amendment 9) by an overwhelming majority to limit both the growth of the Jewish racist party, Kach, and also the growth of a consolidated Palestinian vote:

> A list of candidates shall not participate in Knesset elections if any of the following is expressed or implied in its purpose or deeds: (1) Denial of the existence of the State of Israel as the state of the Jewish people; (2) Denial of the democratic character of the State; (3) Incitement to racism.[18]

Since PLP regards the State of Israel as 'belonging to all its citizens, Jews and Arabs' it can hardly be charged with racism, but the Supreme Court may at some future date rule that this clause in its statutes denies 'the State of Israel as the state of the Jewish people', for the latter means implicitly that the state belongs to the Jewish people *everywhere*, not merely those who actually live in Israel. This is not a position that the PLP can accept, since it can only mean to Palestinian Israelis that they are lesser citizens than Jews who at some future time decided to make Israel their physical as well as spiritual home.[19]

Technically, as an anti-Zionist party Rakah is also at risk. In 1977 Shmuel Toledano, who as the Labour prime minister's adviser on Arab affairs had gained a reputation for his liberal attitude to Arabs, recommending the banning of Rakah if necessary in order to maintain the fragmentation of the Arab sector.[20]

Rakah enjoys two forms of protection which do not apply to the PLP. It can claim a respectable longevity of political practice dating back to the Mandate days, including support (even by its Arab members) for the 1947 United Nations Partition Plan. Older members of the Labour Party would probably resist attempts to outlaw it. More practically, Rakah has fulfilled a critical role in Soviet–Israeli relations since the diplomatic break between the two states in 1967. Furthermore, because of its pro-Moscow stance it has become clear that its support among Palestinians is limited. It therefore serves as a useful outlet for Palestinian radicalism while failing to unite all Palestinians behind its banner.

For the time being Rakah is more secure than the PLP, but its future cannot be assured. The formation of a Palestinian coalition which provoked a crisis in electoral politics might persuade the government of the day to force Rakah to pledge its explicit loyalty to the Ninth Amendment in a way it could not do without risking self-destruction.

In view of the growing electoral power of Palestinian Israelis, it must be concluded that by the Ninth Amendment the state has given notice that, while allowing democracy within certain limits, it will not allow democracy the possibility of redefining the identity of the state to modify its Jewishness. For dissident groups, like Abna al Balad, the Ninth Amendment came as proof, if proof were needed, that the aims of the state and of themselves were mutually exclusive. Likewise, despite the existence of specifically (Jewish) religious parties, there would be no point at all in the Islamic Association seeking to participate in national political life.

If the Ninth Amendment proves inadequate to stem the advance of the Palestinian vote of 'loyal dissent', the state may seek alternative methods to block the purposes of the Palestinians and of those Jews sympathetic to them. The most frequently aired argument in recent years has been that the citizen's right to vote should be contingent on the full discharge of national duties, meaning the completion of military service. As has been noted, military service has for some years been the qualification for certain state welfare benefits. There is already, therefore, a precedent for invoking military service as a basic qualification for full civic benefits.[21] Alternatively, in view of the inherent weakness of government under Israel's proportional representation system, Labour and Likud might seek a change of system to raise the threshold for Knesset representation or introduce a constituency system to blunt the impact of the Palestinian anti-Zionist vote.

Palestinian demography: the regional dimension

There is another important dimension to the demographic debate, a regional one. Ever since the foundation of the state in 1948, successive governments have endeavoured to intersperse Palestinian population concentrations with Jewish settlements. This policy is constantly threatened with failure. The Palestinian proportion in western and central Galilee, the Little Triangle, and the northern Negev, steadily increases. Wadi Ara, abutting the north-west tip of the West Bank, is totally (98 per cent) Palestinian, and the rest of the Little Triangle is also overwhelmingly so. In the northern Negev, the Beersheba region is predominantly Palestinian bedouin outside the town itself. The Northern District (all north of a line from the northern side of Haifa to the West Bank) became more than 50 per cent Palestinian at the end of 1985.[22]

Furthermore, although there are strong disincentives to settling outside these areas, there is increasing Palestinian encroachment, both by natural increase and by migration, into mixed localities. In Galilee there is Palestinian penetration of previously entirely Jewish settlements, for example Nazaret Illit and Carmiel. There is also progressive Palestinian expansion westwards, with penetration of coastal towns, Hadera and Nahariya, and south east of Tel Aviv at Rehovot and Rishon le Zion.[23]

Haifa is the kind of case that causes anxiety in Israel, for it combines a sense of decline on the edge of Israel's Jewish heartland with the Arab demographic threat. Its population of 225,000 is both ageing and shrinking. Fifteen per cent is over 65, well above the national average. In 1984 2,500 more people left the city than came to it. The Jewish birth rate in the city declined by 25 per cent in the decade 1975–85. Jewish natural increase is only 3.2 per thousand, partly on account of the high death rate, while the Palestinian natural increase is 20 per thousand. The Palestinian community grew by 143 per cent between 1981–6 and increased overall from 5.7 per cent in 1980 to 8.2 per cent of the city population in 1986. Palestinians have expanded into the poorer Jewish areas, especially Hadar Ha-carmel, as Jews move up the hill.[24]

Successive governments have attempted to thwart such developments, and to diffuse the Palestinian population by interspersing it with settlements. But the Northern District has a history of demographic

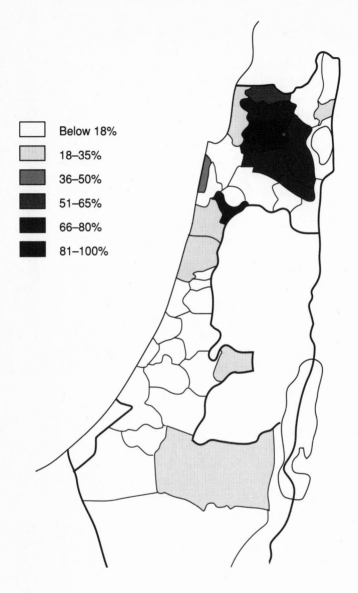

Map 4   Palestinians in Israel by natural region

Source: Statistical Abstract of Israel No. 37 (1986) pp. 35–37. This map
includes the population of East Jerusalem.

defeat for the Jews. Following the events of 1948–9 the state at first achieved a ratio of 29:21 in the Jewish favour,[25] but found it impossible to maintain. In spite of its efforts during the thirteen years 1972–85, the Northern District's Jewish population only increased by 95,000, a figure insufficient to rival Palestinian population increase.[26]

During the decade 1985–95 the government plans to settle 181,000 Jews in the Northern Region to swing the balance back in Jewish numerical favour.[27] On present estimates the Palestinian population of the Northern District will be about 483,000 in 1995 compared with 387,000 Jews. If the planned additional 181,000 settlers materialize, it would ensure a Jewish majority until the end of the century but for not long thereafter. However, the discussion is hypothetical since there is no likelihood of this target being achieved. The demographic pattern will probably be nearer to the table below, making the Northern District about two-thirds Palestinian by the year 2010.

Table 2   Northern District Population Projection (assuming no Jewish immigration, in thousands [rounded])

	1985	%	1990	%	1995	%	2000	%	2005	%
Jews	349	50	371	47	387	44	408	43	429	40
Palestinians	351	50	418	53	484	56	550	57	631	60

Source: Based on national population projection in *ISA 1986*, p. 63.

The pattern of Jewish population movement in Israel is little different from that in other industrialized and industrializing countries with the predominant movement being towards the economic centre of the state (the central coastal plain), and away from the periphery (the north and the Negev). Since the development towns of the Northern District, with the exception of Carmiel, are in a state of economic stagnation, one geographer forecasts 'massive (Arab) penetration of the Jewish cities in the Galilee (such as Upper Nazareth) up to a threat to the continuation of their Jewish existence'.[28] In the south too, in the Beersheba–Arad–Dimona region, precisely the area where the bedouin are consolidating their demographic hold, 1,500 Jews moved away in 1985 alone.[29] The only areas where large numbers of Jews wish to settle is within commuting distance of the two metropolitan areas of Greater Jerusalem and Tel Aviv. This implies a partial gravitation back toward the Jewish–Arab demographic pattern of the Mandate (with the notable exception of Jaffa, Haifa and coastal Arab villages), with large Palestinian areas inside Israel echoing the 1947 Partition Plan allocation of Arab areas south of Hebron and in Galilee.

State failure to evolve a fresh Arab policy

In spite of these demographic indicators, which have been well known since the early 1980s, there has been a failure to evolve a coherent policy in response to developments since 1966. The identity and temperament of the ministers charged with special responsibility for Arab affairs 1984–8, Weizman, Arens and Milo, reflects the ambivalences implicit in state treatment of its minority. In his *Arabs in the Jewish State*, Lustick characterized state policy from the rise of Palestinian nationalism in 1975 as either 'integrationist' or overtly repressive, in both cases implying the creation of new control mechanisms.[30] Neither characteristic has implied any fresh approach.

The 'integrationists', predominantly Labour, proposed wooing the Palestinians by improvement of the quality of life, cessation of land expropriation, development of employment opportunities and the advancement of accommodationist young professionals within the system. It also advocated, in the words of one expert, 'the adoption of a strong uncompromising stand against hostile elements and the creation of appropriate means to deal with the roots of the problem . . . We must not shrink from taking practical measures against Rakah, which has proven its ability to change the balance of political forces and to use its success as a lever for nationalist agitation.'[31]

Integrationists have no intention of allowing the growth of an independent Palestinian economic sector. They feared the growth of economic power more than the growth of political power. As long as the Palestinians remain weak economically, it was argued, they would be unable to use their political muscle.[32]

The other position, of overt coercion, was characterized by the attitude of Ariel ('Arik') Sharon who, as minister of agriculture in the first Likud administration, adopted a stringent policy of evictions and house demolitions against bedouin and villagers, an offensive 'I have launched to stem the hold of foreigners on state lands.'[33] Where Labour politicians had spoken in euphemisms about 'developing' the Galilee, and preventing 'illegal settlements', Sharon and many like-minded supporters of the Israeli Right spoke frankly of judaizing the Galilee, of demolishing the homes of 'foreigners', and if necessary, expelling trouble-makers. In this trend there was less talk than among integrationists of co-opting 'positive elements' or of doing anything to improve the quality of life for Palestinians within the Israeli State.

In practice, it is difficult to distinguish between integrationist and coercionist trends, since the objective remains broadly the same, and since both groups recognize the need for some integration and some coercion. It is essentially a matter of balance and degree.[34]

There is a good deal of overlap between Labour and Likud, except in one vital respect. As in the West Bank and Gaza so also in Israel, the Labour Party takes a closer and more manipulative interest in the Palestinian community. Its concern about integration of positive elements derives from its understanding of the importance of social and economic organization. While many right-wing politicians advocate direct repression, Labour Party officials recognize the importance of maintaining sophisticated control mechanisms.[35] Labour remains anxious to manipulate, forestall, co-opt and control any Palestinian attempts at social organization. Thus, while Likud appears more threatening to Palestinian interest in the long term, it has been far less interfering and manipulative in daily life than Labour.

The absence of a fresh policy, a 'coherent, explicit and comprehensive approach', to use Ian Lustick's phrase, and the ambivalence between integration and coercion can be seen in government reports during the past fifteen years. In September 1976 a secret government memorandum written by the Northern District Commissioner, Israel Koenig, was leaked in the press. Koenig, who had held the post since 1966, was concerned by the disintegration of state control through village notables and the opportunities a democratic system might afford to radical Palestinians, particularly in view of Rakah's victory in the Nazareth election of 1975. He advocated renewed efforts at Jewish settlement to thin out Palestinian population areas, and to confine the latter;[36] the establishment of 'a policy of reward and punishment for leaderships and communities which express any kind of hatred of the state and Zionism'; and 'a special team to investigate the personal habits of the leaders of Rakah and other negative types and bring its findings to the attention of the electors'.

In the economic sphere Koenig urged the use of central marketing agencies to 'neutralise and place difficulties in the way of Arab agents'. Socially, too, 'The government must find ways to neutralise the giving of grants to families with many children in the Arab population, either by making them conditional on the family's economic position, or by transferring responsibility for the grants from National Insurance to the Jewish Agency or Zionist Organisation which will give them only to Jews.'[37] He wanted to encourage Palestinians to emigrate. 'Travel abroad for studying should be made easier, and it should be made harder to return and arrange work – such a policy will encourage emigration.'

Koenig's memorandum provoked a public outcry from Palestinians and a substantial number of Jews, who called for his dismissal. Prime Minister Rabin denied having seen the memorandum and refused to dismiss Koenig.[38]

Eleven years later, in October 1987, the Hebrew daily *Ha'aretz* published leaked details of a report entitled *Principles for Government Policy Regarding the Minority Sector in Israel*, commissioned by the Likud minister Moshe Arens and drafted by his adviser for Arab affairs, Amos Gilboa.[39] Like Koenig, Gilboa recognized the growing solidarity of the Arabs with fellow Palestinians in the occupied territories, and the danger of a monolithic Palestinian entity straddling the 1949 Armistice Line. 'The main consequence of this process,' Gilboa wrote, 'is the strengthening of feelings of bitterness and frustration, the development of a spirit of national identity under an alien power, and an awareness of the organisational, economic and demographic power that they possess.' The apparent new element in official thinking was Gilboa's recommendation 'to aim for a situation of *equality* [my emphasis] and integration between the minority population and the Jewish majority by providing the resources needed, and to create the conditions whereby the minority population can feel it is an integral part of the state.'

This objective seemed to represent a *volte face* in official thinking, allowing for the first time the possibility of genuine and full Palestinian participation in the life of the Jewish State.

Other leaked parts of the report, however, suggested that far from the empowerment of the Palestinian community implicit in the foregoing, the real intention was continued co-optation, but within a revised framework appropriate to changing circumstances. For example, the report recommended that one aim should be 'to forbid the establishment of an independent Arab party with links with the PLO and to ban bodies acting towards the implementation of autonomy for Arabs in Israel; and to forbid and frustrate any illegal or subversive activities'.

'Outside the formal framework of the legal parties,' it continued, 'there is a certain amount of Israeli-Arab organisation directed towards a separation from the Israeli official system,' and it named the committees for the Heads of Arab Local Councils, for Arab Education and for the Defence of Arab Lands. As already noted, the Committee for the Heads of Arab Local Councils was first founded by Labour as a means of control and also to thwart the growing local power of Rakah. After 1975 it became a coalition of different Arab political viewpoints (as reflected in municipal and council elections) in an effort to obtain budgetary equality with Jewish local councils. In the absence of a political party representing specifically Arab concerns, it helped organize civil rights protest activities. By 1988 it had not made any statements suggesting secession from the state. Similarly the Arab Education Committee was concerned with the content and quality of education in the Arab sector. It did not have a political agenda, except in the sense that the disparity between the Jewish and Palestinian education budgets was itself a political issue. As for the Committee for the Defence of Arab Lands, this remained a one issue movement devoted to the prevention of the further expropriation of Arab lands. Rakah, which had played a substantial part in the creation of this committee, remained firmly committed to the territorial integrity of the Israeli State within the 1949 Armistice Line.

Gilboa's identification of these organizations indicated that his view of 'dissidents' was not confined to the extra-parliamentary groups like Abna al Balad which genuinely challenged the legitimacy of the state, but included 'loyal dissenters', the Rakah and PLP voters.[40] In order to prevent external assistance to such 'hostile' groups, he suggested that foreign money should only be transferred to Arab bodies with the prior permission of a regulatory body (or subject to new legislation) to ensure that no money came from unapproved sources.[41] He also recommended that all Arab institutions should either be integrated into official government institutions or, where this was undesirable, that such bodies should be ostracized.

Although his specific recommendations were different from those of Koenig, Gilboa's apprehension concerning growing Palestinian assertiveness and his concern to contain and control this phenomenon appear broadly the same. Thus, while the new notion of equality with the Jewish majority was adumbrated, there was no sign of any real change in government policy.[42]

The Gilboa report was complemented by the publication of two other government reports. The first of these, the Markovitch report (commissioned in late 1986 and completed in early 1987), concerned the question of illegal Palestinian housing. In spite of a decision taken by Peres, Weizman and Bar Lev (the police minister) in August 1985 to suspend the policy of demolition, this had been resumed after Weizman's replacement by Moshe Arens in Yitzhak Shamir's new cabinet in autumn 1986. No one was quite sure how many illegal homes there were, and estimates varied considerably.[43]

Many structures had 'grey' status, that is they were declared illegal but the owners were not necessarily required to demolish them. Some had been declared illegal because they had no permit, others because they had been put to a use not originally permitted, for example living accommodation used for agricultural or trading purposes or *vice versa*.

The Markovitch report recommended the destruction of 500 out of a total of 2,332 homes currently under demolition orders in the Triangle, Haifa and Jerusalem.[44] Furthermore, it recommended the evacuation (and demolition) of tens of hamlets and bedouin concentrations both in the Galilee and in the Negev. Some of these bedouin settlements were little more than *tanakat*, shanties built from old oil drums and other pieces of metal sheeting. Others, however, were far older settlements. For example, the hamlet of Aryan, near Ar'ara in Wadi Ara was already over 140 years old but was scheduled for demolition on account of its proximity to two settlements built in the mid-1980s, Katzir and Hinanit.[45]

The other report produced by the (Labour) minister of economic planning, Gad Ya'cobi, concerned the economic development of the Northern District up to the year 2000.[46] The overall purpose of the plan was to create incentives to draw more settlers into the region and to discourage emigration, especially among the younger generation. Although it looks at the whole Northern District, it is those areas with large Arab constituencies which command the report's main attention. These areas are the western Galilee uplands, lower Galilee from Acre eastwards to Nazareth, and coastal Galilee, from Rosh Hanikra to Acre. Twenty-eight thousand Jews live in forty-five settlements in the uplands of western Galilee, compared with 150,000 Palestinians living in twenty-four villages. In other words the average Palestinian settlement contains 6,250 inhabitants compared with 622 inhabitants in the average Jewish settlement.

Despite a smaller and richer Jewish population and the fact that already more lands are in Jewish than Palestinian hands, the report proposes to increase Jewish landholdings and to contract Palestinian-held lands further.[47] Lands for the Jewish sector are to be appropriated by 'adjustment of landownership', a euphemism for expropriation from neighbouring Palestinian communities. For example, Jabal Kamana near Carmiel, considered by the report to be a reserve area for development happens to be the ancestral home of certain bedouin.[48] In another case, lands pertaining to Saffuriya village above Nazareth, are earmarked for appropriation for industrial development of Nazaret Illit. Nazareth has much greater need of this land than Nazaret Illit, since it has double the population and less land available.[49]

At the time that the Ya'cobi report was in circulation, unemployment in Nazareth among Palestinian workers stood at 22 per cent, the highest in the country.[50] Yet no land allocations for industrial development were made in the report for Palestinian localities, on the technical grounds that they could not be, since these localities did not hold approved master-plans.[51]

The growing damage and dangers

If the population were static, the existence of such proposals to benefit the Jewish but not the Palestinian community would imply governmental intention to reinforce the status quo rather than to accelerate a deterioration for Palestinians. However, by the end of the century, the time limit for the Ya'cobi proposals, there will be an additional 200,000 Palestinians in Galilee. Simplistically, one might assume that the progressive demographic change will lead to a shift in power in the north in favour of the Palestinians. Looking, however, at the economic implications, this is not so.

It has been calculated that every 1 per cent in population growth forces a country to spend an extra 4 per cent of its national income on demographic investment (opening up new land, factories, schools, hospitals, and so on) merely in order to 'stand still'.[52] In the case of the Palestinian population of Israel, increasing at an annual rate of 3 per cent, this would mean in terms of the Palestinians' proportionate share of Israel's 1985 GNP, the allocation of an additional $400 million or so each year, or about $530 per head of population, merely to stand still. There is no prospect of such additional funds being available. In 1986 only 4 per cent of the national development budget was allocated to Palestinian localities, working out at $5 per head.[53]

For the foreseeable future Palestinian areas will continue to lack any economic infrastructure of their own. Palestinian labour will remain predominantly unskilled and casual, since nothing has been done to improve the qualifications of school-leavers. One may confidently predict, therefore, that the unskilled labour market will be flooded with substantial additional numbers of Palestinians seeking employment. Nationally that figure could be about 100,000, of whom the overwhelming proportion, 75,000 or thereabouts, will be in the Little Triangle and in Galilee.

Unless employment opportunities are expanded, the increase in the Palestinian labour force will depress the value of Palestinian labour, leading to increased unemployment, increased poverty and greater economic disparity with the Jewish community. Already unemployment among Palestinians is about 50 per cent higher than among Jews.[54] The polarization between employment and conditions for Jewish and Palestinian labour will be likely to intensify. This will lead not only to an increasing sense of impotence and anger, but also an increasing availability of manpower, not otherwise employed, to give these emotions concrete expression. In other words, such an economic situation may well lead to civil unrest.

Closely related to the dismal economic expectations for Palestinians are the educational ones. At the beginning of the academic year 1987/88 there were 230,000 Palestinian children enrolled in the state education system. In the year 2005, when the newborn children of today will be nearing the end of secondary education, school enrolment will have almost doubled to a figure of between 400,000 and 450,000. In order to keep pace with the present inadequate levels faculty, building and equipment must be doubled by the end of the century. It is difficult to see this happening, since by 1987 there was already a shortage of 1,400 classrooms, or 40 per cent of the total classroom requirement in the Palestinian sector,[55] and an annual need for 300 new classrooms to keep up with population growth.[56] A school construction fund exists, with a current budget to construct fifty-two rooms for the Palestinian sector, compared with 498 rooms in the Jewish sector, revealing that while Palestinian children comprise 23 per cent of all Israeli school-children, they receive only 11 per cent of available funding.[57]

In 1985 a Ministry of Education report recognized that inequalities existed and recommended a phased programme gradually to improve standards, with the eventual aim of parity with the Jewish sector. However, the proposals were shelved owing to financial stringencies and in 1987 Palestinian education faced a 10 per cent cut in its budget, leading to further reductions. Instead of enrolling the 4,000 extra teachers necessary to bring Palestinian schools into line with Jewish ones, it was decided to cut 400 teaching posts.[58] The prospects, therefore, in the field of education are extremely gloomy.

The implications for community health in Galilee are serious too. Unless resources are developed and directed toward serving the majority of the population the health risks are considerable. At present there is a prospect of a population of over 600,000 Palestinians without access to hospitals within their own localities. The lack of proper sewage disposal and of safe drinking water will lead to massive pollution of the water sources of northern Israel with serious consequences for the whole population. Although Palestinians will suffer most, Jews will not remain unaffected. In summer 1988 an outbreak of polio in the Jewish town of Nahariya and the mixed city of Acre was blamed on sewage and water facilities in western Galilee.[59]

The longer these problems are left unaddressed, the harder it becomes to rectify them. No government will feel able to allocate the large share of the economic, education and health budgets necessary to achieve approximate parity with the Jewish sector. It is rapidly reaching a stage where a solution will only be available if an outside donor, for example the United States, considers the problem so important that it earmarks funds specifically to resolve the crisis. However, it is unlikely that even this would occur since, other reasons apart, it would be highly unpopular with the Jewish electorate.

The prospects for the Palestinian Israelis are bleak: continued political emasculation, economic weakness and high unemployment, increasingly unhealthy living conditions, and a collapse of the education system. The latter will encourage an increasing drop-out rate as Palestinians find the education they are offered inadequate. As in the Gaza Strip, Galilee Palestinians will seek their education on the streets, and it is likely therefore to be a political one.

One cannot help feeling that the state has seriously underestimated the radicalization of its young Palestinians. No one who meets Israeli Palestinian families can fail to be struck by the dissonance between the mild, almost placatory, manner of the older generation and the assertive nationalism of the younger one. Palestinian youth, imbued like youth everywhere with a passionate belief in changing things, is likely to follow the example of Gaza and the West Bank, resorting to disorder in order to force the state to take their grievances seriously. It follows, therefore, that the longer the state postpones dealing with these issues, the more terrible the clash of interests will be.

There is a danger that Israel may not be galvanized into a policy decision before a total physical and psychological separation of

Palestinian West Bank and Palestinian Israel is seen as absolutely imperative. This will be so if Palestinians both sides of the Armistice Line set themselves a new objective of political unity for all Palestine. This is not the make-believe dream of PLO supporters. It is the logical step that will be taken by a growing minority which has ceased to believe it can ever be accepted on an equal footing within the state.

The process has already commenced. In 1987 the Palestinian community, led by Hadash/Rakah, began a programme for national and civil equality by holding a widely observed one-day strike on 24 June. Although not very much attention was given to this strike by the Jewish sector, the demands of this programme are significant:

1 A complete withdrawal from the occupied territories and the establishment of an independent Palestinian state under the PLO.
2 Recognition of the refugee right of return, or to compensation.
3 Recognition of the Arab community in Israel as a national minority and as an indivisible part of the Palestinian Arab people, with full national and civil rights in complete equality with Jewish Israelis.
4 Repeal of land seizures and the return of confiscated land.
5 Return of land to refugees who are still inside Israel, and return of all *waqf* property and repeal of all legislation preventing the sale or lease of land to Arabs.[60]
6 Repeal of those provisions for the Druze community which detaches it from the Palestinian community.[61]
7 Repeal of all discrimination against peasant rights, and protection of bedouin rights in the Negev.
8 Repeal of all discrimination against Arabs in the nationality law, in local government, employment, education and health.
9 Participation of the Arabs in central and local government on an equal footing.
10 The establishment of an Arab university in Nazareth, and the creation of an industrial plan for the Arab sector on an equal footing with the Jewish sector.[62]

The radical nature of these demands scarcely requires elaboration. They indicate a strong identity of view with Palestinians elsewhere regarding the right to self-determination in the occupied territories, and the right of the refugees to return. The sense of grievance over the fate of all refugees, internal or otherwise, is strongly felt by virtually all Palestinian Israelis.[63] More seriously for the Jewish State, these demands indicate a refusal to accept the legitimacy of the measures taken against them since 1948. It is most unlikely that Palestinian Israelis expect to achieve much of this programme, but their willingness to remain Israeli citizens will depend upon how the state responds.

As in the case of the occupied territories, so also the question of Jewish Israeli attitudes towards the Palestinian minority in Israel is fundamental to the long-term prospects of Jew and Arab in Palestine, for popular attitudes will severely limit political options. State policy for the last forty years has already helped to mould popular attitudes towards Israeli Palestinians. This was not an inevitable product of conflict with neighbouring states or with the PLO, for the state could have chosen to make a distinction between Israeli and other Palestinians, and to have demonstrated this by its actions.

In fact, as chapter 6 describes, state policy towards its Palestinian minority has encouraged the Jewish public to treat Palestinians as untrustworthy sub-citizens. Not all Jews have taken this view, but the majority have. In an address to the Jewish–Arab Council for Peace Education in December 1985 Dr Sammy Smooha revealed the following Jewish attitudes to Arabs reflected in his survey work: 58 per cent did not believe it was possible to trust Arabs, 44 per cent believed that Arabs would never be as 'advanced' as Jews are, and 47 per cent wanted Palestinians to be encouraged to leave Israel.[64] Such findings echo those of a Van Leer Institute survey in 1980, which reported that 36 per cent thought Palestinians were 'dirty' and 42 per cent thought they were 'primitive'.[65]

In 1987 Dr Smooha collated the findings of surveys made in 1976, 1980 and 1985 which suggest that attitudes have remained largely static, and that on the whole there is a low level of consensus or amity between Israeli Palestinians and Jews. While 86 per cent of Palestinians consider the achievement of economic and social equality as both important and urgent, only 13 per cent of Jewish Israelis agree. On the contrary, 59 per cent of Jews view the achievement of economic and social equality as either not particularly important or actually unimportant. In fact most Jews are hostile to the idea of equality, for the same survey shows that 54 per cent of Jews want Israel to continue to favour Jews 'to a considerable degree', while another 22 per cent want Jews to be favoured 'to some degree'.[66] In other words, 76 per cent of Jews are hostile to granting Palestinian citizens equality. Sixty-six per cent of Jews advocate positive discrimination in favour of Jewish applicants for both university places and employment in the public sector. Only 19 per cent oppose such discrimination.

The same survey reveals that only 9.5 per cent of Jewish Israelis over the past decade have been willing to grant equality to Palestinian Israelis at the cost of some Zionist-Jewish characteristics of the state. One must assume that this group votes for one of the leftist Israeli parties: Rakah, PLP, Citizens' Rights Movement (CRM), Mapam or one of the smaller groups. The remaining 90.5 per cent of Jewish Israelis adhere to a 'control' policy towards Palestinians, reflecting the stance of the two main parties. A breakdown of this 90.5 per cent does not encourage optimism regarding the prospects for inter-communal amity. Thirty-seven per cent, identified broadly with Labour, believe Arab needs should be considered 'along with liberal supervision', in other words these support the integrationist control approach. An almost equal number, 36 per cent, support the overt coercion approach associated with Likud. The remaining 17.5 per cent advocate that Palestinian Israelis should be stripped of their civil and political rights and, if need be, expelled.[67]

There is some discrepancy with other surveys, but they all indicate that most Israeli Jews are not currently willing to allow Palestinian citizens a greater say in national affairs. For example, in 1984 a *Ma'ariv* poll reported 10.5 per cent of Jews advocating unconditional equal rights for Palestinians. Forty per cent considered equality should be contingent on fulfilment of national service, while another 20.5 per cent believed equality should be conditional on peace with the Arab countries. The remaining 28 per cent opposed the granting of equality under any conditions.[68] A *Ha'aretz* poll conducted in October 1987 found that 35 per cent of respondents believed Palestinians should not have freedom of speech, while 50 per cent wished to curtail their civil rights.[69]

It is instructive to compare these findings with those of a survey carried out immediately in the aftermath of the 1967 war.[70] At that time only 42 per cent of respondents considered that Israeli Palestinians should remain under the controls of the existing status quo, while 23 per cent believed they should enjoy equal rights. Twenty-eight per cent favoured their expulsion, half of these naming the occupied territories as the destination. Accepting that expulsion to the occupied territories no longer implies a solution in the way it might have done immediately after 1967; the conclusion must be that Jewish attitudes towards the Palestinian minority have indeed hardened in the period 1967–85.

Dr Smooha's 1985 survey work also indicated that 24 per cent of Jewish respondents favoured the denial to Palestinians of the right to vote in Knesset elections, compared to 40 per cent in the *Ha'aretz* poll two years later, in October 1987. As mentioned in chapter 8, 68 per cent opposed any electoral list running for seats in the Knesset if 'it accepts the rules of democracy and recognises Israel's right to exist but objects to the State's Jewish-Zionist character', reflecting support for Basic Law: The Knesset (Amendment 9) of 31 July 1985.[71] In other words, by 1986 probably two-thirds of the Jewish Israeli electorate favoured banning both Rakah and PLP from the Knesset elections. Assuming the stability of present Jewish attitudes, if the state finds itself under pressure from the Palestinian vote, it will be able to ban Rakah and the PLP under Amendment 9 in the knowledge that such a measure would enjoy majority Jewish support. Dr Smooha concludes 'Full participation by Israeli Arabs in Israeli democracy is, therefore, conditional upon their acceptance of the Jewish-Zionist character of the State', a manifestly self-contradictory statement.[72]

It may be arguable whether Dr Smooha's findings are corroborated by other opinion surveys. A survey of Jewish Israeli youth conducted in early 1987 revealed that 70 per cent of respondents wanted to prevent the participation of Rakah in Knesset elections, while 90 per cent wished to ban any party openly supportive of the PLO.[73] Furthermore, 80 per cent of respondents considered that Jews had more rights than Israeli Palestinians, and slightly over half of these considered Palestinian Israelis had either few or no rights. Forty per cent of respondents supported equal rights for all Israeli citizens, but 50 per cent favoured a reduction in the rights Palestinian Israelis already enjoy, and 40 per cent opposed the right of Israeli Palestinians to vote in Knesset elections.[74]

Opinion polls may be fickle yet it is difficult to dismiss the general consistency of surveys conducted in recent years in Israel. The message for Palestinian citizens is that they are generally unwelcome. A poll in 1984 indicated that 54 per cent of the Jewish population preferred to live in a state without any Arabs.[75] It is difficult to see any Israeli government being able to liberalize the situation for its Palestinians under such circumstances or, indeed, for Palestinians to conclude that they can ever hope to achieve equality by parliamentary means. During the 1970s when Israel, in spite of the 1973 war, was at the height of its power and self-confidence it was possible for the state to encourage Jews to be more accepting of Palestinian citizens. No such encouragement took place, and it is doubtful whether any regime could soften public attitudes once Jews feel more on the defensive against the Palestinian threat, whether this threat is military, civil or purely demographic. If public attitudes cannot be softened, the state will find it virtually impossible to act against the tide of public opinion.

Consequently, it must be concluded that when the Palestinian vote impinges on the Jewish monopoly of state power, steps will be taken to disempower the minority by changing the election procedure. If this results in Palestinian civil disobedience, increasingly overt coercive measures will be taken to enforce submission to Jewish rule. In the end, if conflict between Jewish determination to monopolize power and Palestinian Arab determination for equality becomes unremitting, the state will seek more drastic solutions to the problem. For some Zionists, however, the question lies in how Israel can survive such a moral trial and still remain the focus of hope and fulfilment for the Jewish people.

11
THE CHOICES
THAT MUST
BE MADE

The Uprising has precipitated the most serious challenge to Israel since its foundation, at precisely the time when it is less sure than ever of the direction it should take. The election of 1984 reflected the growing uncertainty and polarization of the Israeli electorate as the smaller parties of Left and Right gained at the expense of Likud and Labour. In the 1988 election this uncertainty and polarization deepened, with growing apprehension concerning the Uprising, regional security, the resurgence of the religious parties and the economy. The contrast with the self-confidence of 1967 could scarcely have been more striking.

Government, public opinion and 'the present continuous'

Yet the spectrum of opinion between an unyielding position, associated with Likud and the Right, and a more accommodating one, associated with Labour and the Left, has been evident in government policy since 1967. The former tendency found expression in 1967 in the Land of Israel Movement – the vanguard of New Zionism – which held, in the words of one of its leaders, that 'there is no alternative of going back to old boundaries, we are condemned to be strong.'[1] The latter tendency inclined towards reaching a settlement and 'feared the possible consequences for Israeli democratic society of rulership over an unwilling national minority which, in view of the differences in birth rate between Arab and Jew, was a potential majority.'[2]

In practice it was possible for government from 1967 to 1976 to embody both movements' point of view, since Israeli governments are 'large compromise-oriented bodies which strive to generate consensus in policy making. They reflect a wide spectrum of public opinion and are consciously created with that purpose in mind.'[3] Public opinion and governmental policy remained virtually identical, to the point that the absence of consensus over the future of the territories was embodied in an implicitly agreed policy of 'the present continuous'.

In reality, however, the government was indeed caught between the historic Zionist claim to all Eretz Israel and its security needs on the one hand, and on the other the possibility of a comprehensive peace if it conceded the territories which it had captured. Ostensibly it made no choice between these two options, but in practice, since the continued status quo implied retention of all Eretz Israel, it chose the former. All the Land of Israel Movement needed was an absence of government obstruction. The peace tendency – later expressed in Peace Now – was inevitably in the weaker position, since it could agree on what should not happen (indefinite retention of the territories) but not upon what should.[4]

Inevitably the government, albeit dominated by Labour, tilted increasingly toward the Land of Israel Movement view. The views of Dayan, Peres and Rabin carried the day. While some politicians made pronouncements both before and after the June War that Israel had no territorial ambitions, the day after the cease-fire began Dayan expressed another view, 'I don't think that we should in any way give back the Gaza Strip to Egypt or the Western part of Jordan to King Husayn.'[5] His integration of Israel and the territories, his view that the Arab population should retain Jordanian citizenship while Israel retained sovereignty over the territory, and his call to allow individual Jews to purchase land in the occupied territories (in addition to the government's security plan) all indicated the way things were going in practice. By 1973 forty-four settlements had been established and another fifty were planned.[6]

Some of Dayan's colleagues may have been opposed to all this but they were equivocal. Abba Eban, for example, warned that economic integration implied a policy of apartheid but he also made the quite contradictory statement that 'increased immigration will add to the strength of our gains in war; it is not enough to occupy territories, we must settle them too.'[7] In any case, the view of Dayan, Peres and Rabin prevailed because it was clear that this was what the public wanted.[8] A poll in November 1974, for example, revealed that three-quarters of the Jewish population wanted an expansion of the settlements, while two-thirds favoured annexation, a process which was implemented informally. Although it never formally endorsed it, the government implicitly accepted the Allon security plan of July 1967 which envisaged permanent retention of the eastern ridge of the West Bank, most of the Jordan valley, and the western coast of the Dead Sea, leaving Jericho in a narrow bridge between Jordan and the West Bank population concentrations.

Regional compromise or autonomy?

The territorial definition of security and the establishment of settlements meant that Labour 'had embarked upon a programme without accepting the ideology that underlay it'.[9] Its policy for a peace agreement remained blurred between retaining all or part of the occupied land and a solution whereby the Arab inhabitants returned to Jordanian sovereignty, or accepted self-government.[10] Labour called this approach 'regional compromise', which implied compromise solely within the occupied territories. It proposed to hang on to areas of strategic or political importance: (1) the Jordan valley (in order to insulate Palestinian enclaves from the Arab world to the East and to provide the first defensive line in a conventional war); (2) East Jerusalem including its environs where Jewish settlements with the appearance and function of fortresses had been built; (3) certain areas along the 1949 Armistice Line both of tactical value but also ones where dormitory areas for Tel Aviv and Jerusalem had developed. In effect this 'regional compromise' offered Jordan or some other Arab authority sovereignty over three enclaves, the populated areas north of Jerusalem (Samaria), similar areas south of Jerusalem (Judea), and the northern section of the Gaza Strip.

When Likud assumed power in 1977, explicitly embracing the ideology which Labour had in theory avoided, it accelerated Dayan's legacy of integration and settlements. Many Israelis may have been uneasy at Likud's explicit statements that none of the territories was negotiable, but this did not imply that they were committed to their return. Labour and its supporters were willing to abide by the autonomy scheme envisaged at Camp David, if it led both to military control of the territories and to a settlement with Israel's neighbours. The Camp David Accords allowed for the election of a self-rule body for the inhabitants of the occupied territories, and a peace treaty between Jordan and Israel which would determine the final status of those territories at the end of a five year period. While Egypt and the United States understood 'autonomy' to lead towards increased self-government with an implicit eventual outcome of full independence in association with Jordan, Likud had a fundamentally different view. It had no intention of ever relinquishing sovereignty of the occupied territories. Ideologically, despite its secular basis, it identified with the religious view expressed by Rabbi Z. Y. Kook, 'I tell you explicitly that the Torah forbids us to surrender even one inch of our liberated land.'[11] Likud proposed retaining sovereignty over two vital ingredients, land and water, but to allow the Arabs to organize their own lives within the municipalities and villages with regard to education, health, municipal services, and so on. Implicitly, even these services would come under the more general oversight of the Israeli ministries to which they related.

It proved impossible to implement self-rule partly because the Palestinians rejected its purpose, and partly because both Likud and Labour rejected the idea of Palestinian elections since these would lead to demands for a Palestinian state under a PLO government.[12] Both parties tried to create unelected Palestinian self-rule bodies, Village Leagues in the case of Likud, and mayors appointed in consultation with Jordan in the case of Labour after it shared government from 1984. Both formulas were rejected by the overwhelming majority of Palestinians.

Labour remains willing to hand sovereignty of the Arab population concentrations to Jordan but such sovereignty would be nominal in view of the size and vulnerability of the areas concerned. The offer of regional compromise is as far as public opinion allows it to go in its policy of trading territory for peace. Likud sticks to its Land of Israel ideology, insisting that its own version of autonomy and a 'peace for peace' arrangement with Jordan remains the only option. For most Israelis and for Israel's leading strategists, the Labour and Likud proposals are 'the only two options that are worthy of discussion.'[13]

In practice, the difference between the two options is slight. Neither accepts a return to the 1949 Armistice Line even with minor modifications, the interpretation which even the United States put on Resolution 242. Neither brooks a compromise in Israel's sovereignty over Jerusalem or the possibility of a Palestinian state. As Prime Minister Rabin said in the 1970s there will be 'no third state between Israel and Jordan'.[14]

Regional compromise maps based upon strategic considerations – produced by two leading strategic institutes, the Leonard Davies Center (the Hebrew University) and by the Jaffee Center for Strategic Studies (Tel Aviv University) – indicate that the area of disagreement

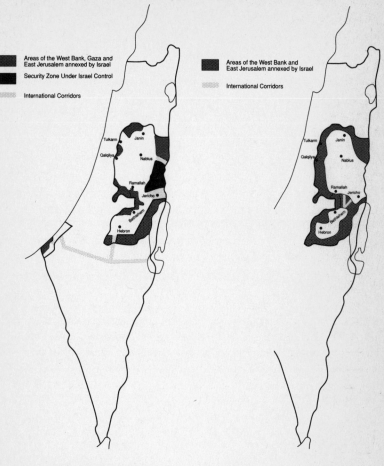

Regional Compromise I
Jaffee Centre
Tel Aviv

Regional Compromise II
Leonard Davies Institute
Jerusalem

Map 5   Regional compromise scheme: two strategic views

between Labour and Likud is more one of principle than of practice. It is inconceivable that the three Arab population areas under the regional compromise scheme, Judea, Samaria and Gaza, would be significantly different in real status from the autonomous areas envisaged by Likud. Both schemes would allow the Arab inhabitants to retain administrative powers in about 60 per cent of the territories and lose the remaining area absolutely. Both allow for some Palestinians to become Israeli citizens: under Likud's Eretz Israel scheme, Palestinians who opt for Israeli citizenship would enjoy civil but presumably not political rights. Under Labour's regional compromise, about 20 per cent of the Palestinian population might be incorporated into Israel, or might be transferred to the Arab enclaves.[15]

The real difference is that Labour is more sensitive to the international implications of state policy. It prefers to pursue a peace process which will satisfy the United States and other important members of the international community that it is not being unreasonable. Its preferred option, still, is to transact a deal with Jordan to make the latter responsible for the Arab enclaves. This, it hopes, would achieve a durable and internationally agreed settlement on its eastern front. With Husayn's renunciation of the West Bank in August 1988, Labour explicitly reiterated that it would opt for self-rule as the alternative, although one must assume this means conferring autonomy only on the areas allocated to the Palestinians in the regional compromise scheme. Likud believes it can impose a self-rule settlement which would not compromise its ideological rights to all the land. The difference lies less in the end product than the means to achieving it.

The Jewish settlements

The general tendency of the Israeli electorate to favour retention of the Jewish settlements suggests that Labour's position must remain closer to Likud's than its regional compromise indicates. These settlements, associated more in people's minds with Likud than with Labour, constitute major inroads into the proposed Arab enclaves.[16] The increase in settlers is occurring within the commuter catchment areas of metropolitan Tel Aviv and Jerusalem, suggesting that these areas might be irremediably integrated into the Israeli State, despite the twin facts that 40 per cent of West Bank Palestinians also live in these metropolitan areas and that the new settlements themselves draw more Palestinian labour into the areas to service them.

These metropolitan areas are increasingly viewed as vital to Israel for demographic as well as strategic reasons. As an authoritative strategic study states 'East of Greater Tel Aviv, the need to provide for an expanded population located on the Samarian foothills is especially compelling . . . Prospects for the center's (*the coastal plain*) expansion have significant implications for future boundary changes, because the location of the ecumene (*national population concentration*) sets limits on Israel's political and strategic abilities to compromise on its outer, national boundaries.'[17] Consequently, border adjustments are proposed to meet this Jewish demographic need.

Furthermore, a general expansion of the settlements is still planned. For example Ariel, ten miles south west of Nablus and with 8,000 members in 1988, is scheduled to grow to 100,000 persons by the year 2010 to become the capital of Jewish Samaria.[18] Although it is unlikely that Ariel will reach anything like its target, the inducement to move into better housing at lower cost, supported by regular cheap bus services into the metropolitan areas is bound to attract more settlers whose motivation is economic rather than ideological.[19] It was estimated that by 1990 the settler population would reach 100,000 (excluding 120,000 in East Jerusalem).[20] Although this remains substantially behind World Zionist Organization targets, an annual increase of 10,000 settlers could be expected until the mid-1990s,[21] giving a population of about 200,000 (exclusive of East Jerusalem) by the end of the century.

The choices still to be made

The immediate choice which Israel must make in response to the Uprising concerns the borders with which it could live in order to bring the increasingly unsustainable state of affairs in the occupied territories to an end. Neither regional compromise nor self-rule addresses the challenge of the Uprising satisfactorily. The Palestinians will accept neither. It is faintly possible that the PLO, in its anxiety to acquire a state, would accept an Israeli-controlled security zone in the Jordan valley. But this would be conceded reluctantly and would be unlikely to enjoy the acquiescence of the territories' population. It would almost certainly lead to political unrest at a later stage. Nor would it enjoy the satisfaction of Israel's own Palestinians, for whom the return of the occupied territories to Palestinian rule is now a fundamental part of their political baggage.

The situation within Israel's currrent area of control is not moving in Israel's favour. On the contrary, the tide of events is flowing increasingly strongly against its interests. As General Harkabi states, 'The longer the conflict remains unresolved, the more the conditions that Israel can obtain will worsen.'[22] The sooner it forges a decision and pursues its implementation, the greater its chance to achieve more rather than less of its strategic goals. As the tide turns increasingly strongly against it, through the Uprising, through demographic change, and through increasingly articulate and organized demands from Israeli Palestinians on behalf of themselves and their co-nationals in the occupied territories, it will become progressively harder for Israel to realize its strategic objectives through negotiation.

The fundamental choice is whether Palestine/Eretz Israel shall be one state or two. Likud has made its choice, but it is one bereft of a solution. For its Eretz Israel policy commits the state to unremitting conflict with its unwilling Palestinian subjects, and in the end it may be forced to abandon the option.

Labour has yet to make an unambiguous choice. If it opts for a two state solution it will be less a matter of telling the Palestinians how much they can have than a case of assessing how much Israel can retain to meet its own security consistent with meeting the Palestinians' need for political stability, without which Israel's own security objective cannot be achieved. The durability of a two state solution will depend less on what Israel is prepared to give away than on the provision of adequate political and economic security for both states. The political or economic stability of Israel may be desirable to the well-being of a Palestinian state, but without the stability of the latter Israel will find itself back at war with the Arabs. In other words, it is almost as important for Jews as for Palestinians, that any Palestinian state is viably proportioned.

A pragmatic assessment of this kind will cause immense strain within Israel. It is not easy for Israelis to perceive the security of Israel as rooted in its adversary's well-being. Furthermore, Israel being a credal society the drawing of any borders implies an ideological position on the Zionist spectrum. Following the June 1967 war all schools were issued with new maps of Eretz Israel bereft of all borders, even those of the 1949 Armistice, let alone the 1967 cease-fire line. Three things were clear from this map: that official policy viewed the 1949 Armistice Line as no longer valid (despite Resolution 242); that the borders of Eretz Israel were yet to be determined; and that the government was anxious to avoid a controversy between those who, at one end of the spectrum, considered all the territories should be returned and those at the other for whom the conquests of 1967 were insufficient. In the words of Shlomo Avineri, 'The debate about Israel's borders is thus far more complex than the debate about security guarantees: it goes to the very essence of how Israelis see themselves as a society and nation.'[23]

For the New Zionist school of thought the greater the territory under Israeli control, the more Jewish and the more Zionist the state will be. For Labour and the Peace Movement Zionists, the greater the territory under Israeli control, the less Jewish and the less Zionist the state will be, because of the presence of the Arabs. Were it not for these Arabs, both schools of thought would be happily reconciled.

At the heart of the ideological question stands the City of Jerusalem. Virtually all Zionist Israelis of both schools of thought remain committed to its retention as the united eternal capital of the Jewish people. Yet a united Jerusalem under sole Israeli sovereignty is bound to remain essentially a city of dissent. The city's Palestinians and some of its Jewish ultra-orthodox will continue to challenge the legitimacy of the Jewish State.

There are two reasons why the Palestinian people will not acquiesce in the permanent loss of Jerusalem to Israeli sovereignty. One is ideological, carrying similar force to that of the Zionists: Jerusalem is the most holy city of Palestine for Muslim and Christian Palestinians, and its natural capital. The second reason is a functional one. Jerusalem, as Labour's regional compromise planners are fully aware, joins the northern part of the West Bank (Samaria) with the southern part (Judea). Palestinians can accept no final settlement which denies them this strategic land bridge. On the issue of Jerusalem the ideological and strategic requirements of Zionist Jew and Palestinian Arab are at loggerheads. They can only be reconciled by some agreement to share the city.

Closing the gap

The Palestinians will accept nothing less than a return to the 1949 Armistice Line, while the Israelis insist on retaining large areas of the territories for security or ideological purposes. A substantial gap lies between the two, which may only be bridged when one or both parties fear the greater danger of failing to compromise on even 'minimalist' demands.

For several years the PLO has espoused the two state solution less ambiguously than Labour. Under international pressure it might be persuaded to accept Labour's regional compromise plan and might even sign a peace treaty based upon it. But even so, such an arrangement could have little prospect of durability as a final political settlement since it would provide inadequate space or sovereignty to the three Palestinian enclaves, while doing nothing for the refugee population. A place of abode in Palestine for the refugees currently outside it remains fundamental to any solution.

In order to achieve an agreement which would meet Israel's minimum security needs and Palestinians' minimum political ones it might be possible to envisage a durable two state solution along the following lines:

1 In Jerusalem either joint sovereignty over the whole city, or redivision of the city along the old lines, possibly with special international status for the Old City;
2 In the occupied territories minor border rectification to eliminate the Latrun salient, and the provision of small monitoring zones along the Jordan river or the eastern escarpment for Israel for a generation;
3 Israeli removal of all settlers, from East Jerusalem as well as elsewhere since all are deemed illegal by the world community and would be a cause of recurrent friction;
4 The provision of territory south east of the Gaza Strip (and possibly the area between Beersheba and the West Bank) to the Palestinian state as envisaged in the 1947 Partition Plan, to allow for essential population expansion, and as a symbolic token of the fact that Israel bears some responsibility (to avoid argument let us not try to quantify it here) for the creation of and failure to resolve the 1948 refugee problem and that symbolic amends for this would be a conciliatory factor. This is land which has relatively low population density and could be ceded with less cost than any other part of Israel once designated for the Arab state.
5 Demilitarization of the Palestinian state, or an international surveillance force, for an agreed period.

If Israel could obtain a cast-iron assurance of no further claims by Palestinians living outside the 1949 Armistice Line, it might deem such a bargain painful but worthwhile. This, it should be stressed, is not a proposal (there are no prescriptive solutions in this book) but merely conjecture of how the minimum requirements of each party might be satisfied. Only negotiations between Israel and the PLO (or alternative

Palestinian authorities) can indicate whether such conjecture is well founded.

Israel will welcome such a bargain far less than the Palestinians. But giving adequate satisfaction to the Palestinians of the occupied territories is now urgent if the Uprising (or successive uprisings) does not begin to turn the thoughts of Israel's own Palestinian population from civil rights to secession from the Jewish State.

The fundamental choices for the Jewish State

If it wishes to avoid further conflict with the Palestinian people, Israel must move rapidly within its own borders too. After forty years, Israeli Palestinians still patiently seek equal rights despite the fact that the gap between Jew and Arab is either static or actually growing.

This raises a more fundamental choice for Israel than that implicit in sloughing off the occupied territories. It must choose whether it is willing to retain its present geographical configuration in the knowledge that the Palestinian minority will continue to grow and may become half or more of the Israeli population around the year 2050. The state has only sixty years until then in which to deal with the challenge implicit in this demographic change either by control mechanisms or by empowerment of the Palestinian inhabitants.

If it chooses the latter course, it must come to terms with the idea of becoming an Arab-Jewish state, at face value a highly unattractive option. It would have to find the substantial funds with which to achieve equality of the Palestinian and Jewish sectors in national life, reallocate land in the light of past seizures from the Palestinian community and restructure the discriminatory areas of state activity, for example the Law of Return and quasi-governmental Zionist organizations, to ensure that all citizens could benefit equally.[24] Such measures have a reasonable chance of ensuring future communal harmony inside the state. This is the only basis on which Jewish Israel can genuinely be reconciled with the region in which it lives.

If Israel opts for retention of the Palestinian areas of the state but decides to control rather than empower its Palestinian citizens, this would drive the latter ultimately to seek secession rather than equality. It would also cause friction with a Palestinian state in the occupied territories, which would find it difficult to stand by while Israeli Palestinians were suppressed. In other words, the control option practised for the past forty years will, if continued, lead to renewed conflict with the Palestinian people. A viable two state settlement must be accompanied by empowerment of Israeli Palestinians.

If Jewish Israelis find the prospect of an Arab-Jewish state inside the 1949 Armistice Line an unacceptable one, they must choose how to retain Israel's Jewish identity. Since Israeli Palestinians will not leave their homes willingly, safeguarding the Jewishness of the state can only be done by excision of the high Palestinian population areas, offering them autonomy (if they will accept it) or annexation to the Palestinian state in the West Bank. It so happens that these high Palestinian population areas lie relatively close to the West Bank's border: in the south the bedouin concentrations north and north east of Beersheba; in the west the Little Triangle and Wadi Ara; in the north across the vale of Jezreel, central and western Galilee. The vale of Jezreel could presumably provide an international corridor. Excisions of this kind would remove virtually all Palestinians, and the lands on which they live, from within the Jewish body politic. It would leave Israel overwhelmingly and permanently Jewish, but it would not bring Israel into a productive relationship with its neighbours.

The dangers of procrastination

To moot such possibilities in current circumstances may seem outrageously unrealistic. Yet these are the hard decisions which Israel will face unless the Palestinians settle for far less than they have indicated they are likely to do. Unless Israel secures an agreement the tide is likely to continue flowing against the Jewish interest. The sooner Israel secures a political settlement from the Palestinians, the more advantageous it is likely to be. With the progressive growth in Palestinian awareness of their potential power both sides of the Armistice Line, the less advantageous will be the terms Israel can hope for. Speed of peace, like speed of war in the past, is emphatically in Israel's interest.

It seems as if Israel is being asked to make all the concessions. But it must be remembered that it is not Israel but the Palestinians who have so far endured all the losses, in 1947–9, in 1967 and progressively throughout the period by land seizure. Furthermore, Israel can derive concessions only from the PLO, but it has refused to countenance any negotiation with the PLO, leaving the latter's disposition, be it conciliatory or adversarial, irrelevant. When it decides to speak with the PLO (or the Palestinian authority at that time) it may secure a

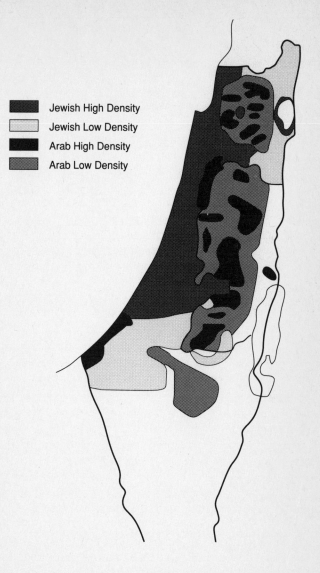

Map 6   Population distribution in Palestine/Eretz Israel

Based on: *Statistical Abstract of Israel No. 37* (1986) and Arnon Sofer, 'Geography and demography in the Land of Israel' (University of Haifa, cyclostyle 1987) Map 1.

satisfactory agreement. But if it does not, it rather than the PLO will still be saddled with unbearable problems. In this respect the PLO has the incomparable advantage of having much less to lose. As long as it repudiates the PLO as a negotiating partner, Israel is likely to continue to find itself in the unenviable position of having to resolve the deteriorating situation in the West Bank and Gaza Strip alone. The situation demands that it propose a solution that the people of the territories will accept, a far harder task than hammering out a deal with a PLO leadership with is more susceptible to external pressure than the leaders of the Uprising.

In the short term the prospect is either for continued coalition government, offering electoral safety to both Labour and Likud by sharing the same boat, or possibly after the next general election, for one party or the other to form a government with a small majority which is insufficient to push through a controversial solution. Neither party is likely to stray far from the centre ground of public opinion. Any attempt – without majority public support – to resolve the problem of the territories, would probably precipitate the greatest internal crisis in the history of the state, with fragmentation and bitter polarization of Israeli society.

Strong civil government can only occur once public opinion has shifted decisively in one direction or another, and such a change is likely to take years rather than months to achieve unless some unforeseeable *deus ex machina* occurs to change the whole appearance of things. In July 1988 a 'senior source', evidently General Amram Mitzna, commanding Central Command (which includes the West Bank), indicated not only that the Uprising was likely to last for years but that if the solution lay in negotiations, those negotiations could only take place with the PLO.[25] Furthermore, it was authoritatively suggested that about 75 per cent of the general staff believed in the need for territorial concessions.[26] Implicit in this leak was the intention by certain members of the general staff to persuade public opinion that the government must act soon to find a political solution.

One foreseeable possibility must be that in the event of a progressive deterioration in the situation, the military will feel compelled to go further than leaked statements. The grave danger in such circumstances would be a transition from civil government to military control of the state. Either the government might feel compelled to bring in the army with a declaration of a state of emergency in order to implement its solution, or it might be warned by the army to retreat from a solution which the general staff believed would be disastrous for the state.[27]

If the situation continues to deteriorate, growing fear will favour those who offer political certainties rather than doubts. The path to peace, advocated by the doves, will be strewn with grave uncertainties and a nation gripped by apprehension may not have the courage to live with them. One must accept that the political drift, albeit still modest, confirms that the Jewish public is more likely to choose the solutions advocated by the Right.

The threat of transfer

The rightist view that Eretz Israel is the Jewish birthright and that it therefore belongs more to Jews than to Arabs (a notion with which most Jewish Israelis already agree), leads naturally to the conclusion that the Palestinian 'strangers' in their midst must either accept the Jewishness of Eretz Israel or depart. The most outspoken exponent of these ideas is the leader of Israel's small right-wing Kach party, Rabbi Meir Kahane. He is explicit, 'I want to make life hard for them [the Palestinians]. I want them to think: "It makes no sense to go on living here; let's take our compensation payment and leave." . . . I would only use force on those who don't want to leave . . . I'd go all the way, and they know that.'[28] Furthermore, Kahane believes,

> it is not the Arabs of the Occupied Territories who are the problem. We can get rid of those Arabs now. The real problem is that there are many Arabs in Israel who have Israeli citizenship . . . once the Arabs have a majority in this country, they're going to do what any self-respecting nationalist would do. They are not going to accept living in a country called a Jewish state, in a country with a Law of Return that applies solely to Jews. Once the Arabs have gained a majority, they'll change the laws and nature of this State, and they'll be right, completely right. And this is why I want to move them all out now.[29]

In the early 1980s Kahane and his party, Kach, were dismissed as a lunatic fringe, a frightening one but nevertheless outside the national consensus. There was something unsettling in his claim that he said publicly what other people only thought. Had his thinking been confined to a lunatic fringe there would have been no need to ban his party in the 1988 election. In fact it was widely expected that Kach might increase its Knesset representation from one to seven seats.[30]

However, the idea of 'transferring' the Palestinian population, as expulsion is more delicately described, is widely held. The Van Leer poll among Jewish youth in 1984 revealed that 57 per cent of respondents, aged 15–18, thought that the Palestinians in the territories who refused Israeli citizenship (presumably without enfranchisement) ought to be expelled.[31] At the right-wing Tehiya Party conference in spring 1986, its leader Yuval Ne'eman declared that transfer for at least half a million refugees 'out of the Land of Israel' was a precondition for peace negotiations. At the end of the conference Tehiya called on the government to help West Bank and Gaza residents to emigrate and to expel subversives. It proposed annexation of the territories and the granting of citizenship to those Arabs pledging allegiance to Israel.[32] In November 1987 Reserve General Rehavem Ze'evi established the Movement for the Transfer of Palestinians. 'We have lit a torch,' he exclaimed, 'and it shall burn.'[33] His Moledet Party, campaigning explicitly for the removal of Palestinians, won two seats in the 1988 election.

It was widely feared at the time of Ze'evi's statement in November 1987 that about 25–30 per cent of Jewish Israelis supported the transfer idea. In fact the proportion was already substantially higher, over 40 per cent.[34] One poll suggested that 30 per cent of the Jewish electorate thought annexation of the territories and the transfer of the population elsewhere in the Middle East was 'most desirable', while 42 per cent found the proposal 'acceptable'.[35] It should be noted, however, that the same poll found an even higher number of Palestinians approved the expulsion of Jews from Palestine: 35 per cent found this notion 'most desirable' and 53 per cent 'acceptable'. The difference is that the Palestinians do not have the means to execute expulsions, though this is what Jews would justifiably fear were the roles reversed. From these results it was extremely difficult to tell whether there was a stable quorum of between 35–40 per cent favouring expulsion, or whether the proportion was actually increasing, as one authoritative poll was suggesting when it reported that by midsummer 1988 one in two Jewish Israelis favoured expulsion.[36]

With such broad public support it is not surprising that many Likud politicians also support transfer. These apparently include General Ariel Sharon who, before his invasion of Lebanon in 1982, implied that the Palestinians might have to be expelled, warning darkly that they should 'not forget the lesson of 1948'.[37] The following year, the Deputy Speaker of the Knesset, Meir Cohen, stated 'that Israel had made a great mistake by not expelling 200,000 to 300,000 Arabs from the West

Bank in 1967'.[38] As *The Jerusalem Post* commented at the time, the failure of Likud to reprimand Cohen gave the impression that 'he articulates the tacit premises of official policy.'[39] More recently Gideon Patt, Likud science minister, threatened Israeli Arabs that if they did not behave themselves they would be put on trucks and taxis and sent to the border.[40] In summer 1987 the Likud deputy minister of defence, Michael Dekel proposed the transfer of West Bank Arabs. Like Meir Cohen, he was not disciplined.

Among Israel's settlers, too, it is hardly surprising that the idea of expulsion is generally supported.[41] Belief in the need for transference has been long-standing in the Land of Israel Movement. One recurring theme is that a proportion of 30 per cent or more Palestinians could not be integrated into the Jewish State. This has great significance for Israeli Palestinians who will probably be 30 per cent by 2020.[42]

Within the army there is a division of opinion between those who support expulsion and those who prefer territorial compromise. As General Aharon Yariv, himself a former chief of military intelligence, remarked as early as 1980 there was a widely held opinion in favour of exploiting a future war to expel up to 800,000 Arabs. He warned that such a plan already existed and that the means of implementation had been prepared.[43] Another former chief of military intelligence, General Shlomo Gazit, warned in a lecture 'the solution for them [the Palestinians] must be found outside historic Eretz Israel.'[44] Since then, however, he has warned against the transfer idea as 'an entirely false Messianism . . . that is not realistic'.[45]

What frightens Palestinian Arabs is the fact that the idea of transfer is not the exclusive property of the extreme Right, nor yet of the broad (Likud) Right. Exponents and practitioners of population transfer permeate the Israeli establishment, the Labour Party as well as Likud. They cannot forget it was Labour's leaders who oversaw the expulsions of 1948, nor that it remained an option for consideration after 1967. In recent years open statements have been rare, but three examples indicate that Palestinian fears of Labour's intentions are not groundless. In 1984 Yitzhak Navon, ex-president of Israel and the leading Sephardic member of Labour, stated during the 1984 election campaign, 'the very point of Labor's program is to have as much land as possible and as few Arabs as possible.'[46] Early in the Uprising, when Israeli Palestinians demonstrated in support of those in the occupied territories, President Haim Herzog warned them 'against another chapter in the Palestinian tragedy',[47] while his colleague Defence Minister Rabin warned the same Palestinians 'you should remain as you have been until now, loyal, and enjoying a calm life. In the distant past you have known tragedy, and it would be better for you not to return to that tragedy.'[48] Israeli Palestinians understand perfectly what his warning implies. Rabin himself, with Yigal Allon, carried out Ben Gurion's instruction to expel between 50,000 and 70,000 inhabitants from the two cities of Lydda and Ramla in the summer of 1948.[49]

There can be no doubt that the strongest weapon with which Israel can coerce the Palestinians into settling for less than they want is the implicit or explicit threat of mass expulsion. It may seem that Palestinians are unduly paranoid concerning the danger. The task would be impossible to achieve in time of peace, and it would be impossible to achieve without considerable bloodshed, since many Palestinians would resist to the death rather than be removed. In order to execute a mass expulsion, those implementing such a scheme would probably need to create a powerful incentive to flee.

Currently a majority of Israeli Jews probably still oppose the idea of expulsion, including some leading Likud members, like Moshe Arens, for whom expulsion remains morally abhorrent. But there is good reason to fear that if the situation continues to deteriorate in the occupied territories and inside the Palestinian areas of Israel, the proportion of Jewish Israelis favouring expulsion will continue to increase. An autonomy arrangement, or some other political solution which leaves Israel in control of the territories while solving the question of Arab self-government, would almost certainly reduce substantially the number favouring expulsion. But as has been seen, no such solution can be in prospect since it is unacceptable to Palestinians.

The Jewish State is to a great extent responsible for the unhealthy public attitudes to Palestinians, both inside Israel and in the territories. When leading servants of the state make demeaning or abusive remarks about Palestinian Arabs in public it is bound to encourage those who favour transfer. There have been a substantial number of such remarks, from the prime minister, Knesset members and army generals, referring to the Arabs as 'two-legged animals', 'drugged cockroaches', 'a cancer in the flesh of our country', 'Arab scum'.[50] Others refer to Palestinians as 'foreigners', a definition which finds a ready echo among adherents of messianic Zionism. When troops had difficulty suppressing the Uprising, ex-Chief of Staff Raphael Eitan who still commands considerable respect in the army, enjoined 'instead of chasing after Arabs with clubs, we should be shooting them in the head. I have no doubt that this will happen in the end.' He also reportedly urged that rioters should be deported *en masse*, 'without taking into account what the rest of the worlds says.'[51] The generation of a contemptuous attitude towards the intended victims is a natural prerequisite for public acquiescence in an expulsion policy.

Likewise, the reluctance of the Israeli establishment to punish those who maltreat or illegally kill Palestinians only encourages further excesses in the future. The light sentences served by those responsible for the massacre at Kafr Qasim in 1956,[52] the pardon of soldiers and officers guilty of murder in the period 1977–8 in south Lebanon,[53] the punishment, or lack of it, of those implicated in the Sabra/Shatila massacre of September 1982,[54] and the deliberately delayed publication of the Karp report on settler violence against Palestinians,[55] are all examples of state reticence in punishing Jewish political offenders properly. The light punishment of the Jewish Terror Against Terror (TNT) in 1984 hardly discourages its admirers, particularly when leading statesmen described those convicted for murder or attempted murder as 'basically good boys', or when most of the convicted had their sentences reduced by presidential decree, after pleas from the religious establishment.[56] In November 1987, the Landau Commission reported that Shin Bet (or Shabak, the General Security Services) operatives had routinely resorted to torture of Palestinian detainees, and had routinely committed perjury in Israeli courts over the previous sixteen years. It recommended against prosecution of those who had committed either offence, and accepted the legitimacy of 'a moderate amount of force' and 'non violent psychological pressure' in order to obtain information. These, and many other less notable examples, encourage Jewish Israeli society to think it can get away with excesses against Palestinian Arabs.

The bleak prospect

However, as one commentator on the Landau report wrote 'I am convinced that the commission's conclusions constitute a national disaster. They make all the pessimistic predictions made by Professor Yeshayahu Leibowitz come true. The secret service state, against which he warned us since 1967, has come about. Anyone who believes that the licence to use moderate physical force will only be invoked towards Arabs is very wrong.'[57] After the commencement of the Uprising 500 Israeli mental health professionals protested the moral cost of continued occupation of the territories: 'All of us have been swept into a current of fear, violence and racism. We are losing our sensitivity to human suffering, our children are being raised on racist, discriminatory values, and IDF soldiers are being placed in morally impossible situations.'[58] If respect for the rule of law continues to deteriorate, 'it appears likely,' in the words of another Israeli, that 'by the beginning of the twenty first century the State of Israel will have become an interesting combination of South Africa and Northern Ireland . . . a cruel non-democratic state structure with constant internal fighting and bloodshed.'[59]

The prospect is of a steady erosion of law and order both in the occupied territories, where Israel will face recurrent outbursts of popular feeling, and within Israel itself where the Jewish population is likely to be increasingly polarized as the implications of demographic change begin to bite into the sense of Jewish (rather than Israeli) identity. A government which tries to bridge a crumbling national consensus is unlikely to halt this deterioration without resort to martial law. It remains an open question whether the military would cleave to the imperative of an orderly Israeli withdrawal from the territories, continued control of the Palestinian population or whether it would conclude that the only military solution is expulsion.

The real danger for the Palestinian people in such a situation is that those who wish to expel them, who comprise an *armed* element of Israeli society, settlers and their friends in the army, will begin to implement their own solution unilaterally. Half a million, or one in seven Jewish Israelis, have firearms in their possession.[60] The existence of an element within the Israeli armed forces which might either commit atrocities or 'look the other way', cannot be ignored in view of the brutality used by some troops attempting to crush the Uprising. Nor can one ignore the kind of acts contemplated by Jewish underground groups, to blow up civilian Palestinian buses, an echo of the wilder end of the Palestinian terrorist spectrum. Speaking of those members of TNT arrested in 1984, General Harkabi observed,

> they are rational people whose chief motivation stems from their awareness that annexation of the West Bank together with its Arab population would be disastrous and tantamount to national suicide – unless that population were thinned out and made to flee by means of terrorism . . . the logical, rational conclusion of the policy that aims at annexation. Such terrorism is neither a punishment nor a deterrent; it is a political instrument.[61]

As Israel Eldad, mentor of the far Right has written, 'Had it not been for Deir Yassin, half a million Arabs would be living in the State of Israel. The State of Israel would not have existed. We must not disregard this, with full awareness of the responsibility involved. All wars are cruel. There is no way out of that. This country will be Eretz Israel with an absolute Jewish majority and a small Arab minority, or Eretz Ishmael . . . if we do not expel the Arabs one way or another.'[62] 'One way or another' is a chilling phrase for many Jewish Israelis who believe that

> The solution of the transports, the trucks, is not the end of the story. There is a further stage, which the proponents of racist Zionism do not usually refer to explicitly, since the conditions for it are not yet ripe. But the principles are there, clear and inevitable. This is the stage of genocide, the destruction of the Palestinian people.[63]

In a situation where a determined group believed that the Palestinians must be expelled before their idea of the Jewish State disintegrated, an attempt to restrain them might lead to civil war.

Can the outside world help Israel avoid disaster? The answer must be in considerable doubt. Kahane may well be correct when he says 'If the United States believes that Israel is in line with its interests, then there's nothing Israel can't do.'[64] The United States has put pressure on Israel to conform to international norms only at a minimalist level. It has taken no effective steps at law enforcement. Apart from the occasional rebuke, the United States and other Western friends of Israel did not see law observance as the crucial safeguard of civilized values for Israel as well as for the inhabitants of the territories. Had they done so, they would have obliged Israel not to change the status of Jerusalem in 1967, nor to build a single settlement in the occupied territories. Since Israel has remained dependent upon American economic aid since 1948, this would not have been difficult to achieve had the latter been more strongly committed to law observance than to its own strategic interest. This may seem like a naïve argument, but it will prove infinitely more naïve to have opted for short-term self-interest if in the long run the United States' most trustworthy ally in the Middle East is destroyed by its inability to conform to international norms of behaviour.

One must also conclude that the continued arming of Israel and its adversaries will fuel the fire of conflict and danger. For it is only when Israel recognizes that its supremacy is no longer assured that it will be able to make the painful concessions necessary for its survival in the Middle East. There is no sign of this happening yet and in the meantime life becomes more dangerous. The continued supply of strategic and tactical weaponry is a serious distraction from the greater danger facing Jewish Israelis inside the Land of Israel. Unless they are able to come to terms with their Palestinian neighbours, and define with them how the Land of Israel/Palestine can be shared, there can be precious little security for anyone.

When one surveys the nature and depth of the problem within the area of Palestine/Eretz Israel, the performance of interested outside powers seems lamentably inadequate. Resolution 242, a fine statement for 1967, now seems a flawed key to peace. With the inter-communal dimension rapidly overshadowing other aspects of the conflict, a more profound process of reconciliation is needed, in which 242 can be no more than an opening gambit.

It may seem futile to end this political review on a moral note. Yet understanding and forgiveness are vital prerequisites to peace and inter-community co-existence in the Middle East. They are qualities supposedly fundamental to Judaism, Christianity and Islam, despite the intolerance their more ardent devotees have so often expressed.

For outside powers, particularly ones imbued with the values of one of these religions, there is a responsibility to assist the process of reconciliation. Of them all, the United States has the greatest potential role, one which it has so far failed to play. If it took a more neutral stance it could help each protagonist to discard its respective demonology and to understand the genuine fears of its adversary. By proclaiming the PLO as anathema for so long it has authenticated Israel's negative perceptions of Palestinians and persuaded the Palestinians that they face a Jewish–American conspiracy. It has been a poor friend to both.

Ultimately, of course, reconciliation is a direct affair. Israeli and Palestinian leaders must dare to meet face to face. Even so, no reconciliation will be possible without, as General Harkabi insists, self-criticism. It is a punishing challenge for both communities, for implicit in the exercise of self-criticism is the willingness to change attitudes and perceptions, to put values of human dignity before those of ethnic identity. To risk allowing our attitudes and perceptions to be changed, as a leading psychologist has written, is one of the most frightening prospects most of us can face.[65] Yet it is only through such change that reconciliation can come about. The willingness to take this path demands great courage. It is easy to be downhearted by the challenge this poses. The majority in both communities incline towards the enemy stereotypes. Yet in both camps there are women and men who labour against the tide and who refuse to give way to despair. One must pray that they will prevail. After all, they live in a land in which miracles have been known to happen.

NOTES

PROLOGUE: UPRISING

1   *Guardian*, 12 December 1987.
2   Ibid., 15 December 1987.
3   Ibid., 5 January 1988.
4   Ibid.
5   See fortnightly issues of *Middle East International* no. 316 of 9 January 1988 onwards.
6   *Wafa* telex, 12 December 1987.
7   See for example Shyam Bhatia's report in the *Observer*, 10 January 1988.
8   One theory was that UNLU central committee had 16 members, 8 from Gaza, 8 from the West Bank, with religious representation: 6 Sunni Muslims and 2 Christians, and political representation: 8 drawn from Fatah, PFLP, DFLP and the Communist Party. See *Israel and Palestine*, no. 140, February–March 1988. Another was that its committee comprised three members each from Fatah, DFLP, PFLP, CP and Islamic trends; see for example, Zvi Gilat, *New Outlook*, March/April 1988.
9   Communiqué no. 16, 13 May 1988, in *Facts Weekly Review* (Jerusalem) 8–21 May, 1988, no. 10.
10 Israeli troops were seen by UN officials urinating into Khan Yunis refugee camp water supply. *Guardian*, 14 December 1987. Conscripts opened fire despite strict instructions regarding the use of firearms. One plain clothes Shin Bet (secret police) was seen taking careful aim and shooting at a group of retreating Palestinians. Ibid., 19 December 1987.
11 Ibid., 12 December 1987; *Middle East International*, no. 316, 9 January 1988.
12 *Guardian*, 12 December 1987.
13 Ibid., 19 December 1987.
14 Ibid., 19 January 1988.
15 By 16 October 1988 sixty-seven had died of tear gas related cases, *Middle East International*, no. 336, 21 October 1988. Pregnant women and children were the most vulnerable. For details see *Israel and Palestine*, no. 140, February–March 1988.
16 Eric Silver in the *Observer*, 24 January 1988.

17 Ibid.
18 In Ramallah, a predominantly Christian and 'moderate' town, merchants repeatedly mended their steel shutters. Locksmiths worked free of charge, and were provided with food by local restaurateurs, *The Sunday Times*, 31 January 1988.
19 United Nations and charitable society food supplies were prevented from entering the camps. *The Independent*, 20 January 1988.
20 *Guardian*, 19 January 1988.
21 Peres suggested the abandonment of the Gaza Strip, offering it to either Egypt or Jordan or granting it unilateral autonomy as a demilitarized zone. He backed down but was blamed for inflaming Palestinian unrest. Ibid., 10 December 1987; *Middle East International*, no. 315, 19 December 1987. While he agreed with Prime Minister Shamir, that the PLO was to blame, his Labour party colleague and Defence Minister Rabin was busy denying it, *Middle East International*, no. 316, 9 January 1988. Rabin's deputy, the Defence Ministry co-ordinator for operations in the occupied territories, Mr Shlomo Goren, claimed the PLO was indeed responsible for the trouble. *Guardian*, 14 December 1987.
22 *Guardian*, 22 December 1988.
23 Ibid., 13 January 1988.
24 *Middle East International*, no. 316, 9 January 1988; see also *The Jerusalem Post*, 10 September 1987, in which the government is reported to have denied receipt of a message from Yasser Arafat, conveyed by Knesset Member Charlie Biton who had met him in Geneva, and also the discussions between Likud MK Moshe Amirav and the two Palestinians, Faysal al Husayni and Sari Nusayba. See further on PLO offers of negotiations, Abdul Wahab Darawsha's claim, *Ma'ariv*, 4/5 December 1986, in *Israeli Mirror*, no. 760.
25 For examples of different reactions across the political spectrum, see *The Sunday Times*, 3 January 1988; *Middle East International*, no. 316, 9 January 1988; *Observer*, 24 January 1988; *Guardian*, 12 January 1988.
26 *Guardian*, 14 December 1987.
27 After renewed calls for his expulsion from Likud (*The Sunday Times*, 3 January 1988) he was finally expelled.
28 'Holding on to the occupied territories,' Lahad stated, 'is a burden for Israel, from the human aspect, and the national aspect. We are situated in an area where we are not liked, where people treat us as occupiers. Our soldiers are prepared to defend Israel, to sacrifice their lives if necessary, but they don't like fighting women and children.' *Observer*, 17 January 1988.
29 *The Sunday Times*, 3 January 1988.
30 *Middle East International*, no. 316, 9 January 1988.
31 *The Sunday Times*, 24 January 1988. *Israel and Palestine*, no. 140, February–March 1988 gives a figure of 30–40,000.
32 *Guardian*, 22 December 1988.
33 In the bedouin town of Rahat, and in the mixed Arab-Jewish cities of Jaffa and Lod (Lydda) there were violent scenes between demonstrators and police. In Abu Ghosh, an Arab village west of Jerusalem well known in Israel as the 'good Arab village', stones were hurled at passing buses on the Tel Aviv-Jerusalem highway. *Middle East International*, no. 316, 9 January 1988.
34 Ibid.

35 Ibid., no. 317, 23 January 1988.
36 Partly resulting from a US government warning to its citizens not to travel to Israel during the disturbances. Ibid.
37 Gad Ya'cobi, speaking on Israeli TV, 22 March 1988, in *The Other Israel*, March–April 1988.
38 *Middle East International*, no. 316, 9 January 1988.
39 *Guardian*, 13 January 1988.
40 *Middle East International*, no. 318, 6 February 1988.
41 *Middle East Report (MERIP)*, May–June 1988, p. 51.
42 *Facts Weekly Review*, 29 May–4 June 1988, quoting from UNLU Communiqué no. 19 of 5 June 1988.
43 At the summit in Algiers in June 1988 King Husayn backtracked from the stance taken before the Uprising, by acknowledging the PLO's right to negotiate on its own behalf for the Palestinian people. *The Independent*, 9 June 1988.
44 *MERIP*, May–June 1988, p. 47.
45 This was underlined on New Year's Day, barely three weeks after the outbreak of the Uprising, when hundreds of demonstrators used the Friday prayer at the ancient al Azhar university to demonstrate in solidarity with the Palestinian people. This demonstration reflected pan-Islamic bonds working parallel to Arab nationalist ones. Ten days later two leading Muslim clerics, Hafiz Salama and Umar Abd al Rahman, called for a *jihad* against Israel and the abrogation of the peace treaty. Hafiz Salama also rejected Mubarak's call for an international peace conference. *Guardian*, 12 January 1988.
46 Ibid., 26 January 1988.
47 *Middle East International*, no. 318, 6 February 1988.
48 Six months later, however, it used surrogate Palestinian forces to evict Fatah from the Beirut camps.
49 Some Jordanian deputies even used the opportunity of a parliamentary session to criticize the application of martial law, in effect since 1967, which made rallies, demonstrations and party political activity illegal. Ibid., no. 316, 9 January 1988.
50 The United States abstained from Resolution 605 on 22 December, but on 4 January supported the resolution calling on Israel to drop its plans to expel nine Palestinians from the territories. US abstention on the first resolution constituted a strong censure of Israel. Its support for the second was the first time the United States had voted against Israel since 1981, when it had condemned Israeli annexation of the Golan. When Israel flouted the 4 January resolution some days later by expelling four of these Palestinians, the United States felt it could not damage its relationship with Israel further by joining the rest of the Security Council in a resolution of condemnation. Ibid., no. 317, 23 January 1988.
51 *Guardian*, 9 July 1988.
52 Telseker Institute poll in *Hadashot*, 12 April 1988, translated in *Israeli Mirror*, no. 776.
53 See *Ma'ariv*, 19 May 1988; *Ha'aretz*, 5 April 1988; *Koteret Rashit*, 20 April 1988; *al Hamishmar*, 29 March 1988, all translated in *Israeli Mirror*, no. 777. Also see the open letter from Ansar 3 (Ketziot) in *Facts Weekly Review*, no. 15, 19–26 June 1988.
54 For example, see *The Independent*, 24 August 1988 and *Middle East*

International, no. 331, 5 August 1988.

55 *Facts Weekly Review*, 19–26 June 1988, no. 15.

56 Ibid., 16–29 October 1988, no. 28.

57 *The Independent*, 12 & 23 May 1988.

58 *Middle East International*, no. 335, 7 October 1988.

59 *The Independent*, 30 September 1988.

60 *Israel and Palestine*, no. 144, September 1988, individual cases cited.

61 *Facts Weekly Review*, 24–30 April, 1988, no. 8.

62 By October 1988 this service was still highly inadequate.

63 *Facts Weekly Review*, 12–18 June 1988, no. 14, and 27 June–2 July 1988, no. 16.

64 See *Middle East International*, no. 328 of 25 June 1988 and *al Hadaf newsletter*, no. 7, July 1988 which show that the hot summer winds, a major accident during army training, and the inadvertent spread of fire from burning garbage explained some of these fires.

65 *Facts Weekly Review*, 18 September–1 October 1988, no. 26.

66 There were indications of growing tension between the army and Shin Bet on the one hand and the Israeli government on the other, the former feeling angry and demoralized at the way in which they were required to contain what was essentially a political rather than a military problem. *Guardian*, 9 July 1988.

INTRODUCTION: THE LEGACY OF THE PAST

1 Petah Tiqva, see Neville Mandel, *The Arabs and Zionism before World War I* (Berkeley, Los Angeles and London, 1980) pp. 35–6.

2 Mandel, *The Arabs and Zionism*, p. 38.

3 Ibid., p. 39.

4 Ibid., pp. 7–31.

5 Ibid., pp. 47–8.

6 For example, Rashid Rida, the Syrian Arab Muslim thinker, wrote in 1902 warning that the Jews sought national sovereignty in Palestine, *Al Manar*, iv, 21 (1902), pp. 801–9, quoted in Mandel, *The Arabs and Zionism*, p. 46. In 1905 a Christian Arab, Negib Azoury, published *Le Reveil de la nation Arabe*, and warned that 'Two important phenomena, of the same kind but opposed . . . are currently emerging in Asiatic Turkey: these are the awakening of the Arab nation and the latent effort of the Jews to re-establish the ancient kingdom of Israel on a grand scale. These two movements are destined to unremitting conflict until one of them prevails. The fate of the entire world depends upon the outcome.' Azoury, *Le Reveil de la nation Arabe* (Paris, 1905) p. V, (my translation). See for a discussion of Azoury, Albert Hourani, *Arabic Thought in the Liberal Age* (London, 1962) pp. 277–9; Mandel, *The Arabs and Zionism*, pp. 50–52.

7 Both newspapers were Christian-owned. Christians were more opposed than Muslims at first since they felt the direct rivalry of Zionists in trade, particularly with the West.

8 Britain had made several vague promises of independence to the Arabs during the course of the war. For the various declarations and pledges see George Antonius, *An Arab Awakening* (London, 1938) Appendices A–E.

9   See the speech on the Balfour Declaration given on 2 December 1917, in *Speeches, Articles and Letters of Israel Zangwill* (London, 1937) pp. 331–8.

10 The full text of the memorandum of July 1919 of the General Syrian Congress in Damascus presented to the American (King-Crane) Commission of Inquiry, may be found in Antonius, *The Arab Awakening*, Appendix H.

11 The relevant articles, 4 and 11, may be found in Doreen Ingrams, *Palestine Papers, 1917–22, Seeds of Conflict* (London, 1972) pp. 177–83.

12 For example see Beatrice Stewart Erskine, *Palestine of the Arabs* (London, 1935) pp. 69–119; see also for statistical evidence of growing Jewish economic control, Elia Zureik, *The Palestinians of Israel, A Study of Internal Colonialism* (London, 1979) pp. 54–9.

13 The proposed council was to be composed of ten government appointees, plus eight Muslims, two Christians and two Jews. It is unlikely that such a legislative council would have improved the situation for Arabs substantially. Britain was unwilling to moderate the pro-Zionist provisions of the Mandate in the 1920s, pressure was growing on European Jews to emigrate, and the Zionists had access to growing sources of capital for economic control of the country. Yehoshua Porath, *The Emergence of the Palestinian-Arab National Movement, 1918–29* (London, 1974) pp. 144–58.

14 Resolution of the 12th Zionist Congress, Carlsbad, 1921, quoted in Porath, *The Emergence of the Palestinian-Arab National Movement*, p. 146.

15 The remark of Dr Eder made after the 1921 Jaffa riots, quoted in William Ziff, *The Rape of Palestine* (New York, 1938), p. 171 and quoted by Sami Hadawi, *Palestinian Rights and Losses in 1948 – A Comprehensive Study* (London, 1988), p. 17.

16 See Porath, *The Emergence of the Palestinian-Arab National Movement*, pp. 258–73.

17 The largest single seller was the Beiruti Sursuq family, which sold about 30,000 dunums (one dunum = 1,000 sq.m., or approximately ¼ acre) near Tiberias to the Zionists in 1901, and in 1920 a larger area, 240,000 dunums, in the Plain of Esdraelon, leading to the dispossession and eviction of 8,000 peasants from 22 villages. Mandel, *The Arabs and Zionism*, p. 22, and Hadawi, *Palestinian Rights and Losses in 1948*, p. 66.

18 Cmnd. 3686, *Report by Sir John Hope-Simpson on Immigration, Land Settlement, and Development* (London, 1930) quoted in Erskine, *Palestine of the Arabs*, p. 103.

19 Hadawi, *Palestinian Rights and Losses*, pp. 51–60.

20 With regard to the strategic acquisition of land, see Kenneth Stein, *The Land Question in Palestine, 1917–39* (North Carolina, 1984) reviewed in *International Journal of Middle Eastern Studies*, vol. 20, no. 3, August 1986.

21 Yehoshua Porath, *The Palestinian Arab National Movement, 1929–39* (London, 1977) pp. 283–4.

22 Ibid., pp. 284–94.

23 J. C. Hurewitz, *The Struggle for Palestine* (New York, 1976) p. 159.

24 Leading Zionists had successfully persuaded the United States to support the inclusion of the Naqab in the Jewish State to allow for its development and the absorption of Jewish refugees and to provide an outlet to the Red Sea. See *Ad Hoc Committee on the Palestine Question*, Document A/AC, 14/32 of 11 November 1947, appendices B and C, reproduced in Walid Khalidi, *From*

Haven to Conquest (Beirut, 1971) pp. 697–8. Bedouin rights in the matter, as the UNSCOP report made clear, were almost wholly disregarded, *United Nations Special Committee on Palestine*, Document A/364 of 3 September 1947, pp. 11, 54.

25 It is arguable whether the Jews would have been in a majority by May 1948. The actual partition was made on the mistaken assumption that the Arabs were 407,000 compared with 498,000 Jews. Ibid. A footnote disclosed that another 90,000 bedouin in the Negev had not been included in these figures, ibid. In fact the census of 31 December 1946 shows that there were altogether 510,000 Arabs as against 499,000 Jews in the proposed Jewish State. This was explained in the minority report of the *Ad Hoc Committee on the Question of Palestine*, Document A/AC 14/32 of 11 November 1947, Appendix 1, Annex 1. The difference is explained by a miscounting of the bedouin population in UNSCOP's report, compared with the *Ad Hoc Committee*, pp. 306–7. The text is reproduced in Khalidi, *From Haven to Conquest*, pp. 645–99.

26 Article 11 of United Nations General Assembly Resolution 194 (III) of 11 December 1948.

27 The argument over Resolution 242 revealed that while the PLO would accept it within the corpus of the other UN resolutions on Palestine, the United States wished to exclude all resolutions on Palestine except 242, and thus deny the right to self-determination explicitly recognized in other UN resolutions. Alan Hart, 'The conspiracy against Arafat's PLO', *Middle East International*, 27 June 1986.

CHAPTER 1 PALESTINE: THE INTERNATIONAL CONFLICT

1 See the thesis elaborated by L. Carl Brown, *International Politics and the Middle East: Old Rules, Dangerous Game* (Princeton and London, 1984) to which I am indebted for many insights into great power politics in the region.

2 Eisenhower and Nixon, for example, both saw the fight against communism as their foreign policy priority. Eisenhower saw Israel as an impediment and Nixon saw it as an asset. See Stephen Spiegel, *The Other Arab-Israeli Conflict, Making America's Middle East Policy from Truman to Reagan* (Chicago, 1985) p. 2.

3 On the arguments in Washington for and against the creation of Israel, see ibid., p. 4. On its misgivings once it had decided to support the creation of Israel, see Simha Flapan, *The Birth of Israel, Myths & Realities* (New York and London, 1987) pp. 157–9.

4 In 1948 it reminded the Soviet Union that giving the Negev to the Arabs would be tantamount to providing Britain with a base. At the same time it explained to the United States that to oppose Israeli control of the Negev would be tantamount to driving Israel into the arms of the Soviet Union. Flapan, *The Birth of Israel*, p. 45.

5 Bernard Reich, *The United States and Israel* (New York, 1984) p. 182.

6 A. J. Klinghoffer, *Israel and the Soviet Union* (Boulder, Co. and London, 1985) p. 18.

7 Ze'ev Schiff and Ehud Ya'ari, *Israel's Lebanon War* (New York, 1984) p. 31, quoted in Stephen Green, *Living by the Sword, America and Israel in the Middle*

East, 1968–87 (London and Boston, 1988) p. 155.

8   'US objectives and policies with respect to the Near East', *National Security Council* 155/1, quoted by Stephen Green, *Taking Sides: America's Secret Relations with a Militant Israel, 1948–67* (London, 1984) p. 115.

9   In the period 1951–3 the US gave $159 million to Israel in official development aid compared with $20 million *in toto* provided to Arab states in the same period. Ibid., p. 116.

10 Ben Gurion proposed to Eisenhower that the United States should replace France as Israel's main arms supplier in 1960, but the latter declined and remained opposed to supplying weaponry. Ibid., p. 152.

11 Airgram A 434, from US Embassy Tel Aviv to Dept of State, 17 December 1963, in Carrolton Press Declassified Documents Reference System, 1977/62D. See also the memo of the American Israel Public Affairs Committee (AIPAC) Director I. L. Kenen's memo of 26 November 1963, both quoted in Green, *Taking Sides*, pp. 185–6.

12 Green, *Taking Sides*, pp. 186–7.

13 Jon Kimche, *Palestine or Israel – the Untold Story of why we Failed* (London, 1973), p. 258.

14 Richard Nixon, *Memoirs* (New York, 1987) p. 481 quoted in Klinghoffer, *Israel and the Soviet Union*, p. 86.

15 *The Washington Post*, 15 August 1979.

16 With a total of 200 MiG 19's and 21's, see Klinghoffer, *Israel and the Soviet Union*, pp. 81–5, and Green, *Living by the Sword*, p. 9.

17 *The New York Times*, 8 July 1968, quoted in Green, *Living by the Sword*, p. 14.

18 Green, *Living by the Sword*, pp. 56–61.

19 Klinghoffer, *Israel and the Soviet Union*, p. 146.

20 Paragraph 1 of the MoA of 1 September 1975, quoted by Ali E. Hillal Dessouki, 'The politics of strategic imbalance: Israel and the Palestinian question', in Michael Hudson (ed.), *Alternative Approaches to the Arab-Israeli Conflict* (Washington, 1984) p. 15.

21 Paragraph 9 of MoA, Dessouki, 'The politics of strategic imbalance', p. 15.

22 Spiegel, *The Other Arab-Israeli Conflict*, p. 429.

23 Ibid., p. 406.

24 Said to Thomas A. Dine, chief of the American Israeli Public Affairs Committee in autumn 1983. Bernard Gwertzman 'Reagan turns to Israel', *The New York Times*, 27 November 1983, quoted in Spiegel, *The Other Arab-Israeli Conflict*, p. 406.

25 It signed friendship and co-operation treaties with Egypt (1971), Iraq (1972), Somalia (1974), the People's Democratic Republic of Yemen (1979) and Syria (1980).

26 Arab communists have been the perennial target of most Arab security services.

27 In October 1984 US Congress passed a law, known as Section 535, detailing three conditions to be met before the Administration can deal with the PLO: (1) recognition of Israel's right to exist; (2) acceptance of resolutions 242 and 338; (3) renunciation of terror.

28 US General Accounting Office, *US Assistance to the State of Israel – the uncensored draft report for 1983*, p. 7.

29 See the assurance given by President Johnson, cited in M. Riad, *The Struggle*

for Peace in the Middle East (London, Melbourne and New York, 1981) pp. 80–81.

30 Klinghoffer, *Israel and the Soviet Union*, pp. 78, 86.

31 State Department to Ambassador Barbour, 14 September 1967 in Carrolton Press Declassified Documents Reference System, 1980/201A, quoted in Green, *Taking Sides*, p. 245.

32 *The New York Times*, 5 March 1980, quoted in Aryeh Y. Yodfat and Yuval Arnon-Ohanna, *PLO Strategy and Politics* (London, 1981), p. 129.

33 Paris Declaration of 26 March 1979.

34 In April 1981 Reagan's first Secretary of State, Alexander Haig, visited Israel where he was told of the plan to strike south Lebanon. 'A basic change in attitude of the United States towards Israeli military action in Lebanon appears to have given a new flexibility to Israel's Army and Air Force.' *The New York Times*, 8 April 1981, quoted in Green, *Living by the Sword*, pp. 154, 157.

35 Edward Shaheen, *The Arabs, Israel and Kissinger* (New York, 1976) p. 199, quoted in Hudson, *Alternative Approaches*, p. 23.

36 Klinghoffer, *Israel and the Soviet Union*, pp. 119, 167. This was tried again in 1986–7 when Gorbachev's *glasnost* brought the Soviet Union and the United States closer together.

37 Spiegel, *The Other Arab-Israeli Conflict*, pp. 337–40.

38 The rivalries between Arab states, and their identity as accommodationist or radical has changed over the years. In the 1960s radical Egypt opposed accommodationist Libya; in the 1970s accommodationist Egypt opposed radical Libya; Syria and Egypt, the young radicals of the 1950s, broke after 1973 as Egypt became accommodationist; in the 1980s Iraq became accommodationist as it fought against a radical Iran.

39 Shimon Peres, Chatham House, 22 January 1986.

40 Text of the Reagan Initiative, Department of State, *Current Policy*, 417, 1 September 1982.

41 *Time Magazine* survey, 24 May 1982 and Abdul Sattar Kassem, *Public Opinion Survey in the West Bank and Gaza Strip*, May 1983, both quoted in Murad A'si, 'Israeli and Palestinian public opinion and the Palestine question', in Elia Zureik and Fouad Moughrabi (eds), *Public Opinion and the Palestine Question* (Beckenham, 1987) pp. 191–2.

42 *The New York Times*, 21 May 1983.

43 SA–5 surface to air missiles, and SS 21 TBMs. See Green, *Living By the Sword*, pp. 228–31.

44 Meron Benvenisti, *Demographic, Economic, Legal, Social and Political Developments in the West Bank: 1986 Report of the West Bank Data Base Project* (Jerusalem, 1986) p. 23.

45 Amos Kenan, in Rael Jean Isaac, *Israel Divided: Ideological Politics in the Jewish State* (Baltimore and London, 1976) p. 94.

46 Article 1 of the 1949 (IVth) Geneva Convention reads 'The High Contracting Parties undertake to respect and ensure respect for the present Convention in all circumstances.' The International Red Cross Commentary to Article 1 by Jean Pictet elucidates the meaning of the phrase 'ensure respect' as follows: 'the proper working of the system of protection provided by the Convention demands in fact that the Contracting Parties should not be content merely to apply its provisions themselves, *but should do everything in their power to ensure*

that the humanitarian principles underlying the Conventions are applied universally' (emphasis added).

47 In November 1987 the European Parliament declined to renew three trade and financial protocols with Israel, until Israel allowed the occupied territories the same access to the European market which Israel itself enjoyed. In March 1988 the European Parliament again refused to renew the protocols, but this time its reason was no longer the principle of equitable access to European markets, but Israel's violent response to the Uprising.

CHAPTER 2 THE JORDANIAN DIMENSION

1 Another 19 per cent were wholly opposed to any negotiation; opinion poll by Abd al Sittar Kassem in A'si, 'Israel and Palestinian public opinion', p. 193.
2 Mohammad Shadid and Rick Seltzer, 'Political attitudes of Palestinians in the West Bank and Gaza Strip', in *Middle East Journal*, Winter 1988, vol. 42, no. 1, p. 27.
3 The precise definition of the promise became the subject of bitter controversy between the Arabs and Britain, particularly with regard to Palestine.
4 Porath, *The Emergence of the Palestinian Arab Nationalist Movement* p. 178, citing *al Karmil*, 30 June 1923. In 1923 Abdallah met Weizmann in London, to seek support for the enlargement of his Amirate in return for Jewish settlement on both banks of the Jordan. Yosef Gorny, *Zionism and the Arabs 1882–1948* (Oxford, 1987) p. 87; Simha Flapan, *Zionism and the Palestinians* (London and New York, 1979) p. 333.
5 Abdallah maintained neighbourly relations with the Zionists and in 1932 he offered to lease them 70,000 dunams of the fertile Ghor valley. An agreement was reached in January 1933, and although the option was never taken up, it was renewed repeatedly up to 1939.
6 Porath, *The Emergence of the Palestinian Arab Nationalist Movement*, p. 73.
7 Ibid., p. 230.
8 Flapan, *Zionism and the Palestinians*, p. 253. By his stance, Abdallah forfeited the Nashashibi faction's support for the Greater Syria scheme. Many of the Nashashibi faction lived in the areas allocated to the putative Jewish State.
9 Ben Gurion hoped for a foothold on the East Bank and the eclipse of his implacable adversary, the Mufti. 'I would suggest,' he wrote in 1934, 'that Abdallah be given supreme religious authority over all Moslems in Eretz Israel, in return for opening up Transjordan to us'. David Ben Gurion, *My Talks with Arab Leaders* (Jerusalem, 1972) p. 39, quoted by Flapan in *Zionism and the Palestinians*, p. 133. In 1937 he met Abdallah, who sought the injection of Jewish capital into Transjordan to reduce his dependence on Britain and a Jewish State in Palestine to co-operate economically and militarily against his primary Arab enemy, the House of Saud, which had ousted his father from the Hijaz in 1924. Flapan, *Zionism and the Palestinians*, p. 255.
10 Ibid., p. 256.
11 Ibid., p. 285.
12 More unrealistically, he also asked the Jewish Agency to persuade the United States government that Hashemite rule in the Arabian peninsula would serve US interests better than the regime of the Ibn Saud. Sasson to Sharett,

22 March 1948, Central Zionist Archives S25/3909, quoted by Flapan, *The Birth of Israel*, p. 39.

13 Golda Meir's report to the People's Council, 12 May 1948. Israel State Archives 51702 p. 4, quoted by Flapan, *The Birth of Israel*, p. 39.

14 'Future course of events in Palestine', memo, 4 May 1948, US Nat. Arch 501. BB Pal/5–448 quoted by Flapan, *Zionism and the Palestinians*, pp. 336–7.

15 Flapan, *Zionism and the Palestinians*, p. 327–8.

16 BBC Summary of World Broadcasts, part iv, no. 50, period 3–9 May 1948, p. 59, cited by Flapan, ibid., p. 332.

17 Mahmoud, *King Abdallah and Palestine*, pp. 96–7, cited by Flapan, *Zionism and the Palestinians*, p. 324; Bar Zohar, *Ben Gurion*, vol. 2, p. 773; Ze'ev Sharef, *Three Days*, p. 62, both cited in Flapan, *The Birth of Israel*, pp. 140–2.

18 John Bagot Glubb, *A Soldier with the Arabs* (London, 1957) p. 142.

19 Morris, 'Operation Dani and the Palestinian exodus from Lydda and Ramle in 1948', in *Middle East Journal*, vol. 40, Winter 1986.

20 The Zionists knew this. See Ben Gurion *War Diaries* (Tel·Aviv, 1982) pp. 886, 956, entries for 18 December 1948 and 17 January 1949, quoted by Flapan, *The Birth of Israel*, p. 255.

21 Flapan, *The Birth of Israel*, p. 145.

22 Ibid., p. 148.

23 Pamela Ann Smith, *Palestine and the Palestinians, 1876–1983* (Beckenham, 1984) p. 90.

24 Ibid.

25 Ibid., p. 223, n. 36.

26 Flapan, *The Birth of Israel*, p. 150.

27 Smith, *Palestine and the Palestinians*, p. 101.

28 For example, in Nablus, a city of over 40,000 inhabitants in the 1960s, there were only 6,000 eligible voters. Moshe Ma'oz, *Palestinian Leadership in the West Bank* (London, 1984) p. 52.

29 Smith, *Palestine and the Palestinians*, p. 100 names members of Nashashibi. Tuqan, Salah, Dajani, Abdul Hadi and Khalidi families.

30 Ibid., pp. 91–6.

31 10,000 Jordanian dinars. Arthur R. Day, *East Bank/West Bank* (New York, 1986) p. 111.

32 Roger Owen, 'Economic history of Palestine under the Mandate, 1919–1948', a paper given at the Welfare Association International Symposium, Oxford, January 1986.

33 Smith, *Palestine and the Palestinians*, p. 103.

34 Ibid., pp. 106–7.

35 This assurance was given by the US Ambassador to the United Nations but subsequently confirmed by US President Johnson in his letter to Husayn, dated 12 April 1968, in Riad, *The Struggle for Peace in the Middle East*, pp. 80–1.

36 See U.S. News & Report, 2 Sept 1974, in Ma'oz, *Palestinian Leadership on the West Bank*, p. 121.

37 Public address by Schultz on 20 November, quoted in Marantz and Stein, *Peacemaking in the Middle East: Problems and Prospects* (Beckenham, 1985) p. 152.

38 In fact, only the Israeli sponsored Village Leagues and one or two parliamentarians supported Husayn. See *Middle East International*, no. 270, 7 March 1986.

39   Abdul Sittar Kassem poll, in A'si, 'Israeli and Palestinian public opinion', p. 190.

40   Ibid., p. 193.

41   Shadid and Selzer, 'Political attitudes of Palestinians'.

42   On her visit to Israel in May 1986 Prime Minister Thatcher called for the emergence of a moderate Palestinian leadership to replace the PLO.

43   *Al Hamishmar*, quoted in *The Jerusalem Post International*, week ending 3 May 1986. On the closure of twenty-five out of thirty-seven PLO offices, see *Middle East International*, no. 279, 11 July 1986.

44   *Observer*, 29 June 1986.

45   Jordan's Minister for the Occupied Territories, Marwan Dudin, was brother of Mustafa Dudin of the Village Leagues. Ibid.

46   *Ma'ariv* suggested that the US Ambassador in Tel Aviv was acting as the primary postman between Amman and Jerusalem. *The New York Times* claimed Husayn and Peres had met in the Wadi Araba desert, see *Middle East International*, no. 292, 23 January 1987.

47   See the *Observer*, 22 June 1986, and *Middle East International*, 30 May 1986. See also Wolf Blitzer, 'Jordan: a divided nation', in *The Jerusalem Post International*, 2 May 1987, arguing that indigenous East Bankers fear a return of the West Bank to Jordanian rule.

CHAPTER 3   GOING HOME? THE REFUGEE ISSUE

1   Almost every year the General Assembly records its regret that Resolution 194 (III) of 11 December 1948 with regard to the refugees has not yet been implemented.

2   This point was made shortly after the 1967 war by A. H. Hourani, 'Palestine and Israel', *Observer*, 3 September 1976, reprinted in Walter Laqueur, *The Arab-Israeli Reader* (London, 1970) pp. 325–32.

3   The poll was taken by the Israeli Institute for Public Opinion Research, a predecessor of the present Israel Institute for Applied Social Research. See Murad A'si, 'Israel and Palestinian public opinion', p. 155.

4   Benny Morris, *The Birth of the Palestinian Refugee Problem 1947–1949* (Cambridge, 1987) p. 257.

5   Ibid., p. 269 and footnotes.

6   Ibid., pp. 278–83 and footnotes.

7   See chapter 9, page 198.

8   Flapan, *The Birth of Israel*, p. 226.

9   Ibid., p. 231.

10   Transjordan was 'most anxious' to make peace, according to Moshe Sharett, Israel's new Foreign Minister. Morris, *The Birth of the Palestinian Refugee Problem*, pp. 263–4 and footnote.

11   Ibid., p. 277, quoting from Israel State Archives, FM3749/2 Sasson (Lausanne) to Z. Zeligson, 16 June 1949.

12   UN General Assembly Doc A/2470 para 16, 1953, quoted in UNRWA, *UNRWA: Past, Present and Future* (Vienna, May 1986) p. 4.

13   In January 1952 UNRWA had received General Assembly support for a proposal to establish a $200 million development plan, but by 1957 less than $38 million for self-support programmes had been pledged. Ibid., p. 4. For an account of

the Jordan waters issue, see Georgiana G. Stevens, *The Jordan River Partition* (Stanford, 1965).

14 Thirty years later UNRWA ran into difficulties with both refugees and with host governments over its review and final abandonment of ration rolls in the early 1980s and sought the assistance of the PLO to stem refugee protests.

15 The following summary of the negotiations by Palestine refugees is heavily dependent on Flapan's account in *The Birth of Israel*, pp. 218–32.

16 Personal archive of Aziz Shehadeh, quoted in ibid., p. 18.

17 Flapan, *The Birth of Israel*, p. 222, his emphasis, citing Nimr al Hawari, *The Secret of the Catastrophe* (Nazareth, 1955) pp. 376–87.

18 Hawari, *The Secret of the Catastrophe*, pp. 367–8, in Flapan, *The Birth of Israel*, p. 226.

19 Morris, *The Birth of the Palestinian Refugee Problem*, p. 264.

20 In the end the Ramallah Congress was stifled by the Jordanian authorities. Flapan, *The Birth of Israel*, pp. 231–2.

21 John Davis, *The Evasive Peace* (London, 1970) p. 69.

22 It may have been as high as 500,000. Milton Viorst, *UNRWA and Peace in the Middle East* (Washington, 1984) p. 41.

23 By the end of 1967 Israel had only allowed 15,000 to return. Davis, *The Evasive Peace*, p. 69.

24 A'si, 'Israeli and Palestinian public opinion', p. 156.

25 Sammy Smooha, *The Orientation and Politicization of the Arab Minority in Israel* (Haifa, 1984) p. 42.

26 See Ran Kislev, 'Israel's Arabs: coping with duality', *Ha'aretz*, 21 August 1987, reviewing Smooha's work over the period 1976–85. If this finding seems overly bleak, it should be noted that by 1985, while 71 per cent were wholly opposed to a return, 26 per cent were prepared to consider a return of refugees 'under certain conditions' – implying that returnees would not change the Jewish identity of the state or in any way question the system.

27 Mark Heller, *A Palestinian State – The Implications for Israel* (Cambridge, Mass., 1983) p. 59.

28 Yariv's position as expressed in Everett Mendelsohn, *A Compassionate Peace* (London, 1982) p. 80.

29 Meir Pa'il, 'A Palestinian state', in Alouph Hareven (ed.), *Can the Palestinian Problem be Solved?* (Jerusalem, 1983) p. 124. Israel's own anxiety to dissolve the refugee problem is exemplified in its resettlement plans in Gaza, commenced in the 1970s and renewed in 1983 in order to formalize the exchange of population between Palestinians and some 600,000 Jews from Arab lands, the view ascribed to Mordechai Ben Porat, architect of the 1980s resettlement plan, in Viorst, *UNRWA and Peace*, p. 49. Israel claims its motive is humanitarian, but its insistence on the demolition of vacated shelters in the camp in a context of acute overcrowding belies this.

30 Mendelsohn, *A Compassionate Peace*, p. 86.

31 Rosemary Sayigh, *Palestinians: From Peasants to Revolutionaries* (London, 1979) p. 111.

32 Pa'il, 'A Palestinian state', p. 124.

33 Sayigh, *Palestinians: From Peasants to Revolutionaries*, chapter 3.

34 By 1988 only two camps in Lebanon had escaped major violence: Wavell Camp in the Biqa', and Nahr al Bared, north of Tripoli.

35 The estimate of 210,000 displaced persons has remained unchanged since the

1970s, and must be treated with caution.

36 An official estimate for the end of 1985 gives a population of 2,693,700 (*Europa Yearbook 1987*), making Palestinians just over 40 per cent. It has been widely assumed that the Palestinians comprised as much as 65 per cent of the East Bank population. See Valerie Yorke, 'Jordan is not Palestine: the demographic factor', in *Middle East International*, no. 323, 16 April 1988.

37 Roger Owen, *Migrant Workers in the Gulf* (London, 1985) p. 18.

38 See for example Heller, *A Palestinian State*, p. 59.

CHAPTER 4   THE OCCUPIED TERRITORIES: FROM CONTROL TO REVOLT

1 See Meron Benvenisti, *Demographic, Economic, Legal, Social and Political Developments in the West Bank: 1986 Report of the West Bank Data Base Project*, pp. 63–4 indicates a measurable increase in violence from 1982, as does his *1987 Report*, pp. 40–1.

2 The ease with which this network was built up in part resulted from the capture of Jordanian secret service files, and the re-employment of those who had served the Hashemite regime. With regard to the Druzes, see below pp. 131–2.

3 For an example of the way this has been carried out, see Fuad Aziz and Raja Shehadeh, *Israeli Proposed Road Plan for the West Bank, A Question for the International Court of Justice* (Ramallah, 1984). On the more general issue of land use planning, see Mona Rishmawi, *Planning in Whose Interest? Land Use Planning as a Strategy for Judaization* (Ramallah, 1986).

4 Military Order 158 of 1 October 1967. No water installation was allowed without a licence from the military commander. Between 1967 and 1987 there were only five cases of Palestinians being allowed to sink new wells.

5 Israel was able to absorb into higher grade positions the Kurdish and Arab Jews who had previously provided all the unskilled labour.

6 See Meron Benvenisti, *Demographic, Economic, Legal, Social and Political Developments in the West Bank: 1987 Report of the West Bank Data Base Project* (Jerusalem, 1987) pp. 10–11.

7 After the foundation of the PLO in 1964, Jordan had rashly allowed it to establish its headquarters in East Jerusalem. In January 1967 it ordered its closure as its potential threat to Jordan's long term retention of the West Bank was perceived. Ma'oz, *Palestinian Leadership*, p. 111.

8 Saul Mishal, 'Nationalism through localism: some observations on the West Bank political elite', *Middle Eastern Studies*, vol. 17, no. 4, October 1981.

9 Despite the initial belief that Israel would return the West Bank to Jordan, Muslim dignitaries met under the chairmanship of Shaykh Abd al Hamid al Sa'ih, to form a national resistance. Al Sa'ih was expelled and Jordan reimposed its authority over the religious institution. The other early effort at resistance, the National Guidance Committee, set up in Jerusalem, Nablus, Tulkarm, Ramallah, Bethlehem and Hebron, was quickly shunned by the old élite, Jordan and the PLO. It tried to work with the Islamic Conference in Jerusalem, the first oppositional effort in the territories. See Ibrahim Dakkak, 'Back to square one', in Alexander Schölch (ed.) *Palestinians over the Green Line* (London, 1983) p. 71; Mishal, 'Nationalism through localism', p. 483; Ma'oz, *Palestinian Leadership*, p. 88.

10   Ma'oz, *Palestinian Leadership*, p. 97.
11   Ibid., p. 99.
12   Mishal, 'Nationalism through localism', p. 487.
13   As Dayan said in 1967, the West Bank 'would not have a central Arab authority above the municipal level', *Middle East Record*, Tel Aviv, 1967, p. 278, quoted in Ma'oz, *Palestinian Leadership*, p. 89.
14   Israel hoped the election results would, in Dayan's words, 'invest the nominees with political authority by which . . . they can speak for the Arab public who elected them,' and exclude Jordanian and PLO influence. *Jewish Observer and Middle East Review*, 7 April 1972, in Ma'oz, *Palestinian Leadership*, p. 106.
15   Dakkak, 'Back to square one', p. 76.
16   Ibid., p. 80.
17   Ma'oz, *Palestinian Leadership*, p. 120.
18   Ibid., p. 133.
19   Ibid., p. 137.
20   Ibid., p. 149.
21   Shaul Mishal, *The PLO under 'Arafat: Between Gun and Olive Branch* (Yale and London, 1986) p. 118.
22   Dakkak, 'Back to square one', p. 82.
23   Ibid., p. 84.
24   Mishal, *The PLO*, p. 122.
25   Evidence emerged of covert discussions at the behest of the PLO leadership, between West Bank leaders and Israeli and American officials to ascertain whether the autonomy talks might advance Palestinian interests. Ibid., p. 124.
26   Ibid., p. 135.
27   Radio Monte Carlo, 10 November 1979, quoted in Mishal, *The PLO*, p. 137.
28   Ibid., p. 145.
29   The first Village League was established in 1978 but the Village League Movement did not emerge until 1980. See Salim Tamari, 'In league with Zion: Israel's search for a native pillar', *Journal of Palestine Studies*, vol. XII, no. 4, Summer 1983.
30   The following publications of al Haq/Law in the Service of Man since 1984 reflect increasingly adverse conditions: Emma Playfair, *Administrative Detention* (Ramallah, 1986); Joost Hilterman, *Israel's Deportation Policy in the Occupied West Bank and Gaza Strip* (Ramallah, 1986); Emma Playfair, *Demolition and Sealing of Houses as a Punitive Measure in the Israeli-Occupied West Bank* (Ramallah, 1987); Paul Hunt, *Justice? The Military Court System in the Israeli-Occupied Territories* (Ramallah and Gaza, 1987). Also, by the Council for the Advancement of Arab-British Understanding, *Punishing the Innocent – House Demolitions as Collective Punishment on the West Bank* (London, 1987).
31   This process was so invisible that as late as summer 1987 two Birzeit academics asserted that given the apparent demise of PLO influence, the old traditional élite, which had seemed very much on the defensive following the break between the PLO and Jordan in 1986, was reasserting its control of West Bank life. *Middle East International*, 11 July 1987.
32   Daoud Kuttab in *al Fajr English Weekly*, 31 May 1987, in *Israeli Press Briefs*, no. 53.
33   Ma'oz, *Palestinian Leadership*, p. 166; Mishal, *The PLO*, pp. 143–4.
34   Yehuda Litani, 'Islam as a political weapon', *Jerusalem Post International*, 6 June 1987.

35 See Ma'oz, *Palestinian Leadership*, pp. 200–202.

36 Marisa Escribano, 'The Endurance of the Olive Tree: Tradition and Identity in two West Bank villages' (unpublished Ph.D. thesis, Harvard University, 1987) p. 164.

37 For example, at Kobar, a village a few miles north west of Ramallah, 60 per cent of village income comes from labour in Israel, and 15 per cent from labour in the West Bank. Ibid., p. 62.

38 Histadrut treatment of its West Bank and Gaza workers is described by Marty Rosenblut, 'Migrants in their own land', 'No commitment'; on Palestinian trade unions see Joost Hilterman, 'Israel's Iron Fist', all in *International Labour Reports*, issue 24, November/December 1987.

39 Such agreements resulted less from union strength than the goodwill of employers, for example Birzeit and al Najah universities, one or two taxi fleets, and hotels in Jerusalem.

40 A frequent form of intimidation was to place soldiers or Shin Bet agents outside a union office, and to note the details of ID cards of those entering. Another was widespread use of administrative detention under the British Defence (Emergency) regulations 1945, which required no formal charge or court hearing. See Hilterman, 'Israel's Iron Fist', p. 13.

41 Ibid.

42 These were the Carpenters and Building Workers' Union, February 1987, and the Gaza Commercial and General Services Workers' Union, April 1987.

43 Jerusalem and Palestine have had a special place in the Muslim world since the beginning of Islam. See Yehoshua Porath, 'The political awakening of the Palestinian Arabs and their leadership towards the end of the Ottoman period', in Moshe Ma'oz (ed.) *Studies on Palestine During the Ottoman Period* (Jerusalem, 1975) pp. 351–5. It was inevitable, given this background, that the Zionist settlement of Palestine awoke a specifically Muslim reaction. The Arab revolt of 1936 owed its origins in part to the religious inspiration of Sheikh Izz al Din Qassam in 1935. See Porath, *The Palestinian Arab National Movement*, pp. 133–9, 194.

44 It was, for example, widely overlooked that some of the most serious disturbances had been triggered by interference with Muslim holy places. See Ma'oz, *Palestinian Leadership*, pp. 157–8.

45 As one Palestinian told Yehuda Litani of the *Jerusalem Post*, 'I have not become religious, nor have I joined the Muslim Brotherhood. I still like whiskey and would not mind joining you for a drink later tonight. But I keep Ramadan mainly for political reasons.' Attendance of unprecedented numbers of worshippers at the al Aqsa mosque did not mark a return to Islam. 'Rather, it expresses a deep disappointment with all other political means.' *Jerusalem Post International*, 6 June 1987.

46 The decision for example, to establish a university in Gaza, and that it should be Islamic, had been partly a PLO one. Adam Roberts, Boel Joergensen and Frank Newman, *Academic Freedom under Israeli Military Occupation* (London and Geneva, 1984) p. 49.

47 For a while the Muslim Brotherhood had its headquarters in Jerusalem, following the growth of state oppression in Egypt in the early 1950s. Smith, *Palestine and the Palestinians*, pp. 188–9.

48 Thomas Friedman, 'An Islamic awakening', *The New York Times*, 30 April 1987.

49 In Gaza it allowed the establishment of an Islamic University in 1978, which expanded rapidly from 120 students to 2,800 in 1987 and 5,000 by 1987, creating the impression of a Muslim takeover of the Gaza Strip. See Roberts, Joergensen, Newman, *Academic Freedom*, p. 49, and Thomas Friedman, 'An Islamic revival is quickly gaining ground in an unlikely place: Israel', *The New York Times*, 30 April 1987. In 1980 it turned a blind eye when a mob of fundamentalists marched on the leftist and secularist Palestine Red Crescent office to burn it.

50 See Eli Rekhes, 'Violence: the next stage?', *Jerusalem Post International*, 21 November 1987.

51 Elaine Ruth Fletcher, 'Islam and the Strife', Ibid., 6 February 1988.

52 *The Independent*, 26 September 1988.

53 See Escribano, 'The Endurance of the Olive Tree', p. 62.

54 See Hillel Frisch, 'Corrupting the revolt', in *The Jerusalem Post*, 12 September 1984, and Joost Hilterman, 'The emerging trade union movement in the West Bank', *MERIP Reports*, October–December 1985.

55 To which UNRWA headquarters had moved definitively in 1978 (having relocated there temporarily 1976–7).

56 For examples and an explicit condemnation of the use of Unicef, WHO and UNDP funds, see Union of Palestinian Medical Relief Committees, *Twenty Years of Occupation: an overview of health conditions and services in the Israeli occupied territories* (Jerusalem, 1987, mimeograph) pp. 22–3.

57 See David McDowall, *The Palestinians* (Minority Rights Group pamphlet, London, 1987) pp. 24–5 for a summary of the Zubaydat story, which is more fully told in Salim Tamari and Rita Giacaman, *Zbeidat, the Social Impact of Drip Irrigation on a Palestinian Peasant Community in the Jordan Valley* (Birzeit, 1980) and Alex Pollock, 'Aspects of poverty and underdevelopment in the northern sector of the Jordan Valley', (The Arab Thought Forum, Jerusalem, n.d); Harold Dick, 'A strategy for economic development under prolonged occupation: empowerment and entrepreneurship', a paper given at the Welfare Association international symposium, Oxford 1986.

58 These limits included production quotas on most market garden produce, and a blanket prohibition on the planting of new, or replacement of old, fruit trees – a catastrophe particularly for the Gaza citrus growers.

59 e.g. T. H. Tulchinsky, 'Medical services in Gaza', Around the World, *The Lancet*, 21 February 1987 quoted in Union of Palestinian Medical Relief Committees, *Twenty Years of Occupation*, p. 4.

60 The figure given in fact by the Israeli Ministry of Health, *Review of Health Services in Judea, Samaria and Gaza*, 1986, p. 11. There exist great variations from locality to locality, for example, an IMR of 49 per thousand in a village close to Jerusalem, and 91 per thousand in three villages close to Ramallah. UPMRC, *Twenty Years of Occupation*, pp. 4–5.

61 8 per 10,000 compared with Israel 28 per 10,000 and Jordan 22 per 10,000. UMRC, *Twenty Years of Occupation*, p. 5.

62 Ibid., p. 6.

63 Ibid., p. 8.

64 Ibid., p. 7, citing Meron Benvenisti, *1986 report*, p. 17.

65 In 1977 Israel had abolished the cheap government health service accessible to everyone in favour of a health insurance scheme, which it claimed 38 per cent of

the population had joined. In fact in Ramallah only 19.5 per cent were subscribers, in Jericho only 14 per cent, and the actual user rate far lower, UMRC, *Twenty Years of Occupation*, p. 10.

66 Ibid., p. 11.

67 Ibid., p. 20.

68 See also M. Barghouti, R. Giacaman, C. Smith, *The Medical Relief Committee: a Model for Mobilisation* (Jerusalem, 1986, mimeograph); Union of Palestinian Medical Relief Committees, *Annual Report for 1985* (Jerusalem, 1986, mimeograph); Gaza Medical Relief Committee, *Health in the Gaza Strip* (Gaza, 1986, mimeograph) and R. Giacaman, *Reflections on Community Participation in Health Promotion Activities in the Israeli Occupied Territories* (Birzeit, 1987, mimeograph).

69 There is little available on the women's committees. See Rita Giacaman: *Reflections on the Palestinian Women's Movement in the Israeli-occupied Territories* (Birzeit, 1987, mimeograph), *Palestinian Women and Development in the Occupied West Bank* (Birzeit, 1983, mimeograph), and 'Health and underdevelopment in the occupied territories: a theoretical framework' in *Birzeit Research Review*, no. 3, Spring 1986; Joost Hilterman, 'Organising under occupation' in *Middle East International*, 20 March 1987; Yvonne Haddad, 'Palestinian women: patterns of legitimation and domination', in Khalil Nakhleh and Elia Zureik (eds) *The Sociology of the Palestinians* (London, 1980).

70 See Palestinian Agricultural Relief Committee pamphlet, 'The Palestinian Agricultural Relief Committee Household Economy Program' (June 1988).

71 *Facts Weekly Review*, 17–23 April, 24–30 April, 1988, nos. 7 & 8.

72 Ibid., 21–27 August, 1988, no. 23. Israel closed down the Union of Charitable Societies, and other urban-based 'non-popular' institutions in late August 1988.

73 *Al Fajr English Weekly editorial*, 19 April 1987, in *Israeli Press Briefs*, no. 53.

74 A poll in early 1983 indicated that in the West Bank only 45 per cent favoured a Palestinian-Jordanian dialogue, 41 per cent opposed the rapprochement, 32 per cent favoured a joint Jordanian-Palestinian negotiating team, 19 per cent were wholly opposed to it, and 43 per cent said that any peace team should include only Palestinians – the result of the second of two surveys carried out by Abdul Sattar Kassem in January 1982 and March–April 1983, A'si, 'Israeli and Palestinian public opinion', pp. 192–3.

75 Just over half of the population, 54 per cent, according to the same poll, preferred not to rush into negotiations but wait until the time was ripe. Ibid., p. 192.

76 *Al Fajr English Weekly*, 31 May 1987, in *Israeli Press Briefs*, no. 53.

77 *Facts Weekly Review*, 31 July–6 August 1988, no. 20.

78 Ibid., 16–29 October 1988, no. 28.

79 Shadid and Seltzer, 'Political attitudes of Palestinians', p. 22, and poll carried out for *Time Magazine* in April 1982, A'si, 'Israeli and Palestinian public opinion', p. 191.

80 Only 72.2 per cent supported the current PLO leadership. Shadid and Seltzer, 'Political attitudes of Palestinians', p. 23.

81 Only 16.9 per cent of respondents in 1986 favoured a final two state solution to the Palestine-Israel conflict, compared with 33 per cent in 1983. Compare Shadid and Seltzer, 'Political attitudes of Palestinians', p. 25 with A'si, 'Israeli and Palestinian public opinion', p. 194.

82 Compare, A'si, 'Israeli and Palestinian public opinion', pp. 188–99 and Shadid and Seltzer, 'Political attitudes of Palestinians', p. 25.
83 Shadid and Seltzer, 'Political attitudes of Palestinians', p. 26.
84 Ibid.
85 Editorial, *Facts Weekly Review*, 7–13 August 1988, no. 21.
86 Finding of the Abdul Sattar Kassem survey, in A'si, 'Israeli and Palestinian public opinion', p. 194.
87 One of a number of similar remarks to author, September 1987.

CHAPTER 5   THE ISRAELI PALESTINIANS: HOW THEY ARE CONTROLLED

1 This viewpoint has been put to me more than once during the course of researching this book, as if the implication of what is going on inside Israel with regard to its Palestinian minority will go away if nobody talks about it.
2 Statement to the Anglo-American Committee of Enquiry, as reprinted in *The Jewish Case: Before the Anglo-American Committee of Inquiry on Palestine as Presented by the Jewish Agency for Palestine*, p. 66, quoted by Ian Lustick, *Arabs in the Jewish State*, (Austin, 1980) p. 88.
3 For an example of such fears see the Van Leer poll on Jewish youth in Israel, 1987 in *New Outlook*, February 1988.
4 See below on the demographic challenge to Israel, pp. 221–30.
5 Lustick, *Arabs in the Jewish State*, p. 41.
6 Its provisions could also be applied outside areas under a military commander by local authorities. Sabri Jiryis, *The Arabs in Israel, 1948–66* (Beirut, 1968) p. 54.
7 Although in theory everyone moving in or out of closed areas was required to obtain a permit from the military government in practice it was only used against Arabs. See Israel, *Report of the State Controller on the Ministry of Defence for the Financial Year 1957–59*, no. 9, February 1959, p. 56, cited by Jiryis, *The Arabs in Israel*, p. 200.
8 The British Mandate Defence (Emergency) Regulations 1945 were condemned by the Knesset in 1951 as 'incompatible with the principles of a democratic state' but were not cancelled. In fact Britain had cancelled the regulations with effect from midnight, 12 May 1948, two days before its mandate ended. Israel refuses to recognize this cancellation, since it was not published in the Palestine Gazette. See André Rosenthal, 'The 1945 Defence Regulations – valid law in the West Bank?' (unpublished paper, February 1984) and David McDowall, 'Are Israel's Defence Regulations valid?', *Middle East International*, no. 292, 23 January 1987.
9 This was the assessment of the Palestine Conciliation Commission in 1951. Hadawi, *Palestinian Rights and Losses*, p. 94. For background see Jiryis, *The Arabs in Israel*, pp. 58ff.
10 Under the Law of Absentees Property, the State confiscated the assets of the Muslim *waqf*. Mosques and other specifically religious buildings were excepted. In 1946 the *waqf* properties had accounted for one-tenth of all land in Palestine, as well as 70 per cent of all shops in some Arab cities. Lustick, *Arabs in the Jewish State*, pp. 59, 189–90; compare with Jiryis, *The Arabs in Israel*, p. 63, which states that, according to the Committee of Enquiry on

Palestine in 1936, one-sixteenth of the total land area of Palestine was *waqf* property.

11 See Chapter 11, note 60.

12 For these and other cases, see Jiryis, *The Arabs in Israel*, pp. 65–71.

13 The main legal instrument was the 'Emergency Articles for the Exploitation of Uncultivated Lands' (*Offical Gazette*, no. 27, 15 October 1948, (b), p. 3, cited in Jiryis, *The Arabs in Israel*, pp. 72–3).

14 Don Peretz, *Israel and the Palestine Arabs* (Washington, 1958) p. 142, cited by Lustick, *Arabs in the Jewish State*, p. 60.

15 Lustick, *Arabs in the Jewish State*, pp. 99, 107–8.

16 In 1950 the estimated number of Palestinians employed in the Jewish sector was only 3 per cent of all employed Israeli Palestinians, whereas by 1961 this proportion had increased to 12 per cent. Y. Ben Porath, *The Arab Labour Force in Israel* (Jerusalem, 1966) pp. 51–7, in Reinhard Wiemer, 'Zionism and the Arabs after the establishment of the State of Israel', in Alexander Schölch (ed.), *Palestinians over the Green Line*, p. 43.

17 To give one example, Umm al Fahm in Wadi Ara, which had lost 34,000 of its 125,000 dunums by 1966, lost another 65,000 dunums over the next decade. See Lustick, *Arabs in the Jewish State*, p. 179, and compare with Jiryis, *The Arabs in Israel*, p. 80.

18 While on average, each Arab village in 1948 had 9136 dunums, by 1974 this had fallen to 2,000 dunums. Tawfiq Zayyad, 'The Arabs in Israel', in J. Zogby (ed.), *Perspectives on Palestinian Arabs and Israeli Jews* (Wilmett, Illinois, 1977) p. 50; Lustick, *Arabs in the Jewish State*, p. 179, lists a representative number of Arab villages.

19 Since the mid-1970s Israel has intensified efforts in Galilee with fifty-eight new settlements between 1977 and 1981. Schölch, *Palestinians over the Green Line*, p. 15. In 1980 alone thirty *mitzpim*, or observation posts, were constructed overlooking Palestinian villages in Galilee, and another twenty were planned. Despite these efforts, the state had only persuaded about 300 additional Jews to settle in western Galilee by 1986. Benvenisti, *1986 Report*, p. 46.

20 *al Ittihad*, 30 December 1985 and 18 March 1986, in Peter Lagharn and Hatim Kana'aneh, 'Development needs and potential of Israel's Arabs' (Galilee, 1987, mimeograph) p. 25.

21 Lustick, *Arabs in the Jewish State*, pp. 132–3, 190.

22 Ibid., p. 131.

23 Ibid., p. 132.

24 McDowall, *The Palestinians*, p. 33, n. 84.

25 Erik Cohen, *Integration vs. Separation in the Planning of a Mixed Jewish-Arab city in Israel* (Jerusalem, 1973) in Lustick, *Arabs in the Jewish State*, pp. 131–2.

26 *Israeli Statistical Abstract 1986*, p. 55. During this same period, 1973–85, it was only possible to increase the Jewish population marginally, 27,400 in 1974 to 29,300 in 1985. See Lustick, *Arabs in the Jewish State*, p. 131, and *Israeli Statistical Abstract 1986*, p. 55. See also *Ha'aretz*, 29 April 1986, in *Israeli Mirror*, no. 754.

27 *Ha'aretz*, 17 January 1986, in *Israeli Mirror*, no. 748. For other examples, see Kol Ha'ir, 15 February 1985, in *Israeli Mirror*, no. 725–6; *Jerusalem Post*

International for weeks ending 4, 11, 18 July 1987, and *Israeli Mirror*, no. 762 of 22 July 1987 with press translations from *Ma'ariv*, 24, 26 and 30 June 1987, *Ha'aretz*, 28 June and 6 July 1987, *Yediot Aharonot*, 26 June 1987 and *Hadashot*, 30 June and 2, 5 July 1987.

28 Reported in *Ha'aretz*, 2 July 1987, translated by *Israeli Mirror*, no. 762.

29 Ruth Gavison, 'Minority rights in Israel: the case of army veteran provisions', in International Centre for Peace in the Middle East, *Relations between Ethnic Majority and Minority*, (Tel Aviv, 1987) p. 21.

30 Lustick, *Arabs in the Jewish State*, p. 102.

31 However, the Negev bedouin were allowed into Beersheba one day per week without a permit, and some of the Druzes of Galilee were allowed almost complete freedom of movement.

32 *Davar*, 26 January 1962, quoted by Jiryis, *The Arabs in Israel*, p. 46.

33 Lands belonging to Deir al Asad, Ba'na and Nahf.

34 On 31 December 1963 there were 224,850 Jews compared with 157,944 Palestinians. *ISA 1964*, p. 15, cited in Jiryis, *The Arabs in Israel*, p. 90.

35 For background on the location of Druze villages, see Salman Falah, 'The history of Druze settlements in Palestine during the Ottoman period', in Ma'oz (ed.), *Studies on Palestine during the Ottoman Period*.

36 The Jewish Agency had cultivated links with the Druzes during the 1930s and this increased their reluctance to join the revolt. They were also aware of Syrian Druze relations with the Jewish Agency, hoping it could persuade the French President, Léon Blum, to advance Druze interests inside Syria, under the French mandate. See Porath, *The Palestinian Arab National Movement*, pp. 243–5, 270–3.

37 For an analysis of the different Druze behaviour in Lebanon, Syria and Israel, see Kais Firro, 'Political behavior of the Druze as a minority in the Middle East – a historical perspective', in *Orient*, vol. 27, no. 3, September 1986.

38 See Chapter 11, note 61.

39 The British census carried out in May 1946 indicated there were 92,000 bedouin living in the Negev, and 35,000 living elsewhere. See United Nations, *Ad Hoc Committee on the Palestine Question* (Document A/AC 14/32, 11 November 1947) Appendix C.

40 Ibid.

41 Lustick, *Arabs in the Jewish State*, p. 134; Penny Maddrell, 'Note on the Israeli Bedouin' (unpublished mimeograph, n.d.).

42 Chaim Weizmann, Israel's first president, and Yigael Yadin, army commander, met sixteen bedouin shaikhs in 1951 promising that their honour, weapons and lands would be preserved. Arieh Leo Cohen, *The Beduin in Israel* (Kfar Menachem, 1978) p. 28, quoted by Maddrell, 'Note on the Israeli Bedouin', p. 2.

43 Maddrell, 'Note on the Israeli Bedouin', p. 2.

44 Lustick, *Arabs in the Jewish State*, pp. 134–5.

45 For details, see Maddrell, 'Note on the Israeli Bedouin', p. 3.

46 Ibid., p. 9.

47 Jiryis, *The Arabs in Israel*, pp. 165–6.

48 Lustick, *Arabs in the Jewish State*, p. 177.

49 Wiemer, 'Zionism and the Arabs', p. 57.

50 Raja Khalidi, *The Arab Economy in Israel* (London, 1988) p. 116, table 4.1,

extrapolating from *Israeli Statistical Abstracts*, for 1954, 1964, 1966, 1974, 1984 and 1985.

51   Khalidi, *The Arab Economy*, p. 120.
52   Ibid., p. 121.
53   Ibid., p. 129.
54   Ibid., p. 127.
55   Although it remains in line with the proportionate demographic increase of Palestinians in Israel. Ibid., p. 117.
56   In 1967 Palestinian unemployment soared to 17.7 per cent compared with a national rise to 10.4 per cent. In 1985 the Palestinian rate was 9.5 per cent compared with a national rate of 6.7 per cent. Ibid., p. 118.
57   Ibid., p. 133.
58   Ibid., p. 135.
59   Ibid., p. 43.
60   Samih Ghanadiri, *al jamahir al arabiyya fi isra'il – banurama al idtihad wa'l tamayiz al qawmiayn* (Nazareth, 1987) p. 115.
61   Maddrell, 'Note on the Israeli Bedouin', p. 5. See also *The Jerusalem Post*, 18 January 1987, 8 July 1987.
62   *Israeli Statistical Abstract, 1986*, p. 55, and *al Ittihad*, 7 February, 1986, quoted in Laugharn and Kana'aneh, 'Development needs', p. 27.
63   See Yitzhak Oded, 'Land losses among Israel's Arab villagers', *New Outlook*, September 1964, p. 14, in Lustick, *Arabs in the Jewish State*, p. 171.
64   Estimated at 24,000 built on state land by 1977. Lustick, *Arabs in the Jewish State*, p. 195.
65   The area around Beersheba is littered with squalid unserviced 'illegal' settlements which suffer harassment and arbitrary transfer. See Maddrell, 'Note on the Israeli Bedouin', p. 6.
66   Smooha, *The Orientation and Politicization of the Arab Minority in Israel*, p. 81.
67   The actual figures for 1985 were 2.03 (Palestinian) and 1.08 (Jew), *Israeli Statistical Abstract, 1986*, p. 269.
68   Ibid.
69   Ghanadiri, *al jamahir al arabiyya*, p. 111.
70   The Law for the Encouragement of Capital Investments. See Lustick, *Arabs in the Jewish State*, pp. 186–7; Khalidi, *The Arab Economy*, pp. 162–3.
71   Lustick, *Arabs in the Jewish State*, p. 186.
72   Maddrell, 'Note on the Israeli Bedouin', p. 6.
73   See Mahmud Bayadsi, 'The Arab local authorities: achievements and problems', *New Outlook*, October–November 1975, p. 59, quoted by Lustick, *Arabs in the Jewish State*, p. 188.
74   Ghanadiri, *al jamahir al arabiyya*, p. 119.
75   Jiryis, *The Arabs in Israel*, p. 172.
76   Lustick, *Arabs in the Jewish State*, p. 183.
77   For details, see ibid., p. 188.
78   *The Jerusalem Post*, 11 January 1986, quoted in Khalidi, *The Arab Economy*, p. 163.
79   In 1950 it was 46.2 per thousand (Jews) and 56 per thousand (Palestinians). *Israeli Statistical Abstract 1986*, p. 4.
80   Ibid. Life expectancy for Palestinians by 1983 was three years less than for

Jewish Israelis. Ibid., p. 122.

81 In the north these are in Safad, Nahariya, Tiberias and Haifa, serving the urban population. There is virtually no ambulance service based in Arab population areas. See Laugharn and Kana'aneh, 'Development needs', p. 14–15.

82 Hatim Kana'aneh & Fuad Farah, 'Sewage problems in rural communities: an exchange of ecological balance' (Galilee Society for Health Research and Services, unpublished manuscript) p. 3, in Laugharn and Kana'aneh, 'Development needs', p. 12.

83 Such is the geological structure that there is virtually no filtration effect on water. Kana'aneh and Farah, 'Sewage problems', in Laugharn and Kana'aneh, 'Development needs', p. 13.

84 Arraba, 1978–9; severe contamination in Rama, al Reina, and Maghar villages, 1981–2; Laugharn and Kana'aneh, 'Development needs', p. 13.

85 Before approaching central government about the costs of sewage planning and construction, a council must prepare and gain approval for their master and detailed sewage plans. The average cost of such plans together is about $60,000 and, should approval be given, it costs on average $75,000 to lay 1 km. of sewage. The Galilee Society for Health Research and Services, 'Activities in the field of sanitation' (Galilee, Feb 1984).

86 There is a problem with solid waste also, since there are no authorized dumps in any Arab village in Israel.

87 The Galilee Society for Health Research and Services, 'Revolving Loan Fund Program for sewage systems planning in Galilee' (unpublished proposal, Galilee, 1984) in Laugharn and Kana'aneh, 'Development needs', p. 13.

88 Ben Porath, *The Arab Labor Force in Israel*, p. 53, cited in Lustick, *Arabs in the Jewish State*, p. 184.

89 Ernest Stock, *From Conflict to Understanding* (New York, 1968), p. 66, cited in Lustick, *Arabs in the Jewish State*, p. 185.

90 Nationally, one in four of the 0–17 age group is Palestinian. However, Palestinians constituted over 57 per cent of this age group in the Galilee by 1983. Laugharn and Kana'aneh, 'Development needs', p. 30.

91 Ghanadiri, *al jamahir al arabiyya*, p. 142. In 1987, out of 980 senior posts in the Ministry of Education only 32 pertained to the 23 per cent of children who are in the Palestinian sector.

92 In 1949 only 11,000 Palestinian children attended school. By the school year 1987/88 this number had increased twentyfold to 220,000. *Israeli Statistical Abstract 1986*, p. 583, and Ghanadiri, *al jamahir al arabiyya*, p. 135.

93 *Israeli Statistical Abstract 1986*, p. 578. Palestinian enrolment rate per thousand at primary level 947, but at secondary level 621, compared with Jewish levels 965 and 869 respectively.

94 In 1982 the national average budget per child was 8,328 shekels. For examples of the discrepancy by district, see Central Bureau of Statistics, *Local Authorities in Israel 1982/83: Financial Data*, special series no. 760, (Jerusalem, 1985) pp. 177–83, in Laugharn and Kana'aneh, 'Development needs', p. 31.

95 *al Ittihad*, 16 March 1986, in Laugharn and Kana'aneh, 'Development needs', p. 31.

96 Ghanadiri, *al jamahir al arabiyya*, p. 135; Welfare Association Factsheet on

Education (Geneva, 1985).

97 Ghanadiri, *al jamahir al arabiyya*, pp. 135, 143.

98 Ibid., p. 135.

99 56 per cent compared with 28 per cent, Laugharn and Kana'aneh, 'Development needs', p. 33.

100 *Israeli Statistical Abstract 1984*, p. 734, quoted in ibid.

101 Sam'i Mari, 'The future of Palestinian education in Israel', *Journal of Palestine Studies*, no. 54, Winter 1985, p. 57.

102 *Israeli Statistical Abstract 1986*, p. 592.

103 *Israeli Statistical Abstract 1984*, p. 654.

104 Arab students have 252 hours of study of the Torah and other Jewish religious texts, while Jews do not study the Koran and Gospels at all. Ghanadiri, *al jamahir al arabiyya*, p. 138.

105 See Fouzi al Asmar, *To be an Arab in Israel* (London, 1975) pp. 48–50.

106 Jiryis, *The Arabs in Israel*, p. 47.

107 Ibid., p. 49.

108 In the Fifth Knesset elections, for example, special ballot papers were used, whereby it was possible for the tellers to check on any groups within the different families which disobeyed the Military Government's instruction on the way to vote. Ibid., pp. 51–3. Similar evidence was found in the 1973 elections, see Lustick, *Arabs in the Jewish State*, p. 138.

109 Aharon Cohen, *Israel and the Arab World*, 1964, p. 510, quoted in Jiryis, *The Arabs in Israel*, p. 51.

110 See Jiryis, *The Arabs in Israel*, pp. 28–31.

111 When Labour proposed making its Arab Knesset member, Abdul Wahab al Darawsha the deputy minister of education it provoked an outcry from Likud members of the coalition. See *al Hamishmar*, 29 October 1986, in *Israeli Press Briefs*, no. 49 and Susan Hattis Rolef, 'Empty gesture', *Jerusalem Post*, 18 February 1987, in *Israeli Press Briefs*, no. 52.

CHAPTER 6   PALESTINIAN RESPONSES TO THE JEWISH STATE

1 Jiryis, *The Arabs in Israel*, p. 127.

2 Its greatest success was in the 1977 election when it attracted 4.6 per cent of the vote, but in the elections of 1973, 1981 and 1984 it attracted only 3.4 per cent of the national vote.

3 Smooha, *The Orientation and Politicization of the Arab Minority in Israel*, p. 62.

4 Uri Avnery, *My Friend, the Enemy* (London, 1986), p. 314.

5 Ibid., pp. 316, 324, 326.

6 Ibid., p. 324.

7 *Al Ard* was closed down after thirteen issues as an organ 'opposed to the security of the State and the interests of the people'. Jiryis, *The Arabs in Israel*, p. 130.

8 The Supreme Court ruled that al Ard's aims were 'utterly destructive of the existence of the State of Israel in general and of its existence within its present frontiers in particular'. Ibid., pp. 133ff. When al Ard sought permission to participate in the 1965 Knesset elections as 'the Arab Socialist List', it was

refused and some of its leaders given the option of imprisonment or exile. Lustick, *Arabs in the Jewish State*, p. 128.

9 Ibid., p. 249.

10 Smooha, *The Orientation and Politicization of the Arab Minority in Israel*, p. 4.

11 Abna al Balad worried the authorities sufficiently that an activist and its general secretary from 1983 onwards, Raja Ighbariya, spent four out of the eight years 1980–87 under arrest.

12 Avnery, *My Friend, the Enemy*, p. 316.

13 By 1987 al Ansar was confined to Umm al Fahm, with affiliated groups in Tayiba and Tira.

14 *Sawt Umm al Fahm*, 12 September 1987.

15 Shaikh Abdallah Darwish of Kafr Qasim in Elaine Ruth Fletcher, 'From Marx to Mohammad', *Jerusalem Post International*, 21 November 1987. See also Friedman, 'An Islamic revival'.

16 Friedman, 'An Islamic revival'.

17 For example in Umm al Fahm where it was established in 1985, the Islamic Association had opened seven pre-school kindergarten centres, a clinic, library and bookstores, a student computer centre and was publishing a periodical by 1987. Elaine Ruth Fletcher, 'The new Muslims', *Jerusalem Post International*, 21 November 1987.

18 Smooha, *The Orientation and Politization of the Arab Minority in Israel*, p. 5.

19 Nadim Rouhana, 'The Arabs in Israel: psychological, political and social dimensions of collective identity' (unpublished Ph.D. thesis, Wayne State University, Detroit, 1984) p. 111, in A'si, 'Israeli and Palestinian public opinion', pp. 173–4.

20 Rouhana in A'si, 'Israeli and Palestinian public opinion', p. 173; Smooha, *The Orientation and Politicization of the Arab Minority in Israel*, p. 50.

21 Rouhana in A'si, 'Israeli and Palestinian public opinion', p. 175.

22 Smooha, *The Orientation and Politicization of the Arab Minority in Israel*, p. 5.

23 Ibid., p. 37.

24 Ibid.

25 Kislev, 'Israel's Arabs: coping with duality'.

26 Smooha, *The Orientation and Politicization of the Arab Minority in Israel*, pp. 56–7.

27 Ibid., p. 92.

28 Compare Smooha, *The Orientation and Politicization of the Arab Minority in Israel*, p. 80 with the findings of his 1985 study: 11 per cent accommodationist, 39 per cent accommodationist conditional on certain improvement of conditions for Palestinians; 40 per cent loyal dissent (Rakah and the PLP), 10 per cent dissident. Kislev, 'Israel's Arabs: coping with duality'.

29 Smooha, *The Orientation and Politicization of the Arab Minority in Israel*, p. 153.

30 Avnery, *My Friend, the Enemy*, p. 327.

31 Smooha, *The Orientation and Politicization of the Arab Minority in Israel*, p. 152.

32 Moshe Gabai, 'Israeli Arabs: problems of identity and integration', in *New Outlook*, October/November 1984.

33 Alexander Flores, 'Political influences across the Green Line', in Alexander Schölch (ed.), *Palestinians Across the Green Line*, p. 187.

34   See the Nadim Rouhana survey, in A'si, 'Israeli and Palestinian public opinion', p. 175.

35   *Ha'aretz*, 15 January 1968, in Flores, 'Political influences across the Green Line', p. 189.

36   For example see Burhan Dajani (ed.) *Al Kitab al sanawilil qadiya al filastiniyya li'am 1969*, Beirut 1972, p. 370, quoted in Flores, 'Political influences across the Green Line', p. 188.

37   See 'Ya sha'bna al filastini' leaflet of the Union of the Arab University students committees in the country, 30 March 1976, quoted in Flores, 'Political influences across the Green Line', p. 191. The Union was affiliated to Abna al Balad.

38   'Ru'us al aqlam lil-mu'tamar al-16 lil-hizb al shuyu'i al isra'ili', 30 January 1969, (Haifa, 1969) p. 28, in Flores, 'Political influences across the Green Line', p. 188.

39   *Jerusalem Post*, 2 May 1976, in Lustick, *Arabs in the Jewish State*, p. 331n.

40   Its owner, Mashhour Lutfi , is a staunch supporter of the PLP and a bitter opponent of Rakah. His two editors are Atallah Mansour, the first Arab journalist for *Ha'aretz* and for many years viewed by the Israeli establishment as a 'good Arab', and Daoud Kuttab, a centrist in his Palestinian nationalism and ex-editor of the East Jerusalem paper *al Fajr English Weekly*.

41   *Moment*, October 1986 in *Israeli Press Briefs*, no. 50.

42   Lustick, *Arabs in the Jewish State*, p. 268.

CHAPTER 7   DILEMMAS OF THE JEWISH STATE

1   Abba Eban, *The New Diplomacy* (London, 1983) p. 229.

2   Shlomo Avineri, *The Making of Modern Zionism, the intellectual origins of the Jewish State* (New York, 1981) p. 13.

3   For example Peretz Smolenskin or Moshe Lilienblum who both changed their views after the 1881 pogroms. Ibid., chapters 5 & 6.

4   Ibid., chapter 13.

5   The description given of the views of Aharon Gordon. Ibid., p. 153.

6   As Ben Gurion himself said at the time of the Balfour Declaration, 'within the next twenty years, we must have a Jewish majority in Palestine'. Ben Gurion, *Mi-Ma'amad le Am* (From class to peoplehood) (Tel Aviv, 1933) p. 15, quoted by Shabtai Teveth, *Ben Gurion and the Palestinian Arabs: from Peace to War* (Oxford and New York, 1985) p. 40.

7   Sharett, *Diaries* (Tel Aviv, 1970) vol. i, p. 112, quoted by Flapan, *Zionism and the Palestinians*, p. 154. Sharett had no doubt at all that 'our fate in Palestine will be determined not by political formulas but by the number of Jews.' Minutes of the Jewish Agency Executive, 22 November 1936, quoted by Flapan, *Zionism and the Palestinians*, p. 154.

8   Gorny, *Zionism and the Arabs*, p. 2.

9   Meron Benvenisti claims that the official statistics underestimated the West Bank population by 27 per cent and the Gaza population by 16 per cent, by the end of 1987. *Jerusalem Post*, 18 March 1988. By autumn 1988 Palestinians

under eight years of age already outnumbered Jews, 630,000 to 590,000. *The Times*, 19 October 1988.

10 Weizmann to Weltsch, 13 January 1924, quoted by Flapan, *Zionism and the Palestinians*, p. 72.

11 His words were addressed to a Mapai (Labour) conference. Wiemer, 'Zionism and the Arabs after the establishment of the State of Israel', p. 46.

12 Ibid.

13 Ibid., p. 47; *ISA 1986*, p. 63. In fact, the reality is proving less adverse than Bacchi described, with a prospect now of 4.1 million Jews and 1.2 million Palestinians inside the 1949 Armistice Line.

14 *Jerusalem Post International*, 14 December 1985.

15 Israel Radio, 14 May 1986, in *News From Within*, 20 May 1986. See also *Jerusalem Post*, 5 May 1986.

16 In *Judische Rundschau*, 1919, quoted by Flapan, *Zionism and the Palestinians*, p. 127.

17 Survey by Professor Steven Cohen, cited in Avishai, *The Tragedy of Zionism*, p. 354.

18 10,000 of these immigrants were Falashas from Ethiopia, *News From Within*, 15 November 1985. On emigration, see Bank of Israel emigration figures, quoted in *Ha'aretz*, 31 May 1985, in *Israeli Mirror*, no. 734.

19 *ISA 1986*, p. 66.

20 *Middle East International*, 19 December 1987.

21 National Insurance Institute figures, *Jerusalem Post International*, 5 July 1986.

22 Ibid.

23 See for example, Haim Sadan, 'Israel's big problem', *Jerusalem Post International*, week ending 16 August 1986; Pinhas Landau, 'The issue that just won't go away', in *Jerusalem Post International* week ending 23 May 1987; Bernard Josephs, 'Israelis seduced by the "good life" in America', in *The Jerusalem Post*, 21 September 1987.

24 *Jerusalem Post International*, 5 July 1986.

25 Avraham Schenker, *New Outlook*, March/April 1988. An expectation of 800,000 *emigrés* by the end of the century is based upon Hanoch Smith statistical estimate, based on the current *emigré* level of 12,000 per year. *Ha'aretz*, 18 May 1988, in *Israeli Mirror*, no. 779. General Matti Peled claimed in 1985 that 420,000 Jews had already left Israel. *Hadashot*, 3 December 1985, in *Israeli Mirror*, no. 745.

26 *Jerusalem Post International*, 27 December 1986. According to the Council for the Prevention of Emigration, 27 per cent of high school students thought of emigration and another 15 per cent said they would be pleased if their families left. *Ha'aretz*, 18 May 1988, in *Israeli Mirror*, no. 779.

27 Ephraim Ya'ar, 'Emigration is a normal phenomenon', *New Outlook*, January 1988.

28 *Jerusalem Post International*, 5 July 1986.

29 Ibid., 12 December 1987.

30 Isaac, *Israel Divided*, p. 152.

31 Histadrut Executive Committee Protocols, Tel Aviv, 5 Sept 1929, quoted in Teveth, *Ben Gurion and the Palestinian Arabs*, p. 84.

32 Sadan, 'Israel's big problem'.

33 Yael Lotan, 'Israel's national schizophrenia', in *al Hamishmar*, 10 October

1986, translated in International Centre for Peace in the Middle East, *Israeli Press Briefs*, no. 49.

34 For example, see Nathan Scharansky's claim in *Jerusalem Post International*, 23 August 1986.

35 For example, see *Jerusalem Post International*, week ending 28 March 1987, and Walter Ruby, 'The row over refugee status', in ibid., week ending 25 April 1987. For an angry denunciation of Jewish American assistance to Soviet emigrants, see Shmuel Katz, 'The Soviet Jewry emigration hoax', ibid., week ending 17 August, 1985.

36 For example, see *The Independent*, 20 June 1988, and *The Sunday Times*, 26 June 1988.

37 Reuven Ahlberg, 'The case against Greater Israel', *Jerusalem Post International*, 26 February–3 March 1984. Only in Israel is the birth rate higher than the replenishment rate. Ibid., week ending 14 December 1985.

38 Ibid., week ending 7 November 1987.

39 Some estimates predict an even steeper decline, of 20–25 per cent by the end of the century. Ibid., 17–24 June 1984.

40 *Guardian*, 24 October 1987.

41 G. Sheffer, 'The uncertain future of American Jewry-Israel relations', *The Jerusalem Quarterly*, no. 32, summer 1984, p. 70. Intermarriage is increasing with about 25–30 per cent of young Jews currently marrying non-Jews. *Jerusalem Post International*, 31 October 1987. Allowing for the fact that some Jews do not marry, the intermarrying proportion among those who do marry is 45 per cent. Jews 'lost' by intermarriage used to be offset by those Gentiles who embraced Judaism on marriage, but the latter has declined from 44 per cent in the early 1970s to only 12 per cent since 1980. Ibid.

42 Report of Dr Donald Feldstein to the American Jewish Congress, reported in *Jerusalem Post International*, 8–14 April 1984.

43 David Rosenberg, 'The UJA's optimistic fundraisers', ibid., 21 February 1987.

44 Sheffer, 'The uncertain future of American Jewry-Israel relations', pp. 68, 78. See also the *Guardian*, 24 December 1987 which reported a poll in summer 1987 showing that 63 per cent of American Jews 'cared deeply' about Israel, a 15 per cent drop since 1983.

45 Even before the Uprising a substantial majority of American Jews considered public criticism of the Israeli government to be acceptable, with under-forty year olds feeling less attached than their elders. The decline in commitment is slight but it is real. Almost 50 per cent of American Jews, according to a poll in 1983 were 'often troubled by the policies of the Israeli government'. Sheffer, 'The uncertain future of American Jewry-Israel relations', p. 77.

46 Compare S. M. Cohen, *Attitudes of American Jews toward Israel and the Israelis*, (New York, Sept 1983) quoted in Sheffer, 'The uncertain future of American Jewry-Israel relations', p. 79, with Alex Brummer, 'The heart and mind of the Jewish voter', *Guardian*, 13 April 1988.

47 Sheffer, 'The uncertain future of American Jewry-Israel relations', p. 80.

48 For example, see the findings of Professor Steven M. Cohen in 1986, summarized in *Jerusalem Post International*, week ending 9 May 1987.

49 Rosenberg, 'The UJA's optimistic fundraisers'.

50 See on this question two contrasting books, one by an anti-Zionist Israeli, Akiva Orr, *The Unjewish State* (London, 1985) and a Zionist one, Norman

Zucker, *The Coming Crisis in Israel – Private Faith and Public Policy* (Cambridge, Mass., 1973).

51 In 1986 the amendment was defeated by 61 votes to 47, in 1985 it was defeated by 62 to 51, and in the previous Knesset (1981–4) it was defeated by a far closer margin of 58 to 54. *Jerusalem Post International*, 15 February 1986 and Moshe Samet, 'Who is a Jew?' in *Jerusalem Quarterly*, no. 37, 1986, p. 134.

52 *Jerusalem Post International*, 19 December 1987.

53 For more on Rabbi Kook, see Avineri, *The Making of Modern Zionism*, chapter 16, and Ehud Sprinzak, 'The iceberg model of political extremism', in David Newman (ed.) *The Impact of Gush Emunim* (Beckenham, 1985) pp. 27–8.

54 In 'The War', in Arthur Hertzberg, *The Zionist Idea* (New York, 1969), quoted by Avineri, *The Making of Modern Zionism*, p. 195.

55 Z. Y. Kook, 'Between the people and its land', *Artzi* (Jerusalem, 1983) p. 10, quoted in Yehoshafat Harkabi, *Israel's Fateful Decisions* (London, 1988) p. 150.

56 Sprinzak, 'The iceberg model of political extremism', p. 37.

57 Bernard Avishai, *The Tragedy of Zionism: Revolution and Democracy in the Land of Israel* (New York, 1985) p. 250.

58 The essential theme of Sprinzak's article.

59 *Deuteronomy*, I v 8; for a fuller discussion of God's promise, see Gwyn Rowley, 'The Land of Israel: a reconstructionist approach', in Newman (ed.) *The Impact of Gush Emunim*.

60 I have relied on Shlomo Avineri's description of *Altneuland* in *The Making of Modern Zionism*, p. 99.

61 *Igrot* (Letters) (Tel Aviv, 1971–4) vol. i, p. 71, quoted in Teveth, *Ben Gurion and the Palestinian Arabs*, p. 5.

62 The mayor of Arad, *Jerusalem Post International*, 15–21 January 1984.

63 See *News From Within*, 1 November 1985 listing the development towns most hit by high unemployment. During the 1980s there was a net loss of 15,000 from Beersheba and Dimona. All development towns in Galilee face stagnation. In 1987 the Palestinian population in Galilee grew by 19,000 while in the same year 2,500 Jews left. *Koteret Rashit*, 3 February 1988, in *Israeli Press Briefs*, no. 58.

64 *Jerusalem Post International*, week ending 29 August 1987.

65 Benvenisti, *1986 Report*, p. 51.

66 Ibid., p. 52.

67 Ibid., p. 56.

68 Benvenisti, *1987 Report*, p. 61.

69 For descriptions, see William Frankel, *Israel Observed* (London, 1980) pp. 172–83.

70 Ibid., p. 181.

71 Thomas L. Friedman, 'Israel's tangle of farm troubles', *The New York Times*, Sunday 13 September 1987. *Kibbutzim*, since they are larger-scale ventures, have been better able to absorb spare labour by building factories.

72 Ibid.

73 David Ben Gurion, 'Our action and our direction', in Yaacov Becker (ed.), *Mishnato shel David Ben Gurion* (Tel Aviv, 1958) vol. ii, pp. 525–6, quoted by

Avineri, *The Making of Modern Zionism*, p. 202.

74 Harkabi, *Israel's Fateful Decisions*, p. 63.

75 Avineri, *The Making of Modern Zionism*, p. 219.

76 Ibid., p. 223.

77 Magnes, 'Like all the nations?' (pamphlet, Jerusalem, 1930) quoted in Flapan, *Zionism and the Palestinians*, p. 175.

78 Leibowitz' own verdict, *al Hamishmar*, 13 February 1983, in *Israeli Mirror*, no. 636.

79 Keller, *Terrible Days*, (Amstelveen, 1987) p. 164.

80 Avishai, *The Tragedy of Zionism*, p. 303.

81 Ibid., p. 305.

82 Israel Radio, 14 May 1986, in *News From Within*, 20 May 1986.

83 Weizmann to Einstein, 30 November 1929, quoted in Flapan, *Zionism and the Palestinians*, p. 71.

84 When asked early in 1986 why there would be no elections in the occupied territories, Peres replied that elections were not possible because of the potential for terrorist subversion. Stated in response to a question following his address at Chatham House, 22 January 1986.

85 *Israel and Palestine*, no. 140, February–March 1988.

86 Avishai, *The Tragedy of Zionism*, p. 303.

87 Quoted in *Middle East International*, no. 336, 21 October 1988.

88 Avishai, *The Tragedy of Zionism*, p. 303.

89 Ibid., p. 299.

90 Dahaf poll for the Van Leer Institute, October 1987, reported in *Ha'aretz*, 26 October 1987, *Jerusalem Post International*, 7 November 1987, and *New Outlook*, February 1988.

91 In March 1982 51 per cent (already alarmingly high) disapproved of press freedom, increasing to 65 per cent by March 1983. By this date 58 per cent disapproved of criticism of government defence and foreign policy. Research by Dr Mina Tsemach, Dahaf poll, reported in *al Hamishmar*, 20 March 1983, in *Israeli Mirror*, no. 642.

92 Survey carried out by Dr Sammy Smooha, *New Outlook*, July 1986.

93 *Observer*, 12 June 1988.

94 Along with the law courts and doctors, *Jerusalem Post International*, 7 November 1987.

95 Avishai, *The Tragedy of Zionism*, p. 265.

96 Ibid., p. 340. For 1988 election results, see the *Jewish Chronicle*, 11 November 1988.

97 For a full discussion of the role of the Israeli military, see Yoram Peri, *Between Battles and Ballots, Israeli Military in Politics* (Cambridge, 1983) pp. 268ff.

98 Ibid., p. 274.

99 Ibid., p. 277.

100 Alex Mintz, 'Arms production in Israel', *Jerusalem Quarterly*, no. 42, spring 1987, p. 94.

101 Simha Bahiri, 'Guns or milk and honey', *New Outlook*, September/October 1986 and Simha Bahiri, 'Military and colonial aspects of the Israeli economy since 1967', *New Outlook*, May/June 1987.

102 Bahiri, 'Guns or milk and honey'.

103 See below, p. 229.

104 Frankel, *Israel Observed*, p. 24.
105 Benny Morris in *Jerusalem Post International*, 13 December 1986.
106 Professor Yoram Dinstein, assessing the implications of the Israeli election results, Chatham House, 2 November 1988.
107 Frankel, *Israel Observed*, p. 25.

CHAPTER 8   THE PAST REVISITED

1 Israel Zangwill, *The Voice of Jerusalem* (London, 1920) p. 104.
2 Ibid., p. 93.
3 Teveth, *Ben Gurion and the Palestinian Arabs: From Peace to War* p. 94; 'there was no comparing the value of Eretz Israel for the Arabs with the importance it held for the Jewish people', conversation with Fuad Bey Hamzah, April 1937; Ben Gurion, *My Talks with Arab Leaders*, p. 124, quoted by Flapan, *Zionism and the Palestinians*, p. 135.
4 Abba Eban, *The Voice of Israel* (London, 1958) p. 11.
5 Eban, *The New Diplomacy*, p. 224.
6 Max Nordau's writings quoted in Christopher Sykes, *Two Studies in Virtue* (London, 1953) p. 160, and David Hirst, *The Gun and the Olive Branch* (London, 1977) p. 20. Ben Gurion was similarly evasive, see 'Towards the Future', in *Hatoren* (1914–15), quoted in Teveth, *Ben Gurion and the Palestinian Arabs*, p. 25.
7 Herzl was by no means alone in this naïve optimism. The kind of ideas expressed now strike us as patronizing, but were *avant-garde* compared with European colonial attitudes elsewhere, Avineri, *The Making of Modern Zionism*, pp. 98–100.
8 Ahad Ha'am, 'Emet me Eretz Israel', in *Kol Kitvei Ahad Ha'am* (Tel Aviv, 1946) p. 24 quoted by Avineri, *The Making of Modern Zionism*, p. 122.
9 Yitzhak Epstein, 'The hidden question', a lecture given to the 7th Zionist Congress, subsequently published in *ha-Shiloah*, quoted in *New Outlook*, December 1985, and Gorny, *Zionism and the Arabs*, p. 43. Another was Eliyahu Sappir, Jerusalem born and bred, who drew Jewish attention to anti-Zionist propaganda in the Arab press in 1900, in *ha-Shiloah*, a leading literary journal in Russia until the First World War. Gorny, *Zionism and the Arabs*, p. 41.
10 Ahad Ha'am, *Letters* (Jerusalem, 1923) vol. 5, p. 161, quoted in Gorny, *Zionism and the Arabs*, p. 65.
11 Moshe Elgin in his review of Yizkor (Forward), 3 June 1916, quoted by Teveth, *Ben Gurion and the Palestinian Arabs*, p. viii.
12 Walid Khalidi, *From Haven to Conquest*, pp. 189–90.
13 Ibid.
14 Curzon's memorandum of 26 January 1919, in Doreen Ingrams, *Palestine Papers, 1917–1922, Seeds of Conflict*, p. 58.
15 See Teveth, *Ben Gurion and the Palestinian Arabs*, chapter 12. For the similar views of Yitzhak Ben Zvi, who succeeded Weizmann to become Israel's second president, see Gorny, *Zionism and the Arabs*, p. 73.
16 Speech to the Inner Action Committee, 12 October 1936, quoted by Flapan,

Zionism and the Palestinians, p. 134. See also Teveth, *Ben Gurion and the Palestinian Arabs*, p. 37.

17 Gorny, *Zionism and the Arabs*, pp. 165–6.

18 Palestinian national identity, as distinct from other parts of Syria, was developing as early as 1920. One of only two pre-war newspapers of consequence in Palestine was entitled *Filastin* and spoke of Palestine as a distinct entity. Mandel, *The Arabs and Zionism*, p. 127. In 1914 a circular distributed and published in the press, and entitled 'General Summons to Palestinians – Beware the Zionist Danger' warned that the 'Zionists desire to settle in our country and expel us from it' and was signed anonymously by 'a Palestinian'. Ibid., p. 220.

19 It has been a long-standing characteristic. Take, for example, Ben Gurion's testimony to UNSCOP in 1947 'there is a marked difference and inequality between the two peoples. There is a difference between a *nation* living in the twentieth century, and a *people* living in the fifteenth century, some of them in the seventh century.' (emphasis added). Quoted in Flapan, *Zionism and the Palestinians*, p. 132.

20 Teveth, *Ben Gurion and the Palestinian Arabs*, p. 131.

21 David Ben Gurion, *Yoman* (Diary), 19 July 1936, and Moshe Sharett in the Mapai Political Committee, July 1936, Beit Berl, both quoted in Teveth, *Ben Gurion and the Palestinian Arabs*, p. 157. It is impossible to say whether at an earlier stage Ben Gurion might have accepted such an offer as a basis for Jewish Arab relations in Palestine. But by 1936, with the growing danger to European Jewry, he would contemplate no limitation on Jewish immigration to Palestine.

22 Grunwald, 'The industrialisation of the Near East', *Bulletin of Palestine Economic Society*, February 1934, vol. 6, no. 3, pp. 78–9, cited in Fred Gottheil, 'Arab immigration into pre-State Israel, 1922–31', in E. Kedouri and S. Haim, *Palestine and Israel in the 19th and 20th centuries* (London, 1982) p. 147.

23 Increasingly Palestinians from the central uplands (the present West Bank and Galilee) and Syrians and Lebanese were drawn into the rapidly expanding coastal economy. During the years 1922–31, 39 per cent of the increase in the Arab population in the part of Palestine that became Israel in 1948 had come as immigrants from other parts of Palestine, Lebanon or Syria. Gottheil, 'Arab immigration', p. 150.

24 See for example the case made by Henry Cattan, *The Palestine Question* (London, 1988) pp. 32–40.

25 Avi Shlaim, *Collusion Across the Jordan* (Oxford, 1988); Flapan, *The Birth of Israel*; Morris, *The Birth of the Palestinian Refugee Problem*; Tom Segev, *1949 – The First Israelis* (New York, 1986); Charles Kamen, 'After the Catastrophe I: the Arabs in Israel 1948–51', *Middle Eastern Studies*, vol. 23, no. 4, October 1987.

26 These points are well borne out in William Louis and Robert W. Stookey (eds), *The End of the Palestine Mandate* (London, 1986).

27 Flapan, *The Birth of Israel*, p. 76.

28 In February 1948 Ben Gurion knew that the Arabs of Western Galilee (allocated to the Arab state) had no wish to fight. Ben Gurion, *War Diaries*

(Tel Aviv, 1982) p. 253, entry for 19 February 1948, in Flapan, *The Birth of Israel*, p. 73.

29 Ben Gurion to Sharett, 14 March 1948 in ibid., p. 73.

30 One was even made between Arab Jaffa and Jewish Tel Aviv in autumn 1947. Flapan, *The Birth of Israel*, p. 74.

31 Ben Gurion, *War Diaries*, 28 January 1948, p. 187, in ibid., p. 73.

32 For example Musa Alami, who had represented the Palestinians in the Arab League, and therefore knew Arab thinking very well. See Flapan, *The Birth of Israel*, p. 68.

33 On Ben Gurion's rejection, see ibid., p. 160.

34 Ibid., p. 174.

35 In the words of Flapan, 'acceptance of the UN Partition Resolution was an example of Zionist pragmatism par excellence. It was a tactical acceptance, a vital step in the right direction – a springboard for expansion when circumstances proved more judicious'. Ibid., pp. 32–3.

36 Ben Gurion, *Memoirs* (Tel Aviv, 1974, Hebrew) vol. 4, p. 278, quoted in Flapan, *The Birth of Israel*, p. 22. See also Teveth, *Ben Gurion and the Palestinian Arabs*, pp. 102, 136, 185, and Flapan, *Zionism and the Palestinians*, p. 265.

37 Ben Gurion's speech to the Histadrut Executive, 3 December 1947, quoted in Michael Bar Zohar, *Ben Gurion: a political biography* (Tel Aviv, 1977, Hebrew) vol. 2, p. 641, and repeated in Flapan, *The Birth of Israel*, p. 32.

38 Bar Zohar, *Ben Gurion*, p. 704, quoted in Flapan, *The Birth of Israel*, p. 43.

39 This approval of expulsion was in the offensive around Mishmar Hamek (western Galilee). In fact it proved unnecessary since mass flight occurred as a result of the approach of Jewish troops. Morris, *The Birth of the Palestine Refugee Problem*, pp. 112, 115f. On the question of destruction of Arab property see examples on pp. 112, 127, 155.

40 Benny Morris, 'The causes and character of the Arab exodus from Palestine: Israel Defence Forces Intelligence Branch Analysis of June 1948', *Middle Eastern Studies*, vol. 22, no. 1, January 1986, pp. 5–19, and Morris, *The Birth of the Palestinian Refugee Problem*, chapter 3.

41 Benny Morris, 'The harvest of 1948 and the creation of the Palestinian refugee problem', *The Middle East Journal*, vol. 40, no. 4, Autumn 1986, p. 684.

42 See Benny Morris, 'Operation Dani and the Palestinian exodus from Lydda and Ramle in 1948', ibid., vol. 40, no. 1, Winter 1986.

43 See the assault orders given by the Irgun commander, in Morris, *The Birth of the Palestine Refugee Problem*, p. 96.

44 For details of Deir Yassin, see the eyewitness account of the Red Cross delegate in W. Khalidi, *From Haven to Conquest*, pp. 761–6; the version given by Menachem Begin in *The Revolt* (London, 1951) pp. 162–5, which denies a massacre took place; Hirst, *The Gun and the Olive Branch*, pp. 124–9 which quotes extensively from primary sources; Christopher Sykes, *Crossroads to Israel* (London, 1965) pp. 416–18; Nicholas Bethell, *The Palestine Triangle* (London, 1979) pp. 354–5; see also David Gilmour, 'The 1948 Arab exodus', *Middle East International*, 21 November 1986 which cites the evidence of a Haganah intelligence officer in the area who says he was refused permission to warn the inhabitants to leave the village before the Irgun attacked.

45 Morris, 'The causes and character of the Arab exodus', p. 9.

46   Begin, *The Revolt*, p. 164, quoted in Hirst, *The Gun and the Olive Branch*, p. 129.

47   Morris, 'Operation Dani', p. 94.

48   On the atrocities in the Galilee, see Morris, *The Birth of the Palestinian Refugee Problem*, pp. 229f; and Nafez Nazzal, *The Palestinian Exodus from Galilee 1948* (Beirut, 1978). The worst atrocities in the Galilee occurred at Eilabun and Safsaf. In southern Palestine the most notable case was at Duwayma, on 28/29 October 1948, where at least 100 died, and possibly as many as 580 (claimed missing and never accounted for by the village *mukhtar*). See *Davar*, 6 September 1979, and *al Fajr English weekly*, 31 August 1984 which carried a resumé of an article appearing the previous week in *Hadashot*; and Morris, *The Birth of the Palestinian Refugee Problem*, pp. 222–3, which gives an account and explains how this precipitated further mass flight in the area.

49   Minutes of Israeli Cabinet Meeting, 17 November 1948, Kibbutz Meuhad Archive, section 9, container 9, file 1, quoted by Segev, *1949 – The First Israelis*, p. 26. Benny Morris apparently sought access to Israeli state archives concerning atrocities, but his appeal to the Israeli Supreme Court was rejected in October 1986. See Amnon Kapeliouk, 'New light on the Israeli Arab conflict and the refugee problem and its origins', *Journal of Palestine Studies*, no. 63, XVI no. 3, Spring 1987, p. 17.

50   Weitz had written in 1940 'the only solution is Eretz Israel . . . without Arabs . . . and there is no other way but transfer . . . not one village or tribe should remain'. Diary of Joseph Weitz, quoted in *Davar*, 29 September 1967, reprinted in Uri Davis and Norton Mezvinsky, *Documents from Israel, 1967–73* (London, 1975), p. 21.

51   From 'Our Arab policy during the war', memorandum to the political committee of Mapam by Aharon Cohen, director of Mapam's Arab Department, 10 May 1948, quoted in Benny Morris, 'Joseph Weitz and the Transfer Committees, 1948–9', *Middle Eastern Studies*, vol. 22, no. 4, October 1986, p. 522.

52   Morris, 'Joseph Weitz', passim, see especially pp. 532–3.

53   Morris, 'Operation Dani', p. 104.

54   Shertok to Zaslani, 25 April 1948, quoted in Morris, *The Birth of the Palestinian Refugee Problem*, p. 133.

55   Quoted by Ben Gurion, *Medinat Yisrael Hamehudeshet*, pp. 164–5, in Morris, *The Birth of the Palestinian Refugee Problem*, p. 141.

56   Segev, *1949 – The First Israelis*, p. 29.

57   Morris, 'Joseph Weitz', p. 550.

58   Ibid., p. 556.

59   *The Complete Diaries of Theodore Herzl* (New York, 1960) vol. I, p. 343, quoted in Hirst, *The Gun and the Olive Branch*, p. 18.

60   Adolf Bohm, *Die Zionistische Bewegung* (Berlin and Jerusalem, 1935) vol. I, p. 706. Herzl offered to move the native population to alternative sites outside Palestine, paying the cost of transit and compensation for loss, and a resettlement loan.

61   Memo to the Zionist Executive, May 1911, quoted in Walter Lacquer, *A History of Zionism* (London, 1972) p. 231, quoted in Flapan, *Zionism and the Palestinians*, p. 259.

62 Zangwill, *The Voice of Jerusalem*, p. 100. See also 'Before the Peace Conference', in *Speeches and Articles of Israel Zangwill*, p. 341.

63 Flapan, *Zionism and the Palestinians*, p. 82.

64 See the Minutes of the Joint Meeting of the Zionist Executive with the Special Political Committee, 1 December 1930, and notes of a private meeting with the British Prime Minister and Foreign Secretary, House of Commons, 4 December 1930, both cited in ibid., p. 70.

65 When the hard-line Zionist Menachem Ussishkin proposed a transfer of the Arab population in December 1929, the Jewish Agency executive condemned it. Jewish Agency Executive minutes, 30 April 1930 and 15 December 1929, in Gorny, *Zionism and the Arabs*, p. 242.

66 Flapan, *Zionism and the Palestinians*, p. 246; Teveth, *Ben Gurion and the Palestinian Arabs*, p. 181.

67 Ben Gurion, *Memoirs* (Tel Aviv, 1974, Hebrew) vol. 2, pp. 330–1, quoted in Flapan, *Zionism and the Palestinians*, p. 246.

68 *New Judea*, August/September 1937, pp. 222–4, quoted in Flapan, *Zionism and the Palestinians*, pp. 261–2.

69 Ibid.

70 Jewish Agency Executive minutes, Central Zionist Archives, Jerusalem, 12 June 1938, quoted in Flapan, *Zionism and the Palestinians*, p. 263.

71 Morris, *The Birth of the Palestinian Refugee Problem*, pp. 221–4, 243–7. In 1952 the matter of Israel's Arabs was discussed for the first time since the war by the Labour (Mapai) party. Some members favoured expulsion of the remaining Palestinians. However, it was recognized that in peacetime, bearing in mind Israel's precarious international position, it could not be done. Wiemar, 'Zionism and the Arabs', p. 36.

72 Menachem Begin and Yigal Allon, and Pinhas Sapir and Abba Eban, respectively, private diaries of Yaacov Herzog, cabinet secretary, cited in Yossi Melman and Dan Raviv, 'A final solution of the Palestinian problem', in the *Guardian Weekly*, 21 February, 1988.

73 The scheme only lasted for three years. It was made public by Ariel Sharon in November 1987, when advocating Arab emigration, ibid. See also Wiemar, 'Zionism and the Arabs', p. 47.

74 By IIASR, A'si, 'Israeli and Palestinian public opinion', p. 154.

75 *Christian Science Monitor*, 3 June 1974, quoted in Naom Chomsky, *The Fateful Triangle* (London, 1983) p. 116.

76 Flapan, *The Birth of Israel*, chapter 7. See also the short report 'No rush towards peace in 1949', in *The Jerusalem Post International*, week ending 21 February 1987.

77 It was still opposed in principle to the partition of Palestine (because of its fear that Abdallah would be the beneficiary) and insisted on the establishment of an independent state in the Arab part of Palestine, which would 'eventually annex the Jewish part.' Flapan, *The Birth of Israel*, p. 205.

78 Sharett believed that Egypt was implicitly recognizing Israel and favoured an Israeli proposal to change the name of the Arab League to an 'Oriental League', of which Israel was to be a member. Ibid., pp. 206–7.

79 Morris, *The Birth of the Palestinian Refugee Problem*, pp. 221–4, 243–7.

80 *Foreign Relations of the United States*, Washington 1971, annual report for 1949, pp. 637–9, 742–3, 796–800, in Flapan, *The Birth of Israel*, p. 209.

81 The approach was made to the Israeli office in Paris (which had become the focus of Arab contacts), Divon to Sasson, 25 January 1949, *Israel State Archives*, 3749/2 in Flapan, *The Birth of Israel*, p. 209. In 1953 in spite of an undertaking in the 1949 Israeli-Syrian Armistice Agreement not to develop water resources originating in the demilitarized zone, Israel commenced a major water diversion. Under the 1953 United Nations/United States joint plan to divide the Jordan headwaters equitably between the three parties (Israel, Syria and Jordan), Israel was to enjoy 33 per cent of the water, in spite of the fact that only 23 per cent of it originated from Israeli territory. In fact Israel and the Arab states failed to reach an agreement, and Israel acted unilaterally. Israel was wholly opposed to any United Nations supervision of water withdrawals. See Stevens, *The Jordan River Partition*, p. 30, and Green, *Taking Sides*, pp. 77–9, 89. When Syria also tried to obtain some of these waters, 3 miles within its own borders, in March 1965, Israel attacked with artillery and tank fire. Green, *Taking Sides*, p. 191.

82 Flapan, *The Birth of Israel*, p. 210.

83 The offer was enthusiastically supported by George McGhee, special assistant to the US Secretary of State, who believed it had been one of the best opportunities to solve the refugee problem. Flapan, *The Birth of Israel*, pp. 210–11.

84 Avi Shlaim, 'Husni Zaim and the plan to resettle Palestinian refugees in Syria', unpublished paper submitted to the Refugee Documentation Project, York University, Toronto, 1984, cited in Flapan, *The Birth of Israel*, p. 211.

85 Morris, *The Birth of the Palestinian Refugee Problem*, p. 243.

86 See Yemima Rosenthal, *Documents on the Foreign Policy of Israel* (Jerusalem, 1987) vol. 4, May–December 1949, quoted in 'No rush towards peace in 1949', *Jerusalem Post International*, 21 February 1987.

87 Eliyahu Sasson (from Lausanne) to Z. Zeligson, 16 June 1949, Israel State Archives, 130.02/2447/2 quoted in Morris, *The Birth of the Palestinian Refugee Problem*, p. 277.

88 Avi Shlaim, 'Conflicting approaches to Israel's relations with the Arabs: Ben Gurion and Sharett, 1953–56', *The Middle East Journal*, vol. 37, no. 2, (1983) pp. 13–14, quoted in Green, *Taking Sides*, p. 104.

89 Ibid.

90 See text of correspondence quoted in Green, *Taking sides*, pp. 117–19.

91 Enclosure to memorandum from Allen W. Dulles, 8 February 1961, pp. 2–3, quoted in ibid., p. 113.

92 Telegram 29 from US consulate-general, Jerusalem to Secretary of State, 21 July 1964, NSF Country File – Israel, vol. 2, cables 4/64 to 8/64, Lyndon Baines Johnson Library, quoted in Green, *Taking Sides*, p. 192.

93 See Dov Goldstein, 'Nasser was waiting for Eshkol', *Ma'ariv*, 5 June 1987, in *Israeli Press Briefs*, no. 54.

94 As one senior US official commented in 1954: 'On the Arab side, small scale infiltration persists on the part of individual and small groups acting on their own responsibility. There is no evidence of organised military activity by the Arab states acting in concert or by any individual Arab state.' Executive Secretary James Lay, memorandum, 6 July 1954 appended to National Security Council document 155/1, quoted in Green, *Taking Sides*, p. 119.

95 In fact the Jaffa riots exploded out of a clash between two Jewish political

groups, see Hirst, *The Gun and the Olive Branch*, pp. 46–7.

96 Ibid., p. 90, and Porath, *The Palestinian Arab National Movement*, chapter 9.

97 Article 9 of the Palestine National Charter as amended by the Palestine National Council in July 1968.

98 *Life*, 12 June 1970, p. 33, quoted in Ariel Merari and Shlomi Elad, *The International Dimension of Palestinian Terrorism* (Tel Aviv, 1986) p. 18.

99 Interview in *al Akhbar*, Beirut, 4 August 1973, quoted in Merari and Elad, *The International Dimension of Palestinian Terrorism*, p. 20.

100 Merari and Elad, *The International Dimension of Palestinian Terrorism*, p. 5.

101 Dialogue with Black September, *al Sayyad*, Beirut, 13 September 1972, quoted in Merari and Elad, *The International Dimension of Palestinian Terrorism*, p. 24.

102 See Helena Cobban, *The Palestinian Liberation Organisation* (Cambridge, 1984) pp. 154–6.

103 Ibid.

104 Merari and Elad, *The International Dimension of Palestinian Terrorism*, p. 54.

105 For example, Sabri Jiryis and Afif Safieh.

106 Sixty-six civilians were deliberately killed by troops when their homes were demolished over their heads. See John Bagot Glubb, *A Soldier with the Arabs*, pp. 309–10. Other examples of reprisals in which civilians were foreseeably the primary victims include (1) the attack on Samu, West Bank, 1966, eighteen civilians killed; (2) air attack on Irbid, June 1968, thirty civilians killed; air attack on Abu Za'abel factory, Egypt, February 1970, seventy civilians killed; air attack on Bahr al Baqr school, Sha'a province, Egypt, forty-six schoolchildren killed; air attack Beirut, July 1981, over 200 civilians killed. For an essay on Israeli terrorism against its neighbours, including civilian targets, during the 1950s, see Livia Rokach, *Israel's Sacred Terrorism: a study based on Moshe Sharett's Diaries* (Belmont, 1980).

107 The best account is in Jiryis, *The Arabs in Israel*, chapter 3, and interviews thirty years later with the perpetrators, in *Ha'ir*, 10 October 1986, reproduced in *News From Within*, 23 October 1986, which suggest that some of them feel little remorse.

108 Civilians were taken from their homes and shot, see the eyewitness account of a survivor in Paul Cossali and Clive Robson, *Stateless in Gaza* (London, 1986) pp. 17–18.

109 See 'West Bank story', published in *Private Eye*, 10 November 1967, and the statement made by an anonymous soldier in 5th Reservist Division, dated Tel Aviv, 10 September 1967, 'we fired such shots every night on men, women and children. Even during moonlit nights when we could identify the people, that is – distinguish between men, women and children. In the mornings we searched the area and, by explicit order from the officer on the spot, shot the living, including those who hid, or were wounded (again: including the women and children).' It was issued as a statement from the office of *Haolam Hazeh*, and published in *Israel and the Geneva Conventions* (Beirut, 1968).

110 The findings of the Kahan Commission enquiry into the events in Sabra/Shatila camp, 16–18 September 1982, make it difficult to disbelieve that senior military commanders either intended an atrocity to happen, or deliberately ignored the possibility of one happening even though they knew the barbarous propensities of their auxiliary Lebanese Forces. Furthermore, as the Kahan

enquiry reveals, some Israeli troops realized what was happening on the first night but did nothing about it. See McDowall, *The Palestinians* p. 34, note 104.

111   Harkabi, *Israel's Fateful Decisions*, p. 207. He originally wrote the book in Hebrew, *Hachravot Goraliot* (Tel Aviv, 1986).

112   Hisham Sharabi, 'Its time for uninhibited debate', *Middle East International*, 10 October 1987.

113   Sabri Jiryis, *Shu'un Falistiniyya*, May/June 1987, quoted by Sharabi, 'It's time for uninhibited debate'.

CHAPTER 9   THE OCCUPIED TERRITORIES: THE PROSPECTS

1   *MERIP*, May–June 1988.

2   Ibid., September–October 1988; *Middle East International*, 9 September 1988.

3   Central Bureau of Statistics statement on 9 July, quoted in *Facts Weekly Review*, 7–13 August 1988, no. 21.

4   Bank Hapoalim statement, in *MERIP*, September–October 1988. Also reported in *Facts Weekly Review*, no. 26, 18 September–1 October 1988.

5   Resulting from a reduction in payment of taxes and municipal dues, and the security costs and damage from the Uprising, estimated at 10 million shekels, *Facts Weekly Review*, no. 26, 18 September–1 October 1988.

6   Ziad Abu Amr, 'The *intifada* is on a stony road', *Middle East International*, 11 June 1988.

7   Zucker, *The Coming Crisis in Israel*, chapter 4.

8   Abdul Wahab Darawsha, then a Labour MK, was the messenger. *Ma'ariv*, 4–5 December 1986, in *Israeli Mirror*, no. 760. Likud MK Moshe Amirav confirmed that Nusayba and al Husayni transmitted a message from Arafat seeking a meeting with Israel's Prime Minister, *Koteret Rashit*, 20 January 1988, quoted in *New Outlook*, April 1988.

9   Hanna Sinyura, editor of the pro-Fatah *al Fajr* newspaper, had sought to change the terms of the debate with regard to East Jerusalem by putting himself forward as a candidate in the 1988 Jerusalem Municipal elections. Sinyura probably had the assent of the PLO leadership, but like Sari Nusayba who had met with Moshe Amirav, he awakened fears among many Palestinians that, far from calling Israel's bluff, he was playing into its hands.

10   Central Bureau of Statistics, *Projections of Population in Judea, Samaria and Gaza up to 2002* (Jerusalem, 1987) gives five projections. I have used projection 3, which assumes a moderate decline in fertility, in the West Bank from 6.5 to 5.0 and in Gaza from 7.2 to 5.7, but which also assumes a negative net migration of 8 per thousand in the West Bank and 6.5 per thousand in Gaza. This is probably a conservative estimate. Projection 4, with the same fertility rates, assumes zero net migration, which may prove more accurate unless there is an upturn in the Gulf economy. Projection 4 estimates 1,429,000 in the West Bank and 992,000 in Gaza, giving a total of 2,421,000 in all.

11   Reported in *The Jerusalem Post*, 18 March 1988, reprinted in *Israeli Mirror*, no. 775. See also Gaza figure of 634,000 for the end of 1986, given in *Ha'aretz*, 13 October 1988, in *Israeli Mirror*, no. 772.

12   For example in education. In 1984 the school population (aged 5–14) was

222,000 in the West Bank and 146,000 in the Gaza Strip. By 2002 these populations will have increased by 54 per cent (the West Bank) and 68 per cent (Gaza), putting commensurate pressure on teaching faculty and facilities, CBS, *Projections of Population in Judea, Samaria and Gaza up to 2002*, p. xx.

13 *ISA 1986*, p. 696.

14 Jordanian-Palestinian Joint Committee, *Report on the Housing Project in Support of National Steadfastness in the Occupied Territories* (Amman, 1986) p. 4, quoted in United Nations, *Living Conditions of the Palestinian People in the occupied territories – report of the Secretary General* (A/39/233) p. 37.

15 This figure does not include Israeli housing schemes for refugees in the Gaza Strip, since the authorities require a refugee family to demolish its old dwelling on relocation. It thus only constitutes housing replacement. There are at least 140,000 substandard or delapidated homes out of a total stock of 182,000. Ibid.

16 For example, see communiqués nos. 14 and 16 of 22 April and 13 May respectively, in *Facts Weekly Review*, nos. 7 and 10 of 17–23 April and 8–10 May 1988 respectively.

17 Cossali and Robson, *Stateless in Gaza*, p. 54.

18 Escribano, 'The Endurance of the Olive Tree', pp. 166–7.

19 Ibid.

20 Ibid., p. 168.

21 Assuming the refugee proportion of the whole remains at 43 per cent and 70 per cent respectively.

22 Hypothetically, if all the refugees were to leave the West Bank and Gaza Strip this would reduce the respective populations in 2002 to their 'natural' level of about 700,000 and 200,000. In the West Bank this would return the population to its late 1970s level, and Gaza to a level slightly below that following the refugee influx of 1948.

23 Benvenisti, *1986 Report*, pp. 20–1.

24 Gwyn Rowley, 'The occupied territories: the deeper realities', in *Focus*, Winter 1987, p. 35.

25 See for example a report of a recent Tel Aviv University opinion survey in the *Observer*, 12 June 1988, which announced a 'sharp swing to the right' and predicted that parties to the right of Likud would win 15 per cent of the vote in the November election, while Labour and Likud were level pegging.

26 A'si, 'Israeli and Palestinian public opinion', pp. 164–5.

27 A poll carried out by the Israeli Institute of Applied Social Research (IIASR). Ibid., p. 155.

28 *Newsweek* poll, quoted in *Middle East International*, 23 January 1988; a similar survey by *Hadashot* and published in *Time Magazine* 8 February 1988 reflected a similar balance, 63 per cent supporting government policy and 27 per cent believing the government were too soft. *MERIP*, May–June 1988. In May 1982, also, at a time when the authorities were treating the territories with considerable severity [see American-Arab Anti-Discrimination Committee, *The Bitter Year* (Washington, 1983)], 77 per cent of those polled supported government policy and only 14 per cent opposed it. *The Jerusalem Post*, 11 May 1982, in A'si, 'Israeli and Palestinian public opinion', p. 167.

29 IIASR poll, in A'si, 'Israeli and Palestinian public opinion', p. 154.

30 From 1968–72, opinion in favour of retaining the territories increased and then receded, in Gaza's case from 85 per cent to 69 per cent, and in the West Bank's

case from 91 per cent to 47 per cent. IIASR poll in A'si, 'Israeli and Palestinian public opinion', p. 165. The following year, 1973, 66 per cent of Israelis opposed the return of the Gaza Strip, while 58 per cent opposed the return of the West Bank. *The New York Times*, in ibid. At the end of 1977, 67 per cent of the public were against any withdrawal from the occupied territories even in return for peace with all the Arab states, IIASR poll, quoted in *The Jerusalem Post*, 29 January 1978. But compare with a poll one month earlier during the euphoric period of Sadat's trip to Jerusalem, which suggested that 41 per cent of the public would be ready to give up the West Bank for a 'true peace', with only 21 per cent opposed. DAHAF poll published in *The Jerusalem Post* on 25 December 1977. Both polls quoted in A'si, 'Israeli and Palestinian public opinion', p. 166. In 1980 *The Jerusalem Post* reported that 60 per cent of the public opposed trading the West Bank for peace. Among young people the proportion was higher, 76 per cent, *The Jerusalem Post*, 20 May 1980. In two polls published by *The Jerusalem Post* in January and June 1983 a slight majority of respondents opposed any withdrawal from the occupied territories: 42.3 per cent against withdrawal, 39.8 per cent for, *The Jerusalem Post* 2 January 1983; 50 per cent against any concessions to Jordan, 43 per cent against giving back any part of West Bank in exchange for peace. *The Jerusalem Post*, 10 June 1983 in A'si, 'Israeli and Palestinian public opinion', p. 169.

31 *Jerusalem Post*, 1 February 1984, in A'si, 'Israeli and Palestinian public opinion', p. 169.
32 DAHAF poll, in ibid., pp. 170–1.
33 Conducted during 1985–7 by Modi'in Ezrachi, and published in *Ma'ariv*, March 1986 and 12 May 1987.
34 Compare with Smith Poll in *Jerusalem Post International*, 11 October 1986 which showed 50 to 52 per cent unwilling to concede any territory, and 37 to 41 per cent in favour, and with Sammy Smooha's survey in ibid., 16 August 1986 which concluded that out of a sample of 1,200 Jews, 42 per cent would oppose any territorial compromises, and a similar percentage would *not* oppose a full withdrawal.
35 Modi'in Ezrachi survey in *al Hamishmar*, 6 April 1988, *Israeli Mirror*, no. 776.
36 Dr Asher Arian, 'National security and public opinion', quoted in *The Other Israel*, May–June 1988.
37 For example, see *The Jerusalem Post*, 31 March 1981 and 8 May 1981: 62 and 75 per cent respectively favoured expansion of the settlements, while 30 and 24 per cent respectively opposed it. A'si, 'Israeli and Palestinian public opinion', p. 167, and compare with Modi'in Ezrachi results in *Ma'ariv*, March 1986 and 12 May 1987 which indicated about 37 per cent unwilling even to freeze new settlements and approximately 25 per cent willing to consider freezing new settlements but retaining old ones.
38 Modi'in Ezrachi in *Ma'ariv*, March 1986.
39 Compare *Jerusalem Post International*, 7 November 1985, 14 June 1986, and Abraham Rabinovich, 'City's changing demography' in ibid., 6 June 1987. The former claims an ultra-orthodox population of 85,000 in 1985, which would be 26 per cent (not 27 per cent as claimed) of 328,000 Jerusalem Jews. The latter article presents the view of Professor Uziel Schmelz who argues that the percentage is much lower, only 20 per cent. Even if this lesser percentage were true, the non-Zionist proportion of the city is still around 40 per cent.

40 But 19 per cent did accept a need to set up a Palestinian state in the territories. IIASR polls of January and July 1974, in A'si, 'Israeli and Palestinian public opinion', pp. 157–9.

41 Ibid.

42 During the decade 1967–77, one analyst argued that 80 per cent of Israelis were fairly consistently opposed to any deal with the PLO, and believed a Palestinian state would endanger the security of Israel. Louis Guttman, *The Jerusalem Post*, 11 November 1977, in A'si, 'Israeli and Palestinian public opinion', p. 166. Towards the end of 1979 another poll suggested that even if the PLO recognized the right of Israel to exist beforehand, 63 per cent of the Jewish electorate would still oppose negotiations with the PLO, and 72 per cent would continue to oppose the establishment of a Palestinian State. *Jerusalem Post*, 16 October 1979, in A'si, 'Israeli and Palestinian public opinion', p. 167.

43 IIASR poll, published by *The Jerusalem Post*, 29 January 1978, in A'si, 'Israeli and Palestinian public opinion', p. 167.

44 In 1983 the proportion of Jews favouring the establishment of a Palestinian state was no more than 7 per cent, and this had barely changed by the end of 1987. Compare DAHAF poll, in A'si, 'Israeli and Palestinian public opinion', pp. 170–1, with the 8 to 10 per cent in a study of 2,000 urban men under the age of thirty-five, by Efrayim Yucktman-Ya'ar of Tel Aviv University and Mikha'el Inbar of the Hebrew University reported in *The Jerusalem Post*, 25 December 1987.

45 Compare a poll in 1985 showing that only 15 per cent favoured talks with the PLO (if it recognized Israel and renounced terrorism) in *Ha'aretz*, 23 August 1985 and *Israeli Mirror*, no. 736, which indicated no change in a decade, and a 1987 poll which indicated that 37 per cent would now talk with the PLO (if it recognized Israel and renounced terrorism), *Yediot Aharonot*, 23 September 1987 and *Israeli Mirror*, no. 765. However, one must accept the contradictory and unreliable nature of these polls. Compare the above, for example, with the following: over a three year period, June 1983 to September 1986 there was a slight hardening of opinion, from 48 per cent favouring negotiations if the PLO renounced terrorism and recognized Israel, falling to 43 per cent by 1986. Those who disagreed with this view increased from 41 to 52 per cent. Smith Institute polls reported in the *Jerusalem Post International*, 11 October 1986.

46 One poll claimed that a third of the electorate now favoured negotiations with the PLO, and that this would rise to 50 per cent if the PLO renounced terror and recognized Israel. Arian, 'National security and public opinion', quoted in *The Other Israel*, May–June 1988. By September 1988 another poll confirmed that half Israel's Jews would accept talks with the PLO on these conditions. *The Times*, 7 September 1988.

47 'The political and social positions of youth in Israel', 1987, an opinion poll by DAHAF for the Van Leer Institute, Jerusalem, published 1987, reported in *New Outlook*, February 1988.

48 Even though it excluded self-determination and negotiations with the PLO. *The Jerusalem Post*, 12 October 1982, in A'si, 'Israeli and Palestinian public opinion'. p. 167.

CHAPTER 10   ISRAELI PALESTINIANS: THE PROSPECTS

1   *Yediot Aharonot*, 10 February 1985, in *Israeli Press Briefs*, no. 32.
2   *News From Within*, 26 August 1986.
3   Private communication to author, dated 17 December 1987.
4   For a harsh verdict on leftist attitudes, see Arnon Sofer, 'Geography and demography in the land of Israel in the year 2000' (Haifa, 1987, mimeograph) p. 16.
5   *ISA 1986*, pp. 27, 28.
6   Ibid., Table II/19 p. 63, gives two hypotheses. The first of these presumes a (Jewish) migration balance of 5,000 per year in the 1980s and nil in the 1990s. The second assumes a migration balance of 15,000 per year in the 1980s and 5,000 per year in the 1990s. In fact by 1988 the indications were that migration was below even the first estimate, on which the projections are based: in 1990 Palestinians will be 19.28%, in 1995 20.9%, in 2000 22.3% and in 2005 23.75% of the population (I have rounded this upwards in view of the lower than expected Jewish immigration). It is possible that either or both Jewish and Palestinian population figures may fall beneath those estimated if the birthrate is lower and migration negative. Generally speaking, however, Israel's official population statistics and forecasts are notable for their accuracy.
7   *ISA 1986*, p. 4.
8   Ibid., p. 63.
9   Ibid., p. 58.
10   Ibid., p. 60.
11   Ibid., p. 63.
12   In 1981 63 per cent of Arab voters voted for Zionist parties (29 per cent for Labour and 12 per cent for affiliated Arab lists), and 37 per cent for Rakah. In 1984 52 per cent voted for Rakah and the PLP, and 48 per cent for Zionist parties (23 per cent for Labour). Yehuda Litani, *Ha'aretz*, 27 July 1984, in *Israeli Press Briefs*, no. 27. See also *Jerusalem Post International*, 2 November 1985.
13   77 per cent of the Arab electorate voted in 1988 compared with 73 per cent in 1984. For a breakdown of the Arab vote, see *Israel and Palestine*, no. 146, November 1988.
14   Jiryis, *The Arabs in Israel*, p. 133.
15   The Central Elections Committee, reflecting Likud's predominance in the Knesset and benefiting from the abstention of five Labour members, voted to disqualify PLP. Its decision was overturned by the Supreme Court. Keller, *Terrible Days*, pp. 105–6.
16   *Ha'aretz*, 27 July 1984, in *Israeli Press Briefs*, no. 27.
17   Keller, *Terrible Days*, p. 108.
18   Quoted by Amos Shapira, 'Confronting racism by law in Israel: promises and pitfalls', in *Relations between Ethnic Majority and Minority*, p. 33.
19   This view is not shared by Shapira, who argues that 'the phrase . . . need not be interpreted as adversely reflecting on the civil and political rights of the non-Jewish citizens of Israel.' Palestinians, however, find this argument unconvincing. See, for example, Anton Shammas, 'A stone's throw', *New York Review of Books*, 31 March 1988.

20 *Ha'aretz* supplement, 28 January 1977, quoted in Lustick, *Arabs in the Jewish State*, p. 263.

21 Discharged Soldiers Act 1949, welfare provisions regulations of 1970, see Ruth Gavison, 'Minority rights in Israel: the case of army veteran provisions', in *Relations between Ethnic Majority and Minority*, pp. 20–1.

22 *ISA 1986*, p. 35.

23 See Sofer, 'Geography and demography in the land of Israel in the year 2000', p. 8. There is allegedly expansion westwards by the bedouin in the northern Negev.

24 *Jerusalem Post International*, 30 August 1986.

25 *ISA 1964*, p. 15.

26 Sofer, 'Geography and demography in the land of Israel in the year 2000', p. 9.

27 Ibid., p. 9.

28 Ibid., p. 11.

29 Ibid., p. 10.

30 Lustick, *Arabs in the Jewish State*, pp. 252ff.

31 Ori Stendhal, 'Rakah tries to seize a decisive position in the Arab street', *Ha'aretz*, 31 January 1976, in Lustick, *Arabs in the Jewish State*, p. 255.

32 The Histadrut has supported this approach. Its modest development of employment opportunities since 1984 is to absorb unemployed Palestinian labour but its policy is to retain control firmly in Jewish hands.

33 *The Jerusalem Post*, 8 August 1977, in Lustick, *Arabs in the Jewish State*, p. 258.

34 Moshe Arens, for example, in spite of belonging to Likud, acted as an integrationist as Minister without Portfolio, making the first admission by any Israeli cabinet minister that the Palestinians suffer from inequality and discrimination, although he opposed Weizman's return of Area Nine, and obstructed the restoration of Kafr Bir'am and Iqrit to their Palestinian owners. Ronnie Milo, Arens' successor, was closer to the coercionists. It would also be difficult to describe all Labour ministers as integrationists. Gad Ya'cobi's development plan contains no hint of integration or of economic development for the Palestinian sector.

35 Before 1948 Labour Zionism appreciated more than Revisionist Zionism, the importance of labour unions and other co-operative strength. Through the operation of Military Government in Arab population areas inside the frontiers established in 1949, it also learnt the value of keeping a close monitor on all economic and social activities as well as political ones.

36 *al Hamishmar*, 7 September 1976, quoted in Keller, 'The Koenig Affair', *Israel and Palestine*, March 1986, and Keller, *Terrible Days*, pp. 94–103.

37 Ibid.

38 Koenig remained in his post until 1986 when he resigned in protest over the decision to suspend demolition of 'illegal' homes.

39 The following material, including translated excerpts from *Ha'aretz*, 25 October 1987, are quoted from *al Hadaf newsletter*, no. 4, and separate translation.

40 In another recommendation, Gilboa targeted Rakah by suggesting measures to reduce the number of Arab students studying in Eastern Bloc countries (virtually a Rakah monopoly). There was no suggestion that this reduction should be accompanied by an end to the discriminatory educational policy which forced Palestinians to go abroad if they wanted a university degree.

41 The first indication of implementation of funding restrictions was in July 1988, *al Hadaf newsletter*, no. 7, July 1988 referring to *The Jerusalem Post*, 18 July 1988.

42 Regarding the plan for financial equality with the Jewish sector, Gilboa proposed the allocation of NIS 235 million to the Palestinian community over the five year period 1988–93, with NIS85 million of this sum devoted to developing the municipal sector, i.e. public services like sewage disposal, electricity, town planning and construction of basic facilities. *Ha'aretz*'s leak of the Gilboa report coincided with a strike call by the Committee of Heads of Local Arab Councils because of underfunding of Palestinian councils and municipalities by NIS50 million. *al Hadaf newsletter*, no. 4.

43 For example one total of 8,000 in the mid-1980s, another of 24,000 by 1977. Keller, *Terrible Days*, p. 109; Lustick, *Arabs in the Jewish State*, p. 195.

44 Ghanadiri, *al jamahir al arabiyya fi isra'il*, p. 113.

45 A few houses were demolished in early 1988, and another thirteen homes in the period 1 May–15 July 1988. All the victims were required to pay the expenses of the demolition crew, the police and border guards. *al Hadaf newsletter*, no. 7, July 1988. Fifteen more homes were demolished in Tayiba on 8 November 1988. The lack of decision concerning implementation of the Markovitch report was understood by Palestinians to indicate a desire on the part of the Likud element within the government to await the election of a new (Likud dominated) government empowered with a clearer mandate from the electorate to deal firmly with this issue.

46 *al Ittihad* Arabic daily obtained and published details of the report in early July 1987. See Ghanadiri, *al jamahir al arabiyya fi isra'il*, pp. 35–46, based on articles by Najir Majalli in *al Ittihad* appearing on 3, 5, 6, 7, 8 July 1987.

47 Ghanadiri, *al jamahir al arabiyya fi isra'il*, p. 46.

48 Repeated attempts to remove these bedouin, declaring their settlements as 'unlicensed' have so far been unsuccessful, despite the denial of services such as water and electricity, and the imprisonment of family heads. See B. Michael, 'The village that must not remain', *Hadashot*, 16 November 1984, in *Israeli Mirror*, nos. 713–14.

49 In 1985 Nazareth had a population of 47,000 compared with 25,500 in Nazaret Illit. The former has 7,500 dunums of land compared with 9,500 dunums belonging to the latter. Ghanadiri, *al jamahir al arabiyya fi isra'il*, p. 11. See also for earlier comparative figures, Henry Rosenfeld, 'Nazareth and Upper Nazareth in the political economy of Israel', in *Relations between Ethnic Majority and Minority*, p. 51. Saffuriya is a sensitive case, since refugees from the village in 1948 (and those subsequently evicted) almost all live in Nazareth. Morris, *The Birth of the Palestinian Refugee Problem*, p. 201.

50 Ghanadiri, *al jamahir al arabiyya fi isra'il*, p. 42.

51 Only 10 out of 204 clauses on development plans in the report refer to the Arab population, and these emphasize the importance of preventing encroachment onto state land and unlicensed building. Ghanadiri, ibid., p. 46.

52 Paul Harrison, *Inside the Third World* (London, 1981) p. 250.

53 Ghanadiri, *al jamahir al arabiyya fi isra'il*, p. 118.

54 In 1985 there was 6.4 per cent unemployment among Jews and 9.5 per cent among Palestinians, *ISA 1986*, p. 318.

55 In addition, a further 2,000 rooms were required for technological and scientific

purposes to bring the provision in the Palestinian sector into approximate comparability with the Jewish one. Ghanadiri, *al jamahir al arabiyya fi isra'il*, p. 140; *Jerusalem Post Magazine*, 11 September 1987. In Nazareth 161 class-rooms (the equivalent of eight schools) are rented rooms mainly in private houses. Sarah Graham-Brown *Education, Repression and Liberation: Palestinians* (London, 1984) p. 47, and *al Hadaf* factsheet 'Discrimination', 1987.

56 *al ta'lim al 'arabi fi isra'il: qadhaya wa matalib* (Arab Education and Requirements in Israel: Issues and Requirements) (Shafa 'Amr, 23 May 1984).

57 Ghanadiri, *al jamahir al arabiyya fi isra'il*, p. 141.

58 *Jerusalem Post Magazine*, 11 September 1987.

59 The polio virus was found at Acre, Nahariya, Carmiel and Abu Sinan. *The Independent*, 8 October 1988.

60 Internal refugees numbered 45,800 when Israel asked UNRWA to hand over its activities in 1952. They had either fled, or been expelled from their homes during or after the hostilities of 1948–9. Israel also cleared Arabs away from border areas and systematically removed remaining ones from villages and towns which were already partially abandoned. Kamen, 'After the Catastrophe I: the Arabs in Israel, 1948–51'. Most were settled in Nazareth and Shafa 'Amr. A third wave of movement occurred in the late 1950s when refugees attempted to settle in old village or kinship groups. Roughly one in four Israeli Palestinians was a refugee in 1950, making their present day numbers probably in the order of 180,000–200,000. As in the occupied territories, the sense of grievance is compounded by awkward social relations with the non-refugee community. Like refugees the world over, they quickly discovered that their presence was not welcome and feelings of rejection and difference have persisted. Less than 20 per cent of refugee marriages are with local people. Only 10 per cent of refugees have more friends among locals than among the refugee community. Refugees and locals even vote differently in local elections. See Majid al Haj, 'Adjustment patterns of Arab internal refugees', in *International Migration*, vol. XXIV, 3 September 1986.

61 In April 1987 the government publicly recognized that while it preferred Druzes over other Palestinians it had not treated them equally with Jews, and announced it would do so in future, in view of their military service. However, this did not affect plans to seize more land. Druze villagers of Bayt Jann found themselves in conflict with government forces to prevent seizure of land for nearby Jewish settlements. Nor has the statement led to any substantial effort to develop Druze villages economically on the scale enjoyed by Jewish settlements. See Ghanadiri, *al jamahir al arabiyya fi isra'il*, pp. 173–88. There can be no expectation that the Druze community will suddenly identify with other Palestinians rather than the state. The Druzes have always carefully assessed the balance of forces at play before deciding how their own community interest is best served, and in the long term if they see the tide turning in the Palestinian favour in the north, they may dissociate themselves from the state apparatus.

62 Ibid., p. 92.

63 Nearly 90 per cent of Palestinian Israelis consider the refugees have an absolute right of return to the Israeli parts of Palestine; only 4 per cent think they have no right, opinions in fact, almost exactly inverse to those of Jewish Israelis. Smooha, *Orientation and Politicization of the Arab Minority in Israel*, p. 42

gives 85 per cent and Kislev, 'Israel's Arabs: coping with duality' on Smooha's more recent work gives 82 per cent 'absolute' yes, and another 14 per cent supporting return under certain conditions.

64 *News From Within*, 21 January 1986.
65 Out of a sample of 1,200 respondents. Minah Tsemach, 'Attitudes of the Jewish majority in Israel toward the Arab minority', Van Leer Foundation (Jerusalem, 1980) in A'si, 'Israeli and Palestinian public opinion', p. 150.
66 Out of a sample of 1,200 Jewish and 1,200 Palestinian Israelis. Kislev, 'Israel's Arabs: coping with duality'.
67 Ibid.
68 *Jerusalem Post International*, 24 June–1 July 1984.
69 *Ha'aretz*, 26 October 1987, in *New Outlook*, February 1988.
70 A survey of 2,500 adult Israelis carried out by the Israel Institute for Applied Social Research, in A'si, 'Israeli and Palestinian public opinion', p. 153.
71 Sammy Smooha, 'Political intolerance: threatening Israel's democracy', *New Outlook*, July 1986.
72 Ibid.
73 A survey of 612 respondents, aged 15–18, Dahaf research for the Van Leer Institute, published October 1987, reported in *New Outlook*, February 1988, and in *Jerusalem Post International*, 7 November 1987.
74 For modest indications of greater acceptance of Palestinians by young Israelis, see *New Outlook*, February 1988.
75 Gallup Poll, 17–19 June 1984 in *Hadashot*, 24 June 1984, *Israeli Mirror*, no. 692–3. 31 per cent could not see a way to get rid of them, 31 per cent proposed paying them to go, 20 per cent favoured forcible expulsion, and 15 per cent thought they should go to a state on the West Bank.

CHAPTER 11   THE CHOICES THAT MUST BE MADE

1 See Isaac, *Israel Divided*, p. 67.
2 Ibid., p. 79.
3 Ronald Mark Sirkin, 'Coalition, conflict and compromise: the party politics of Israel', (unpublished Ph.D. dissertation, Pennsylvania State University, 1971) pp. 363–4, quoted in Isaac, *Israel Divided*, p. 10.
4 Isaac, *Israel Divided*, p. 101.
5 *The New York Times*, 12 June 1967, quoted in ibid., p. 108.
6 Isaac, *Israel Divided*, p. 129.
7 *Davar*, 11 September 1967. Pinchas Sapir, the Finance Minister, warned that 'integration means converting Israel into an Arab state' but did little to stop the process.
8 See Isaac, *Israel Divided*, pp. 108–25.
9 Ibid., p. 131.
10 The latter option was envisaged by Defence Minister Shimon Peres in 1975 when he made the mistake of calling for the 1976 municipal elections.
11 Rabbi Pichnik, *Year by Year, 5728* (Jerusalem, 1968, Hebrew), p. 109, quoted in Harkabi, *Israel's Fateful Decisions*, p. 148.
12 Prime Minister Peres, in spite of his call for Palestinian self-expression (in his Chatham House speech, January 1986) repudiated Prime Minister Thatcher's

call for municipal elections during her visit to Israel in May 1986.

13 Leonard Davies Institute seminar, Hebrew University, Jerusalem 1982, quoted in Gwyn Rowley, 'Developing perspectives upon the areal extent of Israel' (Sheffield, 1988 [mimeograph]) p. 7.

14 *MERIP*, May–June, 1988, p. 40.

15 For a discussion of the Eretz Israel and regional compromise schemes, see Gwyn Rowley, 'Developing perspectives'.

16 In fact the increase in the number of settlers, approximately 20,000, has been as great during the first two National Unity Government years, when Labour controlled both the premiership and the defence (occupied territories) portfolio, as it was in the latter part of the Likud administration, 1982–4. Benvenisti, *1987 Report*, pp. 52–5.

17 Saul Cohen, *The Geopolitics of Israel's Border Question* (Jaffee Centre for Strategic Studies, Tel Aviv University, Jerusalem 1987) p. 93.

18 World Zionist Organization information, 1987, cited in Rowley, 'Developing perspectives', p. 15.

19 $260,000 for a living unit in Tel Aviv, compared to $120,000 for equivalent accommodation in Ariel with a loan on easy terms. Moreover, it was planned to attract Jewish immigrants of retirement age. Oral information from Dr Gwyn Rowley, Sheffield University.

20 Benvenisti, *1987 Report*, p. 54.

21 Ibid., pp. 53–4.

22 Harkabi, *Israel's Fateful Decisions*, p. 60.

23 Shlomo Avineri, 'Ideology and Israel's foreign policy', *Jerusalem Quarterly*, no. 37, 1986, p. 8.

24 The World Zionist Organization, the Jewish Agency and the Jewish National Fund.

25 *Guardian*, 9 July 1988.

26 Ibid.

27 These possibilities are briefly discussed in Peri, *Between Battles and Ballots*, pp. 284–5.

28 Raphael Mergui and Philippe Simonnot, *Israel's Ayatollahs* (London, 1987) pp. 85, 49.

29 Ibid., p. 48.

30 *The Times*, 7 September 1988.

31 Avishai, *The Tragedy of Zionism*, p. 299.

32 *News from Within*, 15 April 1986. Ne'eman's colleague, Geula Cohen considered that 'inducing the Arabs' to leave would be humane as Jordan is part of the Land of Israel, so going there would not be emigrating.

33 *The Jerusalem Post*, 23 February 1988, quoted in *New Outlook*, April 1988. Ze'evi's arguments regarding transfer are less to do with security than with the Jewishness of the state, in particular the issue of mixed marriages.

34 A poll conducted over a two year period showed that in August 1985 35 per cent supported the expulsion of Palestinians from the occupied territories, a figure which dropped to 29 per cent in early 1986 before rising in the autumn to 38 per cent in 1987. Opposition to expulsion was about 60 per cent. Smith Institute poll, in *Jerusalem Post International*, 11 October 1986. The editor of the Gush Emunim settler magazine, *Nekuda*, wrote in January 1988, 'half a year ago, 90 per cent of people would have objected to transfer. Today, 30 to 40 per

cent would argue that it's not a dirty word or an inhuman policy. On the contrary, they would argue it's a way to avoid friction.' Quoted in *Jerusalem Post International*, 30 January 1988. Another poll in early 1988 indicated *Nekuda* was probably right, that the proportion in sympathy with transfer was about 40 per cent of the Jewish electorate. Tel Aviv University poll, in the *Observer*, 12 June 1988. A poll carried out earlier by Tel Aviv's Telseker Institute showed that 50.4 per cent of respondents agreed with Ze'evi's proposal for population transfer, but only 14.4 per cent thought the proposal practicable. *Hadashot*, 19 July 1987, in *Israeli Mirror*, no. 762. This finding was confirmed by a poll by IIASR and the Hebrew University which found that 50 per cent favoured transfer. *The Times*, 24 August 1988.

35 A survey by Efrayim Yucktman-Ya'ar of Tel Aviv University and Mikha'el Inbar of the Hebrew University, published in *The Jerusalem Post*, 25 December 1987, and quoted in *MERIP*, May–June 1988.

36 *The Times*, 24 August and 7 September, 1988; *Israel and Palestine Political Report*, no. 144, September 1988.

37 Avishai, *The Tragedy of Zionism*, p. 298. See also Yossi Melman and Dan Raviv, 'A final solution of the Palestinian problem', *Guardian Weekly*, 21 February, 1988.

38 *New York Times*, 4 April 1983, quoting remarks Cohen had made on 16 March 1983, in Chomsky, *The Fateful Triangle*, p. 116.

39 Quoted in *Jewish Post and Opinion*, 30 March 1983, in Chomsky, *The Fateful Triangle*, p. 116.

40 Melman and Raviv, 'A final solution of the Palestinian problem'. Aharon Pappo, a Likud activist, and Zvi Shiloah of the Land of Israel Movement, have both argued that expulsion would be humane, and Yosef Shapira, a National Religious Party government minister suggested that Palestinians should be paid to leave. *The Jerusalem Post*, 23 February 1988.

41 The results of a questionnaire on security matters, distributed among rabbis, yeshiva students and Torah scholars from the occupied territories were discussed in the November 1987 issue of the settler magazine *Nekuda*. Although only half responded, among those who did, 62 per cent wanted to *encourage* the Palestinians to leave, while another 15 per cent wanted to *compel* them to leave, *New Outlook*, January 1988.

42 See on Jewish fears, Wiemar, 'Zionism and the Arabs', pp. 50–1.

43 *Ha'aretz*, 26 May 1980.

44 *Yediot Aharonot*, 15 January 1982, quoted in Chomsky, *The Fateful Triangle*, p. 117.

45 *Ha'aretz*, 2 March 1988.

46 Avishai, *The Tragedy of Zionism*, p. 340.

47 *Jerusalem Post International*, week ending 23 January 1988.

48 Quoted from the Hebrew press in *al Hadaf newsletter*, no. 5.

49 See Benny Morris, 'Operation Dani and the Palestinian exodus from Lydda and Ramle'.

50 These remarks are attributed to Menachem Begin, General Raphael Eitan, General Ben Gal, commanding the Northern District, and the Mayor of Rosh Pina.

51 *Ha'aretz*, 29 February 1988, quoted in *New Outlook*, April 1988.

52 See Jiryis, *The Arabs in Israel*, chapter 3.

53 Notably the Daniel Pinto affair, see Pori, *Between Ballots and Battles*, pp. 272–3, 275, 277, 286.

54 See the Kahan Commission report.

55 *The Karp Report: an Israeli Government Inquiry into Settler Violence against Palestinians on the West Bank*, originally completed in May 1982 was only published in February 1984. It 'bears out the suspicion that a systematic miscarriage of justice is being perpetrated in the West Bank . . . The police, deferring to the army, fail to stand on their own rights, and the army tends to look benignly on those [settlers] it views as its soldiers.' *Jerusalem Post* editorial, 9 February 1984.

56 Israel's two former chief rabbis, Ovadim Yossef and Shlomo Goren supported the immediate release of TNT detainees in May 1985. *Ha'aretz*, 30 May 1985, in *Israeli Mirror*, no. 736. On the intervention of sixty rabbis, see also *Ha'aretz*, 25 September 1984, in *Israeli Mirror*, no. 704.

57 See *Kol Ha'ir*, 6 November 1987, and other commentaries on the Landau Report in excerpts reproduced in *Israeli Mirror*, no. 868.

58 *Koteret Rashit*, 3 February 1988, *Israeli Press Briefs*, no. 58.

59 Meir Pa'il, 'Zionism in danger of cancer', in *New Outlook*, October–December 1983.

60 Estimate in *Ma'ariv*, 20 September 1985, in *Israeli Mirror*, no. 742.

61 Yehoshafat Harkabi letter to *Ha'aretz*, 11 May 1984, in Jansen, *Dissonance in Zion*, p. 108.

62 Israel Eldad, *Deot*, Winter 1968, in Davis and Mezvinsky (eds) *Documents from Israel*, p. 187. His views do not seem to have moderated since then, see *Yediot Aharonot*, 26 February 1988, in *Israeli Mirror*, no. 776.

63 Yoram Peri, *Davar*, 3 August 1984, in *Israeli Press Briefs*, no. 28.

64 Mergui and Simonnot, *Israel's Ayatollahs*, p. 64.

65 Carl R. Rogers, *On Becoming a Person, A Therapist's View of Psychotherapy*, London, 1967) p. 333.

INDEX